WE

Peter Essex was
educated in Australia, Great Britain and South
Africa, where he now lives. Among his interests
are nature conservation and the languages and
cultures of South Africa. *We the Enemy* is his
second novel.

By the same author

The Exile

PETER ESSEX

We The Enemy

FONTANA/Collins

First published by William Collins Sons & Co. Ltd 1986
First published in Fontana Paperbacks 1987

© Peter Essex 1986

Made and printed in Great Britain by
William Collins Sons & Co. Ltd, Glasgow

Conditions of Sale
This book is sold subject to the condition
that it shall not, by way of trade or otherwise,
be lent, re-sold, hired out or otherwise circulated
without the publisher's prior consent in any form of
binding or cover other than that in which it is
published and without a similar condition
including this condition being imposed
on the subsequent purchaser

It was the regalia of royalty; a python skin fashioned by the mightiest witch doctors of all into a coil thicker than a man's leg. It contained body parings from all the Zulu kings: from the first – Shaka Zulu, to the last – Cetchwayo ka Mpande. It held too a smudge of vomit from every man of every regiment that has ever taken up the war shield in the king's name. It symbolised the resolve and unity of the Zulu nation, and it was called . . .

INKATHA!

To Vulindlela
my guide and mentor

Zululand

Before dawn:
Wednesday, 22nd January, 1879.

PROLOGUE

The seventh new moon since spring – the Hlolanja; the seeking dog saw us encamped in the deep Ngwebini ravine of the Nqutu hills. Twenty thousand Zulu men with but one mind: to wash every spear, every last sharp blade in the life blood of the white soldiers – just one hill away.

As a black tide under a black sky the valley seethed with silent men, and I was one. From end to end, from side to side it breathed. And we were waiting, waiting for the empty eye socket of that moon to draw down and lose itself beyond the land. Not one camp fire twinkled in the Ngwebini that night.

There was time to think, and as always with thoughts there were those for the ears of a friend and those that would die in the chest. Now there are important things that must be told, things that must change yours and the lives of many others. But let me not begin with the meal before the water is boiling . . . Let us go back to the Ngwebini ravine.

It was almost time for the birth of the morning sun – neither night nor day. A man's mind carries further than his eyes then, mine did. For it was then that I was told that the Zulu nation, like the black bull under the sacrificial axe of the war doctor, was about to die.

Understand me; Zulus there would always be, as plentiful as the reeds in the river. But people alone do not make a nation. People are born and people die and there is no hillside without a grave. No, it is its land that gives a nation its pride, its spirit, its sense of belonging on earth.

The first agonising cut had been made – the English soldiers had crossed the Buffalo river and were thrusting ever deeper into the land of Zulu. The black bull was bellowing, but soon its gall and liver and heart would be taken away and it would die . . . A nation would die. There were those who thought differently to me, and had I not had the curse of such bewitched eyes, it would have been easy to join them in their confidence. For as the sun greeted those twenty thousand glinting spears a flash flood of battle lust surged through that valley that promised to sweep the English to the sea. Who was I then to be thinking of defeat?

I was a young warrior in the regiment Ingobamakhosi – the bender of kings. I had a thick shield of ox-hide in the regimental colours of tan with a great black spot at the base; a stabbing spear, one armslength of assegai wood with a heavy steel blade deeper than a grown man's chest. That was what I owned and that was what I was – holder of the King's spear, bearer of the King's shield.

Sigewelegwele, the commanding induna of the Ingobamakhosi, did not share my uneasiness. He believed in victory. He was certain of it. He also believed that the attack should be made on the English position below without delay. Ours was a bachelor regiment, nearly the youngest of King Cetchwayo's warriors, as sharp and keen to draw blood as *umtente* shoots in spring. Yet I was thinking of defeat.

My thoughts however remained my thoughts. I was not even near enough to hear the words that were voiced at the war council that morning. The decision must have gone against Sigewelegwele though because he returned to the regiment, eyes low, jaw tight, an angry man.

The sun had risen well by then, breaking through the clouds to chase away the last chill of night and we were warming on the hillside like lazy rock rabbits. What made Sigewelegwele decide to choose me to do his dirty work I could only wonder at. Perhaps I was simply the first one those hawk eyes rested upon when he looked up. A nod was good enough to send me scrambling to his side. He said: 'How can our commanders let us lie here for another day? When the leopard holds the monkey in its jaws does it not bite?'

'It bites, Father.'

'The army has had no food since yesterday's dawn. Now we must wait in this valley for another day and another night. We will be withered and weak before we attack.'

Into my mind had worked a splinter of understanding as to why he had chosen mine from amongst the sea of faces there. The twinge of it disquieted me.

'You . . .' Sigewelegwele was pointing, his tone friendly, his memory amazing, he terrified me. '*You* are Umzeze of the Ntombela clan.'

'Yes, Father.'

'Your home therefore is within the smell of the breeze.'

'Yes, Father.'

The splinter had grown into a stick. My induna was about to order me to go down to the plains beneath the hills, where the cattle of my people grazed, what was left of them. In the plains below besides cattle, as Sigewelegwele well knew, there were British scouts looking for the Zulu army.

'Umzeze do you know what I want you to do?'

Indeed I knew only too well.

'Then take whoever you wish to help you and go at once.'

What Sigewelegwele wanted me to do was to bring about a battle. If the commanders would not lead his army – his impi to the British, then he Sigewelegwele would lead the British to the impi. I, Umzeze, was to be as the honey bird is to the gatherer. I had to look willing and yet be unwilling.

'I will go,' I said, 'to the hills to the north. There are many cattle there.'

'You will go to the south.' He prompted quietly. 'To the plains. There are even more cattle there.' Sigewelegwele was at his most frightening when he spoke in such a way.

I left for the lowlands where the cattle grazed; and the English scouts roamed, taking with me a band of young herd boys, *udibi* whose job it was to herd cattle and carry the warriors' sleeping mats. Sigewelegwele was as treacherous as a glancing spear, but I thought I had a plan to better him.

I knew every bush, every rock and furrow, every last ox from those parts, knew them by name. Was I not the son of that very valley? Moving with the stealth of the heaven herd I would gather the oxen while the thunder rumbled harmlessly by.

Herding oxen is the simplest thing to do. Take care of the lead bulls, let them think that they are choosing the direction, and they will tread with you to the end of the earth. Confuse the leaders however and as many oxen as you have is as many directions you will have to run.

All was going well. Despite the scattering of man and beast that war brings about, my *udibi* boys brought together a small herd of strays. We had seen the English scouts at a distance – hired *baTlokwa* horsemen who rode like the wizards of the night, but we hid in the shimmer of the heat, moved in the shadows of the clouds. They did not see us. We would have tricked them all the way back to the impi too, but for those *udibi*.

Sharp only on one side, like a knife, were those brainless pups. No sooner had we reached the shadow of the Nqutu hills than they started puffing up like little lizards. I did this – did you see me do that. Sticks became spears, and they became heroes in their own eyes. Being so close to the impi I myself didn't see any harm in it, I was more amused than angered by their antics. Inattention comes in the same brew as good humour, and so it was I hardly noticed the spoilt formation; the slowed stride of the herd. Perhaps Sigewelegwele had judged me well.

Perhaps also, those British mercenaries, the *baTlokwa* scouts would have seen us anyway. The ground was open and flat there and there was one more ridge to cross to reach the impi when one of my herders looked back pointing wildly, then broke into a stamping war dance. Out he stormed hardly bigger than his own defiant stick. 'There it is,' he shouted, 'there is the *baTlokwa*. Leave them to me – I will eat them up.'

I remember I laughed out loud. Is it not easy to remember the very last time of anything? Then a chill trickled through me and I too turned.

Over the rise to the west, riding hard down upon us they came, no shadows these, these were the merciless mountain men: the *baTlokwa*. A whole troop of them, dressed in their British uniforms.

Who caught who then is a question the ancestors must puzzle over. Those hill ponies came at a gallop that struck sparks from the rocks, their riders had their long guns out and aimed like pistols. . . And us? We ran for the ridge my brave *udibi* boys and I, the ridge and the Zulu army in its shelter.

The sudden drop into the ravine below caught even myself by surprise. One bullock tumbled over the edge bleating as it plunged, the rest reared back milling everywhere just as the horsemen reined up. A huge rifle with a sweaty black *baTlokwa* face peering down the sights was my last memory before I jumped.

My spear and my shield, to my disgrace, I lost in that jump. I still had my life though, and never did that have a sweeter taste. Like sputum on the wall I clung to that rocky face. The *baTlokwa* were still there, if I tilted my head sharply I could see them on the lip of the ravine, and they could have shot me away with ease . . . They had no further interest in me though. For before them, packed so tightly that neither rock nor grass broke through was a valley of shields. As far as their eyes would take them their gaze was returned by that silent seated host – Cetchwayo's impi – they had found it, and, at that moment, Sigewelegwele got his fervent wish. The eagles of war were launched.

Up sprang the Umcityu regiment with a bellow that almost drowned out the ragged volley from the horsemen. *Nanziya izitha!* – There goes enemy! You could not mistake the full throated shout of the umKosana their commander. *uSuthu!* Like lightning strikes winter grass the war cry set the army aflame. *uSuthu!* Burning its way out of that valley with a tempest of battle lust to drive it on roared the regiments.

The Umcityu, uNokenke, the Nodwenu men with their pure white shields, what a proud sight they made. Next to sweep below me was my own regiment the Ingobamakhosi with a stamp that made the very rocks shake. Was I mistaken, or did I see Sigewelegwele himself look up to me and raise his spear in mock tribute: a salute to the sputum on the wall. I could either dry up or slide off and who would notice?

The King's own regiment, the uThulwana, were the last to storm from the ravine, taking with them the fading echoes of the impi's royal war cry – *uSuthu! uSuthu! uSuthu!* Soon even that sound ceased and the warm cooing of the rock doves called the valley once more to rest.

Drawing my legs up close to my chest gave me room to sit upon that shelf. There would be time to prepare myself; time before the sun dried me to my bones; before my ancestors' voices welcomed my spirit. As a Zulu I had no fear of death. What is there to fear in going home?

'Umzeze . . . Umzeze!'

The third or fourth time my name was called I heard it with my ears.

'*Umzeze!* Get off your testicles and look up!'

There was nothing ancestral nor welcoming about that voice. That voice belonged to Mabuso my friend since clay oxen days.

Mabuso was poking over the cliff edge all that remained of a cross-berry tree with its branches cut short – a huge log that a cripple could have climbed. I well remember the feel of that sappy bark under my hands. My ancestors would have to be patient.

'I thought I would save you for the English guns,' my friend said. 'Listen, you can hear their thunder from here.'

And so you could. You could not see them for there was still the broad flat Nqutu plateau between where we stood and the British camp, but the battle at the place called Isandhlwana had begun, and we were late.

We ran. I without shield or spear, Mabuso with both, stabbing at the air in anticipation of what was to come. And what was to come?

The Zulu impi was stretched across the entire plateau. With only the reverse aspect of their shields towards us, and at that distance, it was impossible to tell which regiment was ours. Ahead was row upon row of running men, we simply followed on.

To the right of us the retreating *baTlokwa* horsemen were still to be seen; halting now and then to spring to the ground and rattle off a volley into the Zulu ranks from across their ponies' backs. They didn't even cause a flinch.

Lightning, lightning of heaven it glitters and shines –
Sun, sun of the Zulus, it consumes all.

Twenty thousand voices filled out that chant. It swelled through those rocky hills, it rolled back the rumbling gunfire, it filled the chest and strengthened the knee. And all the time we were running, right across that plateau, it was with us. Then we reached the rim, and the first of many dead men. There it was the British turn to roar, and for the moment the cold rage of their cannon took our breath away.

Had I wanted to, I couldn't have stopped then. Half-running, half-falling, I crashed down that mountainside like a hurtling boulder. Half-lamb, half-leopard, I bounded into the midst of the foremost warriors, and onwards.

The British were ahead, you could see a blur of faces, of white helmets, blood red jackets and raised rifles. Stretched into a broken line, two deep, halfway around the base of the Isandhlwana. There seemed so few of them. One bloody charge would sweep them away – so we charged. *uSuthu! u – Sss – uthu!* – with the hiss and the boom of a breaking wave that war cry flung us forward; blind to the falling; careless of death. *uSuthu!*

They cut us down like thatching grass, those red-coated reapers; their line would smoke and flame, and Zulus would scream and fall, and creep in agony beneath their riddled shields. Close enough to see the frowns on those fiercely bearded faces, we were halted in a river of blood.

That was where I found Mabuso again, or rather he found me; flat on my belly in the long grass listening to the scything bullets, and hoping for a revival of my courage. I felt a tug at my ankles, there he was, next to me, smiling stupidly, clutching a dangerous looking muzzle loader. He pointed the thing towards the British and fired. Eh! He knew he'd ended the war with that shot. With a shout he stood up, perhaps to take the surrender. What he took was a bullet, dead centre in his stomach. Stupid Mabuso. Dear Mabuso.

I wanted to be true to my friend, true to our pledges. He begged me to – to kill him and end his agony. As it was I held him, felt his warm blood spew onto my shoulder, and shut my ears to his groaning pleas. I loved him, you see. Judge my weakness in that light.

Mabuso's spirit would have an abundance of good company. From all around in the long grass came the sound of pain, a lowing, groaning drone of death. And, to ensure the maintenance of that dirge – the never ending bullets.

Perhaps my friend's death drove me from my senses. For suddenly I found myself standing, a target for every British rifle there. And not only was I standing – I was shouting, yes with all the power of my lungs:

'*Mahlamvana who quenched the fire – did he order us to lie at the feet of the English? – No!*'

And the answer came, '*No! No! No!*'

'*Thou who was spat out by the elephant – is this how we are to die?*'

'*uSuthu!*' The chest of the army rose. '*uSuthu!*' The horns began to lower.

Dew melts before the sun – perhaps that explains it – explains why so many of those white men stood there neglecting to raise their rifles – they knew they were about to be overwhelmed; they wanted to close with us and make an end of it.

There was much more that I still shouted but the ground was trembling with the stamp of feet, the air was frayed with the rattle of spear on shield. Who was to hear one voice? Many Zulu were dead, but many many more were up. The war cry roared out – the British fire faltered – chest, horns and loins the Zulu impi pounded down. I with them.

With them yes, and at the same time alone. Like a herder caught in a storm I was rocked and wrenched this way and that. There wasn't any shelter for the shieldless there. From all around I could hear the thud of spear striking flesh, the shout – '*Ngadla!* I have eaten!' – yes, and see too the fountaining blood as the British line took the shock, then convulsed like a stepped-on snake coiling and striking left and right.

How they fought. There wasn't a bayonet that wasn't dripping as rifle and all it clattered down. There wasn't a man on the ground who hadn't fought a hero's fight.

All the way back to their wagons and tents we mauled them. They closed up back to back – clubbing, bayoneting and shooting, as the spears rained down.

Yelling defiance they retreated until, slipping in their own blood, the steepness of the Isandhlwana stopped them. There the last of them died.

It was a long, terrible – bloody day. A day of events of which you might say: that, I shall never forget. But as bark falls from an ageing log, so memory strips away with time.

I was in the shade of the Isandhlwana when the last throat had cried its final cry. I had a war spear, long-bladed and thick with blood, I remember. But whose spear and whose blood? Surely all that should be clearer than the muddy puddle of memories that remain for me of that day.

The last white man to die in that battle had been a white induna – an officer. He'd had blood all over his face. Down the rocky Isandhlwana he'd stormed, snarling, whirling his sword into a silver arc as it slashed left and right. As mad as a wounded lion, a score of Zulus toppled before his blade – then suddenly it was I he was attacking.

I remember that well because, you see, that man has visited me on countless nights since then . . . He stands there his chest heaving, his tunic blotched and torn. There is a moment when he draws back that furious sword, and that's when my spear finds his open chest and sinks in as far as I can drive it.

Still he tries to hack me, that induna. He strains – his face is savage with effort. Then he sinks, he topples like a lopped tree. I have killed him, so it is for me to liberate his spirit. I do it: I slit him from rib to penis, his bowels spill out – his spirit is free. That is as much as the dream permits me of the washing of my spear. It is enough.

I turned my back on the Isandhlwana, walked the short distance to the river, and there I sat listening to the water, letting it wash away a thousand screams, until a moon no thicker than a fingernail-cutting was well into the sky.

As Sigewelegwele had said, my kraal was within the smell of the breeze. I didn't go straight there however. Mabuso's home was an easy half a day's walk further west. I wanted them to know how a son of their kraal had become a hero. Especially I wanted to relate to Indewe, Mabuso's sweetheart, the story of how her lover remained at Isandhlwana. What praises I had practised, what deeds they would be told of. . . How different it was when I saw her waiting the next day with her friends at a bend in the road.

Hau! I tried. She'd loved a live hero, she didn't need him to be dead to be convinced of his bravery. Those maidens' wails shrivelled the words in my throat. I turned and walked slowly away until I could no longer hear the crying and was once more alone. So I thought.

Leather rasping on acacia thorns gave my pursuer away. It was Fana, one of Indewe's friends, and the garment that was caught was a beaded loin cloth that had, in her progress, been snared and hitched to one side by the offending thorns. She was indeed a full grown woman – that knavish acacia shrub left no room for any doubt.

With a delicately balanced clay water urn and her dignity to contend with, to have jerked would have seen a loss of both. Her extrication needed to be at the same time slow and balanced – which made it all the more revealing, intriguing. Let me say, it brought a breath of life back into me.

Not for an instant was her lofty urn in danger – nor her dignity. With the modesty that comes with breeding she kneeled until the captive flap of beadwork unsnagged and once more cloaked its treasure. Then, eyes lowered, she passed me on the track. Charmed by the graceful mobility of her departing buttocks, a fresh thought had entered my mind. The burden of my sadness I left hanging to that acacia bush – it was my turn to follow.

Only once did she glance back to see me coming on. My reflection over hers at the water's edge was the next she saw of me. The urn dipped into the reed pool and sucked at our reflections.

'I have killed in battle,' I told her. 'I must be purified.'

'I saw your spear was head down as you walked.'

'Yes.'

'But you warrior are as blind as you are brave. Have you never seen these beads I wear? See the red, that is for my crying eyes as they look at you. See the white, that shows the purity of my love for you.'

What could I say? To be truthful I had never really paid much attention to the messages that women weave into their beadwork, not until that day. Fana stood from the river facing me. It was true what she said; I had been blind. Here was a woman with the pattern of love in her beads, in her soft eyes, in her sweet mouth.

'You wish to wipe your axe? Am I to be your cleanser?' Her words were as sibilant as the rustling reeds.

'Yes you must do that!'

'Yes, we must do that.' Her tone repaired the harshness of my words. 'We must because you have killed, and need the fortification of the act. We must *hlobonga* to purify you – we must have sex without breaking in and protect you from the disease that killing brings. But I do it, not as a duty, I do it because I love you. I always have.' One pace then brought Fana's full soft body against my hardness. 'Remember,' she whispered to me. 'Please remember.'

The will of the man must be stronger than his penis to *hlobonga*. For after it is all done, and both of you are drained and weak in the knee – the woman must still be able to command the dowry of a virgin. The man must be free to go his way. I wiped my axe there amongst the supple river reeds, and not just once. Fana said it would be cleaner by repetition, and who was I to argue? How was she to know that loving me would be her death?

A summons was waiting for me when I reached my home kraal that night. A summons that instructed me to make full haste to King Cetchwayo's royal kraal – Ulundi. He who was spat out by the elephant – the branch that extinguished the flame – the laurie of Menzi – the King of the Zulus, wished to see *me*: immediately . . . Why should this be?

The question remained in my throat. When the lion roars, lesser beasts are silent . . . I hurried to the place of my King; to Ulundi.

Ulundi crowned the grassy dome of the mountains that surround it as a headring might top an induna's regal brow. It was a vast place. The biggest and most powerful war kraal in all of Zululand.

Power, let me tell you about power. This Cetchwayo was a man who knew what the word meant. A nod of his proud uSuthu head, a wave of his huge arm, and a man – no a score of men would march up to the royal slayers, chanting grateful praises at every step. When he frowned the nation pondered, when he smiled the warmth of it reached across the land. No man could marry without his consent. Thus all life both the beginning and ending of it was by royal favour. Not a witchdoctor's brew or thought existed without the knowledge of it reaching Ulundi. Not an ox was born, or a patch of ground tilled that the King did not hear about it. His praises were sung every morning:

> *Thou, Mahlamvana, who quenched the fire*
> *Kindled by the white people . . .*
> *Thou, the laurie of Menzi,*
> *Who flashed out the red flash from the Intumeni heights*
> *Which extend to the sea . . .*
> *Thou the worster of the elephant with a tuft of hair*
> *Bandylegged one through the overcoming of brothers . . .*

First light was the time for the sharp voice of Cetchwayo's praise singer to pierce the mind, and excise any dark doubts the citizens of Ulundi may have had regarding their King. I was still stretched out upon my sleeping mat and being thus restored when they came for me, two of the King's bodyguards, stern-eyed, hard-voiced. I was, they said, to be quick.

'Thunder that pealed from atop Isandhlwana hill.'

The spate of praises drew us as we trotted past the blur of rush huts and fences of woven branches that led to the King's quarters.

'He who stabs kneeling like a calf . . .' We were getting closer, the outpouring was coming louder. My stomach was dropping deeper.

'There is the elephant.'

Indeed there he was, King Cetchwayo fat and healthy returning from his morning walk, the royal anus wiper happy to have done his duty one fulfilled pace to his rear.

'Here is Umzeze, Noble Elephant!'

I was announced. Noble Elephant seated himself and regarded me with a look that bent the voice back in my throat, as I cried out the Royal salute *Bayede!* and advanced.

Nothing in Zululand happens that the King doesn't hear of it. So it was with my demented act at Isandhlwana.

'Fill the vessel of my ear,' Cetchwayo demanded. So I did. I told him everything that had passed on that day. And, when I had finished, he made me go over it again, and again, testing me with questions, turning my mind inside out as though he were probing for something, some piece of evidence perhaps. I could hide nothing.

That man took me sip by sip until he'd drained me like a gourd.

'You stood up spearless and shieldless. *Why?*'

Once more I told him of the cattle, the *udibi*, the charge of the *baTlokwa* horsemen and my tumble at the ravine's edge. 'My shield and spear were lost to me there I am ashamed to say.'

'There is no shame in it,' Cetchwayo said. 'You are a man among men, Umzeze. At a time when the indunas had lost control you sprang up weaponless, your contempt for the English bullets raised the regiments to their feet. I and my indunas are proud of you, Zulu.'

They didn't look proud of me. The indunas seated behind Cetchwayo were scowling about like leashed wildcats. Sigewelegwele was there, as was Tshingwayo and the legendary Mbopa whose spear blade had ended the rule of Shaka Zulu so long ago. There were other indunas, I didn't recognise them all.

'The English. Tell me about the English.' The request drew my gaze back to the King.

'They fought bravely, High One.'
'Yet we beat them.'
'We beat them, Father.'
I thought I was to be dismissed. There was a long silence touched only by the distant lowing of the royal herd and the morning call of inKankane ibis. Cetchwayo's eyes were shaded with thought, his lips tight with doubt. As big as he was in every way and as powerful, I felt only pity for him then. Perhaps that was why, when he asked me whether I thought the English had been truly vanquished, I said:

'Yes, King.'

He saw the lie. He saw that I was at odds between my mind and my mouth, and I think he saw the reason for it too. There wasn't another man who noticed the intimacy that flowed between King and subject at that instant. He knew what I knew. We were allies, locked into an unvoiced truth. More English soldiers would return with more guns – the Zulus were brave but bravery could not turn aside a musket volley.

'Of course you are right.' Cetchwayo nodded. I was dismissed, perhaps to be permitted to return to the tranquillity of my home. On my knees then, I backed hopefully out of sight.

It was not to be. I spent the rest of that day, together with other warriors who had washed spears, being doctored and fortified. It was night time before I returned to the visitors' compound, my hut, and a further urgent summons to attend upon my King.

He was eating when I arrived, huge haunches of dripping meat. Gratefully he wasn't disposed to share. Swallowing whilst stretched out prone, though respectful, will bring about frightful winds – agony in the presence of a king.

It soon became apparent to me as to why he had summoned me at that late hour – it was a time for privacy. Apart from one full breasted serving girl we were alone, screened by the dense arched mimosa walls of his eating hut. Despite that, Cetchwayo breathed his words to me in tones that barely bridged us.

'You, Umzeze, lied to me this morning.'
'Yes, High One.'
Here was the King of all Zululand, and here was a self-confessed liar. He had but to raise his voice and the slayers would have come pounding in to rearrange my body parts. I was

apprehensive, but not terrified. I was puzzled, and more than anything else, excited. Cetchwayo had not brought me here to have my neck. He had brought me here because he had something important to say to me.

'The English have thrust a spear deep into the belly of our nation,' he said. 'Do you know, Umzeze, that for every ten brave men who left for Isandhlwana, one did not return. Can there ever be tears enough to mourn such a tragic loss?'

My mind went back to Mabuso, the bravest of them all.

'Always have I looked up to the English indunas as a child looks up to a respected father. It was they who lifted the crown to my head. And now they show themselves to be no better than the Boers – natural cheats who lie about land boundaries, whose words have less substance than a gadfly reflection. Why? I ask myself, why? I would never have been stupid enough to take up my war shield against them, and the English know it. They want me to be weak so they can rob me. I am strong so they must crush me. But first, being so Christian, so civilised, they must endeavour to find a reason. They scatter false accusations in the wind and the dust settles at my door.'

It was dark. The glowing coals in the hearth needed new sticks to give us light, but the King gave no such order. The serving maid gathered the board and what remained of the food and departed. Of Cetchwayo all that I could see then was his eyes, glinting, floating within the smoke haze, as though there was nothing else of him. Mouthless, his words then seeped into my mind. Cetchwayo had had a dream . . .

'I was standing in the cattle kraal, my departed father, Mpande, came to me. He asked me what blood it was that stained the land. I told him that it was the blood of his people. Mpande was angry with me, saying that the nation and I with it would be eaten up.

' "Your time is nearly over," Mpande told me. "You must look to your heritage. There will come one day a new leader; a Zulu as brave as Shaka; as wise as I am; as loved as you are Cetchwayo, my son. He will be called Okhethiwe. And when he comes the regalia of kings must be his – my sacred assegai – the hearth stones of Zulu – the Inkatha of Shaka. These and other things that you now own are his inheritance. For without them, where will he get his power? See to it Cetchwayo my son." '

That was Cetchwayo's dream. And that was the reason why I had been summoned to him. I was to be the guardian of the ultimate symbol of Zulu unity.

'Shaka Zulu's royal Inkatha is to be in your charge,' Cetchwayo said solemnly. 'Hide it. Preserve it. Take it to a secret place far from here where it will be safe for many lifetimes. That is what the spirit of King Mpande has demanded. This is what you Umzeze, hero of Isandhlwana, have been chosen by me to do. Do not fail me.'

I didn't fail him. In the month of *newaba*, the seventh month when the tender green shoots of summer are starting to tickle forth – the British came again. This time as my king and I had foreseen, nothing could stand in their way. Like the branded footprints of some wanton giant, black smouldering kraals marked their savage progress across the land. And every razed kraal brought them one step closer to their objective – Ulundi.

Ulundi, and the guiltless puzzled man who called that place his *indlu ezinkulu enobukhosi* – his great royal house.

'They crowned me in the morning and overthrew me in the afternoon.' Those were the last words I ever heard from my King. He spoke them on the eve of that last hopeless battle, and no words could have summed up his rule better than those. The British wanted Cetchwayo's land for their own people. To get it they had to break his power – so they did.

In the rays of first light they marched over the Mbilane river across the Mahlabatini plains and up the grassy slope towards Ulundi.

With their trumpets baying and their drums snarling out the time. With the yellow sun bright on the brass of barrels, badges and sharp steel bayonets, they came. Blue-coated horsemen bobbing within a square frame of scarlet tramping foot soldiers. Five thousand of them, shoulder to shoulder, they thrust that final massive wedge of death into the heart of Cetchwayo's ravaged country.

But death to a Zulu warrior, to any true Zulu is but a stepping over to the ancestors, and by no means an end of existence – nothing to cause fear. It was easy that day for the indunas to exhort their regiments. With their kraals in ashes; with their king on his knees, what was there left to live for?

For me, observing from a nearby hillside, my agony was as great as any of those bleeding warriors. Perhaps it was greater. I watched the impi rise up and charge, slowly at first, then faster and faster until it seemed like the black wave of their momentum would dash them across the British as a storm sea swamps a rock. It was just an illusion. They weren't even near the square when the British volley fire ripped into them, again and again and again. They faltered. They turned, and fled.

I watched as startled Zulus dashed into the smoke columns of burst cannon shell, to spear the death-dealing enemy that sprang from within.

I watched in agony as the Zulu impi torn and shattered by shell and machine gun lifted themselves for one last charge. I didn't need to see more. Cetchwayo's dream had transformed itself into a reality before my eyes. And I was part of it.

Ulundi was burning and there were flames all around me as I took the Inkatha from its sacred place. British horsemen were jumping the thorn barricades, their long pennant lances were red with Zulu blood. I saw Mvulaba, the King's war doctor, fall screaming into the flames. Where the King was I did not know. I thought about only what I had to do: *preserve the Inkatha of Shaka Zulu for he who was to come*. I took it and ran from that place of death.

For days on end I hid from the British, not daring even to forage for food for fear of showing myself. I had to think of a way of hiding the Inkatha so that I could transport it. It was no small matter to hide a thing as thick as a grown man's thigh and as round as a coiled python. It needed a container; a big container – something that would not arouse suspicion. Something that would last for many lifetimes.

A basket, that was what I needed. A big urn-shaped *iquthu* basket; woven so tightly that it was water-tight; woven of the hardy *umchobozi* reeds that did not tire with age. Yes, and Fana would weave it for me. She had the fingers that could do such a job.

Fana, how she cried when I limped into her kraal, as thin-ribbed as a toothless dog. How she worked on that basket. *Hau!* There was never another woman like my Fana.

For ten days and as many nights we hid amongst the *umchobozi* rushes while her nimble fingers wove a tight *iquthu* basket around that magic thing.

For a hundred days – more perhaps, she walked behind me carrying the royal Inkatha on her head like so much grain.

Many good hiding places I found and just as many I rejected, until one day in the far-off mountains of Lebombo, as if Mpande's spirit had called me to it, I found the perfect place. A cave tunnelled high into the cliffs of a mountain ridged like the back of a basking crocodile. The entrance was on a ledge like the one Mabuso had rescued me from.

It was in that cave, in a hole lined carefully with resin and river clay, that Fana placed the *iquthu* basket with its sacred contents finally down to rest.

It was there that I killed her. She knew of my vow to Cetchwayo – she knew that only I could know of that hiding place. Half-smiling, half-crying she turned to me. I did what I had to do.

I didn't fail my King.

* * *

The flame that had once topped a tall new candle was flicking up little writhing black smuts in its final spluttering efforts. It had burned all night and was about to die, it didn't matter. It was coming dawn and it wouldn't be needed much longer. Like the shrunken old Zulu spread on the sagging steel divan there – it had served its purpose.

With as much dignity as his pain and trembling joints would allow, he drew himself upright. Sinuous shoulders took the strain. Eyes as deep and peaceful as grave pits, peered almost expectantly at the whitening window panes. Perhaps he saw something in those pale sooty squares that the other man there couldn't see.

Stripped of the dignity of darkness then, the room and its tatty contents were exhibited. Corrugated iron walls in a dozen shades of blistered peeling paint began to creak as the sun worked its heat into them. The only other piece of furniture there, a rough pine packing case, held the other person there – a man, middle-aged, slightly built if you could believe the outline of the blanket-draped shoulders slumped against one wall.

The candle burned invisibly for a while, then died with a noisy little splutter that widened the eyelids of the seated man. He yawned into a stretch that shrugged loose the cloaking blanket. Then stood, and crossed to the bed and the old man he called his father.

'No,' he smiled. 'No Father. You did not fail your king. You did what you had to do.' But in his heart he wished that Umzeze had failed. He had a strong intuitive feeling that Shaka Zulu's Inkatha, interred by his father in the Lebombo mountains so long ago was destined to receive the kiss of life. Certainly it wouldn't be his lips that bestowed it. The Inkatha would best serve the Zulu nation as a memory. It was a relic of a barbarous age. An age of despotism, sorcery and godlessness. Such a symbol was the last thing his people needed.

Mancoba, son of Umzeze was a Christian. Not a tribal Christian, not one of those who when things went wrong dithered between *Unkulunkulu* the God of Gods and the cross of Jesus – who prayed to the ancestors on Monday, Christ on Sunday and got blind drunk in between. No he had bathed in the clear flowing waters of the Word, and he wasn't going back to the bubbling mudpools of Satan. Not even to dip his toes in. Not even for his father.

Mancoba cradled the old man's head and shoulders and gently lowered him back onto the mattress. It surprised him, how light the wasted body had become. He noticed that around one thin wrist Umzeze wore a *muthi* amulet, a charm from the tribal Inyanga doctors to ward off the consumption that was wasting him. On a strut next to the bed lay an assortment of roots and leaves, most of them wrapped in dirty newspaper.

'You must take the medicine *I* brought you from the chemist,' he sighed. 'Inyanga *muthi* is not going to help you get better.'

'Nor is the chemist's medicine,' came the stubborn reply. 'The truth is, son of mine, that I am dying. You know it, and I know it. I summoned you yesterday evening that the secret of secrets could be opened to you. I have carried it in my chest since my youth and now I am going home. There was much to tell and the effort of it has spent me. . . You have heard it all now though, and I am glad. . . Now I can happily go.'

'Father. No! . . . Listen!'

It was a plea from the soul, a plea completely misinterpreted.

'Of course I must go, my son. There comes a time for all of us to go. Just pray that you one day may leave by as fine a gate as has been opened for me.'

What Umzeze lacked in strength he invested in fervour. His frail arms were irresistible as they drew his son down to him.

'Our people suffer as they have never suffered, my son. They have become so used to being trodden upon that now they know no better – is the floor of the hut unhappy with its position? The Indian landlords and merchants cheat us. The Boers use us as though we were a nation of slaves. And the English. Eh! The English see it all; their words never end and their deeds never begin . . . But I tell you my son, the time is coming when Zulus will say – enough! Perhaps it will be in your lifetime, Mancoba; when this new Shaka will show himself to the nation. And the strength of the Inkatha will rally the nation to his side. Ah! If only *I* could have seen it.'

'In my lifetime?'

The prospect was abhorrent. A leader who derived his power from the pagan symbol of Shaka Zulu could be nothing but a heathen. And *he* Mancoba; an Anglican, a devoted Christian, was to be the vehicle of restoration of this bloody symbol. *Never!* Someone else would have to be chosen for this task. He drew himself from his father's arms.

'Umzeze . . .'

He was about to utter those words of denial when abruptly he stopped. The consequences of some other person assuming this mission were equally unthinkable. The Inkatha would be resurrected. Whether Mpande's prophecy held any truth in it or not, some despot would see the potential of Shaka's Inkatha, and use it to seize power. The world was filled with the agents of the devil. No. If the burden of the Inkatha had to be borne on his shoulders, then so be it.

With that revelation comfortably positioned to cushion his fall to deceit, Mancoba said:

'Yes . . . I will do it.'

And what those few words meant was I will accept the burden of this custodianship. *Yes.* And by the grace of God that evil thing will never see the light of day.

The words, however, held quite a different meaning for old

Umzeze. He believed that his pledge to Cetchwayo ka Mpande had been provided with succession. His son would do it.

Happy the dying man who perceives his life's task as having been fulfilled. Umzeze lifted a contented smile to the man standing beside him. Mancoba smiled back, and hoped that the sadness drawing his lips was not visible.

Mancoba sighed, turned away, and with the apathy of the too far fallen, signed the quickest of cruciforms across his chest. He bade his father, 'Stay well.'

'You go well.' Umzeze coughed. 'Come back soon. There is more to tell you.'

The January sun is quick and strong. Mancoba stood for a moment in the opened doorway of Umzeze's shack until the glare was bearable. He glanced back once, and somehow it made him feel better that he could now only dimly perceive the figure of his father in the gloom.

'Yes,' he said. 'I'll come straight home.' Then he hurried out into what could only be a better day.

It started well enough. He was late for work, but that was not bad. His employment in the cool subterranean archives of the Natal Provincial Reference Library was of a solitary nature. It was to replace the old volumes and manuscripts that were stored there back in correct order and sequence once they had been used – not to find them when they were required. He was not expected to be bright enough to do that, just to replace them. As it was a rarity for anyone to return anything before tea time, his lateness went unnoticed.

Mancoba enjoyed his job, his record attested to that – twenty years without one day's sick leave. No one called him 'boy', or raised their voice to him. In fact, no one called him anything. In the sepulchral atmosphere of the archives, books were the only things ever properly identified, or authors, or index numbers long and complicated. Nothing else mattered in that stern high-ceilinged silence.

There was plenty of time to do the job – which he enjoyed; and to read – which he adored. Of course all the available reading material was of an historical nature. But that accident of circumstances had produced a surprising result. Mancoba the illiterate sweeper had, after years of molelike diligence, become Mancoba the educated historian.

It rained on and off for the best part of that day, which kept all but the most hardy and persevering researchers at bay, and allowed Mancoba, almost without interruption to indulge in his passion for dusty manuscripts. At closing time he replaced in its little crypt a copy of Bishop Lee's *Once Dark Country*, and with the biblical quote – 'Go ye into all the world and make disciples', he stepped into the hustle-bustle of an emptying city.

Home was a squat tin shack – one of a thousand that covered an urban hillside like a spew of dumped scrap . . . Inside the shack lay a sick old man who coughed loudly and incessantly, and made the long sweaty nights longer, and more sweaty. But although Mancoba would have wished these things otherwise, it was not the ugliness nor the plaguing sickness that caused him to dawdle that evening on his return to the township. The cause for his lack of haste was Umzeze's injunction: 'Come back soon – there is more to tell you.'

Mancoba wished to hear no more on the previous night's subject – not another word. He would tell Umzeze precisely that. He reached the shack an hour later than was normal. He pushed the door back slowly on its ailing squeaky hinges. He quietly set down his purchases of bread and tinned fish, then drew a new candle from its packet and lit it.

Umzeze would speak no more on any subject. Umzeze of Isandhlwana; Umzeze, the bravest of the brave, was dead.

Mancoba knelt next to the sunk-eyed slack-jawed thing that had said: 'Come back soon – there is more to tell you'; and Mancoba sobbed.

He sobbed so grievously that the noise of it brought the neighbours in. Some of them shed a gentle tear in sympathy, and some just looked. Most of them said that Umzeze had been a fine man. All of them were puzzled by Mancoba's massive grief. He had been an old man had he not? A sick man. They did not understand. Nor did Mancoba enlighten them.

His sorrow was for a simple man who had died in the belief that his torch of duty was now held by another. The fine gate that he had passed through was a false gate, and there was not a single Christian tenet that could help relieve that agony. Thus Mancoba cried for himself, because he wished that he could have done it in a truer way. And he cried for Umzeze, whose sin it was to have *not* failed his king. He cried for a long time. And the neighbours shook their heads and most of them said:

'He was a good son this Mancoba. Listen to him weep.'

So that was how Umzeze's secret became Mancoba's secret. But, whereas Umzeze had borne it with the strength of pride, to Mancoba it was a terrible burden. He prayed about it as the years passed by. He prayed for guidance and for strength, and perhaps that was what he got. For as he grew older the belief grew in him that in the end it would not be enough for him to die with Umzeze's testament left unexecuted – his secret intact. It came to Mancoba that the very reason for this secret should be expunged from his conscience. After all it was still vaguely possible that someone would inadvertently stumble upon the hiding place of this pagan relic. His tortuous vow of silence would then have been in vain. Everything would have been in vain.

So he thought about all that Umzeze had told him. He thought about the cave, tunnelled high into the cliffs of a mountain that was ridged like the back of a basking crocodile. He thought about the contents of a large *iquthu* basket. And he prayed:

'Lord give me the means to do what I must do. Lord guide me safely to this distant place, then give me the strength to destroy the Inkatha of Shaka Zulu . . . Oh! Lord, thy will be done.'

*   *   *

Perhaps that is how it all came about . . . Perhaps the events that occurred thereafter were the legacy of the will of God.

1

The Lebombo mountains sweep down along the coastal plains of South-East Africa and form a spine some thousand kilometres long that links three nations. One of these nations is that of the Zulus. The southernmost tail of the Lebombo vertebrae belongs to the Zulus. They call that place Ingwavuma – salute the leopard.

It is a rough and wild country of thirsty rolling mountains, of thorn and rock and aloe. But where the valleys run deep towards the west, there are dark green forests of stinkwood, wild fig, and milkwood trees that filter out the sun some forty metres from the ground. The mark of the leopard is there and people fear it. They fear too the strike of the black mamba, and the toothy jaws of inGwenya the crocodile who waits at the river ford. The predators of that place are many and quick, but the absolute agents of terror of those sunless gorges are far more intelligent, and far more spiteful than mere forest beasts. They are human. They are the *umthakathi* and *baloyi* – the sorcerers and witches of Ingwavuma who kill for the joy of it. For they are moulded with an evil heart.

So hide the waste matter of your body lest it be stolen and made by them into the medicine of death. And watch your step because the vine you tread on could turn into a striking snake. Even the soil of your footprint is enough for the *umthakathi* to kill you with. So beware my friend. And if you *are* struck down, and the *umthakathi* are to blame, then hurry for your time is short. The medicine of the white man will never cure this illness. Now is the time to consult the isangoma. Yes, the power of the sangoma is wonderful. The *amathongo* – the spirits of the ancestors who reside with the sangoma will tell her how to cure you. But be quick my friend. *Be quick!*

There is a sangoma more powerful than any other, indeed, more powerful than any sorcerer or witch. Her powers are extraordinary and her followers are many. The *umthakathi* scatter like chickens before her. They say her eyes are as grey as the summer rain. They say the spirits of the departed chiefs tell her things that no other Zulu knows: great things that concern not just you my friend, but all of us. Her name is Uhlanga.

There is a secret place in the Ingwavuma gorge. They say that if Uhlanga wishes to see you, that she will call you there; call you with the mind . . . And you will answer that call. You will go to her wherever you are, as willingly as the child of the breast. Such is the power of the diviner princess, the great sangoma Uhlanga.

* * *

Doctor Montague Law had made his camp at a beautiful spot beneath a shady fever tree on the shores of a lake called Mandlankunzi. Law had done for the day and he was tired. He tilted back on his camp stool until his shoulders rested against the warm metal bodywork of his Land Rover. He rumpled his shock of thick black hair and yawned. Then, to enhance his comfort further he lifted his legs and weighed them down on a folding metal table. The fact that he crushed some botanical specimens laid out on the table top did not worry him. They had already wilted in the afternoon sun and were of no further interest to him.

What interested him at that moment was the regional weather bulletin for the twenty-four hours that lay ahead. He had a battered portable radio in his hands with a wire aerial that trailed from the tree above him. Once he had heard what he wanted to hear . . . *Northern kwaZulu, fine and warm, winds southerly to south westerly, ten to fifteen knots* . . . he switched off.

The East Coast of Africa, or rather, his little sector thereof, was due to be blessed with the kind of weather conditions that any botanical scientist in the field would call favourable; excellent in fact.

'We're going to have good weather tomorrow.'

The response came in Zulu, somewhat muffled by the canvas walls of a biggish weathered once-beige tent. '*Ngempela* – Indeed, and I hope it lasts.'

If 3 × 7 metres of canvas tentage could be called home, then the space where Monty Law had stretched his lanky frame could be called the garden.

It was the most beautiful garden in all the world, how could it be otherwise, for neighbouring it were the green quilted foothills of the Lebombos; at hand were the virgin lakes of paradise. The place was Ingwavuma. It was nature's last retreat in Southern Africa.

Monty Law sighed. The wooden camp chair creaked and a pair of long, well-hiked legs took up his weight. He ambled down to the water's edge, and, having on nothing more than a pair of old denim shorts to hinder him, on into the lake. He kept walking until friendly little waves were playing up his thighs; the faded blue cloth clung darkly, and the sweat of a day's labour rinsed away from his groin. How he loved the cool lapping sweetness of that water on his sex parts, no human touch could ever be so gentle. He plunged into Lake Mandlankunzi.

'The crocodile will get you in a minute – *khona manje.*' This time there was no tentage to muffle the voice. Somewhat mocking, somewhat concerned, it carried clearly across the water to the swimming man. 'What if they get you. Eh?'

Well what if they did? It was more likely that the bilharzia would get him, but what if they did? Law thought about it as he stroked lazily past a thicket of reeds. *Typha latifolia*, he noted, growing uncharacteristically deeply in the water. Supposing there were crocs in that part of the lake – hungry ones. Who would miss him? The only woman whom he had ever really loved was dead. His parents were dead.

There *was* Kirsten; beautiful sister Kirsten. She was doing the job that he had been groomed to do. She was running the family sugar estates and running them well. He could count on one mourner at his funeral. It was a sobering thought. He would provide enough protein for one adult Crocodylus Niloticus for a few months, and after that everyone, including the croc, would have forgotten that he ever existed.

So Monty Law swam where the crocs swim, floated where the hippos float. But he had an extraordinarily good reason for wishing to survive a while longer too.

The reason was sontekile, a remedy of the isangoma, the witchdoctors of the Lebombo mountains from the times of King Cetchwayo ka Mpande. A remedy of which a long dead missionary had written:

'I despair of ever finding it, or even knowing what it is. Yet I have seen the results of its administration on no less than three occasions. What I observed was a miracle.'

The dated handwriting on the brittle age-tinted square of paper was as clear as if it were inked on the membrane of Law's mind.

'*Sontekile* is a Zulu word meaning twisted thing. Perhaps it takes its name from the appearance of some herb of the Lebombos. I do not know. I have searched for it for many years but have never seen it. My constant prayer is that the heathen isangoma who hold this secret may one day be moved by the hand of God to reveal their knowledge; that all mankind may benefit: that the vile disease of mylotopic paralysis will know a cure.'

Missionary Samuels had written much more on the subject of sontekile, or rather, on his inability to unearth the illusive twisted secret of the Lebombos. He had died in 1870 still thirsting for that knowledge of the isangoma. The only thing that had changed by then was the name of the disease: mylotopic paralysis had become known as multiple sclerosis . . . There was still no cure. To this day there was no cure.

The face of a lovely woman then entered the mind of Montague Law. The picture was so real that he said aloud, 'My sweetheart,' and she smiled her loving smile. But her beauty was as transient as a rose without water. She faded before him as he watched. She drooped and wilted and then she perished, and all because there was no cure for multiple sclerosis.

The strokes of the swimmer lost their elegance, they became fast and stabbing, and took him swiftly further from the shore. This race with his anger did not last long though; it burned him out quickly. It was always like that.

Tired, he turned and floated freely for a while, watching the hovering Malachite kingfishers watching him. He reached out his arms, splayed his fingers and thrust down against the water – an apology for wings. Water gave man his single chance to imitate free flight. He loved the water.

The lovely woman was gone now, and the impotent anger too. Residual in Montague Law, however, was an anguish that was constant. If he could succeed where Samuels had failed, just perhaps that anguish would fade as well.

A distant plume of smoke drew Law's attention to the campsite and suddenly he was cold and hungry. There was freshly caught milkfish on the griddle there, and more than one beer nestling in the coolness of the reeds – compensation for being man. Strokes, swift and stretched, hauled him back to shore. There was one other person who might miss him, one grey-haired Zulu pensioner.

Mancoba looked up from the cooking fire, smiled and raised a thin arm in greeting to his dripping and pensive employer.

He had worked for Doctor Law long enough to know when to talk and when not to talk. Right now the botanist had something occupying his mind. It would be a waste of breath to try and converse with him. Mancoba prodded the sizzling fish. It was almost cooked.

Law stood watching the Zulu at his work for a while. Then he said:

'I'm not giving up, Mancoba. I was thinking while I was swimming. We've been making the same mistakes as Samuels made. He spent a lifetime collecting and researching botanic specimens, and he got nowhere. He involved himself with a few lesser Inyanga – herbalists and isangoma, and that didn't help him either. What he didn't do, and what we have not done either, is to try to get closer to the high isangoma – the priestess diviners of the Lebombos. I think that's a mistake.'

'Samuels,' Mancoba said, 'was a Christian missionary. Those isangoma represented everything he opposed. How could he go cap in hand to them?'

'Exactly . . . he couldn't. But I can.'

'I wouldn't advise it, Doctor Law. These people are evil. They're death merchants. They practise magic rites. They raise the spirits of the dead and deal in vile concoctions. You'd come away tainted from such contact.'

'I might come away with sontekile.'

'No. All they have to offer is trickery.'

'I've got to try.'

'The fish is ready.'

The milkfish was as tender as its promise. The nightness enclosing their yellow circle of firelight, drew in as they ate.

'I've got to try,' Law said again. 'We've been walking these mountains for months and we're no closer to sontekile than we were at the beginning. At this rate we won't achieve any more than Samuels.'

'I can't go with you then' said Mancoba. 'Like Samuels, I don't believe they have anything to offer but trickery and evil.'

They finished the meal in silence. Then Law said: 'Think about it, Mancoba. You were the one who discovered Samuels' manuscript. You were the one who brought it to me. Don't quit now. Remember Samuels' words: "My constant prayer . . ." '

'. . . "That the sangoma who hold this secret may one day be moved by the hand of God to reveal their knowledge." ' Mancoba sighed. 'I too remember every word.'

'Perhaps that day has come.' Monty Law took the coffee pot from the coals, poured for them both and handed Mancoba his cup. 'I wouldn't like to go on alone, old man. You and I have been together for a while now, ever since they kicked you out of the public library.'

'Retired me,' Mancoba chuckled. This was a standing joke. 'With a gold watch and a pension too. But I see I can't dissuade you from doing this thing. I *will* think about it.'

'Sleep on it,' Law said.

Sleep was something that didn't come easily to Law. The slow westwards march of the night stars was a familiar pageant, and beneath it the hour glass of his mind turned again and again and the chronicle of his past trickled by. Somehow it always ended with the same picture. The picture of the woman he had loved.

She had died an awful death. The more so because she'd always had such hope, such vitality, such certainty that everything life had to offer was good. She'd died hitched up between a square squat little robot that made breathing noises for her, and another humanoid with a forever blinking cycloptic eye and a tracking impulse for a mouth. She'd died of an overdose of technology and a shortage of God. She had died of multiple sclerosis.

It always came back to God. Or rather the absence of God in the places where God should be – in the churches and the hospitals. There was nothing but people there, and pain. Lots of both.

Was God with the black Christian sleeping in the smoky glow of the embers?

To a tribal Zulu sleep was a limited death – *ubuthongo*, a time for the *amathongo*, the ancestral spirits, to bridge the gap and make known their wants. Mancoba was asleep, but Mancoba had turned his back on tribalism. So why then was he writhing on a bed of thorns? What presence was it that dared to call upon him and raise him up with a throatful of stammer and babble, night after night?

The old Zulu sank back with a sigh. He would remember nothing of it in the morning. Law, however, would remember quite a lot. There were certain recurring words and phrases amongst the gibberish that came up too often to be forgotten.

In the morning Mancoba would yawn and stretch his sinewed limbs and declare that he had never slept better. Mancoba would come with him, he was sure of it.

In the morning they would break camp and take leave of benevolent, beautiful Lake Mandlankunzi in exchange for a further episode of thorny inhospitality in that barbed spurred forest world of the high Lebombos – looking for a miracle.

Law had an impulse to get up then, to rummage for the photostat he had brought with him of the old manuscript and read it once more. He did not do that. He could feel sleep now, dragging him into its cosy world of fantasy. He did not have to get up – he was word perfect in the passage he wanted to read.

'Perhaps it is God's will that the honour of this discovery should not be mine, nor yet in my time. Yet it will happen . . .'

He had been such a fool. He had wasted months. But now he knew how not to proceed with the search. That was something. Sontekile seemed closer to him then than it ever had before.

Law's optimism was still with him in the morning. Mancoba helped him break camp and pack. He took his accustomed place in the Land Rover. Not another word was said on the subject of his leaving.

Law flogged his Land Rover through the flatlands – the palm veld and flood plains that bound the rolling Lebombos, careless of the pounding he was inflicting on man and machine. His sole concern was getting there.

There was a sangoma's kraal – whose existence they had only heard of – in the green shade of the fever trees within sound of the burbling rushing inGwenya shallows . . . *There*, it was whispered, the most gifted sangoma in all of Zululand held court. Uhlanga of the eyes of rain.

'I hear she has grey eyes,' Law shouted over the clatter of road noise. Mancoba eased closer to hear what his employer was saying. 'It'll take more than that to frighten me.'

The Zulu nodded. Talk was cheap. It would be another matter altogether when he was out of this Made in England steel canister and squatting on a reed mat. He would have a hundred generations of ingrained trickery to contend with then. That was supposing she even agreed to see them. Mancoba was comforted by the thought that Uhlanga would, in all likelihood, contemptuously rebuff Doctor Law's approaches.

Mancoba signalled the lefthand fork that would take them into the foothills. 'You need to be strong,' he advised. 'Strength is what they understand. Especially those such as the sangoma Uhlanga. Be proud with her. Be persevering. Be bold. Look straight into those strange, strange eyes of hers. Let her be the one to drop her gaze.'

'I will,' Law replied. But the words lacked the carry to be heard above the growing low-gear growl of the engine.

Where the rocky steeps started, they nuzzled the Land Rover up to the trunk of a shady knob-thorn tree and left it.

Remaining to be climbed were six hundred metres of mountain, along a donkey track winding through the aloes and rocks. They did not stop until the Land Rover was a toy thing far below and the Maputaland plains stretched to the horizon.

The other side of the mountain, the western slopes were quite different. The soil was moist there, fertile, supporting a thriving evergreen forest. What they sought in those thick, green valleys was a winding narrow pathway twisting its way downwards, finally dwindling out near the riverside kraal of the sangoma Uhlanga. 'Be alert for trickery there.'

They did not have to discover the pathway. Where the track looped by the broken bleached skeleton of a fallen milkwood tree, a guide was waiting – a novice sangoma. Her thin body, all over daubed with white river clay, could almost have been part of the pale decay.

She didn't ask, she didn't indicate, she slid from the tree trunk, stood inquisitively observing them for a moment, then turned and padded away.

Worn and stepped with roots the path descended. They followed.

It could have been the steepness that was taxing his old lungs, but Mancoba remained strangely silent as they worked their way lower. The forest canopy there was almost complete, but where the sky was visible it was dulling.

'It's getting towards evening,' Law said, all he said, all the way down. He didn't stop thinking though. His actions were fluid, almost reflexive; it was his mind that was grasping left and right as they passed deeper into the darkening valley.

And then they heard it; the swish of shallow flowing water, the reedy screech of cicadas. But more than that; quietly subjugating all that – the monotonous throb, throb, throb of a sangoma's hide drum. The spirits were being called in. The neophyte quickened her pace and they followed on.

'Be careful Doctor Law,' was Mancoba's last and most unnecessary piece of advice.

Only a simpleton would have failed to be vigilant in the presence of the sangoma – the great diviner priestess Uhlanga. It would have been an insult to her estate to approach with any other attitude.

The entrance to her hut was designed to admit only those humble or desperate enough to grovel. It was surmounted by the horns of sacrifices past; flanked by protective charms of great power. With the rear end of the crawling apprentice to guide him, Law scraped through – one of the desperate.

Uhlanga was waiting. She had, she said, been so doing since midday. 'You arrive on chameleon's legs,' she stated. 'And with the camouflage of its kind to match. Why have you sought me out?'

Law said: 'Where there is wisdom, is that not where the seeker should come to drink? Even the chameleon must drink.'

She'd likened him to the most despised reptile in Zulu folklore. The beast responsible for the origin of death. Law decided to capitalise on the legend.

'Like the chameleon, I also bear a message. Unlike the chameleon I will deliver it.'

'Deliver it!' Uhlanga – bandoliered with goatskins, cascaded with feathers, beads and bladders, paunched and bulging with mammal ampleness – demanded. She was close enough to reach out and touch if he'd so dared. It was the time divide of a century and a half that really separated them; like an echo chasm ready to whip away the sense of it all – to make the difference between what the scientist delivered and what the sangoma accepted. Law did what he said he would do. He looked boldly into the incredible rain grey eyes of the sangoma.

'Once, a long time ago . . .' Law took a deep and hopeful breath '. . . in the days when King Cetchwayo ka Mpande was a young man, there lived in Durban a missionary doctor called Samuels. Samuels ran a clinic in which he treated black and white alike. He had amongst his patients three white settlers who all presented with symptoms that were alike. Sometimes they would stumble for no reason and fall. The lightest thing would suddenly become too much to hold. A numbness would creep on them and where there was only one person, they would see two . . . bewitched you might say.'

And he had her. The sangoma Uhlanga sat bent towards him, head cocked, attentive. Her upper body, Law noticed, was swaying very slightly as if moved by music. Then he realised there *was* music, soft melodious music. The song of the apprentices, had it been any softer, would have been sheer imagination. They were clapping hands tenderly enough to cup a hovering butterfly. Law listened to it. He felt reassured by its gentleness.

He told Uhlanga how the missionary Samuels had tried every remedy and therapy he knew. But in spite of all his efforts, the disease he recognised as multiple sclerosis had progressed falteringly, but surely through the men's bodies. They became paralysed. They were dying. One morning he had gone to his hospital to find three beds empty – all three patients had vanished.

'Their relatives had come for them in the night. They'd been taken, Samuels was told, to the Lebombo mountains to a sangoma of great repute. This sangoma, it was said, had a cure for such a disease.'

'*Yebo*,' agreed Uhlanga. 'Yes – that is what wise relations would have done.'

'Samuels despaired of ever seeing the men again. He censured the relatives severely for what they had done and sent them back to the Lebombos to bring his patients back again – at least so that they could die under a Christian roof. The relatives returned, but they couldn't find the men, or the sangoma. They begged forgiveness and Samuels forgave them. They prayed for the souls of the three lost men. But their prayers were wasted. You see, the men weren't dead.

'One day, about a year later, when Samuel was digging in his garden, he looked up to see two men approaching. They looked healthy, they had put on weight, but he recognised them in an instant. They were his patients.

'They told a story of a *muthi* called sontekile that had taken away the agonies of their disease. They were cured, they said. And it appeared as though they were. The symptoms never appeared again and both men went on to outlive the missionary . . . The third man never returned. He stayed in the Lebombos and took a Zulu bride. It is said that he outlived them all.'

'They'd been cured by a sangoma of the mountains,' Uhlanga said. 'And that is your message?'

'My message is: what was done before can be done again. There are many people dying terribly from this same disease today. We can help them.'

'You believe the cure to have come out of sontekile?'

'Yes.' That was what he believed. That was what a long-dead missionary had written. The question was, what did she the sangoma believe? She said:

'The men you speak of had been made ill by sorcery. They were saved by the black medicine – the *muthi mnyama*. As clever as you are white man, you will never be able to make such *muthi*; *muthi* that can ward off the evil inflicted by one man upon another. Such a disease is treated by standing the sick man in the sun. His shadow is cut and doctored and the earth, so treated, is then fed to him. Now you have it. Do you think your doctors will be impressed?'

That was what she believed. There was the divide – wider if possible than anything Law had imagined. His strategy had foundered. His western-trained mind was not capable of coping in this world of tribal medicine, where mountain wizards hurl lightning-bolts and *muthi wokubulala* kills from a distance with the sureness of a bullet. He felt frustrated. He felt angry.

A slanting red beam from the dying sun touched on the place by the river; slipped beneath the meagre door and set the hut aglow. In the soft light he could feel the sangoma's pale grey eyes scrutinising him, yet when he looked up she would not hold his gaze. She said softly.

'Then you understand that there is nothing here for you. Nothing that I can give you.' But there was a hesitancy dispersing her words that hadn't been there before. Her words were clear: it was her manner which suggested a desire for further dialogue. It was as though she anticipated something more from him. More of what?

'How. . .? You said you were expecting me. . . How did you know I was coming?' It was a fumble, but Law had come a long way to be here. He too had a need. 'If the spirits informed you that we were coming, then surely the spirits saw importance in my visit. For me to depart empty-handed, would that be what they wanted?'

'You talk lightly about the spirits,' Uhlanga rebuked. 'Do *not* do that. What the spirits want for you has no bearing on what you want for yourself. You think you have travelled far, whereas your journey has not even started. You think you have seen your destination, but your eyes have not even been opened.'

'My search is for sontekile, that's all.'

'No Doctor Law, sontekile has connected you to your search; to me. That is all.'

'You said there is nothing more that you can give me.'

'And that is true. The rest is here for you to take – once you can see to take. Look around you white man – tell me what you see and what you hear. Tell me what you *feel*.'

He saw the apprentices, swaying slowly, singing sweetly – as softly as the rustle of winter foliage. He saw his companion Mancoba seated next to him, his teeth working agitatedly on his lower lip. There were the encircling rush and wattle frame walls, hung with the magic symbols of the trade of the sangoma; the low clay *umsamo*-altar which hid the sangoma's sacred tools. The sangoma Uhlanga – the most powerful priestess diviner in all of Zululand. More than anything, in the blackness of her face, he saw the eyes – the mist-grey eyes. They did not waver now. Now they were viscid and persuasive and they drew at him like the undertow of a shore wave.

'Look around you,' she said again. 'I think you are learning. Yes, I see that you are learning. For you there is much to learn.'

He wondered what it was that he had to learn. He felt the tug of Mancoba's hand upon his shoulder, compelling him to break contact with those eyes. Irritated by this action he turned to see what it was with Mancoba. The old Zulu looked very frightened. His hands were trembling, grasped now tightly beneath his chin – an almost prayer-like gesture.

Law shook his head in reassurance – he was in control.

'No,' mouthed Mancoba. 'No. No. No.' He drew at Law's shoulder.

Law, vexed at the Zulu's lack of understanding, shrugged loose from the grip. He was close now to the knowledge he wanted. Could Mancoba not understand that? He turned back to the sangoma – apologetic for the behaviour of his servant. She nodded; smiled at Mancoba a thin and condescending smile. She said:

'This Zulu weighs you down. He is a burden to you on your journey. Why is he here?'

'He brought me to you,' Law said.

'Then he has done all he had to do.' Uhlanga turned to Mancoba. 'You can go now Zulu.'

Mancoba did not go. He looked from Uhlanga to Law – afraid, but defiant too.

'I stay.'

Uhlanga brushed the statement aside as one would brush contemptuously at an annoying fly. She said:

'Stay then Zulu. But stay still. I see you clearly Zulu. Inside you, you are weak and rotten like a decaying tree. Be careful Zulu, there are storm winds blowing here.' She said to Law: 'And now I will open the way for you.'

At a signal a neophyte came forward bearing in her palms a little carved and polished oxhorn receptacle – a snuff box.

'To open the mind.'

From its place amongst the gall bladders and beads in Uhlanga's hair she plucked a small carved ivory spoon. She heaped it with snuff. She set it to her nostrils and snorted it in. She inhaled that portion, and then more. She took in snuff until her eyes and nostrils were astream with tears and mucus, and her body was raining sweat. Thus she cleansed the passages of her body and cleared the way to her mind. And when that was done and she was free of the feculence that offended the spirits, she sat quietly. And the only sound for a while was the song of the apprentices. The sunglow reddened then faded and lamplight flickered and pushed weakly at the creeping gloom.

'Can you feel it?' Hushed with reverence, the voice of Uhlanga. 'Can you feel it?'

What Law felt was a jolting, cowering fear so sudden that it drew a gasp from him. And with that fear came realisation. He was in danger. He had to get out of there.

'I can feel it.' Uhlanga sighed and closed her eyes ecstatically. 'They are with us.'

The sigh became a yawn. A yawn that set her huge-breasted chest ashudder that drew her mouth into a chasm and arched her neck until the veins rose out like strangler vines. She seemed to be choking. Her hands flew to her throat to join the struggle unlocking a belching eructation-like scream.

Mancoba sprang to his feet, signing the air before him with crosses. Law gathered himself to rise and found himself in that nightmare that forbids the natural motion of the dreamer's limbs. He knew he was moving too slowly to escape.

No such lethargy affected old Mancoba. Behind his defensive barricade of crosses he backed towards the low-arched doorway. He scrambled through it and was gone.

For Law the nightmare deteriorated. He was being buffeted, it seemed, by mighty gusts of air that rushed from nowhere, that whirled and wailed; that whipped at anything loose and snuffed the lamps. Uhlanga's mighty spirits had come to settle in the high beams and whistle their secret words.

And in the darkness Law escaped that nightmare . . . and plunged into another. This time the horror was more enduring.

'Mancoba!'

Law ran, and stumbled and ran again. He found himself at the riverbank, panting and hurt. He stopped there and listened for the sounds of pursuit. The only sound was that of chuckling water. He called again:

'Mancoba!'

The Zulu was in earshot. He was sure of it. The full sharp face of a hunter's moon began riding the mountain peaks, intruding into the gloom of Uhlanga's valley, and with it the river became a lunar festival of swirling silver streamers. There was soft sand underfoot; a sycamore tree invited him to stay and rest. And that was what he did.

He leaned his back against the smooth-barked tree and dug his heels into the sand. His sweat was beginning to cool clammily on him and his legs were bruised. But these discomforts were welcome things. These were realities, good and sensible sensations that had to do with cause and effect. What his intellect was retreating from were events that had no cause, no human cause. Yet he had heard voices, wailing, whistling voices from above him. And no one had been above him. He had felt a tempest blow where no wind could possibly have arisen.

Law pressed his hands against his forehead and tenderly massaged the lids of his eyes. He was so very confused. He wanted so much what Uhlanga had to give him. She had said that she would open his eyes, but could he endure the vision she had to offer? What he had seen had revolted him; had filled him with terror. He had run into the night. His actions had been the actions of a fool.

'A fool,' he said aloud.

His judgement of his actions was not a triumph of logic – it was not meant to be. It was meant to see him through till dawn. He was tired. He would start thinking like a super-scientist in the morning.

He would have to find a place where he could sleep, a place a little further from the kraal of the grey-eyed sangoma. He eased himself up stiffly. He started his journey. He had taken a pace when he saw them. Whitened like marsh wraiths; wading across those moonlit waters – Uhlanga's ochred neophytes. Thankfully they had not seen him.

Law had no doubts as to the identity of the next person to ford the river. It was Uhlanga. He had no doubts as to the action he should take either. He drew himself cautiously from the shadow of the sycamore. He sensed movement, this time behind him. His head exploded in a dazzle of light. He was falling into the middle of the earth.

The pain came later. It came with the realisation that at his back was an earthen floor – at his face was a pair of rain-grey eyes. Pain came with the realisation that he was being lied to.

'You fell. You slipped at the riverside. You bumped your head.'

He had bumped his head all right, against a viciously swung *iwisa* club.

'No don't get up, you're still weak from the injury.'

God! That was the truth. 'Where's Mancoba?' he asked.

'Mancoba? Why should Mancoba mean anything to me? Why were you at the riverside all alone? Why at midnight?'

'Where am I?'

'Were you chasing the sontekile? Does the search for it obsess you so terribly that it drives you from your sleep?'

'Where am I?' Law flared, but his tongue felt thick and disobedient and a light year from his brain. 'Answer me!'

She did not answer. She rose, a giantess, gorging every inch of space in the domed rush hut. She made him a promise however. 'Here, when the time is right, all the knowledge you have ever wished to have, will be given to you. You see you are not who you think you are. You are a special person. You didn't just come to me, you were called to me. Months before you'd arrived in the mountains you had arrived in my dreams. I was chosen to be your teacher, and you my pupil. And now I have told you enough – I must go.'

The last thing Uhlanga did was to hand him a *isihlali*-calabash. 'There is *muthi* in the gourd for your thirst and your suffering – drink it.'

What Law did was to raise himself giddily onto his buttocks and make some rather dismaying discoveries: he was, but for the briefest of goatskin loinpieces, naked. He was a prisoner. Other than for the *isihlali*-gourd and his own bared body, the hut was empty. Behind Uhlanga's departing haunches a sturdy wooden grid dropped into place. And behind that he could see the braced legs and assegai shaft of a guard – his guard.

The rest was not so simple. It was hot. It was daytime. But what day and what time, he had no way of being sure. He'd walked into a midnight trap, how many midnights ago? And why trap him? Why imprison him?

The next few minutes did two things for Law. They taught him a tolerance for empiric agony beyond the human syllabus – and they brought him in a gasping crawl up to the entrance from where he could observe the bright warm world beyond the wooden grid.

What he saw was an engirdling thorn forest – knob thorn, black monkey thorn, umbrella thorn, thickets of *Acacia grandicornuta*. All old friends of the botanist Montgomery Law. To the man at the wooden grid however, they presented a different organic potential. They were nature's barbed-wire barricade. They were hostile.

There wasn't much more to see; a ring of orderly beehive huts like the one he was confined to; a central clearing, empty but for a heap of lightly smoking wood ash and a few earthen cooking pots. He recognised nothing.

This kraal, unlike every other Zulu kraal he'd ever seen, was neat and unlittered by paper and plastic. . . There was something more though. Law's mind, engrossed with pain, took some time to take it in: the total absence of anything modern. There wasn't even a paraffin drum, a bottle or a piece of hitching wire in sight. As though a hundred years had dropped away, the ugly hand of progress had somehow let this place be.

There was the guard with civet skin kilt and *ixlwa*-war spear just outside this hut. There was a pair of laughing doves hunch necked; alert as they quickstepped across the dusty compound – nothing else. There wasn't another living thing to be seen.

Law turned away from it all – not one bit wiser. Uhlanga's *isihlali*-gourd was standing enticingly centre floor. For the thirst and the pain.

The gourd was full and he *was* thirsty, very thirsty. He swirled the liquid around, sniffed it, then lifting it took a tentative sip. Slightly sweet then slightly bitter, Uhlanga had not lied – it eased the dryness in him. He took a little more, then a great draught of it.

It started with a vague uneasiness which he isolated to his stomach, in fact his whole abdomen. It didn't take him long to realise he'd been poisoned. It became a foulness which ebbed outwards, flowed, then surged like a polluted tide through the channels of him until he was filled with it. Black with it. He tried to vomit. He pressed his fingers into his gullet until the spasms rocked him. That made it worse.

He buckled, too sick to care any more. Then, my God! His body began to shiver, shiver and shake, yes, with laughter. The absurdity of his whole situation became so delightfully apparent that he couldn't understand why he hadn't seen it before. Monty

Law the white rat in the lab cage. Doing every bloody thing that was expected of him. How bloody ridiculous – perceive the thirsty animal, now it looks uncomprehendingly around. Now it drinks. Now it writhes. . . Now. . .

Now it tries to pull itself together. It giggles a few more times. Then its trained scientific mind, with massive effort, enforces its ascendancy.

He'd been drugged. He'd ingested with Uhlanga's potion some narcotic, something, he thought, with psychoactive potential. From its action on him so far he figured it to be a protoalkaloid; a potent one, something from the order Cactaceae. Or Convolvulaceae. Or from any of a dozen other plant species that inhabited the rolling Lebombo hills.

His limbs were starting to draw, to become languid and heavy. First the nausea then the euphoria. Law knew he had minutes perhaps only seconds left of realistic thought. He used them to marshal whatever control he had left over his mental activities. He shuffled towards the sunlit doorway.

There were people in the clearing now. Somehow he had expected it. Seated in a semi-circle Uhlanga's apprentices were swaying and clapping and singing their gentle song. Behind them two score of men with white warshields and glinting assegais were deep in harmony. Dividing the picture into little squares was the grid. He reached out for it, but even as he did it shimmered, faded, and was gone.

Gone were the walls. There was no pain, there was no Montague Law. All there was was a harmony of heaven, the sound flowing towards him in molten robes of orange, purple and red, red, red. Beauty beyond possibility. Peace beyond endeavour.

Random chunks of experience began to pass like lighted windows in a midnight train. Faster and faster it came on until there were no compartments – just a blurred and never ending passing strip of yesterdays. . . The colours transformed themselves once more into sound; a baying sound, a human sound. A chant. It was coming from outside the rush hut:

. . . *'Cetchwayo I fear to say the name Cetchwayo*
He who abstains from the food of cowards
And gives to them the anger-heated blood of the lion

He carried off the warshields of the amaSwazi
He felled Mbulazi
Born of Mdayi
He felled Mpoyana
Born of Mdayi
He stripped Mtonga and killed everyone
Come forth; come out and drive away all evil.
Come point your spear at the rising sun and do it.
Come strengthen us brave father of the Zulus
On this morning of mornings.'

The father of the Zulus looked anything but brave at that early hour. His face was screwed up tartly. He looked wryly into the *muthi* gourd in his hands, then back to the face of the single other person there; his doctor of the warspears – Mvulaba. The king drank his strengthening medicine, then composed his features; smoothed his leopard-skin regalia. He drew himself proudly upright.

'Is everything prepared Mvulaba?'

'Everything is prepared my King.'

Cetchwayo held out his hand for the assegai of his ancestors. The burnished blade glowed as it passed from Mvulaba's hands to the king's. The sacred coil of the Inkatha, as potent as the giant python that had given up its skin to sheathe it, looked what it was: proof of the ability of the King to grip the nation; to bind it in loyalty to the house of Zulu. It was time to be strong. Time to be King.

In the greyness, in the misty shadows that precede the dawn it was difficult to see the regiments. You could hear them though. As Cetchwayo left the *indlunkulu* hut he raised his spear. The royal salute thundered out.

'Bayede! Bayede! Bayede!'

Mvulaba was a pace behind, the Inkatha borne full stretch above his head. Their timing was faultless.

Both the king's tread and the sun's first sharp yellow rays touched upon the appointed knoll as one. Cetchwayo's shadow was as great then as the *isiThwethwe* tree.

Closer to the great god *Unkulunkulu* and the ancestors of Zulu, no man could be. Spear arm pointed to the sun, as steady as a rock he stood poised. Then with the lungs of the lion:

'*U!*'

He spat the medicine at the sun.

'*U!*'

The regiments roared. Again he spat.

'*U!*'

Three times he did it. Three times the reply rolled through the valley. Evil be purged – the king our father has stabbed it.

'*U!*'

The boom of it filled the ears, overran the senses, echoed in the mind, long after all else had dimmed and faded; long after an awakening consciousness had dimmed the lucidity of a bygone strengthening of the regiments.

Montague Law shook his head in riddance; then once more as though some stubborn vision still clung to him. He turned his eyes and focused on the *muthi* gourd that had borne him like some magic coracle on a rip-tide of history.

The thing was an arm's length away, and his hand reached out to smash it, shatter it. He didn't do that though, he grasped it instead, quite gently, and complying with that moment of insanity, brought the gourd up once more, almost to his lips.

His thirst was excruciating, and not all of it was physical. There was a part of him that wanted to forsake the familiar world; to free itself from the embarrassment of body and see the vision through. Somewhere a man was calling; a man with the name of Mvulaba – a war doctor . . . *Mvulaba?* Why was that man's aura so cohesive, so strong? He placed the gourd as far from himself as he could stretch. Whatever was in it could stay in it.

And what was in it? What hallucinogenic principle had Uhlanga used on him? A protoalkaloid, a tropane alkaloid? With an effort Law forced himself on a scientific backtrack across the symptoms and reactions he'd just experienced. Botanical, structural types he'd last seen on paper during student days, he tried to remember. They wouldn't emerge. He was tired and thirsty.

God he was thirsty – dehydrated. He couldn't expect his mind to work in that state. Once more he looked over to Uhlanga's *muthi* gourd: for the thirst and the suffering, and the return to yesterday.

He looked down upon his almost naked body and realised that he could hardly see as far as his feet. Night was drawing in. He crawled across to the pale arch of the door. The grid was there as firm as ever. The tree line was ravelled in stark silhouette, and behind that, a dying blood red sky. A night hawk was calling: *Zavolo Zavolo sengel abantabami* – Zavolo milk for my children. The petition however, was fruitless . . . Or perhaps not.

There wasn't a living creature whose language hadn't been translated by the Zulus. The history of the nation was a winding trail of accommodation between man and beast. Again the night hawk called. And soon after that, with a flickering tallow torch and more lies to tell, Uhlanga came through the darkness to him.

Why had he not drunk? Why had he not taken his *muthi*? Did he not know how badly he had been injured by his fall? Did he not know how precious were the herbs, how curative the medicine she had made up for him? Was he intent on killing himself?

Law answered all those questions with a single:

'No.'

He freed his tongue from the glue pot of his mouth. He too had a question.

'Why do you torture me?'

'How do I torture you?'

'You keep me like a trapped jackal with nothing but poison to drink.'

Oh! That was not so. No, on both counts he was wrong, so wrong. 'You were brought in like a jackal, a demented beast snapping left and right. Your head injury had turned you into a mad thing. For three days you lay just where you are now – raving. And I sat there too, cleaned you and held healing potions to your lips. The same medicine that you now call poison.' She took the *isihlali*-gourd and almost pleadingly offered it out.

Refused, she tilted it to her own lips and swallowed.

'Why,' she asked, 'would I do these things you accuse me of having done?'

Why? Because it had to be, that was why. Because there was no other explanation. And yet Uhlanga the sangoma, who had just drunk from the poison gourd, was there before him – as sober as ever before.

She had swapped the constituents of the gourd whilst he had been drugged. Simple!

'You did it whilst I was unconscious.'

'I changed the medicines?'

'Yes.'

'Whilst your mind was elsewhere?'

'Yes Uhlanga, while I was drugged.'

'Whilst you were having visions of the King Cetchwayo and Mvulaba the great war doctor.'

Law's puny flame of defiance died right there. There were alternative explanations. He *could* have been drugged. Then all he had witnessed prior to his narcolepsy: the singing neophytes, the white-shielded warriors, that, *could* have caused such hallucinations. But that still did not explain how she had access to the workings of his subconscious.

In the flickering light of the tallow candle. In that lost Lebombo kraal. In the presence of that awesome Zulu diviner priestess, the white man's arguments, seemed futile and impotent. A lethargy settled over Montague Law then; a sighing indifference to all he had been through.

The question: how did you read my thoughts? – did not get answered because it did not get asked. She *had* done it. That impossibility alone gave her a crippling ascendancy. The blow he had taken to his skull was nothing compared to the assault the sangoma had now delivered to his mind.

When she held out the *isihlali*-gourd again Law took it, and drained it. He neither thanked her nor said another word.

Uhlanga too remained silent. She seemed deep in thought. Occasionally she formed her mouth, as though to speak, but nothing came of it. In the stillness Law drew his limbs in, until he sat crosslegged. That way he felt less vulnerable.

'You have nothing to fear from me,' Uhlanga said. But that was not the message hovering at her lips and the silence continued.

It continued until Uhlanga stood up and crossed to the doorway. Crouched there she said, 'I promised you that when the time was right the knowledge that you seek, that of the sontekile and other matters, would be revealed to you. I see now that the time will never be right. *You* are just another insulting white man. You defile the bush that shelters you. You will go in the morning.'

This time no wooden grill prevented Law from following the sangoma into the open night.

Swimming in a sullen clouded sky the moon was just a glow. He turned his face to it; then to the departing tallow lamp. There was rain in the air. He inhaled the coolness, then on the breath of a sigh he heard himself call: 'Uhlanga . . . Uhlanga.'

*   *   *

You are far from the last place you remember,' she told him. 'You are in a secret place: a war kraal in the Lebombo forest of kwaIsingogo.'

They sat together beside the central leadwood fire and talked. There was trust between them, and, as the flames licked the hard wood into smouldering embers, so the story of the sangoma Uhlanga slowly reduced the sceptic pith of Montague Law.

'You and I, like two travellers at the *umhambeli* pot, share in something – a dream. We see the same man – Mvulaba, not only that, we see him do the same thing, yes, and in the same place. You ask how, but I ask why?'

There she was wrong. To the man squatting there, there was a total absence of reason for anything that had occurred. Now dressed in his own clothes again, he was content to listen.

'Go on,' he said.

'Mvulaba the war doctor is the man whose person seems to linger after the dream is over, is that not so? Mvulaba was killed when the British Redcoats murdered, and burned, and raped their way through Ulundi after the defeat of Cetchwayo's impi. Old Mvulaba died defending the king's *indlunkulu* hut as it went up in flames around him. Did you know that Doctor?'

'No.'

'Then you wouldn't know that the *indlunkulu* hut which usually contained all the king's regalia – the national Inkatha; the sacred hearth stones, his ancestral spear and axe, many other sacred things, was empty at the time. The hut was empty. Mvulaba died defending what, then?'

'Perhaps,' suggested Law, 'after he had seen his beloved king defeated and Ulundi, his home kraal put to the torch, there was nothing left to live for. Perhaps he died defending an ideal.'

Distant thunder, shunted by the northmost hills into a sullen rumble rolled down upon them, smothering Law's ensuing words. 'I think Mvulaba could have done that.'

53

'Ulundi wasn't Mvulaba's home kraal,' Uhlanga said. 'His home was Ondini. The British annihilated Ondini down to the last babe in arms a few days later. Can you imagine the consequences of that hideous act for the departed spirit of the war doctor?'

Law could imagine it: without a single living relative to perform it, the vital ceremony *ukubuyisa* – the bringing home of the spirit – could never have taken place. The spirit of Mvulaba would never have been united with those of his ancestors. It would be homeless – eternally without rest. No worse fate could befall the soul of a Zulu male than that.

'It would be the equivalent of a dead Catholic being denied a requiem,' Law said, then realised that the analogy would go right over this rural sangoma's head. It did not.

'Yes,' she said, 'but Mvulaba had no sin.'

Here was a bone and blanket sangoma who it seemed was at much at home with an owl's claw nostrum as she was with the tenets of Christian dogma. A very strange lady, was this grey-eyed sangoma.

When she said, 'Follow me, there are important things that I wish you to understand before the storm breaks,' Law did not hesitate. He stood up and followed her to a hut slightly bigger than the others in the circle.

'Behold,' Uhlanga gestured, 'our *indlunkulu* – our palace of treasures.'

It was guarded. At the entrance a Zulu warrior stood resting on a war club of brutal proportions.

'Please enter.'

He walked back into a dream. There was King Cetchwayo's ancestral spear; there were the sacred hoe and axe. As if it had been laid there only yesterday – the vessel of kings: the earthen vessel that Cetchwayo had carried to *ncinda*, the rising sun.

'He who abstains from the food of cowards and gives to them the anger-heated blood of the lion.'

'Yes,' Uhlanga echoed. ' "The blood of the lion." But King Cetchwayo was not only brave, he was a visionary too. He knew that the British would one day overthrow him. Mpande, his father, had appeared to him in a dream and told him that. Mpande also told him that the British would try to destroy every vestige and symbol of Zulu unity. So Cetchwayo summoned, one by one, the bravest, shrewdest, and most loyal of his warriors. To each of these men he entrusted the guardianship of one sacred item. He told these brave men that the time would come when they, or their children, or their children's children would be called to account for each item of custody. He told them that one day would come a man who had been chosen by the spirits of all the kings of Zulu from Nkosinkulu to Mpande. This chosen one would gather the Zulu nation to him and heal it, and make it great again. And all these sacred things and insignia of authority would be his . . .'

Law was hardly listening any longer. He walked to the *umsamo* – the altar of the *indlunkulu* where the sacred items lay. He touched the blade of the assegai – sharp and cold. He smoothed his fingertips over the blackened hearth stones; they came away smudged. These things were real. Something, however, was missing.

'Piece by piece, over many years, I have recovered this collection of treasures,' Uhlanga said, 'but as yet it is vitally incomplete. Now the time is overdue for my work to be completed; for everything to be returned.'

'The Inkatha,' Law looked up from the *umsamo*. 'Where is the Inkatha? It was here.'

'Only in your vision, Doctor Law.'

'Where is it then?'

'I've asked that question myself a thousand times,' Uhlanga said. 'My people have searched the hills and the valleys and the plains of kwaZulu. The custodians have been questioned – the ancestor spirits entreated. But still we do not have it.'

'I saw it.'

'Indeed you saw it. It was foretold that you would see it. The custodians were certain on that point.' Uhlanga could not have brought her lips any closer to him without touching. He could feel the warm puff of her breath as she whispered: 'The tortured spirit Mvulaba has come back to us in our hour of trouble. He has the eyes to find it.'

'The eyes to find it . . . the tortured spirit?' With the rapture of deep excitement the significance of those pagan words cut through the intellect of Montague Law. Uhlanga was nodding as a teacher nods who perceives the dawning of comprehension of the pupil.

'*Yes*. It is you. You, Mvulaba.'

'Me Mvulaba? Uhlanga, look at me. I am a white man. What Zulu would ever accept me for what you say I am?'

'Look at *me*,' she answered. 'Look into my eyes. Now what do you see?'

'The colour of rain.'

'And I look into your eyes and I see the blackness of the Ingwavuma night. So which of us then is the Zulu? You are the eyes of Zulu Mvulaba – *mehlo kaZulu*. You are the eyes and I am the skin. You *are* who I say you are.'

Uhlanga smiled. The thatch began to hush with rain – the summer smell of wetting thirsty ground.

'I could do it,' Law said, more in question than affirmation.

'You could.'

'You would take me? You would teach me . . . everything?'

'You are born again to us Mvulaba. Does a mother not teach its child? First to crawl, then to walk, then to run. Yes, I'll teach you everything.'

'I'll do it.'

But Uhlanga sensed his doubts. 'You're tired now.' She beckoned him to leave the *indlunkulu*. 'A seed needs to lie awhile. Come, there is a place prepared for you to sleep.'

But he did not sleep. It was a night without rest for Montague Law. He lay on a thin rush mat on a cattle dung floor – sharing the misty air of that bachelors' *indlu* with a score of sleeping men. It was a comfortless place. But it was not the ache of hip and spine that kept him awake. His true distress was of the mind. Doubts as sharp as flint kept probing at him as the hours passed by – the same doubts, over and over, relentless in their persistence. He was ill prepared and ill equipped to cope with all that lay ahead. He knew it. He was frightened by the thought of it.

'You are the eyes. I am the skin.'

That was to be the form of this ordeal. A subordination of his very senses to the will of this princess of sangomas.

'You are born again to us Mvulaba.'

Mvulaba? It was just a name to him, but to Uhlanga it was a shout of joy – a flame of virtue and hope. And she believed this good inheritance to tenant the soul of this man lying here. This Montague Law. And where will this take you Montague Law? Why to the sontekile . . . but, God, think of the wretched hardship . . . I've thought of the hardship to body and to mind. Then do what you must do . . . I'm afraid. I'm so afraid.

In his fear he rose up and crept from the darkness of the *indlu* into the greyness of the coming dawn. He walked from the secret and mysterious kraal of Uhlanga the sangoma, across the mountains and down into the valley where he had left his vehicle parked – unmysterious and as honest as England.

The engine started as he knew it would, and growled at the shadowed mountain. The wipers wiped away the Ingwavuma dew. He drove his machine back down the winding track and onto the dirt road that led across the flood plains and palm veld, all the way back to the lake called Mandlankunzi. There he drew up under a wide green fever tree and switched the engine off. He sat there for a long time, his hands still locked upon the steering wheel, staring in the direction of the windless flat water. Then he shook his head as though in acknowledgement of some hard-won decision. There was no one there to hear him say:

'Yes. You can do it. You can bring in the Inkatha.'

And he knew he could. Because Mancoba in his babbling dream talk had given him the headstart of a hundred years in the search for the Inkatha of Shaka Zulu. Somewhere there was a Lebombo mountain, crested like the back of a basking crocodile, and somewhere on that mountain was a cave.

'Umzeze's cave.'

Monty Law climbed down from the high-seated Land Rover. He took off his boots and socks and placed them neatly on the bonnet of his vehicle. He removed his shirt and folded it and placed it too on the bonnet.

Wearing nothing but his weathered denim shorts he walked down the bank, through the muddy verge and onwards into the cool still water of Mandlankunzi.

There were no more doubts to sap him. This was the way that Montague Law would die, and Mvulaba would be born. As the water deepened so he began to swim, to fly like a bird to a new life; to a new place, where Montague Law was just a memory. To the place where Mvulaba lived. And as he swam the words of the song of the vision came back to him:

'Let him come now – Okhethiwe

*he who is chosen by the kings.
Let him stand in the space
between heaven and earth.
On his forehead will shine
the mark of the sun.
His seat will be the Inkatha
of Shaka Zulu.
Our hope.
Our destiny.
Our chosen one.'*

Mvulaba would bring this chosen one; this Okhethiwe his magical Inkatha. And Uhlanga would teach Mvulaba as a mother teaches a son. His sap would rise up in the heartwood of Zulu history. *And the knowledge that he wanted would be his.*

He swam on and on. His strokes were smooth and unhurried and they carried him clear across the lake. When he emerged from the water he felt very clean and free. The Land Rover on the other side of Lake Mandlankunzi was no longer visible.

He turned towards the mountains and began to walk.

2

It was the hottest day of a very hot summer – everyone agreed. What wind there was came like the breath of a slumbering dragon – fever dry gusts to stir the dried-up leaves; to dance up a dust devil – to catch the rich, black hair of the woman waiting there and billow it like ink-stained water.

The woman had that look that fashion men adore – part gypsy, part *classique*. She had long springy legs and a fine sculptured torso that showed through the clinging damp patches on her vest. Somehow the sweat failed to detract – as though lifted from the pages of a slightly rumpled *Vogue* magazine – that was the impression she gave.

It was when she moved that impressions became irrelevant – the woman was an athlete.

Now she was moving, turning with shutter speed to bring a gun to bear, a big Colt .45 auto. Two shots tore into the head at the window. There was a door ahead – five shots in the space of five paces and she'd reached it, opened it. She was in a passageway, and moving quickly – too quickly.

She had over-reached her own reflexes – lost control. Slow it down, her mind said – concentrate; see what has to be seen and disregard the clutter. There they are, fire again, and again . . . A balcony ahead with a wooden balustrade. A long drop to the ground with the Colt responding all the way.

There was sweat and there were grazes, somewhere there was pain nagging to be felt, she ignored it all. What counted was the will to win, and that she could really feel. The ground ahead came up and a running man broke loose. Just her and the gun and the sight picture. The Colt seemed to take it in as though it had a will of its own.

The hooter was hooting, the stop watches had stopped. It was over.

Kirsten Law cleared the smoking silver pistol and offered it for inspection. She lifted her ear protectors. The crisp voices of the scorers came to her as they moved amongst the bullet-holed targets, and she smiled.

'C1 – 5 C2 – 5 C3 – 5 . . . D1 – 5 . . . 5 . . . 5.'

She had earned a place in the final shoot; a chance to be a national champion. Somewhere people were clapping. Kirsten was a poor subject for applause. It always surprised her, as though she had strayed into someone else's patch of sunshine. Once she had comprehended that it was really hers, however, it warmed.

It was hers, and what it meant was that she had made it through a world-class field of combat shottists to the finals. She'd used herself up to get there, and now her body was exacting its levy: one thigh informed of a throbbing laming bruise. She didn't remember how it had happened. Her right elbow was hurting – an old injury.

'I feel fine,' she responded to her team captain's enquiry. 'Great.'

'You looked great,' he said. He was receiving nothing from Kirsten beyond his own concerned reflection in her sunglasses.

'There's an hour before the final,' he said, checking his watch. 'I could use some shade, I don't know about you.'

There was some shade but not much of it. The range was wedged between those treeless yellow mountains which mining reports refer to as surface waste dumps; mine dumps was what the rest of South Africa knew them as. It was an excellent place to shoot off pistols in almost any direction. Nothing more than that.

They found their shade. A struggling line of blue gums at the rear of the range. They also found standing there a man; an old grey-headed Zulu, his sweat-stained hat held in hands that were active with discomfort. His name he said was Mancoba. Yes, he had seen the wonderful way Miss Law shot her pistol. No, regretfully he knew less than nothing about such things. He wanted to speak to Miss Law. 'Speak then,' said Kirsten Law.

The manager, as good managers do, presaged disaster. Unfortunately he failed to divert it.

'I have news of your brother.'

'He's dead,' Kirsten said. 'Monty died a year ago.'

'Not now!' The manager stepped in belatedly. 'Whoever you

are, go away.'

Mancoba however had come too far to find this woman to be silenced by one indignant white man. Stubbornly he stood his ground. Apprehensively he spoke on.

* * *

The flags of seven nations hung limply in the torpid heat of that midsummer afternoon. None more limp than the South African tricolour.

The applause for Kirsten was there of course – somewhat more polite than enthusiastic that time. Distinctly unwarming. Fourth place is only good when you're beaten into it, not when you sag there in an apathetic trance. Not when you could have, should have been the winner.

Who could realise how hard she'd tried? Kirsten had been seeing through a haze of shock. The end of the championships had come for her in the shape of a wizened old Zulu who didn't know one end of a pistol from another, but had an astonishing knowledge of a man who was supposed to be dead.

'Your brother is alive Miss Law. He is a prisoner; a prisoner of the mind of the most evil woman alive. Help him, Miss Law, before it is too late.'

Seven hundred kilometres of good tar road separates the mine dumps of the Highveld from the sweet green sugar-cane fields of Natal, and the man in the passenger seat of Kirsten's speeding silver Porsche hardly stopped talking all the way. Begin at the beginning, he was instructed, and he tried.

It was a complicated story however, the pattern having been woven by more than one person. Thus there were several beginnings. To unravel it would require patience from her; from him a skilful hand.

'Have you ever heard of the Inkatha of Shaka Zulu?' he asked.

'Only what I was taught in school.'

'Not many white people know about the true Inkatha and its meaning.'

'Did my brother know about it?'

But Mancoba's question had been simply a test of knowledge – not the right thread to loosen first.

'Doctor Law used to come down to the municipal library where I worked quite often.' That was where Mancoba began his story. 'He loved to study old manuscripts, old books. He was fond of history, and being a botanist too, he especially used to enjoy anything I could find for him that concerned tribal medicine. There was plenty to interest him and we became friends. One day I showed him a very old manuscript that I had unearthed. It told the story of three men who had been cured of what appeared to be the disease multiple sclerosis, by the use of a herbal nostrum called sontekile. Your brother became excited about the possibility of finding and testing what could have been a miracle drug.'

Excited – the word was an understatement in describing the zealot who had set forth in pursuit of the elusive twisted sontekile. Mancoba told her of the expedition to the Lebombos, of Law's decision to go to the kraal of the priestess diviner Uhlanga.

'Uhlanga is of the highest class of diviner known as *abalozi, amakhosi amakhulu*. These people, it is said, have the power to summon the spirits of the ancestors, who then settle in the rafters and call down to those assembled in the hut. It's all sorcery of course, of the most dangerous kind. I am a Christian, I walk in the protection of our Lord Jesus Christ. These things don't touch me. Your brother, though, was not a man of faith. He was easy prey for this woman. He was taken in . . . tricked.'

'By Uhlanga?'

'Yes. Somehow she coerced him to go with her to the mountains. She told him he was one of them; that he had powers that were beyond human powers.'

'She must have promised to show him where the sontekile grows. He'd have walked with the Devil himself to find that cure.'

'I don't know what she promised,' he said, 'I just know what happened. He went into those mountains and he's still there. I blame myself Miss Law. If I had done things differently.'

Kirsten glanced curiously at her passenger, crouched, hardly allowing his skinny frame to make contact with the luxurious upholstery of the Porsche – this man's discomfort was not just of the body. She didn't think he was lying when he said:

'Over this past year I have suffered for my actions.'

'We all suffered.' There was no commiseration in the voice of Kirsten Law. 'We all thought that Monty was dead. Why did you take a whole year to come to me?'

'Your brother is a clever and determined man, Miss Law. What right did I have to interfere? If he wanted to disappear in that manner, for whatever reason, would it have been right for me to report him? The Zulus have an expression – do not defile the tree that shelters you. Your brother was good to me. I could see no harm then in what he was doing.'

Mancoba's answer disturbed Kirsten. It sounded rehearsed, it had the ring of fabrication. In one sentence he was an ardent Christian. In the next he was quoting the axioms of the yesteryear Zulu. For all his remorse this shrewd old *madala* was hiding something. He was trying to manoeuvre her onto ground some distance from the truth. She fell in with it.

'So what changed,' she responded, 'what altered the circumstances enough to bring you to me?'

What had brought him to her? Shock had done that; discovering that he was no longer the sole searcher for the Inkatha of Shaka Zulu. Fear had brought him to her – fear of the capabilities of the man who claimed to tenant the spirit of the dead war doctor Mvulaba.

'I met with your brother about a month ago at a kraal in the Lebombos. Something terrible has happened to his mind. Miss Law, I think that Doctor Law has somehow been driven insane. *Your brother has gone mad.*'

That was the cataclysm that Kirsten Law was suddenly presented with. She halted the Porsche and said what any loving sister would say. 'I don't believe you.'

'The Lebombo mountains, Miss Law, have since earliest times been infested with witches and wizards; sorcerers who rely on the supply of human body parts to conduct their trade. For me, a stranger, to have been in those mountains was dangerous, but it was a danger I was prepared to live with.'

'For my brother's sake?'

'Yes, for his sake. He was like a brother to me too. On many occasions I was tempted to leave. I felt as though I was being watched. I was frightened, really frightened, but I stayed. More than once I came across the remains of some poor soul who had been pegged out and hacked apart for *muthi* by the *umthakathi* – the wizards. But I stayed.'

Ritual murder – that was the tag attached by the police to such an event. And ritual murder, Mancoba told Kirsten Law, had become a common way to die on those sullen peaks. But these were ritual murders with a difference.

'There were rumours that even the hard-arsed district police couldn't ignore. In every mountain kraal one heard the whispers: beware the white *umthakathi*, where there is a killing you will find him near. You can understand, Miss Law, why I was driven to confront your brother. Do you want me to go on?'

There was nothing she wanted less.

'Please continue,' she said quietly. 'Tell me what happened when last you saw my brother. Tell me what he said.'

'He greeted me warmly. He told me that he and I were as close as the saliva and the tongue. He asked me if I had been comfortable and chastised me for my slowness in coming to him. He knew that I had been in the mountains and promised that no harm would ever befall me in the Lebombos.'

'You *were* being watched then.'

'Yes . . . I told him of all the things I had heard, and asked him what truth there was in it.'

'And what did he say?'

'He laughed, as though it was all some huge joke. He said no one knew him better than I did – I must believe what I want to believe.'

Kirsten released her breath in a spasm of relief. 'So there you are,' she smiled. 'It was a rumour and nothing more. My brother is searching for the sontekile. His approach may be unorthodox, so what, there's no more to it than that.'

There was much more to it than that. Mancoba told her how he had shared Monty Law's hut that night.

'I wasn't able to sleep. I wanted to believe your brother but I couldn't. There was evil there, so strong, that I could feel it. It was as though choking hands were at my throat. At the first light of dawn I was still awake. I stood up, and, moving quietly so as not to waken him I searched his hut. I found your brother's diary. He had kept an account of everything he had done and everything he'd witnessed since first he'd gone into the mountains. It was a diary of wickedness, of murder, of strange experiments and rituals. But more than anything it was a chronicled record of a man who was losing his sanity . . . You must help him . . . I think that you are his only hope.'

A passing truck, all lights and sudden turbulence, intruded upon them then. The night had come unnoticed and Kirsten was grateful for it; it would mask the gathering bitterness on her face.

'Of course I'll help him,' she said. 'He's my brother.'

It was quite some time before Kirsten felt capable of driving on.

There were many more things that Mancoba could have told Kirsten as they continued their coastwards journey. He had told her nothing of the other rumour that was sweeping like a bushfire through Ingwavuma; a whisper that the Inkatha of Shaka Zulu had been discovered by the one called Mvulaba. He did not tell her how shocked he had been to discover that he, Mancoba, was no longer the sole searcher for this Inkatha. Nor did he mention the true reason for his nocturnal activity in the kraal of Mvulaba – his need to discover if the rumour was true and, if it was, to destroy the evil Inkatha.

The Inkatha had not been there, but Mancoba knew that now he had little time. If he did not find Umzeze's cave soon, then Uhlanga's minions would. And if that happened; when that terrible day arrived, he would be there to do as God had instructed him to do. He would use anyone or any means to achieve his holy quest. For good reason he did not tell Kirsten Law that.

Mancoba concluded his story by telling Kirsten how he had used the remaining cover of darkness to slip away from the kraal of her brother.

'I've told you my story now,' he said. 'What are we going to do?'

That problem of course had been plying Kirsten's mind for some time. Frustrating her however, like a stone in the shoe of logic, was an enigma: for what reason would one old man become so fanatically devoted to his new employer, that even in the face of the most heinous of anti-Christian actions, he would not desert him?

She neither phrased her question, nor answered his. Monty had been 'dead' for a long time. His rehabilitation was something that didn't have to take place the next day. She would proceed once she was certain who her allies were. 'I don't quite know what our next move should be,' she said. 'I'm going to sleep on it tonight and maybe I'll come up with something in the morning.'

The powerful white lights of her car were ranging on familiar ground now, igniting the roadside hedges of the cane estates into a welcoming promenade of flaming crimsons. The Porsche, like a home-coming thoroughbred seemed suddenly hard to restrain – two huge lime-washed gate posts and three kilometres of gravel brought them to the courtyard of the estate – Prospect Hall. The home since pioneer days of the family Law. Their journey's end.

* * *

She did not come up with something in the morning. She awoke hours before dawn and for a while lay hardly stirring, chasing illusive dream residues that scattered before her like papers in the wind. It was a pleasant but profitless exercise. No revelations came, no messages, no clues.

At about 4.30 a.m. her reverie was penetrated by the new-day sounds of the cane cutters gathering noisily to receive the induna's – the supervisor's instructions at the office. They were bantering and scandalising as only the Zulus know how; their warm resonant voices mingling with the clatter and grumble of cold metal farm machinery carried clear across the paddock separating Prospect Hall from the administrative offices.

There'd been a time when each single sound had conjured for her a vivid image – a shiny black face – a grumbling tractor. She'd known them all once. Now it was just a muddled din. Monty and she had sat wide-eyed on that very bed and giggled at the overhead ribaldry. And on that self same bed they'd fought with pillows and tickled each other half to death.

Over at Great Gran's rickety cheval mirror they'd stood and towelled off the bathwater and taken in each other's naked reflections and giggled a lot more – until one day concerned parents had called a halt to the impromptu anatomy lessons and packed them off for what they hoped would be a more formal education.

They had come together only during school holidays after that. Each with new friends and new secrets that they would have died for. And now she couldn't even remember the sound of her brother's laughter.

Kirsten was dismayed. How was it that two beings, once so

innocently intimate, could wake one morning to the discovery that all they had in common was their differences?

Kirsten shrugged her nightie loose, and walked naked across to Great Gran's cheval. In the soft yellow light of dawn she peered at the glass that had once encompassed the giggling images of two bare-arsed kids. 'Damn it all,' she said. 'Damn it Monty, what the hell do you think you are doing?'

But the other bare-arsed kid was not there to answer. He was a few hundred kilometres north, if Mancoba was to be believed, somewhere in the Lebombo mountains, doing God knows what. But not murder. 'Jesus, he wouldn't do that.'

And where did that leave her? With an old Zulu who for some reason had told a story that she had a problem believing.

She bathed, then dressed, deeply in thought. Breakfast was waiting for her on the porch, served as it had been for generations, by servants equally as experienced in the ways of the family Law. The linen was starched and the silver gleaming. The food was delicious. She hardly touched it.

She found Mancoba sitting as uncomfortably as ever on the guest house steps, gazing like a man marooned, at the oceans of rippling green cane that isolated Prospect Hall from the remainder of Africa.

Committing hat to hand, the Zulu stood. '*Saubona* Inkosikazi.' His manner was deferential.

'*Yebo*, Mancoba – *unjani?*'

'*Yebo*.' He was fine, he'd slept well, he said. Had the Inkosikazi slept well? Had she had time to think about what they should do?

'You never told me what *you* think should be done,' Kirsten replied. 'Well, what do you think Mancoba?'

'We should go to the hills and stop your brother before it is too late.'

'Too late for who – for what? If my brother has been involved in ritual murder, as you say, then it's already too late. Isn't it?'

'Perhaps there is still some way we can help him. He mustn't be allowed to continue.'

'I hear you say *we*, Mancoba. I think you have done enough, old man. I will see this thing through now on my own. I could not allow you to go back.'

'No!'

He tried logic: only he knew the way to Montague Law's secret kraal. He tried emotional appeal: he had led her brother to the hills, he must lead him back. He threatened: the sorcerers would have her before the first Lebombo night had passed. She demolished his case piecemeal:

'My brother will find me, just as in reality he found you. You blame yourself too much for what has happened, *madala* – no one forced him to go there. He went at his own free will, and that is how he must come back. I am his sister, I'll be safe.'

Mancoba was shaking his head vigorously. 'You place too much reliance on a sick mind, Miss Law.'

'And you, Mancoba. What do you place your reliance on . . .? A sister's love for her brother? What is it that really drives you to the Lebombos, old man?'

Perhaps that was the first real opportunity that Mancoba had had to look straight into the deep dark eyes of Kirsten Law. What he saw was a substance as hard as black diamond. What he felt was a gaze reducing him to the dimensions of a cardboard target. There was little left to him in the way of options when he said:

'I asked you before if you knew anything of the Inkatha of Shaka Zulu.'

'And I said that I did not.'

'Yes. Inkosikazi, listen.'

And she listened. She listened carefully without breaking in, for the voice of Mancoba fined down to a whisper. The thread of his tale became as intricate as a spider's web.

She heard the bloody story of Ulundi. The tragedy of a king; of a dream that had sent a warrior and his beloved on a mission that she could never return from. A mission to save the heritage of a nation.

'I searched for Umzeze's cave off and on for years before I met Doctor Law. Before I showed him the old manuscript. His search for the Inkatha is a recent thing. He never knew that I was looking for it all along. He thought I was helping him in his search for sontekile – and I was. The nature of his search has changed, but to this day he doesn't know that the man who hid the royal Inkatha, on King Cetchwayo's command, was Umzeze, my father. He doesn't know that Umzeze described to me the cave that is the hiding place, and how to find it.'

'Yet you never found it.'

'No.'

'Why does Doctor Law want this Inkatha so badly?'

'I don't know.'

Kirsten did not believe him. 'Did my brother ever tell you that the woman he was to marry died from the disease multiple sclerosis?'

'No.'

'You're lying Mancoba. You tricked my brother. You knew that the Thonga-Zulus of that primitive area would kill you as a *noyi* – wizard if you wandered around there without the protection that a white man's presence would offer. So you used him.'

'In a way I did. Yes.'

'Now you want to use me.'

'I need your help Miss Law, and you need mine. No matter what you say you won't find him without me.'

'Perhaps . . . I'll tell you what Mancoba, I'll make a bargain with you. You want the Inkatha just as badly as I want my brother. I'll help you find it. But once we have it I want to put it to a certain use before you finally take it.'

'You want to use it to lure your brother away from the sangoma Uhlanga. Is that it?'

'Yes. If what you tell me is true, then the possession of the Inkatha should end it all.'

'What about sontekile?' Mancoba sounded doubtful. 'He'll just go right on looking for sontekile.'

'I don't think so. I don't think sontekile exists. You're a clever man Mancoba, I think you made up the story just to get Monty to take you into the mountains. You fooled my brother with that story, didn't you?'

'No!'

'Yes. You bluffed him. Somehow you found out about his fiancée, then you faked a document on a blank piece of antique parchment. There must be lots of stuff you could use in a library as old as Durban's. You made something up that you knew would fool my brother, that would excite him. I don't trust you, Mancoba. You've told me some truths, and you have told me some lies. I am finding it hard to decide which is which. My brother, no matter what else he has done, is not a killer. I don't believe that, and I want you to know it. I also don't like having to trade with you like this, but I will. Now, have we got a bargain?'

'It is a sad thing; the way you think,' Mancoba said slowly, 'but yes, we have a bargain. Yes.'

There was no reason not to agree. For Mancoba the setback of not being trusted was slight. Everything was moving in the direction he intended.

Kirsten turned away and walked briskly back towards the old house. There were arrangements to be made. She had come to a decision. Under the circumstances, there was no other course of action besides the one she was taking. Her eyes were frowning, but softening the line of her mouth was the embryo of a smile.

Had Kirsten wanted an example of a real smile she would have had to look no further than over her shoulder. She didn't. She walked on towards the old house on those long springy legs.

Mancoba's pleasure didn't endure. It remained for as long as his sense of accomplishment lasted, and that wasn't long. Kirsten Law was right. He had had to lie quite considerably to bring all this about. And lies, like drowned rats in the drinking hole, had a most inexpedient ability to rise to the surface when least expected.

By the time the back door of Prospect Hall had snapped shut, Mancoba's features were rearranged into a thoughtful frown. His lies were justified. The Inkatha had to be destroyed at any cost. Anyway his lies were minor compared to others that had been told.

Amongst the garaged cars at Prospect Hall he had noticed last night a dark-green Land Rover, the twin, if not the very same vehicle that Doctor Law had driven; then abandoned at the croc pool at Nyamithi with his clothes, and instruments, to fake his own death. Now *there* was a drowned rat, big, bloated and smelly. A lot of lesser stench would pass unnoticed when that one finally emerged. And it was due – it was overdue.

Mancoba had nothing but a blanket to pack and nothing else to do but pack it. He wondered what the white woman was doing and hoped whatever it was she would be quick. He wanted to get going. He hoped she would have the good sense to leave her flimsy sports car at home and take one of the 4-wheel drive vehicles from the garage.

Kirsten Law was indeed doing what she had to do – quickly. At that moment she was sitting at her study desk, one hand drumming an agitated tattoo on the walnut inlay, the other clutching a telephone receiver. 'Yes,' she said. 'That is exactly what I'm saying Mark. I don't want to go next week. I want to go today. I'll tell you more about it when I see you. What I want now is an answer – yes, or no.'

'I'll phone you back,' said Mark Ingram. He hoped the many kilometres of cable that separated his phone from Kirsten Law's would fudge out the annoyance in his tone.

But Mark Ingram's annoyance was a fleeting thing. He was an engineer, a dam builder. A man buying time for thirsty-throated Africa.

He could compute at the tap of a finger everything that was known about the effects of a trillion tonnes of concrete placed in front of a zillion cubic metres of running water. His mind had the capacity of a mechanical grab to take in things material, things technical.

The flow and race of the mind of Kirsten Law however was beyond his ability to grasp. He knew he couldn't hold her if he tried, and paradoxically that was the strength of their relationship – he let her be. One day, he knew, she would be ready for him. There was a time for everything.

Mark Ingram's office was big, bright and modern. Dominating the centre floor was a table supporting a 1:5 000 realistic scale model of his current project. At its plinth an engraved plastic plate read simply:

SUTHU RIVER DAM AND HYDRO ELECTRIC SCHEME.
Consulting Engineers – Ingram Associates
Height above lowest foundation: 110 metres
Length of crest: 782 metres
Volume of concrete in wall: 1 100 000 cubic metres
Storage capacity: 3 275 $m^3 \times 10$
Power generated: 240 MW

It was a huge dam by any standards. Among the giants in South Africa. Ingram ran his finger lightly along the arched crest of the mock up. A crest that would in the near future carry the road link between Swaziland and kwaZulu.

So Kirsten Law, who in the course of three years had refused countless invitations to go with him to the Suthu gorge, suddenly wanted to see the project now, today.

Yesterday she had wanted to win an international pistol shoot. Today she had to see a dam. Ingram would have liked to believe that her motivation was that of interest in the work he was engaged in. It did not, however, ring true. It had to be something else. Something she would not, or could not discuss over a telephone.

He was sure that in the fullness of time, Kirsten's reasoning would become apparent. Right at that moment, however, he was intrigued.

Mark Ingram was a wealthy man. Like many wealthy men he conducted his affairs in a style that often left those around him in a state of bewildered awe.

Soon after having concluded his conversation with Kirsten Law, he was to be seen striding tall across the concrete of the Ingram Associates helicopter pad towards a neat navy-and-white liveried helicopter. His cashmere jacket, flipped to one shoulder billowed in the wash of the already turning rotors like some latterday cloak. The pilot, whose seat Mark Ingram took, was rewarded with a handsome salute. The crescent roar of 400 shp turbines set the window panes atremble. Mark Ingram flew into the morning sun.

* * *

Wealth did not impress Kirsten Law. She had been reared to accept money as a way of life. In greater or lesser quantities, dependent on drought, flood or fire, pestilent aldara borer beetles or even more pestilent mill managers, money was always there. It was the end product of the endless green cane fields of Prospect Hall.

Mancoba, however, despite such bedrock sanctums as *blessed are the poor* . . . and *a rich man shall no more enter the kingdom of heaven* . . . had stepped unwittingly close to the quagmire of envy.

He was impressed. Most impressed.

It was not that he had never seen wealth before; he was Durban-bred, and Durban city was clad with opulence. But a city was a faceless thing. He could put a face to all these riches and that sharpened the punishment of poverty; he was poor, and suddenly that hurt.

He had slept alone in a guest house that could have sheltered a tribe, in a bed that had sucked him in like a womb. He had seen a nineteenth-century mansion of chiselled greystone with deep shady verandahs and a four car garage. There was sugar-cane to the horizon and a narrow gauge railway that fussed across the land and it all belonged to Kirsten Law. More than anything else, though, Mancoba was impressed by the thunderous arrival of the blue and white helicopter that appeared from the west to land right on the lawn of Prospect Hall.

It was unbelievable that one person could command so much. For a moment he wondered why a man would give up all this for a loin cloth and an ideal. Then he was ashamed. This was avarice; it was in him, and he'd never known it had existed.

He was glad when his turn came to board the helicopter. He wanted to go. The man in the pilot's seat kissed Kirsten Law lightly on the cheek, turned, studied Mancoba speculatively for a moment, then returned to his controls. The whine built up until it was physical, until it seemed that the effort of ascent would tear the beast apart. Then they were rising. Prospect Hall became a slate grey roof then a slate grey smudge. As the world expanded so its texture contracted, and Prospect Hall became a slate grey memory.

To Mancoba, whose total airborne experience consisted of a rude fall from a top shelf at the reference library, it was all too much to comprehend. The huge downbeat of the rotors, that chopped the very daylight into flickers, seemed to work its clamour right into his skull. He gripped the edge of the seat, hung on, and prayed.

Within the hour the Ingwavuma plains unfolded – scarred by man's abuse – wrinkled with dry river ruts. To the left the huge granite thumb of the Lebombos came up – the palm of God's hand had opened up beneath them. You had to be a believer to see it that way. Mancoba had that kind of vision. He had prayed. His prayers had been answered. Trusting now, he began to relax.

They flew above the mountains, further north, Mancoba was sure, than his search had ever taken him. As far as Swaziland it seemed.

Far beneath them snaking deeply through the hills, a lazy river ran. Mancoba stared down, starting to enjoy this strange experience. Trying to be one of them. Then suddenly, as though mortally stricken, the engine paled. They were plunging. His body lightened sickeningly and they fell, fell, fell.

There was a rocky gorge and they were swallowed by it – dipping to meet their own muddy shadow. And when he saw again they were skimming the brown river water like a thirsty dragonfly.

They flew on downstream, Mancoba bilemouthed and disorientated, corrected what he could. He was what he was, and they were what they were. They were laughing and he was sick. He wasn't one of them.

And now they were rocketing straight towards the biggest, sheerest, most concrete thing Mancoba had ever seen. He closed his eyes. His stomach rammed into his bowels. Then they were hovering as gently as a fairy above the chunky incompleteness of the Suthu River dam.

Mancoba had no doubts as to where he was. Law, in the past, had spoken about this place many times.

They circled once, then once again; the pilot pointing here, nodding there, excited. His conversation was lost to Mancoba, his inspired gestures said it all. The dam was this man's creation. Even in his misery Mancoba felt compelled to look.

One huge bowed wall had reached half-way across the valley. On the opposite cliff, buttressed into the rock like an Inca temple, its massive twin was rising.

From metal towers on each side of the valley, suspension cables stretched. And along those cables, in yellow buckets as big as houses, the concrete came. Slaves in hard hats shoved and dug and worried at this great provider, like bees around their queen.

They landed in a valley hidden from the dam. Before the whirling blades above them whined to a halt a dusty Land Rover, colour matched to the helicopter, had drawn up nearby. The driver, a hawkish-featured man waved cheerfully, then walked across to the helicopter.

The pilot was the first out. 'Ron,' he said, 'how are you? I brought a friend of mine to inspect all your hard work. Kirsten, this is Ron Davis, my resident engineer.' Kirsten and Davis shook hands.

'Hello,' he said – very English. He had shrewd blue eyes and a patient smile, both of which he turned on Mancoba. 'And you, my friend.'

Was he anyone's friend? The legs Mancoba unfolded onto the ground refused to do more than shuffle him towards the Land Rover. His hearing felt all wrong, their voices were reaching him, hollowed and remote.

'This is Mancoba.'

'Welcome,' Davis said again. 'Tea is on the boil down at the site. You all look as though you could use a cup.'

'I could,' said the pilot.

'*I could*,' said Kirsten Law. Mancoba didn't think they'd be interested in what he thought.

Twenty minutes of dust road brought them to a breeze-blessed plateau, and the site office: a long low asbestos structure with several lesser prefabs gathered close.

Once a kraal had stood there. Driving in, they passed the tangled remnants of a cattle fence. Patches of wispy millet, growing wild at the perimeter reminded of agriculture.

Davis's office provided a distant, almost total view of the building operations: mighty tower cranes with swinging booms, and multi-wheeled machines – all hustle and dust. And wherever you stood, wherever you turned, it reached your ears: the rattle of drills, the rumble of diesels, the thump of compressors, the noise of men pitted against rock.

And tea was on the boil. Several cups of it, sweet and hot enough to do good things inside Mancoba. The pilot's name was Mark Ingram, and he was the man behind the Suthu River dam. Mancoba learned that, and more, by standing well back amongst the steel cabinets, tables and charts, and listening.

Davis, he noticed, was not as relaxed as he'd first thought him to be. He heard that all was not well at the Suthu River dam site. The Pondo nationals, ex-mine boys from the Transvaal Reef, contracted because of their underground and blasting skills, had walked off the job. More than walked off the job.

'They've packed up and gone,' Davis said. 'Yesterday they were underground working in the surge chamber. They refused to turn out for night shift, and, by this morning they were gone. The lot of them buggered off.' He apologised with a coy little wave to the lady.

'Why?' It was the third time Ingram had asked. 'And where the hell would they go? It must be a thousand K's back to Pondoland. So where are they?'

'I wish I knew.' Davis rolled his eyes to the ceiling – no message of enlightenment there. 'It's got nothing to do with wages or working conditions. I had them on a competitive incentive bonus. Whichever shift progressed the most, picked up extra cash. That backfired because the one shift got crafty and left the tunnel in a hellava mess – didn't do their mucking out, and dragged all the equipment as far as they could from the working face. But I stopped that two weeks ago. They were all as happy as hell. Now this.'

'We'll have to go down to the single quarters, Ron. That's as good a place as any to try and find out what is going on.'

Ingram turned to Kirsten Law. 'I'm sorry Kirst. I didn't expect a problem like this. It's a mess, and seeing I'm here, I'm going to have to get involved. I don't know how long Ron and I will be, but I'll organise someone to show you around.'

'No need,' Kirsten shrugged. 'There's no hurry, the dam will still be here tomorrow . . . Besides, maybe I can help you. A good translator is worth her weight in gold.'

Ingram said, 'Okay . . . fine. Let's go.'

He and Davis left the office. Kirsten followed them turning at the door to signal Mancoba to follow – a furtive little gesture that made Mancoba wonder what Ingram had been told about this old Zulu, and his mission in the Suthu River gorge.

The road they took this time was dustier and bumpier, and shared with monster-wheeled machines that thundered out suddenly from bends and corners, and kept Ron Davis nimble at the wheel.

The roadway led on through quiet hills, climbing at first, then dipping down into a lovely open valley. That was where the compound lay. It was nothing like the mine compounds of the Reef. This place was like a township, with stores and banks, a post office, and a clinic with a board outside that boasted 'three years and no fatalities'. There was even a soccer field. Half-time meant a swap – downhill to uphill, yet there it lay, white painted goal posts on an African mountainside. Davis was right. Conditions at the Suthu River hydroelectric scheme were fine.

They drove through a vehicle park blocked by several huge articulated personnel transporters – long loaders that could have swallowed a regiment. Then on, into the living quarters.

'Four and a half thousand men are accommodated here,' Ingram turned from the front seat to speak to Kirsten.

'In a project of this size it costs millions just to lay out something like this with lights and water and sewerage. That all has to be written off. In a year or so this valley will lie completely under water.'

'Asbestos Atlantis,' Kirsten said to no one.

It was easy to see where the Pondos had been quartered. They had painted splendid white designs around the borders of their doors and windows – a reminder of home. Their accommodation was situated at the perimeter of the compound, closest to the river. It looked deserted.

'Best park here.'

Davis drew up under the only shade tree there. Chatting, he, Ingram and Kirsten Law walked away. Mancoba stood next to the Land Rover, disinclined to follow. It would be far more pleasant to rest a while in the dappled shade of the tree, than to walk those dusty streets. Besides, the Pondo affair had nothing to do with him. He had other matters to think about.

He sat there; turned his back on the compound. He looked at the river; the peaceful mountains . . . might have even closed his eyes for just a moment . . .

Suddenly, as though jolted from a daydream, he was alert. A pupil, triggered into bewildered wakefulness by the voice of the schoolmaster: *'Mancoba! Stand! Answer the question.'*

'What question?'

Silly to ask that out aloud. He was alone there. No one to hear, and no one to answer. Silly.

But there was no returning to his previous state of lethargy. There *was* a question to be answered.

Searching for the instinct that had touched him, he stood and began to walk towards the river. The kwaZulu bank of the Suthu wound gently there through an area of sedges and rushes. The opposite bank, the Swazi bank, was rock. Pleated and sheer, it dipped into the river like a curtain. He gave his troubled eyes time to absorb it all. Just a river, just another rocky cliff. A mountain. Yet there was a familiarity about that place. A nagging almost voicelike insistence: *'Come Mancoba. An answer please, Mancoba.'*

'I know that mountain!'

Like dew drops melting on a window pane the trickles of memory were merging. *'Of course you know it, Zulu.'* Merging and flowing till suddenly the glass was clear.

'Umzeze's mountain.'

'Yebo, Zulu!'

'I found it!'

'You took so long. You know now what must be done. It is time now. Remember.'

Oh, how well he remembered; everything his father had told him. And had the day now come?

'Yebo, it is come.'

'This is something I was forced to do. *You forced me father.* I am a Christian. I have a Christian duty. It's an evil thing that lies buried in that mountain, father. There is a greater voice than yours, my father. A greater pledge that I must keep. Forgive me Umzeze *Baba*.'

Tears were blurring Mancoba's vision now, as he turned away, as he ran towards the compound. There would be no forgiveness for him from the spirit of Umzeze and he knew it.

*   *   *

There were three camo-clad policemen standing with Ingram's group outside the Pondo hostel. It was easy to see who the senior of the trio was. He had iron-grey close-cropped hair. The chest and arms of a wrestler were pushing a dirty, dusty shirt to the limit. His back and one big-booted foot rested territorially against a dusty beige Landcruiser.

'What speed, Uncle?' He spoke a Zulu that had been late-learned. 'An old man with the legs of a messenger. Is it an old message that you bring then, Uncle?'

Three faded cloth stars were sewn to each of his shoulders, and to his chest a name tag that spelt 'DENT'; Mancoba had heard of Captain Dent. *uDende*, the locals called him. It was the name, too, of a creeper that grew, tough and wiry in the forests there.

'Come close, Uncle, and let me hear your news.'

The eyes that held Mancoba were raw and blemished with fatigue – he'd missed a lot of sleep this man. But that didn't account for all the tiredness. They had witnessed too much suffering; had taken in too many bad things, uDende's eyes. The captain had the look of one who has lost much faith in human nature. Mancoba wondered what had brought Dent to the compound. It was not for him to ask.

Mancoba knew when not to be an object of interest. He also knew how to use the aegis of a white skin to advantage. The safe space was next to, and slightly behind Kirsten Law. That was where he quietly took himself; there he could listen. The big policeman's attention reverted to Ingram – the eyes, however, constantly reminded the latecomer that he and his feverish arrival had been noted.

'I'd like to tell you it's all under control, Mister Ingram.' Dent didn't say 'but it's not.' He drew himself away from the truck and turned to face the mountain. 'Do you know how big this place is?' He nodded towards the high peaks. 'There's no way I can prevent this sort of thing. These killings have been going on since the dawn of time.'

Ingram had his hands in his pockets, irritably clinking around some loose coins. He did look up to the peaks, but not with any great appreciation. His mind was on four hundred vanished underground workers: his Pondos. He didn't see the connection. 'Ritual murder is nothing new,' he told the policeman, 'you should be able to handle it. Arrest whoever is responsible. End of scare – end of story. I get my workers back, and you get a pat on the back from the Commissioner.'

The implication was there to draw – pat on the back or kick up the arse. Dent could depend on one or the other. There was a cold silence then Kirsten Law said: 'I'm sure the Captain knows exactly who he's looking for.' And Mancoba could see the tension slip from her shoulders when Dent shook his head.

'No, I don't.'

'No idea?'

Captain Dent looked at his inquisitor as though he'd noticed her for the first time. 'You're the sister of the botanist who was killed here last year, aren't you?'

'Yes, Monty Law was my brother.'

'Monty – that's right. I remember you at the inquest. Never did find him. Tragic case. I met him, you know, when he was doing research in the mountains. What brings you back here?'

'I came to see the dam.'

'The dam. Ah, yes.'

So there had been another ritual murder. Mancoba wondered whether Kirsten Law's heart was pounding as anxiously as his was. The policeman looked at him with those dispirited eyes again. It seemed as though he was trying to remember something. Again, abstractedly, he said, 'Ah, yes.' Then continued:

'You know, Miss Law. I could never understand what possessed your brother. I mean, the swamps downriver are lousy with crocs. Every now and again one of the locals gets taken. You'd have thought that an experienced man like your brother would have known better, eh?'

'Yes,' she said. It was all she said. It was time to get this cop well off the subject of Monty Law. Ingram did it for her.

'So,' he demanded from Dent, 'what is your next move going to be? I've got to have my workers back – *now*. You say you have no idea . . .'

'Hold it!' Dent's raised hand supported the command. 'I didn't say that, Miss Law said that. Now I don't know exactly who caused your problem, Mister Ingram, or why. But I *do* have some idea. You're damn right: ritual murder is nothing new. That doesn't make the cases any easier to solve. I was on that mountain all night watching the hacked-up corpse of one of your Pondos. If Miss Law wasn't here I'd tell you what they did to that man. No I'll tell you anyway, they had him spreadeagled, his hands and feet pegged to the ground. He was alive when they skinned him; when they started cutting bits and pieces from his body. They took out his voice box as neatly as a surgeon. Powerful *muthi*, a voice box. Good for comms with the other world. Then they cut off his fingers. Each finger has got a special usage for the *umthakathi*. Then . . .'

'That's enough!' A spasm of disgust juddered Ingram's upper body.

'Well, I thought they might come back for more,' Dent shrugged. 'They didn't. My wait was for nothing. But I'm not empty-handed, not by a long shot.'

'Why do they do it? It's so senseless.' Ingram looked around to the others – to Kirsten Law, to Davis. They nodded. They were like-minded: it was senseless.

Dent said, 'It depends on which side of the kraal gates you were born, doesn't it? It doesn't make sense to us but we weren't brought up to believe in the people of the night – *ba Busiku* – who leave their sleeping bodies and take off into the sky on wings of fire, to murder and cannibalise. We don't believe all that stuff – not any more. But in Europe four hundred years ago *our* forefathers were burning witches wholesale. Makes you think doesn't it?'

Ingram's thought was that something had better be done, and fast. 'Hell, it can't go on like this. This *isn't* the sixteenth century, and we are not building the village pond. Five hundred million rand is being sunk into this valley, Captain. That is a lot of money. Delays can be measured in tens of thousands of rands. What's happened this morning is a disaster.'

'I know that, sir.'

Dent had the policeman's knack of detracting from the word 'sir'. Ingram said:

'So do you think this murder was planned? I mean, was a victim selected, or did they just hack up the first poor sod who happened along?'

'It was planned. These things always are.'

'So what you're telling me is that this killing was set up to warn my Pondos. To scare them the hell out of here.'

'It was planned,' Dent repeated. 'But don't jump to any conclusions as to why it was done. The mind behind this killing is probably so twisted that you would never understand the reasoning, not in a million years. I'll tell you this, Mister Ingram. You think you're doing the locals a big favour by building a dam here. There's a lot of local folk don't see it that way. The Suthu River has always flowed and they've always drawn water from it a bucket at a time – that's all they can carry. What difference is a whole lake full of water going to make, when they can still only get a bucket at a time?'

'I've given them work,' Ingram said. 'The power from the

turbines there is going to boost the whole economy.'

'You've given them a cement wall and a valley full of water,' Dent interrupted, 'and that valley full of water is going to cover hundreds of homes, and even worse, hundreds of burial sites. You're submerging their Westminster Abbeys, Mister Ingram. You're drowning their saints. Do you understand what I'm saying?'

'Of course I know that. But I also know that nearly four months worth of negotiations took place before we even started drilling test holes into this valley. We knew all about the burial grounds, we negotiated with the headmen. Everyone was compensated. It was part of the tender. Everyone was happy.'

'I'm not arguing with you,' Dent said. 'I'm just trying to show you what you're up against. I know that everyone was compensated. They were given more money than most of them would have earned in a lifetime. But money has a habit of running out, and close behind it, the happiness. This isn't the valley of joy you might think it is, Mister Ingram.'

'Are you telling me that the local people did this to try and sabotage me? I find that hard to believe. The dam is their bread and butter.'

Dent didn't answer for a moment. He seemed to be appraising the engineer. It was the same thoughtful scrutiny Mancoba had been subjected to.

'It's more than that,' he said at last. 'It's not just the local tribesmen, and it's not just the dam. Did you ever hear of the Mau Mau?'

'Of course. The Kenya uprising. In the early fifties, wasn't it?'

'Yes. A small band of fanatics from the Kikuyu tribe, bonded together by oaths, took a whole suspicious nation along with them on a killing spree that left thirteen thousand people dead. One of those who died was a nineteen-year-old newly-wed called Wendy Dent. My wife.'

'God,' said Kirsten Law, 'I'm sorry.' Ingram mumbled something consolatory. Dent, however, was not seeking sympathy. He continued:

'I joined the Kenya Police after that – the General Service Unit. We did all the dirty work for the army and the police. When *Uhuru* came four years later, the Mau Mau became overnight heroes. I was kicked out – an imperialist thug. I joined the South African Police and I've been with them ever since; most of the time here in kwaZulu.'

'Yes,' Ingram's tone was brittle, impatient. He didn't want Dent's curriculum vitae. He wanted to know about four hundred missing Pondos. 'Yes,' he prodded again.

'I've got a feel for this place,' Dent went on. 'Sort of like a built-in barometer. Somehow I'm sensitive to the slightest change. I know when things are right and when things are wrong. Right now things are wrong.'

Ingram's mood swung suddenly to anger. 'What the hell have the Mau Mau got to do with it?' he demanded. 'What exactly are you trying to tell me?'

'They're taking oaths in the Lebombos,' Dent said. 'The same kind of bloody anti-white oaths they took in Kenya. I think we've got a huge problem. *That* is what I'm trying to tell you.'

'My God,' Ingram's voice was almost a whisper, 'I don't believe it.'

But it was just words. His face was ashen with the belief of it. Kirsten Law moved to his side. She linked her arm solidly with his. 'Are you quite sure about all this?'

She looked pale too. She had more than a fortune at stake – she had a brother.

'About as sure as I've ever been.' Dent was not enjoying their discomfort. Sincerely he said, 'I'm doing everything I can. As I said to you, I'm not empty-handed. I'm working on something. I've got a prisoner.'

He might have said more, but at that moment a light delivery truck, the progress of which Mancoba had been monitoring since it had turned off the river road, drew up there. The driver craned his neck from the cab; addressed the consulting engineer:

'They need you at the site office, Mister Ingram. Pretoria on the blower for you – the Minister's office.'

'Damn it. That can only mean that the environmentalists have had something to say again.' Ingram spoke to the driver of the light truck, 'I want you to take Miss Law on a Cook's tour of the site. Then on to my house.'

'I'm sure you know what's involved here.' He frowned his final words to Dent. 'I'm sure too we can expect quick results,

Captain.'

To Davis he said, 'Let's go.'

And without a backwards glance they went. Dent laughed that laugh of his. 'You know you couldn't pay me enough to do that man's job. Beyond this dam of his, he's got no idea what's happening in this valley.'

Mancoba silently agreed.

3

Nationality: Thonga-Zulu. *Sex:* Male. *Age:* 25. *Place of residence:* Nkonjane – Suthu River Gorge. *Place of employment:* Ndumu Game Reserve – game guard. *Charge:* Murder – alternatively: accessory to murder. The name on the charge sheet read: September Mabutane.

That was all that Captain Dent's docket told regarding the physical aspects of the life of the man he held as prisoner.

September Mabutane was tall for his race. His features owned that full, proud symmetry – the quality of the classic *nguni* cast – the mould of all things Zulu. At that moment, however, he was bowed and slumped and his features were shaded, so that neither his height nor his pride nor his handsomeness, was apparent.

The cell that held September was painted a cold shadowless grey, that seeped like mountain mist through blanket, skin and bone invading its inmate until he was saturated and heavy. Both body and mind were grey-filled and leaden. September Mabutane felt as though he were dying.

There was a rectangular opening in the wall, too high for groping hands to reach. A louvred affair with a stamped metal grid that gave access to a measure of sound and a lesser measure of sun: a ragged stingy square of light that came and went like a beggar, giving nothing.

There was a concrete bench to sit on; a push button fountain to drink from, and a seatless toilet to excrete on.

The only other things, besides an inmate, permitted by standing orders to be on the inside of a South African Police cell was a Gideons' Bible.

September Mabutane was not thirsty. His bowels were empty. The Bible was a white man's fairy tale that he wanted no part of. The only thing left for him to do was to think, and he thought he was dying. The coldness of the grave had reached up to touch him.

Soon he would cast no shadow. All he hoped was that it would be quick.

It was not quick enough to prevent another interrogation from taking place.

Through the vent above he heard the rumble of a vehicle drawing up in the courtyard outside. The slamming of car doors and the crunch of trodden gravel. Before long, he felt sure, he would hear the rattle of a key entering a lock and the solid metal door of his cell would swing heavily inwards. Who would it be who came to summon him?

It was the one who called himself Shibindji, one of the older policemen, a sergeant. He stood in the little passage that separated the heavy solid door from a further barred door – the final entrance to September's cell.

Shibindji did not look like a policeman. He was scrawny. The blue uniform he preferred hung on his bones like a tribal blanket. He had a beak-like face, and long dead fingers, never without the remnant of a cigarette. At that moment they were gripping a bunch of large keys, and a cigarette.

'You . . . Mabutane,' he said, as though there were others there besides Mabutane. 'Yes you! On your feet. *Yiza!* Come!'

Another policeman joined Shibindji at the grill. This one was dressed in sweaty camouflage, and this one did look like a cop. Together they opened the bars, and for a moment, just for one wild moment, September's mind was seized with the thought of escape. Then he got to his feet, as instructed, and walked quietly with them.

The station commander's office was angular and uncluttered. It was large and square and it held a desk that was large and square. Captain Dent was sitting on it, and his physique, likewise, was in perfect unity. On seeing September he returned some papers which he had been reading to a stack of like-sized papers, tapping the edges until they were as true as a book.

'Ah,' he said. 'September Mabutane. Come in, come in. Stand there my friend. No not there. Shibindji, show our friend exactly where to stand. *That's* right. We want you to be comfortable, Mabutane.'

Comfort was the most unlikely thing that a prisoner would experience in the company of Captain Dent. The Zulu knew that.

What the policeman wanted was the secrets of Abanzanzi – all of them. Everything that was locked in the mind of September Mabutane.

But that was not all that Dent wanted. The possession of Mabutane's knowledge was just the first step. The beginning of the man's usefulness. Mabutane, despite a lack of formal education, was intelligent, surprisingly intelligent. Their previous dialogue had taught Dent that. But intelligence would not provide Mabutane with a shield. It could be his weakness. Dent began.

'Don't shuffle, Mabutane. Do *nothing* you are not told to do. Today I want some answers from you, Mabutane. I want the truth.'

Dent's voice held the prosaic confidence of one whose everyday experience is to receive truthful answers to anything thus asked. He had good reason for believing that. The South African Police were experts in the ignoble art of interrogation. But Dent's primary education in such matters could not be rivalled. He had been taught by the master locksmiths of the mind – the General Service Unit of the Kenya Police. The GSU had called their system 'restoration'. In skilful hands, the GSU method produced fine results and the hands that held September Mabutane were of the most skilful.

'You see September, I really know all I have to know about the murder of the Pondo dam worker. What we must talk about now is Abanzanzi. I want to know about their secrets – their oaths, their hiding places. Especially I want to know who leads them.'

Restoration did not just entail opening the mind. That was simply phase one. Nor was the draining of that mind sufficient. An empty mind was still a hostile mind – a totally useless commodity. The object of restoration was to systematically clean out the polluted areas in the brain – then to refill those spaces with selected material. It was rather like repairing brickwork: the old material often needed to be hammered out first. It was important to use just the right amount of force.

'Tell me all about Abanzanzi. If you do that, if you tell me everything you know then I may let you go. If you don't talk to me . . .' Dent shrugged. It was a large and dismal gesture that reflected the sadness that he would feel in the event of such ingratitude. Then he sat back and lit a cigarette.

It was clearly September Mabutane's turn to respond. He said:

'Yesterday I told you all that it is right for you to know about Abanzanzi, uDende. There is nothing more I can say.'

'You told me no more than is already common knowledge amongst the hill people.'

'And that is all that it is right for you to know.'

'You force me to do things that I don't want to do, Mabutane.'

'I force you to do nothing, uDende. But let me tell you this. You do me honour by punishing me – the more you hurt my body, the more you strengthen my spirit. For you to kill me, uDende, would open a fine gate for me.'

'Oh, I won't kill you,' Dent said quickly. 'I'll simply take you away from everything that is beautiful in your life; your wives; your cattle; the song of the fish eagle at the lakes of Ndumu. All that and more. I'm going to let you rot in that dull cold cell, Mabutane. But now I've lost my patience with you.'

Dent nodded to Shibindji. Shibindji was standing right behind the prisoner. He knew the rules. He knew what next to do.

Dent got up from the desk and left the room. He would distance himself from the breaking-down process. And there were many good reasons for that.

One good reason was that Dent had no curiosity left as to certain types of police methodology. He'd seen it all before – experienced it in fact, in the fullest sense of the word. Never would he forget his final days in Jomo Kenyatta's Kenya. They had laid on a farewell session for him those old police boys of his with a variation: ex-Inspector Patrick Dent at the receiving end of the 500 watt current. Jomo's renegade cops had gone the whole hog on him. For months afterwards he had been torn loose from his slumbers – clutching at the wet canvas hood smothering him, his body a writhing conduit of agony. And then when he was truly awake and truly aware, he had lain there shaking without a single defence against the blackness threatening to flood his mind.

Dent's memories walked him blindly to the front entrance of the police station. There he censored further thought; relaxed his body. A breath that he'd held back for too long he expired, and suddenly all he wanted from life was someone else's job. Suddenly he was in the no man's land that made up the conscience of a cop, and he didn't like what he was seeing there. There was a world outside. He turned to it.

Low cloud was slipping in across the Lebombo peaks. So far that summer had been the driest of four dry years. He'd never known a drought like this before. The mountain folk were still coping, but further down in the plains the ground cover was hoof scarred and juiceless; the *nguni* cattle herds pinched in, listless for the want of sweet grass. There was poverty and hunger there. God, they were taking a long time with Mabutane.

'Captain.' It was Shibindji's voice from close behind.

'Yes, Sergeant?'

'He's passed out.'

I'm not surprised thought Dent – the poor bastard. 'I'm coming right now,' he said. 'Hey, Shibindji look up there. It looks like rain.'

* * *

During the empty months between April and October, if the ground remains unwetted, who will care. Only a fool. The wise men worry when *Ulwezi*, the dripping moon, has come, and gone, and the heavens have not yet melted. Both fool and wise man however are linked in distress if no rain has fallen by November. Then it is time to take action; to discover what it is, who it is, that has offended the ancestors' spirits; to offer sacrifices in appeasement.

Thereafter there is one month left in which to sow grain – December. And if no rain falls during that ultimate month, it is a disaster. Famine is at hand.

That day, despite the best effort of the rain doctors and the sangomas and the hopes of all the Thonga people, no rain fell anywhere in Zululand.

The clouds lay braided to the mountain peaks, as dry as muslin. Their only effect was to minimise the vision of those up on the slopes.

Mancoba was on the slopes.

After Ingram had left in the pick-up van, Dent and Kirsten Law had stood there, talking. The driver who was supposed to take Kirsten on the Cook's tour, waited patiently. Mancoba had taken the opportunity to slip away, not unnoticed, (nothing in the path of the slate-eyed uDende went unnoticed,) but unchallenged. He manoeuvred to keep those below him in sight as he climbed. What he really wished to gain though, was a better view of the crocodile ridged mountain. He had to be sure.

Mancoba found a spot where he could see all he wanted to see . . . and he *was* sure. This was Umzeze's mountain.

He watched uDende tip his hand in careless salute to Kirsten Law; beckon to his men and walk away. They drove off in their Landcruiser with the long whippy radio aerial.

Kirsten Law looked around, hands on hips. She seemed surprised to find Mancoba gone – annoyed.

Mancoba stood away from the shade, cupped his hands and called.

'Here. I'm up here, Miss Law.'

He clambered onto a boulder and semaphored with his arms. 'Here.'

She saw him; gestured irritably for him to return. He shook his head, stood his ground; gestured in return for her to come to him. '*Cheeky*', she'd be thinking. And what could she do about it? The 'Cook's tour' man climbed from his vehicle, the better to see what was happening. She spoke to him. Pointed to the Zulu on the mountain. The driver nodded his head; looked at his watch; returned to his vehicle and lit a cigarette. She began to climb.

Mancoba felt a chuckle rise in his heart. He observed the advancing woman – too wiry to be pretty by Zulu standards. Her breasts were loveless things, that worked like muscle beneath the thinness of her shirt, but her face was very pretty. There was something of her brother there.

A chill passed through Mancoba – a whisper of apprehension at the thought of Monty Law. He cast around in the surrounding bush. The gnaw of excitement in his gut intensified again.

'You didn't wait,' she accused. 'Why didn't you wait?' She was suddenly there. She gathered herself and leapt lightly onto the rock where he stood.

Feline, Mancoba thought, that was what she was. That was the quality she and her brother shared. They were both like cats.

'I didn't want to be with uDende,' Mancoba said. 'He worries me. He sucks your thoughts out like a tick sucks blood.'

'He's a policeman; they're like that. Next time wait.'

Proud like her brother, and pride didn't allow her to ask the reason for his having summoned her there. She had to pretend she had come at her own volition, and this made her angry.

'You didn't tell me anything about these oaths, Mancoba. Did you know about them?'

'The people of this area have always been great ones for oaths. This is nothing new. They take a pinch of earth on their tongue then spit it out – *tsu*!' Mancoba demonstrated the technique. 'Now I may swear to anything and you will be obliged to believe me.'

'That's not the sort of thing that Dent was talking about,' Kirsten Law snapped. 'He says that ceremonies are taking place here where men are swearing to do terrible things, to destroy anything to do with whites.'

'Do you believe him?'

'Why should he lie?'

'Perhaps . . .' Mancoba shrugged. 'Perhaps he's looking for a reason to crack down hard on the local Thonga tribesmen.'

'He's got enough reason already.'

'Maybe he's already gone too far then, and he needs to cover his back. I don't trust him.'

'You don't trust anyone, Mancoba. If you'd stayed with me you could have heard what he had to say yourself. He's got a prisoner. He caught one of the oath takers – got him locked up at Abercorn Drift. Someone called September Mabutane.'

'Did uDende want to know the reason for your visit, and my being here with you?'

'He didn't ask me.'

'He is bound to ask Mister Ingram. Have you told *him* anything?'

'I told him I wasn't happy about the circumstances of my brother's death. That's all.'

'Then that is what Mister Ingram will tell uDende. That's not good.'

'That's for me to decide, Mancoba . . . All you have to concern yourself with is the discovery of the cave where Umzeze hid the Inkatha. That is where the helicopter comes in. Mister Ingram has undertaken to . . .'

'We won't need it,' Mancoba put in. '. . . We don't need the helicopter.'

'You don't understand Mancoba. Those mountains run all the way from here to central Natal. That's a distance of more than a hundred kilometres.'

'No,' Mancoba shook his head. '*You* don't understand. I mean we don't have to *look* any more. I've found Umzeze's mountain. That's why I wanted you to come up here. There it is, one valley away. Look.'

'You mean it? You don't mean it!'

'Trust, Miss Law. See.' Mancoba mimed a pinch of earth onto his tongue. '*Tsu!*'

She laughed, and that pleased Mancoba. It was the first time he had seen her laugh.

'Yes,' he said. 'There it is.'

And suddenly her laughter was gone. She was looking along his upraised arm, at the sweep of the crocodile tail ridge. Shifting cloud was washing through the high gaps giving ponderous movement to the beast.

'Umzeze's cave,' she said quietly. 'Your father must have stood here once, Mancoba. He and Fana. Think of it. Imagine what their thoughts must have been.'

That was exactly what Mancoba was trying not to imagine. He said, 'We can start looking for the cave tomorrow.'

'We can start now.'

'I know these mountains,' Mancoba shook his head negatively. 'You won't be able to see much up there. It would be better to wait until the morning.'

Kirsten Law did not agree.

'Look – the peaks are quite clear in places. Anyway those clouds don't look so thick to me. They'll probably lift.'

'It's quite a climb,' Mancoba warned.

And it was. It took them over two hours to reach the cloud belt, and by then it was past three o'clock. Mancoba's other prediction proved correct too. Once inside the mist, vision was cut down to a few paces.

Neither did it lift. In fact the clouds seemed to thicken; to descend upon them in a swirling white curtain.

Kirsten realised her mistake. She glanced at her wrist watch and estimated that even if they began to retrace their steps at once, it would take them until late afternoon to get back to the vehicle. She decided to catch up with Mancoba; to call off the search for the present.

Mancoba, however was far ahead. Just a fluid grey smudge in the whiteness. She could hear his laboured breathing if she halted, and now and then the clatter of a dislodged stone. She followed all the time hoping for a break in the clouds. The break never came.

What happened was that the mountain became steeper, rockier and more slippery. With every step the mist drew in tighter.

Then she saw that the old Zulu had sensibly stopped and was waiting for her up ahead.

But it wasn't him. Waiting, was a lone kranz aloe, growing head and shoulders from a rock face that was getting on for sheer.

Next to that spiny impersonator she stopped. It was madness to continue. She called out. 'Mancoba,' and when there was no answer; '*Mancoba . . . we must turn back now.*'

No response. She continued for a few uncertain paces, then stopped again. She felt more perplexed than worried. She knew that up to a short while back, she had been aware of the sounds of the climber up ahead. Now there was silence, absolute silence.

The old Zulu could have fallen and hurt himself but that seemed unlikely. Despite those wheezy old lungs Mancoba was as sure-footed and spry as a mountain goat. And besides she would have heard something had he come to grief. She decided to climb on alone a while – to investigate.

She wasn't alone for long. A new companion padded through the silence to join her – fear.

It came with the stealth of a hyena. It nuzzled her groin and slimed its way inwards. It came with the realisation of how incredibly stupid, how totally naive she had been.

Mancoba hadn't fallen, nor had he waited up ahead. Despite her apprehension Kirsten made quite certain of that. There was only one logical route for him to have taken – a steep ravine, shelved like a water course and guarded by an impi of brooding aloes. She searched it to its last grey shadow, but he wasn't there. She called to him again, twice. Then she turned around and started to make her way back downhill through the haze.

That was when she heard the click of a jolted pebble – the sound had come from behind her and above. Someone was there. Someone who didn't, or wouldn't answer to the name Mancoba.

The hyena burrowed deeper now, fear was licking at her spine.

She stopped and waited and whoever it was behind her stopped and waited too. She didn't hear the next sound until she moved again: the scratch of skin against bark and perhaps, yes, a naked footfall. The only other sound was that of her own breath, and that was running ragged.

She had to stop that. She remembered how readily Mancoba's noisy breathing had led her on earlier. Now *she* was providing a homing signal to whoever it was who was stalking *her*. Kirsten did what she thought would be best – she hid.

Flanking the ledge where she presently stood, a tangled tract of dragon bush was anchored to the rock. She drew herself to the ground and carefully climbed beneath the leathery cover. The safe, sweet smell of summer blossoms quilted her and her breathing began to ease.

She began consciously to contest the fear that was hollowing her. She started to formulate a survival plan. Rule one was no further movement without thought. It was the first rule she broke.

She thought she would like to know more about her enemy. She thought that the way to do that would be to gather one of the many stones lying about; to bounce it down the water course. In that way she would be able to see who it was who passed by to follow up the noise.

The first stone proved to be immovably bedded to the ground; the next too large. The third rock she reached for was flattish and shifted readily enough. She eased her hand beneath it; felt something squirming between her palm and the stone. *Pain!* White hot gasping pain shocked up her arm. She wrenched back her arm and a scorpion with it. Thrown back to her neck, it scuttled for her hairline. She hit it, grasped it, threw it down in one reflex of horror. She was on her feet. She broke from cover. She ran.

Other people were running too, careless of sound now. They were converging on her, thrashing through the thorn scrub.

The water course led into a cleft ravine and the cleft ravine channelled her into a narrow, buttressed passage. She was lost. She had been trapped. It would have required the agility of a baboon to scale those sheer rock walls. She tried. Desperation gave her strength – it did not however come close to providing agility. She had one arm that was functional. Her right arm, from hand to bicep was useless, a burning paralysed thing. And one arm was not enough.

It drew her high enough to achieve no more than a jarring, stumbling return to the chasm floor.

And now they were closer.

Now, floating in the greyness, were the silhouettes of her pursuers. They weren't running any more. Perhaps they had realised they didn't need to. With a steady almost unisoned tread they advanced.

Kirsten was on her knees. For one moment, but just a moment, she thought it would be best to face these men, to reason with them – to ask them why they were doing this to her. Then she caught the dull glint of metal – *assegais*. She drove her hurting body up. She knew she didn't have the strength to stay ahead much longer.

It ended less than a hundred stubborn steps from there. Not because she chose to make her stand at that point. She didn't have a choice.

The passsageway through the water course stopped short there, fell away into a swirling grey void. There, in better times, in times of rain, there must have flowed a rainbowed waterfall. At that moment, it was the end point in the flight of a very desperate woman. She turned to face her tormentors.

'What do you want!' *Want – want – want* the hillside mocked her shout.

'Leave me!' *Leave me – leave me.*

A mimic of her panic.

Six men firmed up out of the mist. Slender-hipped hard men naked but for loincloths and *mbatha* charms wound to their wrists. They had clubs, big loosely held *iWisa*, and stabbing assegais. They had arrogance; stone-eyed pitiless arrogance.

They gave Kirsten Law enough time to see all that; to see that there was no further place to run or hide. To see that she was theirs.

They could not have known of the scorpion sting, nor of its effect. Pain was swamping Kirsten Law now, muddying all but one prevailing thought: *there is no mercy in these men* – they must not touch you.

They started forward. She scrambled back. They came at a run. She turned. Hands were groping for her. She committed herself to the waterfall – she jumped.

* * *

Patrick Dent kept regulation hours when he could. And when he couldn't he tried at least to make the time pass as smoothly as possible. The bottom left hand drawer of his big square desk held the means to smooth the passage of time: one litre, (a bit less now) of Courvoisier Napoleon brandy, and one glass. These items he raised to his desk top. There was much more he wished to do before his day was over.

He poured himself a measure – two fingers precisely. He disapproved of glasses filled further than that. He lit a cigarette, then drew on the rawness of it. The alcohol and the smoke eroded through his deeper pains. Like cures like.

'Cheers,' he said to the amber bright glass. 'Here's fucking health.'

Besides the bottle on Dent's desk there was a sheaf of papers – routine stuff, and a black celluloid cassette recorder.

Routine was the last thing on Captain Dent's agenda. He shifted the recorder to within easy reach, pressed the 'play' button, then crammed his huge frame into the inadequacy of his office-issue chair. He leaned back and listened.

Not even the attrition of cheap electronics had managed to erase the agony impregnated into the plastic tape. The sound of the moment was muzzled and guttural. The throat sounds of torture. Once the gagging wet sack had been removed, and the man's frantic lungs had calmed, the recording would improve. There was a thud, then a moment of quiet broken by Shibindji's voice:

'*He's passed out.*'

There was the sound of Shibindji's footsteps diminishing. Then the squeak of Dent's rubber soles – approaching. A telephone was ringing distantly. Dent had never liked the sound of his own taped voice. '*Right.*' It came across too nasal. '*Get him to his cell.*'

The tape ran dead for a moment or two. When next the voice of Dent was to be heard, it was even more hollow.

'*Let's talk, September. Let's talk about Abanzanzi.*'

'Abanzanzi . . .'

As though his system demanded reassurance that its ordeal was over, September Mabutane had gasped then, deeply. There was air in abundance in the cell, but it had not seemed enough for him. *'Abanzanzi.'* He said again. *'I have told you all I can, uDende. You've gnawed it to the bone.'*

'Tell me again.' Dent's voice. *'Tell me what Abanzanzi means.'*

'It means, those who reside below, the dead. The people of the past.'

'Why do you call yourselves that?'

'We were called together by the ancestors, by the mighty spirits of the heroes of kwaZulu. How can we not succeed?'

'What do you mean by succeed?'

'We will grow stronger. To count every Zulu who died a hero is to count the stars. The wishes of the ancestors must be honoured.'

'And what are these wishes?'

'We must follow the river back to its very wellspring.'

'What river? What wellspring? Don't talk to me in Zulu riddles, Mabutane. I'm tired. I haven't got time for that shit.'

There was a long silence and the tape hissed by emptily. Dent remembered the sudden fury that had boiled up in him then. He had wanted to hit out – to send that stubborn black face spinning. Mabutane had sensed his anger.

'There is nothing you can do, uDende. It isn't fear for you that moves me to speak of these things. What little I am telling you, I am telling you because of the power that you have to damage something that is good. I want you to understand something about Abanzanzi so that you can stand back without fear for yourself or your people, and say; this is good. What these men do is good.'

'I've seen the goodness of Abanzanzi. I saw how the Pondo died of it.'

'What you saw was a man who was perceived as being a wizard. He was seen driving thakatha – wizard's sticks into the ground to frighten back the rainclouds.'

'So your people killed him because you thought he was chasing away the rain. You, a game guard, a man of some education, and you believed that?'

'It is not important what I believe. Abanzanzi are travelling to the river's source. The journey is a hard one, a long one. Many mistakes will be made and at times direction lost. But when one day they do

arrive, they will be able to see in both directions – to the future and to the past. Then judgements can be made as to what is right and what is wrong.'

'And I must stand back and let this bloody journey take its course?'

'You must take your view from the mountain, uDende. You are a man of power. You can therefore be strong in leniency.'

Dent stopped the tape recorder right there. For a while he sat, eyes unfocused, deeply in thought. Then as though suddenly aware of an intrusion, he looked down at his fingers. They were drumming dully but militarily on the desk top. He stopped that. Their employment was to bring before him one sheet of foolscap; one pen. He headed the paper explicitly and boldly: *Action against Abanzanzi:* Under that he wrote: *Abanzanzi is tribal, in concept Zulu. Their philosophy is based on the resurrection of outlawed tribal traditions.*

He read what he had just written. Then took deeply from both glass and cigarette and restarted the recorder.

'Mmm . . . What if I told you that I thought you were lying? What if I said you killed this Pondo to frighten all the other Pondos; to chase them away from here, so the dam would never be finished?'

'There may be those who think that way.'

'Mmm. So tell me Mabutane, why I should not step on the neck of Abanzanzi like a snake.'

He wrote: *Police action, to be effective, must aim to crush both the philosophy and structure of Abanzanzi.* The tape ran on:

'. . . look at my people, uDende. Look at them today. Tell me what is left of the greatness of the past. Where are the chiefs and kings whose footsteps shook the earth? Where are they?'

He wrote: *The potency of Abanzanzi will depend on the extent that it possesses the power to be more feared than the security forces.*

'Where are the men?'

Any leniency by the S.F. would be regarded as weakness.

The men, Mabutane said, had been reduced to a tribe of prancing rickshaw boys – out-at-knee garden boys – any kind of Jimboy you could think of – drunk from the white man's alcohol; riddled with the white man's syphilis. Dent let all that pass him by. That was an old lament. What was new, what was interesting, was Mabutane's following statement.

'We the Zulu are to blame for this – no one else. We have let others

take charge of us. We have been led like the bull with the nose ring to new pastures. First it was the missionaries, then the preachers, Anglicans, Catholics, Lutherans, as many religions as there are hairs on a dog's back. And all of them had one message: the old ways, the tribal ways are evil, to follow them is sin. To pay lobola for your bride is sin. To divine with the bones is sin. Eh! And to worship your ancestors, to place them before the son of the Christian God now that is the sin of sins. So the Zulu bull followed, yes, and as sour as the grass tasted, it ate. It grew thin and weaker. Now look at it today. What do you see? A nation without respect for its traditions, a nation without pride in its history, a nation without dignity.'

Neither man had spoken then for a while. Mabutane had looked so dispirited, so tired. The moment had been right for an all out psychological thrust. For some reason Dent had not done that. He had sat there and waited for the Zulu to continue.

'The ancestors have become tired of our ways, sick of our insults, angry with our half-hearted worship. We are a punished people. We must turn back to the old ways.'

'And Abanzanzi will lead the Zulus?'

'Only they know the way.'

'Maybe your leaders don't see it that way. They are Christians you know.'

'Some chiefs have forfeited the right to call themselves our leaders. They have turned against their traditions. They have become impotent and tremble at the words of the missionaries of the Devil and his hell. Well, we are missionaries too. To understand what I am saying we must go back in history; to the days when the Zulu impis were crushed, and the Zulu king exiled from the land of his fathers. King Cetchwayo – the slandered one – appointed certain men and women as custodians of the belief. These custodians were bound by an almighty oath to protect and nurture the legends, the traditions, the poems and sacred beliefs of Zulu. These things, upon which the honour of the nation rests, were taken and stored where no man and no religion could find them and destroy them. They were locked into the memories of the custodians. These custodians are the guardians of our culture, and if you searched until the mountains crumbled and the rivers stopped flowing, you would never find them, uDende. But there are others who try to destroy them, with the gentle violence of the tongue they influence others to believe that the old ways are wrong. These Christians can no longer be

called our leaders. We can no longer follow such weak-kneed men . . . Abanzanzi will give to the nation a true leader. That is our mission.'

'When will it happen? Who is this leader?'

Mabutane had smiled and shook his head. *'You will see,'* was all he said.

He had gone on shaking his head when Dent had probed on the matter of the oaths. There was only one oath that he was prepared to disclose:

' "If I uncover the knowledge of Abanzanzi to one who is not Abanzanzi, then may I die the coward's death. May my wounds carry over; may my spirit suffer in eternal agony." So you see uDende, my story is my damnation. I hope it has not been a wasted sacrifice. I hope your eyes have been opened. I am a lopped tree – use me to make the bridge. You would not be the first white man to cross over to Abanzanzi.'

As if Mabutane had so timed it, at that moment, the tape came to an end. The conclusion of the Mabutane interrogation was on the other side, but Dent made no move to restart the recorder. He remembered his words to Mabutane:

'Well if it's any consolation to you Zulu, you haven't revealed anything to me that I didn't already know.' But that was a lie.

Dent put down his pen and placed his writing into a drawer which he closed and locked. He drew on his cigarette, then stared into the eddying smoke. His eyes unfocused. His mind was in another place, another time. The oaths however had an appalling similarity to the present.

His uniform had been different then: colonial-cut khaki shorts and tunic, creased to a knife edge, strapped with a Sam Browne, gleaming black. He'd had a prisoner then too: the face, he couldn't remember, just the eyes. He would never forget those stagnant pools of poison; lifeless, dull and hating. He would never forget the confession of those oaths:

*If I am sent to bring in the head of a white man and I fail,
  may this oath kill me.
If I fail to steal from the white man, may this oath kill me.
If I fail to report an enemy, may this oath kill me.
If I fail to do the bidding of a leader of the house of Kikuyu,
  may this oath kill me.*

*If I refuse to do my share in driving the white man from Kenya,
may this oath kill me.
If I worship any leader but Jomo Kenyatta, may this oath kill me.
If I am untrue to Mau Mau even in thought, may this oath kill
me.*

The oaths hadn't killed him, *Dent* had, outside a cave on verdant Mount Kenya – a betrayed arms cache. The man had conjured up a *simi* knife from nowhere and come running. He had wanted to die badly that man. Dent's .38 Webley had beaten the oath to it – or had it simply been the instrument of death?

It had not been a human being he'd killed though. The bestial ceremonies of Mau Mau robbed a man of any claim to membership of the human race.

Dent emptied his brandy glass and shuddered. He lifted the bottle and pressed the coldness of it to his forehead.

Inexorably, another picture was forming. He poured again, maybe a drop more than two fingers this time. He gulped it – a man late for an appointment with the past. The alcohol made little difference, he'd blurred the images but that didn't help much. The memory was too vivid. It was all there when he walked through the front door. First the splintered furniture, then Jock the bull terrier lying in her own spilt entrails, faithful tail one last wag from death. Wendy of the eyes of sky – the breasts of Aphrodite, only she possessed neither any longer. She wasn't as lucky as Jock. The Webley .38 . . . two hands to hold it still.

'*Jesus Christ!*' Dent's shout could be heard from the Charge Office. '*Bastards!*'

Shibindji smiled, he'd heard it all before. In an hour or so he would go to his commander's office and sweep up the glass.

What else Shibindji heard was the growl of a motor vehicle, a fast approaching motor vehicle. He made his way to the mosquito screened verandah of the Police Station and watched the oncoming headlights. The driver was a madman.

The madman was Mark Ingram. The Range Rover broadsided to a halt and Ingram flew out of it and up the Charge Office steps almost in a continuation of momentum. He told Shibindji what Shibindji already knew. 'I'm Mister Ingram. I want to see the Captain. I'm in a hurry.'

Sergeant Shibindji did not believe anything that happened in those kwaZulu hills could be that urgent. He said, 'Wait here,' closed the Charge Office door behind him and using a side exit, stepped into the darkness. He felt his way quietly along the familiar outside wall of the building towards the square of yellow light that was his superior officer's window. From what he saw, he judged that Captain Dent would not be seeing anyone that night.

But Shibindji was wrong. Dent saw Ingram, simply because Ingram was not having it any other way.

'Bullshit, Sergeant. Of course he's here. There's his truck right outside. I'll find him myself,' he said. And he did.

If Dent was surprised at the rude and sudden severance of his reverie he didn't show it. He would have offered the man a drink had there been anything left to drink. It said something for his constitution that he could stand without support, and walk without a sway. He walked to the open safe behind his desk, deposited the tape recorder therein, locked it, then turned back to the intruder.

'Ingram,' he said as though finally placing the man. 'What did you say then?'

'I said I'm bloody worried.'

'No, before that.'

'I said she should have been back hours ago. It was bloody stupid of her to go climbing alone, as good as alone, she had that Zulu Mancoba with her. He's not back either.'

'Neither of them back,' said Dent dully. 'Stupid. Yes very stupid.' But there was an epithet that was far more fitting. 'Suicidal.' Yes, that was the word. The *stupid* one was the man standing before him right then. The man who had let her do it. The man who at any moment was going to suggest that the joy of every true blue cop was midnight mountaineering.

'Well,' said Ingram right on cue, 'we've got to go and find her.'

'Not tonight. Tonight we try and get her to find us. I'm going to give you a bunch of flares and a policeman who knows how to fire them. If she's lost, she'll be able to home in on them. If things have gone worse than that . . . well there's not a damn thing we can do tonight. It's black as hell out there.'

'What do you mean – if things are worse?'

Aggravating Ingram's stupidity was his persistence in its application. Dent ignored the question. There was something else worrying Dent – Kirsten Law's fixation with the Lebombos. When they had conversed earlier that day her eyes had been searchingly, almost impatiently drawn to those heights.

'What brought Kirsten Law up here? Why did she come?' Dent asked.

'She had been fed some cock and bull story about her brother's death not being the accident it was supposed to have been.'

'Did Mancoba tell her that?'

'Yes.'

'How interesting. I must speak to that old Zulu when we find him.'

'To hell with him. You concern yourself with Kirsten. If anything happens to her . . . Well, I'm not a forgiving man, Captain Dent.'

'I'm sure you're not Mister Ingram. But don't threaten me again. OK? You'll find I'm not that forgiving either.'

'I guess I'm tired.'

That was the closest thing to an apology the policeman was going to hear.

'Sure,' Dent said reflectively. 'Sure . . . Don't worry. People have been lost before, and found. Kirsten is a tough girl, one night on the mountain isn't going to harm her. By the way, seeing that you're here I'd like to show you something. Maybe you can tell me what this is.'

Leaning against the side of Dent's safe between a shotgun and an FN rifle was a wooden staff. Sharpened at one end, cuffed with hammer marks at the other, it was, but for a lick of white wash at the blunt end, stained to a brownish red. Dent handed it to Ingram. 'Know what it is?'

'Of course. It's the kind of stake we use when marking out a site. Is this blood?'

'Yes,' Dent said. 'It's the stake they used to kill the Pondo. Can you believe; they took him for a rain wizard, so they impaled him with it.'

Ingram examined the stake distastefully before handing it back to Dent. 'Poor bastard,' he said. 'He was helping mark out an additional access road for blasting. Have you made an arrest yet?'

Dent didn't reply to the question. A most interesting thought had just occurred to him. He needed answers more urgently than the engineer. 'Tell me more about these Pondos,' he said. 'You employ them because they're good with dynamite, isn't that right?'

'They get their training on the gold mines,' Ingram confirmed.

'Why?'

'Just something that occurred to me,' Dent shrugged. 'Let's get those flares now and someone to go back with you. Fire off one every half hour. If Kirsten Law is not back before first light we'll start searching for her. We might need some of your men, Mister Ingram, and your helicopter, of course. But let's cross that bridge, if, and when, we come to it. The best thing to do now is to get some rest.'

But Dent ignored his own good advice. Nagging him, with the insistence of a rotten molar, were several most disturbing questions. One of them had to do with Mabutane's statement: '*You would not be the first white man to cross over.*' Who was this madman; this traitor; this first white man? One day he and this traitor to his race would meet, that was inevitable. Dent's visualisation of that event was bisected by the sights of an aimed rifle — his rifle.

The captain from Abercorn Drift lay awake for the better part of that night. He didn't waste his time on riddles however. By the time sleep claimed him, he had evolved a plan for the total destruction of Abanzanzi and the beauty of it was that the Pondos could do it for him. . . . The Zulu bull was not going to sack the fat lands, not while Patrick Dent stood at the gate.

* * *

Kirsten Law's recollection of her fall was mercifully limited. She remembered the frenzy of her body — thrashing limbs, clawing for a hold. Her face contracted with fear, strangely that was very clear. The impact that had ended it, that was brutal in her mind. The debris of a scream was lingering. Had she screamed?

Her body was a maze of agony. There was no forgetting; no escape from that. Pain was her perimeter. The struggle to move was a tentative thing, a slow outreaching to the point of agony, an equally slow retraction — the progress of a snail.

She had broken her fall on a shelf of sorts, that much was clear.

There was rock to be felt, cold and sheer for as far as she was able to stretch up and opposite that, nothing, a grey infinity. She drew back from that.

At times, the ledge narrowed shouldering her dizzily outwards, at times it broadened but it did not end. Not that afternoon. Not that night.

It had to be night because the grey had sombred into a joyless cold black, a blackness so deep that in a way she was grateful for it. She wanted so badly to close her eyes, and now it made no difference if she did. But the surrender of her lids was just the beginning; just a signal, it seemed, for further collapse.

Her right arm had been nothing but a hindrance since the scorpion had stung it. Her left arm now shuddered into failure.

She knew it was the toxin reaching out. She had run, and panicked. She had done everything a scorpion victim is supposed *not* to do. Her tongue felt thick and sloppy. She tested it.

'I had no choice,' she said. The words sounded cloddish – those of a drunk.

'No choice.' She tried again.

'Had to run.'

But her body responded to the apology mercilessly – a vicious abdominal cramp buckled her to her face.

'Please,' she whispered. 'No more.' But the toxin had flowed, by then, to every extremity. There was more to come, and she knew it.

It came upwards – giant pincers that closed across her chest, squeezing, crushing, until breath was a whimpering thing. Until the crushing and the cramping and the bruising was total, a huge and intolerable burden. And suddenly survival was too onerous a thing; she wasn't prepared to bear it any longer.

At that moment the relieving hands of death would have come as a friend. The night was a multiple of such moments. Yet it passed, and in its wake she was still alive.

The greyness was still there in the morning but it had changed. No longer was it a hueless churning paste. Now there was vague light and shadow – the waxy dimension of a poorly lit cellar. Her senses were starting to repair – she could smell. There was a pungent ammonia-like stench. And hear, there was a whistling, whispering in the air. She had never heard such a sound before.

There didn't seem to be harm in it.

Within herself a change had taken place too. There was still a lot of pain, only now it was bearable. Like the mist, the toxic oppression had lifted, she too felt lighter. She could have stood had there been room to stand.

She drew herself shakily to a crouch. Her poorly lit cellar was in fact a poorly lit cave. Light was trickling in from a tunnel, low, hardly bigger than an ant bear burrow. There was enough of it to illuminate parts of her dusty craggy confines – the depths lay blackly beyond vision.

There was enough light for her to discover that she was not alone.

They'd lain as close as lovers, the skeleton and her, bedded into the powdery floor.

She recoiled. She broke the bond. She scrambled in retreat until solid rock pushed hard against her spine. And then she realised where she was and what it was she had found.

'Fana? My God, it's Fana!'

There could be no doubt. And if a century old skull is capable of softening in expression, then Fana's did that. It certainly lost its horror.

Kirsten crawled back to her companion of the night . . . She let her fingers reach out and touch. She brushed the cheekbone as Umzeze must have done; as if those tears had lasted for a hundred years.

The beads had lasted; a triple stranded message of love for the man who had killed her. White for purity in love; red for the flame of passion – *for my crying eyes as they look at you* . . . The *ucu* lay now amongst a straggle of vertebrae in the dust. Kirsten lifted it, and cradled it for a moment, almost afraid to blow the dust away. She placed it in the pocket of her shirt.

Somewhere in the deep shadows of that cave an *iquthu* basket woven from finest *umchobozi* rush lay hidden. And resting inside that – the ultimate symbol of Zulu power. 'The Inkatha of Shaka Zulu.'

She had found it. It was hers. And suddenly she didn't want it. All she wanted was to be away from that insane mountain. She was so, so cold.

The burrow looked much too small to take her. But it was

through there, certainly, that she had arrived so it was through there that she wriggled numbly back towards the sun. She needed light and warmth. She needed to break the umbilicus joining her to that dreadful place.

Rebirth into the summer sun was not the kind thing Kirsten Law had hoped it would be.

Beyond a shoulder-width ledge was a death drop. Birds were circling below, and beneath them a dizzy muddle of shrubbery and rock. From somewhere came a glint of lazy water. There was sun in abundance on the ledge, for some reason however it remained caustic, skin deep.

From the entrance of Umzeze's cave she could see the dry waterfall down which she had fallen. The ledge there ran broader, jutted out to form the lip that had broken her fall, and saved her. Close to the place where she had jumped, a stubborn rockfig tree was wedged into the boulders. Strong patrolling roots had, in their search for water, split a tortuous pathway down the cliff. Kirsten told a disbelieving mind that that was the place to be; an infant could climb those winding tendrils that was the stairway to safety. And it was not far.

That much was the truth. The distance between the cave and the rockfig roots, she judged to be no more than twenty metres. The problem was the hundred metre drop along the route. The problem was the sorcery of vertigo. Even as she lay there she could feel its seductive draw.

'You did it before,' Kirsten reminded herself, 'blind.' Sighted it had to be that much easier. It was poor logic but it worked. It got her about eight fumbling metres away from the cave. It also brought her to the narrowest point along the ledge. 'Do it,' she commanded.

She tried. There were sticky-footed lizards there. They scattered, then, disbelieving, stood their ground, heads turned and watching, waiting for this clumsy pendant thing to fall away.

The rockfig roots were an arm's reach away when she realised they were not what they'd promised to be. They were strong and supportive, but what had looked like easy hand holds from the cave were yards apart. There was no stairway – no safety. There was sheer lichened rock towering upwards.

Her arms were shaking and gripless. She stretched them

upwards nevertheless, reaching for the impossible. And thus the impossible occurred.

An avalanche of sound fell upon her: a roar of thunder. Then Mark Ingram's Jet Ranger burst across the skyline into view.

The woman on the ridge hoped that the smile on her lips was more apparent to the men who had found her than the wetness in her eyes. She waved as they came around. And they waved back.

4

The killing of the Pondo wizard did not have the lacrimal effect on the heavens that it was supposed to. If anything, in the days following his death, the summer sun seemed to become more spiteful, the clouds more reticent. The temperature in the Suthu River gorge rose to a sapping 42° C.

Mark Ingram swabbed his temples against the bicep of his short-sleeved shirt, and contemplated the valley below. The koppie where he stood was stony, and but for a few spiny acacias, shadeless. The locals called the place Rwaqabla – The Frown – he could understand why. What it offered, to he who was prepared to endure a short sharp climb, was an unimpeded downstream view of the outwards reaching walls of the Suthu River dam. To Ingram it was worth the punishment. That view was his fetish. Not a day passed that he was on site, when he didn't take it in.

That afternoon there was no progress to observe. Ingram stood there for a while anyway, his eyes slitted against heat and sweat, frowning, listening. As a surgeon understands the harmonics of the human heart, so he heard the sounds of the Suthu River dam.

There was the whine and rattle of the high wire cables as they plied huge buckets of concrete from the batch plant, where it was mixed, to the form works, where it was poured. There was the growl of monster diesel earth-movers, mucking out the tunnels. There was the clank of hammer on steel as more form works went up. And all these sounds were good.

What was absent from this auscultation was the sound of the blasters: the clatter of rock drills, the thud, the shudder and echo of explosives. No new foundations were being dug. No tunnels were being blasted. The Suthu River dam was ailing. Soon the whole project would be as silent, as pulseless as a corpse. He resolved there and then to give his Pondo workers just one more day to get back on the job. If they had not returned by this time tomorrow he would have to try and recruit new men to replace them. 'Damn them!'

The afternoon shadows were lengthening by the time Mark Ingram climbed from the koppie and returned to his Land Rover. It was a picturesque drive to the plateau where the management personnel were accommodated. He drove reflexively, engrossed by his problems, and the darkening beauty of the hills passed by unnoticed.

Asbestos was not in sight at the lofty level of senior engineers. They tenanted multi-roomed brick and mortar bungalows; homes that would one day house the permanent resident staff of the Suthu River Scheme. There were gardens with lawns and flowers there, and the roads were tarred and guttered.

Their little village was laid out around a well-grassed oval on which some youngsters were playing with a soccer ball. Ingram parked his car, leaned against the bonnet and watched them for a while. Some day he would have kids of his own, kids whom he would teach to kick a soccer ball. A mother's voice called out and the game broke up. They would remember this as a beautiful place, those youngsters. It was time for him too to go home.

Mark Ingram's bungalow nestled privately on a terrace just below the level of the plateau. Only its roof was visible from the oval. The house itself was not visible until you were treading the pathway down the slope.

Ingram was on the pathway when he thought he caught the sound of Kirsten's voice. That didn't surprise him. Kirsten had decided to stay on for a few days, to lick her wounds, as she put it. She was hurt more than she pretended to be, and so secretive about it all. He had noticed the company doctor's car parked up at the oval, old thirsty Ernie Tyrell who liked to do his rounds at sundowner time. He quickened his pace. All three of them would enjoy a pleasant drink on his verandah.

It wasn't Doctor Tyrell to whom Kirsten was talking, it was the Zulu called Mancoba. Ingram saw them both without either of them having seen him. Some instinct told him to stop where he was – to listen. Both of them were standing on his verandah and had either one of them turned, they would have seen him immediately. They didn't.

Ingram did not approve of eavesdropping, but liked mysteries even less. Thus, he made no real effort to hide, nor did he disclose his presence. He felt justified in standing just where he was, quietly listening. Perhaps some of Kirsten's pretence was about to be explained.

'I can't believe that you didn't hear me calling your name,' Kirsten said. 'You couldn't have been that far ahead.'

'We were tricked. You thought you were following me, only it wasn't *my* footsteps you were hearing. I thought you were behind me but it wasn't *you* I was hearing. Those men parted us in the most cunning way one could ever imagine. Suddenly I found myself alone on that mountain, just as you did. We could have been miles apart.'

'I find that hard to believe.'

'Yes,' Mancoba said. 'But that's the truth. If you're trying to accuse me of something bad, Miss Law, then remember that it was you who wanted to climb the mountain that afternoon. I warned you against it.'

'So where have you been? It's been over a week since I saw you.'

'I know.'

'So why the delay? What have you been doing?'

'Searching.'

'What did you find?'

'For one thing, these.'

Kirsten Law inspected the contents of Mancoba's proffered hand. There was the tremble of a lie in her voice when she said, 'What are they? Where did you find them, Mancoba?'

'They are beads. To be more exact they are antique Egyptian beads, of a kind not traded in Zululand for at least a century. They are woven into a love *ucu*. Are they not Fana's beads? As to your last question, Miss Law, they were in your shirt pocket, the one you wore on the mountains. Your laundry maid found them and showed them to me. If they're yours, Miss Law, then take them.'

She did take them. She looked at them for a while, then placed them on the table next to her. There they glowed, a little red fire in the dying sun.

'Yes, I did find the cave. It's in the Suthu River gorge.'

'Below the Crocodile Ridge Mountain?'

'Yes, I wasn't going to tell you, Mancoba . . . I'm still not sure if I can really trust you.'

'Was the Inkatha there? Did you see it?'

'No, but it must be there. It was too dark, and I was too hurt to go searching around.'

'We made a pact, Miss Law. I intend to honour my part. You use the Inkatha to lure your brother out of the hills, then it's mine. You haven't changed your mind have you? You can't do that.'

'No I haven't changed my mind.' Kirsten sounded unsure. 'I wonder though, whether it will work. Do you think it will? Do you think that the Inkatha is what he really wants?'

'Who knows? I told you once before, Miss Law, that something terrible has happened to your brother's mind. You didn't believe me then. Now you've seen the madness for yourself; the insane ritual murder of the Pondo. It's time for you to make up your own mind.'

'I think Monty must be given a chance. God! He has to be . . . I can't believe that Monty would have anything to do with something like that.'

But that was not the sentiment of the listener in the shadows. Mark Ingram had not fully understood all that he had overheard. Several factors however were clear . . . Montague Law was alive. He was enemy number one. Kirsten, his Kirsten, would stop at nothing to protect this maniac. He felt bitterly angry. He felt betrayed. The more so when she said 'You'd better go now. If Mister Ingram sees you here, he's going to wonder why. I don't want that. Come back here tomorrow morning and we'll go to the cave.'

Ingram turned away. Silently, crouching, he walked back up the pathway. He need not have been so careful; it was quite dark by then.

It took him half an hour to work out exactly how to play his hand. It wasn't that good a hand, but at least now he knew who held the knave of trumps.

'Knock knock.'

'Who's there?'

A game they often played.

'Lionel.'

'Lionel who?'

Kirsten appeared from the bedroom. She was smiling. She walked into his arms and kissed him and the scent of her, and the touch of her, found him pretty much as defenceless as ever.

'Lionel?' she persisted. She scamped his nose with her finger tip. 'Come on, Lionel who?'

'Lying'll get you nowhere.'

'Full marks for that,' she said. But for the moment she appeared more puzzled than amused.

'Sorry I'm so late. How does a drink sound?'

'Fantastic,' she said.

Ingram watched her walk to the cabinet. She was limping and doing her best to disguise it.

'See Doc Tyrell today?'

'Yep.'

'And?'

'And, he says I'm fine. Good as new. He says that it'll take more than one lousy Parabuthos scorpion to do me in.' She brought him his drink and stood close to him. 'Let's sit outside, it's nicer there.'

'Nicer *here*,' he disagreed. 'Mmm . . . you've saved my life.'

'Well then, now we're even.'

Ingram laughed. 'Well I don't know about that. If we hadn't picked you off that cliff you'd have wound up as fish feed. One day that ledge will be completely under water. Nope, I think you still owe me one. Now, what did *you* do all day?'

'Oh, I walked around a bit, chatted to some of the engineers' wives, rested a bit. Waited for you. That's all.'

'That's all!' Ingram drew her into him, quickly, roughly. He felt her body wince sharply, and suddenly there was an urgency in him to punish this lying woman; this woman whom he loved. His tongue was phallic, hard, and he raped her mouth with it. His hands began searching for the pain in her. That was what he wanted.

And he found it. A dozen times she caught back on her breath. He heard it and ignored it. He searched and pressed and tongued even deeper. Deep enough to know that it wasn't all pain that she was experiencing. And now each gasp took on a throatier tone. Now her hands were as predatory, as seeking, as his.

In the glow of the lounge lights they stripped, facing each other, glaring like paid combatants. For the first time he saw the bruises on her body and a tenderness rose in him. She didn't want that, she brushed his outheld hand aside. Whimpering like a wounded beast she came for him. There were claws across his back as he sank into the wetness of her.

They writhed and arched. They spoke in guttural. They feasted in each other's juices until there was no more, until both of them were sapless, drained and limp.

Later they did go outside. It was cooler on the verandah. A crisp astringent breeze had come up, he felt it cure him, clean away the torpor of sex. He saw once more the woman who had deceived him – perhaps a little more clearly that time.

'Why didn't you show me the bruises before?' he asked.

'I didn't want to worry you. You've got enough problems.'

'Do you want to talk about it now?'

'I slipped,' Kirsten shrugged. 'I fell down to that ledge. It's no big deal. Honestly. It hurt a bit at the time, but now I'm fine. It was my own stupid fault. I shouldn't have gone climbing up that mountain when I did.'

'Well now you've seen the dam, and you've climbed up, and fallen off the mountain. But what you really came to the Lebombos for is to satisfy yourself that your brother's death was the accident it was reported to be. Have you and Mancoba found out anything to disprove the findings of the inquest?'

'No,' Kirsten hesitated. 'Not a thing. But if you're saying why don't I go home now, then my answer is: I'd like to stay a few more days. If you can put up with me.'

'As long as you don't go mountaineering again.'

'Can't promise you anything,' said Kirsten Law.

And that statement, though said in jest, just about summed it up. She had already committed herself to a course of action, the deliverance of his enemy, her brother. She hadn't a promise left to spare.

Mark Ingram understood the emotions that were driving this woman to do the things she was doing. He could not however, forgive the betrayal. He imagined he must be feeling what the husband feels who discovers his beloved wife in adultery. He would be justified in the course of action that he was about to take. He said:

'I love you, Kirsten.'

And the hollowness in him deepened. Then he lied to her:

'I'm going down to the dam site, so don't wait up for me.'

With the sense of revenge of one betrayed, he walked into the night.

The second shift had come on at the dam. Floodlights were beaming up the wall, casting wrong-side-up shadows like a giant's castle from some Disney movie. Ingram stopped there for a moment, but it was just to look. His real destination lay several kilometres downstream: Abercorn Drift. He wondered how that amazing police captain would react to the news he was bringing him now.

*   *   *

'Sergeant Shibindji, bring us an extra glass,' Dent gave Ingram a smile, that left no room for doubt. The policeman was pleased, very pleased. What else he gave Ingram was his very own, and as yet untouched, glass of Napoleon brandy.

'Have it.' It was amazing how the man made everything sound like an order. 'I just got in myself. Haven't even had time to change. Isn't that right, Shibindji?'

Dent poured a careful tot into the tumbler that the sergeant handed to him.

'Isn't that right?' he said again. 'We've been out all day, haven't we, Shibindji?'

Shibindji nodded solemnly – they had been out all day.

'Tell Mister Ingram where we've been, Shibindji.'

'We crossed the border into Swaziland.'

'And what did we find? Tell him, Shibindji.'

'We found the workers from the dam.'

'You found my Pondos?' said Ingram, incredulous. 'My missing blasting gangs?'

'We found them. I negotiated with them. They will be back on the job tomorrow morning. Almost all of them.'

'Good God!' It was Ingram's turn to smile. 'That's wonderful.' He hated brandy. Warm brandy he detested. That drink however slipped down like velvet. 'When will they *all* be back on the job?'

'When will they *all* be back?' Dent made the question sound ungrateful. 'I stuck my neck out for you, Ingram. Your Pondos were being sheltered by the exile, chief Samuel Mngomezulu. Old

Samuel's got a grudge against King Goodwill of the Zulus. He reckons Goodwill chased him from Ingwavuma because he was too friendly with the Swazis. The way he sees it is that the South African police should have protected him from King Goodwill, so he doesn't like me either. His price for letting you have most of your Pondos back was fifty men, to remain with him and help him with his sugar-cane harvest.'

'Fifty men?' Ingram hoped the relief in his voice wasn't too apparent. The arithmetic of Dent's deal had left him with more than enough bodies to operate two complete shifts immediately. 'Fine,' he said, 'really, that's fine. He can have them for a while – no problem.'

'You can ask Shibindji here,' Dent said.

Ingram didn't know what he was supposed to ask Shibindji. He looked towards the hawk-faced sergeant and found the man nodding in assent. The gesture seemed to be an integral part of him. When Dent was speaking Shibindji was nodding.

'It's true,' said Shibindji.

But it wasn't all true. Shibindji had been privy to all that had happened since Chief Samuel had sent a message across the border that he had four hundred unwelcome Pondos on his hands. Shibindji knew exactly what the truth was. Fifty men would not be returning to the dam, but not because Samuel Mngomezulu had wanted it that way. Chief Samuel had six thousand followers of his own. He didn't need a handful of alien cane cutters any more than he needed the rinderpest. uDende had wanted it that way. The captain was the one who had driven that bargain, and, he'd used up a lot of favours to secure it too.

Fifty selected men had remained on the Swazi side of the border. Dent had gathered them in the shade of some *iminyela* trees, and there he had spoken to them until late in the afternoon. They had left that place calling Dent *Baba Inkosi*, thanking their chief; their father, for the opportunity he was providing to take revenge on the Abanzanzi dogs – and what revenge!

The police captain had formed a deadly fifty-man impi. An impi that was willing and able to carry out deeds way beyond the bounds of the law. *That* was the truth about the fifty Pondos.

'So.' Dent set before himself a sheaf of paper. From his breast pocket he took a pencil. 'Your Pondos will be back on the job tomorrow. That is how long it will take them to walk back here. Now, you said you had some information that might interest me.'

'I have.'

'Shoot.'

'Promise me that Kirsten Law will never know . . .'

'Wait a minute,' Dent directed his eyes to Shibindji, then to the door. The sergeant let himself out. 'It's just you and I now, and you've got my word.'

'Kirsten's brother, Monty Law, is still alive.' Ingram unburdened himself in a rush. He told Dent everything he'd overheard almost word for word. 'I think he's in the mountains – I'm certain he was involved in the killing of the Pondo. He must be mad!'

And Captain Patrick Dent knew that the gods were smiling. His pen fairly skipped across the paper. The statement he took down was somewhat garbled, at times emotional, but he was careful not to interrupt.

'He's got to be stopped,' Ingram touched Dent's hand to stop him from writing. 'By any means. By *any* means.'

Dent had some questions.

'Does Kirsten or Mancoba know exactly where Law is?'

'It didn't sound like it.'

'Have you heard the word *Abanzanzi* before?'

'I don't think so.'

'When do you think Kirsten will go back to this cave to get this Inkatha?'

'Possibly tomorrow morning.'

Dent set his pencil down squarely in the centre of the page on which he'd been writing. It was a gesture of finality. Without asking he recharged both glasses, then raised his in a silent toast.

'I think you're right,' he said. 'Law has got to be stopped. I'll do it as painlessly as possible.' He sounded like someone from the SPCA. 'Leave it to me Mister Ingram, and thank you. You've been a great help. Oh, and by the way, don't try and stop Kirsten Law tomorrow morning or anything like that. Just be yourself and she'll never know the difference. OK?'

That time the brandy tasted ghastly.

* * *

Kirsten Law did notice a change in Mark Ingram. He was quiet. He seemed uninterested in the breakfast she had prepared; toying with his food; gazing from the table-top to the mountains. Gazing in any direction but hers. She didn't comment on it. Her thoughts were elsewhere too.

She left the house soon after he did, better prepared for the mountain this time. This time she had a haversack with rations, a torch and a rope. She wore a loose-fitting gingham blouse and under that a holster containing a Colt .45 auto. She picked Mancoba up about 100 paces from the house, and thereafter did not let him out of her sight.

They found the dry watercourse at midday and followed it downhill to the precipice. It was all there: the dry and rocky waterfall, the mountain fig, its meandering roots like runnels of spilt milk; the ledge that had broken her fall. She pointed out to Mancoba the rocky furrowed brow that concealed the eye of Umzeze's cave.

What else was well hidden was the white man in the shade of an acacia shrub. He was crouched in a clump of Guinea grass, now and then stretching like an inquisitive meercat to improve his line of sight. Though he was not more than 50 paces from Kirsten and Mancoba, neither of them saw him. He was watching them though. The man was wearing nothing but a pair of weathered denim shorts. His hair was black and shaggy, accenting his rather angular features. He was deeply tanned.

And Dent was watching them all.

The policeman wiped away the stinging sweat from the eye piece of his binoculars and focused in. Dent had expected him for some reason to have grown a beard; had visualised him so. This man was clean shaven, and that made a positive ID that much easier. It was Doctor Montague Law.

Dent estimated the range to be over four hundred metres. Slowly he rested the binoculars. Even more carefully he unslung his Winchester .308 hunting rifle. The scope was an old friend, at full zoom it pulled a man in, close enough to touch. Had Dent stroked the trigger at that instant, then Montague Law would have been dead before he'd heard the shot.

It was not a time for killing though. It was a time for observing. Fascinating things were happening in the Lebombos that sunny day.

Dent leaned the Winchester once more against the rock that was sheltering him and took up the binoculars.

Kirsten Law had wound a rope around the thick mountain fig trunk and with the little Zulu braced against the slack, had harnessed herself to it. She began to work her way down towards the ledge – the very same ledge from which they had rescued her just a few days previously.

Whatever else Kirsten Law was, she was no rock climber. They were breaking every rule in the book. Instead of doubling her rope and rappelling it out, she was relying on the friction of the single wind around the mountain fig, and Mancoba's weight to anchor it thus. It was not working. Kirsten's upper body was so tight into the harness she had fashioned that she could hardly move. Mancoba as her rope man couldn't see her to know when to pay out and when to take strain.

The rope jammed into a fissure and Mancoba feeling the slack, paid out. Kirsten had one hand and one foot secure as she tugged at the snagged line. It was a disaster. The rope, when it loosened, had about three metres of play behind it. Kirsten went over backwards. Dent could hear the twang of the line from where he was. The little Zulu didn't have a chance, he was catapulted forward against the tree. There he held on for all he was worth – it wasn't enough. Kirsten's dead weight was pulling him inexorably towards the edge.

It would have been all over then, had Monty Law not broken from cover and rushed to Mancoba's aid. He was a tall man, well shouldered and wiry. He peered quickly over the cliff to ascertain his sister's position, then seizing the rope from Mancoba, he took the strain. Kirsten reached the ledge, completely oblivious to the incredible turn of events at the other end of the rope.

Old Mancoba looked stunned – gazing widemouthed from his rope-seared hands, to Monty Law, to heaven above. He was out of it. Law was doing all that was necessary to save a bad situation.

As his sister crawled along the ledge, so he kept pace from above – selecting sites that would allow her flexibility and balance, and afford him sensitivity and leverage. They made a natural team.

Dent watched, fascinated. Especially he watched the woman. Her face, when he could see it, was set in concentration. Her eyes were a frown, her lips were drawn hard back. There was no hesitation in her movements though, no fear. And all for this thing, this Inkatha?

There was a cave. Dent couldn't see it, but he couldn't see Kirsten any longer either. Her brother was paying out rope and she, it seemed, had been swallowed by the overhang. There could surely be only one cave that Kirsten was interested in. If he had had doubts about the veracity of Ingram's incredible story, they were fading as the day grew older.

Dent had to wait for more than an hour for his answer, but he was a patient man and it was a period of time well spent. He watched Mancoba and Monty Law. Their postures, their gestures were of two men bitterly divided. This was not some argument of the minute. They knew each other well, these men. Their differences were great.

Dent took a swig from his water bottle and immediately felt his forehead bead with sweat. There were some rations in his patrol bag but he was too hot to contemplate food. He lit a cigarette and let the acrid smoke trickle past his nostrils. Then, deeply in thought, he raised his binoculars again. They were still quarrelling; Kirsten Law had still not emerged. And that was when Dent remembered where first he had seen that little Zulu. It had been at the inquest of the 'death' of Monty Law. He had not been called to testify, but he had been there. Mancoba had been the servant of 'the late' Doctor Law.

*   *   *

Though the torch beam did not strip the cave of its deepest shadows, it did show it up to be somewhat smaller than Kirsten had imagined. It did reveal that there were a limited number of places where something as big as the Inkatha could have been concealed.

An upside down army of furry grey bats was tasselling the roof. Bewildered by her presence they were falling and swooping and filling the cave with the trill of wings. She smiled – the sound; the pungent smell that had previously puzzled her, now identified.

The floor beneath the bats was carpeted with their soil. Everywhere else there was dust and beneath that, solid rock. The walls looked solid too. There were however some crypts towards the rear of the cave; slitted little alcoves that would take her with a squeeze. The largest, most promising one was where she began to search.

With the flashlight, a small rock to use as a sounder, and an abundance of hope, she started to probe, and tap, and look for evidence of Umzeze's handiwork.

Half an hour passed. She discarded the small rock in favour of a bigger rock, and began afresh. But the deep crypt was solid, and the lesser crypts were solid. As far as a human arm could stretch, the cave was solid.

Three quarters of an hour later she had tap, tap, tapped her way around the entire perimeter of the cavern. Her shoulder was aching and she didn't have a knuckle that was not skinned. All she had discovered was that Umzeze had not been a man who did the obvious.

The once white circle of light that her torch had provided was yellowing perceptibly.

Fana looked amused. Kirsten had tried to avoid the skeleton this time. Her search however had brought her once more almost to the entrance, the place where Fana lay, grinning in rictus, compelling her to look. So she looked.

She sat there, next to the remains, and switched off the torch. Dispossessed of light, the cave expanded blackly once again. She waited for her eyes to adjust; for the feeble grey trickle that would show the bones of Fana. And with its advent came the knowledge that Kirsten had been seeking: the hiding place of the sacred Inkatha of Shaka Zulu.

She tried to shift the skeleton without damaging it further – an impossible task. Piece by piece the bones dislocated at her touch. She took them and placed them to one side, where they lay together in a single unanatomical heap. Last was the skull. Hesitantly she lifted it, managing at least to keep the jaw intact. She placed it on a ledge as high as she could stretch. That seemed to be the right thing to do.

Fana's sleeping mat was in better condition than its mistress. She pulled it away almost in one piece, and tapped the ground beneath it. It gave back a hollow clunk.

There was nothing more than a thick crust of mud remaining

between her and the contents of the well. Kirsten's hands were trembling as she broke it away, piece by piece. Fragments falling inwards were meeting with a reedy sound – the right sound.

The torch was giving no more than a faint yellow glimmer – it was enough. The well contained a large, sealed, *iquthu* basket. And inside that had to be the Inkatha. Kirsten heard herself breathe the words: 'My God, *the Inkatha.*' Cold little thrills were reaching out inside her; her hands were trembling as she reached down for this treasure of treasures. And even as she took the weight of it, she knew, here was power. Here was a giant rising from its slumber. Whoever dared to walk with it would be a giant too.

The torch failed. Then, as though aware at last of the robber in their midst, the bats came whirling – so close she could feel the beaten air. They were impotent to stop her.

Easing the basket carefully ahead of her, she pushed it towards the light. Her ascent, she hoped, would be a little less frightening than her descent.

It was. She reached safe ground without incident. It was there that more excitement awaited.

'Your brother was here,' Mancoba told her. Unnecessarily he said, 'He's gone now.'

'Gone where? Where did he go, Mancoba?'

Mancoba wasn't hearing her. His senses were totally absorbed in the event that he was witnessing. Kirsten Law, her arms craned over the cliff edge, was drawing intently on the tail end of the rope. Attached to that rope was a fat, squat, urn-shaped woven basket, dusty and stained with age.

'Careful. Careful!' Hoarse with anxiety. 'Give it to me!'

She untied the rope and let him hold it. His hands were trembling as he took it. 'Did you look inside it?'

'No, I did not look inside it.' Kirsten dispossessed him. 'And neither are you going to. Mancoba *where* did my brother go to?'

The Zulu could not take his eyes from the *iquthu.* 'I don't know. How could I know – I had to wait here for you.'

'What did he say? Does he know I'm here? Does he know why I'm here?'

'He knows.'

'And what did he say *for God's sake!*' She felt like shaking this stupid, stupid man. Her brother had been there and now he was gone.

'Couldn't you have done something . . . why didn't you stop him?'

'How could I stop him? You don't know what you're saying.'

It was true. She wasn't thinking coherently. Kirsten took Fana's *iquthu* to a shady place under the mountain fig. She sat there and motioned Mancoba to a place opposite her. 'You're right,' she said quietly. 'What did happen? Tell me, *madala*.'

'Suddenly he was there.' Mancoba told her what he could, but his memory seemed suddenly to have brittled; his story came in fragments. 'Look at my hands.' Raw and blistered, he held them out. 'I couldn't have saved you. He saved you. Your brother. We spoke while you were in the cave.'

Mancoba's message for Kirsten was joyless: 'He is more fanatical then ever, Miss Law. I tried to reason with him. He said I was as a blind man contesting the colour of the dawn – I simply had no conception of what it was all about. I think you have lost, Miss Law.'

'No!' Kirsten cut Mancoba short. 'Monty is going to have to tell me that to my face. To hell with it! I've had enough third-hand messages, supposedly, from my brother . . . I'm beginning to wonder if Monty really is still alive.'

'I would think the same if I were you,' Mancoba stood up and walked slowly to the trunk of the mountain fig. 'But here, where I'm standing now, your brother was standing half an hour ago. He *is* alive Miss Law. But, you don't have to believe me, you will see for yourself . . . He said he wants to talk to you.'

'Why didn't he wait if he wants to talk to me?'

Mancoba shrugged. How could he answer such a question?

'How will we make contact then?'

'He will come to you.'

'When?'

Again the Zulu gestured his ignorance. 'Probably when you least expect it.'

Kirsten said nothing more. She watched Mancoba indifferently as he lifted the *iquthu*; testing its weight. He wanted it so, so badly. He must have sensed the time was right to ask:

'Is this mine now? You don't need it any more.'

* * *

There were several good reasons why Kirsten should have expected her brother to come when he did: Mark Ingram had established a pattern of working very late at the site; she was alone in the cabin; and this was her last night before returning to Prospect Hall.

She did not weigh those factors as a conscious exercise though. It was a gut feeling that told her that the time had arrived. She poured herself a tall glass of wine and added some ice cubes, then made her way through the house, turning off all the lights as she went. The verandah, as usual, was the most comfortable place to be. She drew a chair away from the wall, sat down and allowed her thoughts to take her where they would. She wondered what had become of that gentle, caring human being called Monty Law. She would never accept that that lovely man had become a pathological animal, a murderer.

There was the time when he had brought home the sad-faced wood owl with the limp wing. 'Kill it,' had been the general consensus. 'It's a wild thing. You're just going to prolong its death by nursing it.' He'd nursed it. He'd fed it with rodents and bugs, and sat with it through its hours of pain. Noddy the wood owl still nested in the hollow-trunked kaffir-boom next to Monty's bedroom window; still called out 'Who are you? Who are you? Who are you?' at the fall of dusk.

The answer to Noddy's question was certainly not: a murderer. There were two hundred cane cutters at Prospect Hall who would vouch for that. They called him *Usineke* – the man of patience. They'd never heard him raise his voice in anger.

On an impulse Kirsten took off her shoes and padded silently to the verandah rail. The night was splendid with stars. Her eyes had adjusted. Even so, it was difficult to see much further than the first line of thorn trees. Apart from a faint but ever present rumble from the dam, and the monotonous cooing of a lone cuckoo, all was quiet.

And suddenly he was there. A voice that she thought she had forgotten said:

'Hello Kirsten.'

He was sitting on the arm of the chair she had just vacated.

'I'm sorry I caused you so much heartache. There was no other way.' Hesitant words. Those of a stranger.

She crossed to where he sat. 'It is you?' She touched his cheek. He stood, took both of her hands in his, and pressed them to his chest. She squeezed his fingers. She wanted to hold him, to hug him tightly. Instead she broke away.

'Mancoba told me he'd seen you. He told me to expect you.'

'Ah. I owe you a lot of answers, don't I?'

'Yes you do. Monty, why did you do this to us? Why did you put us through this terrible ordeal? Can you imagine what I've been through?'

'I can Kirsten, and I'm bitterly sorry. If there had been any other course that I could have taken, then believe me I would have. I've come to explain to you why it had to be this way. How much has Mancoba told you?'

'He told me you were searching for a plant called sontekile, that you'd got involved with the sangoma Uhlanga. He said she was a witch, a really evil woman, that you were under her influence.' Kirsten paused, trying to see her brother's features in the gloom. Trying to perceive the effect of these words on him.

'What else did he tell you?' He sounded unmoved.

'Well, he said that . . . he said some pretty ugly things. Things about the state of your mind. He said you were connected to ritual killings.'

'And what do you think?'

No denial, no explanation. Kirsten's words burst from her: 'Jesus, Monty! Does it matter what I *think*! I'm your ever-loving sister, remember. I wouldn't believe it even if I saw you in the act. What I think is immaterial. What is the *truth*?'

'The truth . . .' Monty Law exhaled, almost a sigh, almost a laugh. There was no joy in the sound. 'You want the truth, do you Kirsten?'

'Yes. Exactly that. No matter the pain.'

'Let me tell you why I disappeared. Why I was prepared to go through the whole trauma of my own fake death. Did Mancoba tell you about the ancient manuscript he discovered in the archives of the Durban Library?'

'Yes. Yes he did.'

'Well he had simply no conception, and neither at first did I, of what it was that he was handing to me. He thought he was giving me some everyday tribal remedy, that might, or might not work, but that would interest me enough to get me, and of course himself on the same ticket, into the northern Lebombo Mountains. Fine, his scheme worked, I mounted a little expedition, and off we went. Me, looking for the sontekile – he, secretly looking for something quite different.'

'The Inkatha.'

'Yes. It took me months to realise that sontekile was not just a shrub, or a herb or, in fact, any single organic thing. It was a potion, a nostrum, call it what you like. In fact it was, it still is, a complex formula composed of many constituents. I had been searching for something that didn't exist. So I began my search all over again. And Kirsten, do you know what I found?'

Kirsten, quickened by the excitement in her brother's voice asked, 'What?'

'A modern – no, an ancient – miracle. That's what I found: a compound a thousand times more active than purest cocaine . . . a thousand times more potent than the most powerful narcotic known to medical science. Can you imagine the implications?'

There was no time for hypothesis.

A sudden stirring of foliage on the east side of the bungalow – fright. Then a flutter of wings and the spit-growl of an angry, hungry cat. The cuckoo had stopped calling.

'Genet.' Relief in Monty Law's voice. 'That wild cat's missed his supper. I'm sorry Kirsten, I'm jumpy. It isn't easy, being dead.'

Kirsten laughed softly. The burst of tension had been good for them. It had swept them together. They were closer. She continued the conversation: 'What can you do with something that much more powerful than cocaine, Monty? It would kill you if you took it.'

'Not quite. That's the strange part about it. That's the part that you're going to find hard to believe. Within two hours of the administration of sontekile the respiratory rate slows dramatically. Then the cardiac rate decelerates and the body temperature plunges. Soon after that, there are no measurable vital signs at all. No pulse. No respiration. No temperature. The person is clinically dead . . . But Kirsten, that person's *not* dead.'

Monty Law was quiet for a while. Kirsten could sense questioning eyes on her.

'I also didn't believe it.' He said 'It is unbelievable, that is, until you've seen it with your own eyes, like I have.'

'You've seen this happen?'

'Yes, more than once.'

'Mancoba says that Uhlanga is nothing more than a skilled magician, a trickster.'

'I know what Mancoba says. He has his reasons.' Her brother sounded irritated; the way some one who is overtired is irritated. 'Mancoba has never been where I have been, nor has he been shown the things that I've been shown. I have seen things that no white person has ever seen before, impossible things, Kirsten. Listen to me.'

'I am listening,' she said. 'Don't be upset. I'm scared Monty. You start explaining to me why you disappeared, then, in the same breath, you tell me about drugs that can bring about a state of death that isn't really death. What puzzles me; what frightens me is why you are involved in something so macabre.'

'You know, when you live with a situation, like I have, for so long, you forget how it would affect someone who hasn't been there. The truth is, Kirsten, that though sontekile in the wrong hands would be deadly, it's not used as a poison. Used skilfully and in the hands of an expert, the person to whom it is administered can be revived.'

'Revived? Why give someone sontekile in the first place? Just so that you can *revive* him later? What's the point?'

Law didn't answer. He didn't have to answer. A thin silver sliver of moon had risen above the eastmost hills. It didn't illuminate so much as darken in the shadows. With its rising, however, many things became clear to Kirsten – horrifyingly clear.

'Zombies. Oh! Monty, no!'

'Kirsten, you don't understand.'

'I don't want to understand. I want you to come away. Just come away. This is not you, Monty. I can't believe this. When I was on the mountain, I was chased by a group of men. Did you know that, Monty? Mancoba and I were cunningly separated, and I had to run for my life. Were those your zombies – your *imikhovu*?

Was that your doing ? Oh Monty . . . *Monty* this is *terrible*. You must put a stop to this.'

'I can't stop, Kirsten.' His grasp had the fervour of a drowning man. This time she did not pull away. 'I would never have let anything happen to you, Kirsten. You know that. What happened was a mistake. You wandered into a sacred area, a place of the spirits. That was why you were chased.'

'I nearly died on that mountain, Monty.'

'I die a little every day, Kirsten.'

'Then come away. Come with me. You don't have to do this Monty.'

'Ah! But I do. Can't you see I have to see this thing through? Sometimes I wake up at night and the desire to run away is so overpowering that I want to scream. I clench my teeth and fold my knees into my chest and hold on, because what I have to do here is more important than me. More important than anything, Kirsten. There can be no other course for me.'

'Why does this sangoma Uhlanga not give you what you want? What do you still have to do before she'll trust you?'

'It's not a matter of trust. Uhlanga believes that my spirit and the spirit of a great war doctor called Mvulaba are one and the same. She prophesied the Mvulaba would move me to find the lost Inkatha of Shaka Zulu, and she was right. I *did* find it. Long ago I found it. I *knew* it was in that cave, but, I also knew that once I had brought it to light, the tormented spirit of Mvulaba would beg to be set free. That is how Uhlanga would see it. I'm not sure what the consequence of that would be. So I left it there.'

'I've got the Inkatha,' Kirsten found herself tugging at her brother's hand. 'Let's get out of here.'

'No! Stop it Kirsten. It's hard enough for me.'

'Monty, for God's sake, it's not worth it. So what if you discover some compound a zillion times more potent than cocaine? Is that worth your sanity?'

'Yes, it's worth my life. We're not talking about some hocus pocus *muthi* mix. We are looking at something that might cure hitherto incurable immune system diseases. Diseases like multiple sclerosis.'

'And turn people into *zombies*.'

'No. Not if it's administered scientifically. The use of sontekile is just the first step in the stealing of the human soul, in transforming someone into *imikhovu* – a zombie. I didn't invent *imikhovu*, Kirsten. The Zulu *umthakathi* have been in the business of soul-snatching since the dawn of time.'

'All you want is the recipe.'

'If you want to put it that way, yes, I want the recipe. And, what is more, I'm close to getting it. So close, Kirsten. I can't leave now. Surely you can see that.'

What Kirsten could see was tragedy. She did not know the exact form it would take, nor when it would strike. But it was there. As clearly as if it had been written in that star-sprinkled sky – it was there.

'I've got the Inkatha,' she tried again. 'Surely Uhlanga could be forced into a bargain now: the formula for the Inkatha?'

'If only it was that easy. If only I could pull out now.'

She pleaded, 'Do it.' Tightly she squeezed his hands. 'Monty there's something awful about this place. Do you remember when we were kids at Prospect Hall, how we used to climb up Bulalana Hill where the old kraal used to stand? Remember? Remember how strange we used to feel there, as if our legs had become heavy and we couldn't move? Well, I get that same leaden feeling here. I've had it since the day I arrived. I'm leaving tomorrow. Come with me Monty . . . *please*.'

'If I went home with you now it would be the end of me, and a disaster for my work. Firstly, the newspapers would get hold of it. They'd brand me as a monster, and how could I defend myself? What would I tell them? I've tried to explain to you about sontekile and even you were repulsed. They'd write me up as some modern day Frankenstein; the crazy doctor who sneaks about at full moon, digging up mouldy corpses and administering magic potions. The scientific basis of my work would be ridiculed. I'd be laughed off as a crank. My God! An army of reporters would be sent in to stomp around the Lebombos, and any chance I might have had to complete my work would be trampled into the dust. No, there are a dozen good reasons why I have to remain underground until I've done what I have to do. Please, Kirsten if you want to help me, let me remain "dead". When all this is over, I'll return to Prospect Hall. Then, when I hold out the remedy for the cure of immune system diseases to the Western World, let them try to ridicule me.'

Kirsten could sense in her brother a listlessness as he spoke; a desire to be gone from there. He had said all he wanted to say. But it wasn't quite enough. There was one more matter. One last question:

'The Pondo, who was murdered by Abanzanzi, did you know about that? Were you aware in advance that that was going to happen?'

'No.'

It sounded more like a rejection of her line of questioning than a denial of complicity. Not good enough.

'Why was he killed?' She persisted.

'He was perceived as a wizard. He was seen driving *thakathi* stakes into the ground to repel the rain clouds. But that's not really what you want to know. I didn't know about that murder Kirsten, but even if I had, I would have done nothing to prevent it. You see, part of the formula of sontekile involves the usage of human brain tissue, the pituitary, burnt to carbon, then pulverised. Whether it's a necessary constituent, or just a ritualistic component, I don't know yet. What I do know is that every time sontekile is prepared my chances of obtaining the complete formula improve. I wouldn't lift a finger to prevent a ritual killing. It would be futile anyway, you know that.'

'Yes.'

She did know that. Such killings were as old as Africa. One man could no more influence that cult than he could change the course of night and day. There had to be another way though. That was what she told her brother.

'If there was any other way, Kirsten, I'd take it. There's always been danger for me in what I was doing and now it's increased. Uhlanga is a strange woman. Sometimes it seems as if she has a great affection for me. She has promised me that one day the knowledge that I want will be mine. I feel like a thief doing what I'm doing. If I get caught, even if I'm suspected, then God knows what will happen. I don't have a damn thing to bargain with now. Do I?'

'I would have left the Inkatha in the cave had I known what I know now.'

'No, once Mancoba knew where it was, it was too late. Mancoba wants to destroy the Inkatha. He thinks it's the devil's work. You didn't know that did you?'

'No.'

'Well it's the truth. He believes it's an evil thing. He sees it as his life's work to destroy it.'

'I'll look after it Monty.'

'That won't do, Kirsten. Mancoba would get to it somehow. He's more determined than anyone I know. I can't risk that happening, Kirsten. You'll have to give it back to me. It's the only way.'

'And what would you do with it? Would you give it to Uhlanga?'

'When the time is right. Yes. That's exactly what I'd do.'

'But you said yourself that you didn't know what the consequences of that action would be. What if she decided that it was time for Mvulaba's spirit to be set free; to be properly presented to the spirit world? She might have you killed. She's capable of it.'

'That's a risk I'm prepared to take.'

'Well it's not a risk I'm prepared to take. I'm going to keep it Monty. It's your lifeline. I'm holding it and I'm going to keep on holding it, Monty.'

'*Kirsten*. I want it *now*.'

'No. No, Monty. Trust me.'

'Kirsten, you don't know what you're doing.'

'Not so. But I think *you* might well be in that position, Monty. Don't ask me to give you the Inkatha. I can't. I won't.'

'You're increasing my risks.'

'No, I'm not. Can't you see that?'

'Oh God . . .' He sighed. 'You always were the stubborn one.'

'And the one that got you out of trouble.'

There came the sound of a motor car, still distant but approaching. Her brother swung himself over the balcony rail and dropped lightly to the ground.

'Guard it,' he said. 'Promise me that.'

'I promise.'

'Stay well.' He reached up for her hand – a last touch.

'Go well . . .' she called into the darkness. 'When will I see you again?'

To that question she received no answer.

Turning on the lights inside the bungalow seemed to add

beyond all proportion to the punishing heat. There was no help for that.

The item she wanted to see; the item now masquerading as her 'souvenir', lay on the lower of the guest room bunks: Fana's *iquthu* basket. It was still there, as yet unopened by anyone but herself. Lying next to it, denting the bedspread in its heaviness, the big Colt pistol lay where she had tossed it. If the symbolism of that composition had passed unnoticed before, it did so no longer. Now it was eloquent.

Mancoba could not have the Inkatha, no matter what she had promised. The situation had changed. Her brother's life depended on it. It was hers now to guard and to keep until the time was right.

The Zulu would be told in the morning that neither the basket nor its contents would be surrendered to him. She would tell him that, even before they embarked on the journey back to Prospect Hall.

* * *

It did not happen that way. Mancoba did not arrive at the heli-pad at the appointed hour. Nor was he there half an hour later.

At 08.00 hours, the blades of the Ingram Associates Bell Jet Ranger started to turn. Up front sat a puzzled Kirsten Law; a quiet and frowning Mark Ingram. In solitary occupation of the rear seat – one beautifully woven *iquthu* 'souvenir'.

The blades swung faster until they were a noisy blur; until they had scoured up a sandstorm from the arid dusty soil. The helicopter lifted, hovered for a moment, then, thudded away to the south. The dust settled.

For those left behind, for those in Ingwavuma, that day had all the promise of being as hot and merciless, as any that hot and merciless summer.

5

Amongst the mountain people, the strident blue and white helicopter had become a fairly common sight over the past year. Even so, its appearance in the heavens was always regarded as an event of consequence.

Women, kneeling at the corn-grinding stone would pause, frown into the sky, and hope the flitting shadow of the flying thing would leave their kraal untouched, uncontaminated.

'*Yebo.*' They never ceased to warn the wide-mouthed piccaninnies. '*Yebo*, they are taking away the naughty ones. No one knows where they go to. Be happy my child – be good.'

The bigger boys – those old enough to drive the herds – they knew better. They had listened to their elders at the beer drinks speaking of the white man and his many huge and wonderful machines. Machines that flew, that ran on rails, that floated like metal mountains on the sea. It was all a matter of *kulandelwe izindlela zesimanje* – following the modern ways. Yes, like the great concrete wall that was all but blocking the Suthu River valley. What a marvel that was. What a fine thing for those whose homes were in the mountain. For those in the valley, well, *kulandelwe izindlela ezifikayo*. They would simply have to follow.

It was said there were those in the valley who were preparing to resist, but what chance did they have? '*Akumbethe!*' They would no more endure than the morning dew, yet they were many, and they were Zulus . . . 'and we, we too are Zulus.' And what of the power of the wizards said to support them from the forest called *kwaIsingogo*?

* * *

Monty Law had been waiting since dawn to witness the departure of his sister. He had found a spot on a tumble of rock beneath a spreading Marula tree. From there he knew he would be able to see the helicopter when it rose from the Suthu River gorge. And suddenly there it was; all whirl and perspex in the yellow morning sun. He watched until it was a noiseless flicker between hill and sky, and could have observed it for a moment longer had he moved to open ground. He didn't though. His purpose was achieved, he had witnessed the departure of his sister. Now she was gone.

He lifted his hand, a weary farewell gesture that went on to whisk away an offending fly.

Tiredness. It seemed to habituate the core of him lately. Not just the fatigue that lack of sleep brought about. This was an enmeshing deadweight thing that clung like a sodden, heavy net. The reason for it, well, he'd explained all that to Kirsten. In so doing he'd seen it clearer too. But anguish clarified is not anguish resolved. There was so much still to do. And everything was such a crushing effort.

One more glance in the direction of the departed helicopter and he was on his feet, ambling, head down in thought. He too could have been aboard that shiny helicopter. He could have been away from there, and God knows he wanted that. He longed for that. But before he could dream such dreams, he had a task to complete. Both pace and posture picked up as he distanced himself from the hillside Marula, and such thoughts of freedom.

The going became quite steep. A downhill track, meandering to accommodate tree, rock and ravine. The last stretch covered undulating open ground that led towards a thickly wooded forest. A triangle of tangled bush that nestled in the pubis of two small, rolling hills. The forest was called kwaIsingogo. The hills were part of the Lebombo range; they were locally known as Mawamabi.

The place was a thicket of wicked, climbing river thorn. And where that didn't grow barbed, it was because its equally spiteful cousin, the black monkey thorn was dominant. It was a haven for mambas in the trees and cobras in the grass. It was known to be the home of *Isingogo*, the baboon man who lived on a mono diet of human entrails. For those who had a liking for life, the thicket of kwaIsingogo was best viewed from afar by those who could avoid it; was best not viewed at all.

Law had no choice but to go in – it was his home. Even so, even though he knew that deadly maze to a twig, and did not believe in fabled cannibals, he moved with extreme caution. There were still the snakes, they were very real, very numerous, very quick.

Once hidden by the brush line, he paused, glanced back along the route he had taken. There was not another human being in sight. He sat, haunched, still, observing. His eyes told him he was alone, and he had to believe his eyes. There was no one out there watching him, and yet he felt he was being watched.

Irrational. Then the whole outing that morning had been irrational. There were a dozen good reasons why he should not have been abroad during the day, and yet he'd done it. For some reason he had felt duty bound to participate in that anonymous farewell charade; to march those ten kilometres and wave that lonely hand.

Inside, the thicket was sombre, shaded and quiet. There was a heaviness there, a dusty woodiness that lingered oppressively in the nostrils.

There were pathways, if you knew where to find them, low, tangled game tracks, tunnels, that bent the traveller to his knees or lower. Law knew where to find them. He knew how to traverse them.

Half an hour of such progress brought him to his destination. A clump of beehive huts tucked beneath a canopy of black monkey thorn. The ground cover had been cut away there to open a small clearing. Everything was littered with a snow-like blanket of fallen thorn blossom. Shards of sunlight were cutting through the greenness, touching on the whitened ground, glinting on the spearblade of the sentry standing there.

Law greeted him, then carried on walking towards a hut – a thatch and sapling *indlu*, no different from any of the other huts in appearance, but set on higher ground, a short walk from the central clearing. It was Law's *indlu* – his home. Sharing that senior site was the *indlu* of Mabamba, induna of that regimental kraal. And dominating everything was the big *indlu* – the *indlunkulu* used by the sangoma Uhlanga when she visited the forest of kwaIsingogo.

She was not there that day. There were other Abanzanzi strongholds hidden in the mountains of kwaZulu, how many, Law had not made it his business to find out. But they were sufficiently numerous, or scattered, to occupy Uhlanga for the better part of the month. The sangoma was not due for another two weeks.

Law welcomed the darkness of the *indlu*. As little as it was, that hemisphere of thatch was his. There was a sleeping mat there and a carved wooden head rest on which to lay his head. There was his eating board and spoon, which, when his eyes had adjusted, he saw to be crawling with scullion cockroaches. At the rear his clothes were hanging. Not the tattered old denim that he wore at that moment, but his traditional clothes, his tanned hide *uMutsha* loinskin, and kaross. These he was expected to wear whilst in the kraal. Every other space, on the walls, or the floor, was taken up with bundles of herbs – hanging or stacked, drying or dried, leaves and branches and faggots of twisted roots. The harvest of a year – still vitally incomplete.

Law squatted down using the head rest as a low bench. Fingers groping beneath a rick of yellowing leaves came up with a cardboard-covered notebook, limp-spined with use. He propped it carefully on one thigh, and began to leaf through it. But for a few remaining end pages it had been written out. The script in its early stages was flowing with hope; latterly, cramped tight with frustration. It was the diary of Montague Law.

Sharing the diary's hiding place was a pencil – little more than a stub. He took it, held it poised for a moment, then began to write.

'The tiredness persists. How long can I go on like this? Today I watched sister K. leave – somehow it all seemed so final.

'A year at Isingogo has worn me thin. I feel so black – so down – as never before. If there is a God then let him help me now. For I cannot help myself much further. And if this is my fate then let him help me understand it. My mental endurance is at an end.'

The end of mental endurance – once written, the truth of it was obvious. Insidiously that state had crept upon him, like the advent of some sinister disease – unnoticed until its grip was total. He wrote on:

'There is little time. Uhlanga returns today and I think I must do whatever has to be done now, or never. If sontekile is ever to be mine then, it seems, I will have to demand it. I can not continue to wait until Uhlanga decides I am ready.'

A time limitation. He had never thought about such a thing before. But then neither had he felt before as he did now. He only had to read those early pages to see that. How confident he had been then. Brave words like *drive* and *resolve* had run like cracking whips through those pioneer pages. His cause had seemed so right. He had perceived that cause as a solid stone wall of justification on which to perch – a bystander, an observer – untouched by the blood that flowed around.

It had not worked that way. The blood had seeped its way up. The wall had crumbled under. And now he was belly-deep in the gore – stupefied to find himself where he was. The pencil was moving again:

> 'I think I know what's happened to me now. My mind, in terrible conflict with my will, has chosen to excuse itself from the responsibility of my acts. I hate to apply the word psychotic to myself, but I think I have come close to that awful state of mind. I realised this yesterday.'

Yes, it was then that Kirsten had reached out for him in the darkness and said, 'Is it really you?' In truth he should have answered *no*. For like a face pressed hard and distorted against a window pane, Monty Law was there all right, but hardly recognisable – a stranger on the outside looking in.

Mvulaba . . . Mvulaba. It was he who was seeing – doing – answering. It was he who once having shouldered all the blame had then gone on to usurp his very will.

> 'I must be so careful now. I recognise the symptoms of psychosis, and having done so may yet be able to hold on. I hope so. Two weeks is not that long. Yet even as I write there is a feeling of detachment about the things that I do, and the things I still must do. I am almost too tired to care any more. I must fight this with all my strength.'

Strength? Where is it to come from? said the stranger on the outside looking in. How long will I be able to thus endure?

> 'If I act quickly now, perhaps I will be able to see it through. I must do what I have to do and get away from here, or this place

will dissolve me and suck me in for ever.'

He underlined the word 'must', then sat reading for a while, this chronicle of despair. Even his diary was near its end. Seven more pages remained unpencilled.

*   *   *

'You're mine you bastard.' Patrick Dent breathed the words in an undertone, but he could have spoken louder, there was no danger of being overheard. The proximity of his quarry was an optical trick. He laid down his binoculars, eased into a position, less camouflaged, but more comfortable. He stretched.

'He's gone into the Isingogo woods.' He spoke boldly now, directing his voice towards a clump of nearby tumbled rock. 'It's too late to start anything today. We'll take him out, and his whole bloody gang, in the morning.'

Shibindji was one of the men who appeared above the profile of the boulders in response to Dent's words. The other man was younger, proud-featured, with crisp, black hair furrowed from ear to ear and falling into a mess of plaits in the style of the amaPondo tribe. He was dressed in worn denim overalls, open to the navel.

'Well,' Dent regarded the Pondo speculatively. 'That's where your brother's killers stay, Mzabele. Are you ready to fight the Zulu dogs?'

'*Ewe* uDende.'

'And your men?'

'*Ewe*!' Mzabele nodded – they were ready.

Dent was sure they were. Dent was far from fluent in their language. His sentences were a hodge-podge of Xhosa, Zulu and Fanagalo. Still, Mzabele's eyes said it all. He couldn't wait for the impending confrontation.

'It's too late to set up anything for today,' he repeated. 'Tomorrow morning at first light we'll hit them hard. Now I want all of you here.'

All of them meant Shibindji, Mzabele, and two other, like-overalled Pondos, who emerged rather clumsily from a thicket of Combretum on Mzabele's summons: '*Wosani madoda!*'

Dent frowned at the lack of bushcraft of Mzabele's lieutenants. There was nothing to be done about it in the time available. They had other skills that more than compensated for that shortcoming.

'Come!' he said impatiently. 'Look.'

They came. They stood next to the big policeman. Eyes, schoolboy-wide with excitement followed Dent's extended pointing hand. 'That is the forest called kwaIsingogo – that hill behind it is called Mawamabi . . .'

Simple enough.

'Now, tomorrow morning, as soon as you can see that hill from where we are standing here, you Mzabele and all of your men will move down to the forest edge over there. Do you see where I am pointing?'

Heads nodding. No interpretive problems so far.

'You will spread out on this side of the forest thirty paces apart.'

Consternation. Could everyone count to thirty? Dent stepped off thirty paces. Could they all see how far he was away from them?

'*Ewe.*'

'Good. That is as far apart every man must be. Is that clear?'

'*Ewe.*' Impressed.

'Don't worry, we will go over the whole plan again this afternoon when we get back to your camp.'

'*Ewe.*' This uDende knew about war.

'Now, at the same time that you are at the forest edge, Shibindji and I will be waiting on Mawamabi hill. We will be watching you. We will see when you are in position.'

Dent explained his strategy simply and graphically. It was a winner take all type of plan with no frills. It had to be. Those were the only type of tactics these men would understand and respond to. There would be contingencies of course but he could make no allowance for them. The morning wind for instance. It had been coming from the south-west for almost the entire month but, if it changed, the operation, as it stood, would be a screw up. He did not mention the wind.

He looked at his lieutenants, and they looked back at him. He said, 'Are there any questions?' And there were none. Either he had explained the whole thing brilliantly, or else they hadn't understood a damn thing, and were too scared to admit it. There was one last thing he wanted to say:

'Bawu Inkosi Ingram has asked me to tell you this. His eyes will be on us here tomorrow. These Zulu dogs started this. Now they must be punished. Do not be moved by mercy. There is the enemy: go destroy him. These are the words of Bawu Inkosi Ingram.'

They were not the words of Bawu Inkosi Ingram. Their chief, their father Ingram had said no such thing. They were words from the inventive mind of Captain Patrick Dent. But that was an irrelevance. There were more important issues at stake than the incrimination of Ingram.

He glanced at his watch – 12.00 hours. A swollen sun sat mid sky and everything not made of stone was suffering. He had gone a hellish two days in those hot hills, and the third would be no better. Right now, there was the long dry walk back to base.

'Let's go,' he said.

He was getting too old for this sort of caper.

* * *

Uhlanga, the grey-eyed sangoma, had a piscine affinity with darkness: she moved in it in a soundless, treadless way; supported like a fish in water. And God knows there *was* no water.

The forest of kwaIsingogo was sapless from the drought. The grass was crackle-dry and fallen twigs were noisy underfoot. Still Law did not hear her come.

Suddenly she was there, in the central clearing, her shoal of neophytes, gliding, moon-white in the surrounding blackness. There were greetings:

'I see you all,' said Uhlanga, and, for all the darkness, you had to believe she really could.

'I see you, Uhlanga.'

Law erased the frown from his face, and waited for her to pass him by. She did not. She stopped; moved closer. The acrid dead smell of her trade was with her, it stung his nostrils.

'Are you well, Mvulaba?'

'I am well, Uhlanga.'

'Your work. How is the search progressing?'

'It goes on.'

'Are we any nearer to the royal Inkatha?'

An impulse to snatch her *muthi* necklace arose in him. He was close enough to do it. And then what? The *imikhovu* were somewhere there – they were always there. They would have killed him before the shout *Bulalani Mvulaba!* had died upon her lips. This was not the time for such speculation. The sangoma was waiting for a reply to her question.

'If I knew how near we were to the Inkatha, then I would know where it was – would I not?'

Still she stood there.

'So you would, Mvulaba. And you are the one who will find it, and bring it back to its rightful place – only you. The spirits have pronounced that, and the spirits never lie. So it will happen that way, and it will happen soon. There is no turning against such a prophecy. Do you understand that, Mvulaba?'

'Yes.'

Uhlanga's words had shocked him. But more than that: there was a fearful truth in what she said . . . Mvulaba stirred inside him then – grew a little inside him. Mvulaba thrived on fear.

'Yes,' he said again.

Uhlanga moved on. There were others waiting there to greet, to be greeted. Others more deserving of commendation than Mvulaba, the fruitless searcher. There was Mabamba the regimental commander. There were the officers Ubizo, Umsuto and Habana. All of them were praised.

'*E! Amaqhawe! E!* Look well at these brave men, look well!'

There was a certain ritual to be followed now. The induna Mabamba and his officers, Mvulaba the war doctor, and a few other lesser personages filed into the *indlunkulu* – the big hut.

It was three times the size of the sleeping huts with three thick centre poles to support the dome. Around the perimeters warriors were standing, holding spluttering tallow torches. The floor, cow dung, beaten and polished to a gleam, picked up the torch glow as though itself ignited.

Next to enter were the white-ochred neophytes. Singing, they filed in, and took up their places on the left-hand side, the women's side.

The priestess diviner Uhlanga – Mother of Abanzanzi – Knowledge of heaven – Eyes of rain . . . she and her *imikhovu* bodyguards were the last to come into the *indlunkulu* – almost last.

Behind her three more people made humble progress: two *imikhovu* and between them a man – a prisoner.

He was small. He was old. His shoulders slumped, his head lolled.

'Mancoba,' – an inward gasp of recognition and shock. And Mvulaba grew a little more.

The Zulu took two paces then sagged to his knees, he would have crumpled completely had the *imikhovu* not prevented it. Six more epileptic steps and he was adjacent to the place of Mvulaba, looking down at the man he had known so well. But if he recognised him it was doubtful. Mancoba's focus was in chaos. His eyes were rambling like a drunk, but he was not drunk – he was drugged. He was halfway *imikhovu*.

'Far enough.' Uhlanga brought the procession to a halt. That was where she wanted Mancoba seated – right in front of Mvulaba. Mvulaba would know why.

'Do you recognise him, Mvulaba?'

'I recognise him.'

'Of course you do. This is the man who was with you the first time you came to me enquiring about sontekile.'

'Yes, I remember.'

'Of course you do.'

'The man is old, Uhlanga. Look at him. Look how frail he is. A man like that frightens easily.'

'You think I frightened him?'

'Not by intent, Uhlanga.'

'But why? How? He is a Zulu so how can he be frightened by me? I am sangoma – his gateway to the spirits.'

'He is church-reared, Uhlanga. The Christ spirit is the only spirit he is prepared to admit to.'

'No.' Uhlanga nodded her head, unconvinced. 'If that were so, if he finds my presence so frightening, why then does he bury his feet in ground that I plough?'

Why indeed? Mancoba at that moment should have been safely in Durban – 200 miles from that Lebombo kraal. Uhlanga replied to her own question.

'He has more on his mind than Christianity, this old goat. There are secrets in this man's mind that concern we Abanzanzi. I sense the presence of terrible danger, of a great threat to the existence of Abanzanzi. I think this man knows about it. Tonight I'm going to reach into his mind, and I want you to be there, Mvulaba. I will open him like a calabash, and you Mvulaba can pour him out. I think we will be shocked at what we find.'

They would be more than shocked; they would be outraged.

Uhlanga never exaggerated. When she had done what she intended, Mancoba would have as much control as to the spilling of his thoughts as a calabash of *amasi* milk. And with this outflow would come yesterday's story, the story of the looting of Umzeze's cave. Mancoba might survive it, but Mvulaba – never! His mind was swimming, giddy with panic. He had to think of some way he could stop this. He said:

'Leave the old man to me Uhlanga. As you say he is my responsibility. I know how to handle him. If there are any secrets that . . .'

'You don't listen, Mvulaba.' Uhlanga cut short the plea. 'I said, I *am* going to leave him to you, he *is* yours. But before, he was not a true servant to you. After tonight he will follow you; obey you like a shadow.'

Mvulaba, the war doctor, was to be bequeathed an *imikhovu* – a Zombie servant. Was that what Uhlanga was saying? She was smiling at him – a benefactor's smile.

'In that way he will be of more help to you than an entire impi of warriors.'

Yes, that was precisely what she was saying.

'But first we must empty him – we must take the breath from him.'

We. Was he being invited to share in the disunion of a soul – the secret of sontekile? Was he being offered *that* too? Yes, my God, he was!

'It is time that your eyes were opened Mvulaba. I have been restricting you, hindering you in your search. It came to me in a dream that this was wrong. The wise spirits who guide me, advised me. The Inkatha is so close. We must find it now!'

The wise spirits. They were wiser even than Uhlanga realised. The justice of it! The thief was to be given his prize, and his prize would be the death of him.

There was an alternative, of course. It involved a confession of treachery. And he nearly did it. He said:

'I . . .' and again 'I . . .'

And that was all.

It was too much to expect from him. He was too weak to do it. He had been thirsting for too long in the desert of his ideology to turn away from this well, so suddenly disclosed. He had to have its contents, poisoned or not.

'Thank you.' My God, did he say that? 'I only did what I had to do.'

Mancoba's sad, half-dead eyes turned upon him then. It's the truth, Mancoba. Can't you see it? You were a fool, old man. You came back. You should never have done that.

'We must begin now,' Uhlanga said. 'It's a full night's work that we have ahead of us.'

And so it was. Those who had no right to remain left then. Four tallow torches held by four *imikhovu* gave all the remaining light.

Only two apprentices remained. One of them busied herself in kindling a small fire in the central hearth. The other cuddled to herself a carved wood side drum. She began to beat it. A slow, regular double throb – one resonant, one pitched flat. A rhythm that massaged the listener, perfused him, pushed him along in cadence with it . . . thump – pump, thump – pump. Pushed him towards the slowly opening gate, then onwards to places far beyond; to places where the powers of the sangoma were total.

The fire was burning now. Kneeling, an apprentice applied her lips closely, and blew the flame prongs into buoyant life. Such coal would shimmer hotly until the dawn.

'Mvulaba,' Uhlanga beckoned. 'You must watch me carefully, you must see everything I do and listen to everything I say. Nothing can be repeated.'

She laid out a series of small leather sachets upon the floor and took up the first one.

'umuWane.'

She loosed the binding of the sachet, and tapped a precise measure of fine ground umuWane bark into her palm. She held it out. 'Mvulaba, see.' Impatient suddenly. '*See!*'

'*Yebo*, Uhlanga.' He saw the dirty grey granules of umuWane, and how much there was of it. He saw her transfer them into the mouth of an old ground-down wooden mortar.

'isiThumana.'

A slightly greater measure of this crushed root added to the bowl.

'See, umHlala.'

Another root, dried and pulverised, was added.

'iLabathega, uZililo, green leaves of umBondwe. See!'

Yes, he saw it all. All that Uhlanga was doing. And beyond her; the fire. And beyond that, picking up the fireglow; the dead-fish eyes of Mancoba.

'inTsema!'

A strange herb to use. inTsema was an antidote to many kinds of toxins. Yet into the mortar it went.

Uhlanga opened the last leather sachet as though something venomous and vindictive might spring from it. 'Watch, Mvulaba.'

The command was superfluous. That had to be the constituent upon which sontekile was based. This time nothing of the contents touched Uhlanga's hands. A small metal blade was eased into the sachet, which came away tipped with pitch-black granules. He moved forward, the better to see it.

'Not so close!' A quickly upraised hand warned Mvulaba away. 'Smell it or touch it now, and it will harm you. It must be added to the mixing bowl, then all of it ground into one.'

She did exactly that. She took a pestle of ironwood, one end rounded, like a thigh bone, and began to grind down hard on the compound in the base of the mortar. As she did that, she told Mvulaba all that he wanted to hear.

'This is the love organ of the freshly mated maKhukhumesana fish. Do you know it? Do you know this fish?'

The Tetradon inermis – he knew it. He said, '*Yebo*, Uhlanga.'

'Yes,' she laughed. 'You knew of it but still it held from you its secret. I will tell you its secret. The maKhukhumesana by itself is just a deadly poison. But when the inDlala gland of the neck of the human is wedded with it and ground together with it, you have the power to make the living-dead. You have the power of sontekile. Now watch me, Mvulaba, as you have never watched anyone in your life before.'

'I will do as you tell me.' He hoped Mancoba could not hear him. Mancoba, soon to be *imikhovu*. Slow-eyed Mancoba. Couldn't he see that he was the victim of his own unending meddling, his own deceit?

'Watch, Mvulaba.'

The contents of the mortar, now as fine as pepper, Uhlanga poured into a toy-sized earthen cooking pot. The lid she sealed with spittle and clay. 'No smoke must escape.'

The fire was levelled. Three hearth stones were pushed close into the red, glowing coals. Uhlanga adjusted them very carefully. The pot she then rested in this fulcrum. She was singing now; over and over again:

> 'Awake you Zulu
> The river has no ending
> Awake you Zulu
> The night has come for some.'

The tone was sad and wavering. The voice of one bereaved. She gestured to Mvulaba to sing with her. And so he did for hours perhaps, as time stagnated in the smoky haze in the *indlunkulu* hut.

> 'Awake you Zulu
> And listen to the darkness
> Awake you Zulu
> The night has come for some.'

They smeared him as he sang with umZilanyoni balm. He understood that this was to protect him. He felt the sliding hands of the neophyte gentle and soft, working in rhythm with the song and the throb of the drum. Feet and calves, thighs and groin and nates. Warm, it was warm where she touched. Hands reaching from behind from pelvis to stomach to chest. Breasts brittle with ochre touching like butterflies against his back.

> 'Awake you Zulu
> And listen to the darkness.'

The more the repetition, the sweeter became the verse. The more understandable its meaning.

Uhlanga knew. She knew about his weakness. She knew what he had done. She knew everything. And he was glad.

'Awake you Zulu.'

He lifted up his head and smiled the words, and she smiled back her forgiveness. Please let it be forgiveness.

'The river has no ending.'

He was a rower on the waters of eternity. He had only to ship his oars and drift now. Everything had been arranged, everything had been taken care of for Mvulaba, everything except one immediate thing: the balance of his education.

Mancoba was still there upon the floor. His eyes unblinking. His stare and his expression irritatingly fixed; an expression of rigid accusation.

Impudence! By whose sanction did this man sit in judgement — this schemer of schemes. This arrant thief. This cancer of his soul.

The time had come to be rid of him. To exile him to a place where all thought was implanted from the mind of Mvulaba. It suddenly seemed so proper that it should be so.

Mvulaba was ready.

Sontekile was ready.

The night had come for some . . .

* * *

Patrick Dent's definition of 'first light' was: 'That amount of light required to pick up a sight picture at a range of two hundred metres.'

He lifted his rifle for the umpteenth time in the greyness of that dawn and squinted down the scope.

'Not quite,' he said. 'Shibindji, there's time for one more cup of coffee. Is there anything left in the thermos?'

There was. Shibindji yawned quietly and poured.

As an ambush site Mawamabi hill provided all that was required. Steep, rocky slopes and good concealment; an unimpeded view of the killing ground below. It gave nothing else. There was nowhere on that hill where anything bigger than a mountain dassie could stretch out to sleep. And Shibindji wanted to sleep, that whole long night he'd wanted to sleep. Shibindji hated Mawamabi hill.

'Here.'

He held the coffee-filled mug out to his captain. His captain however had his eye still fastened to the scope.

'Put it down,' Dent said, 'then pass me the signal flare. It's just about time we woke up Mr Monty Law and his Abanzanzi friends. What do you say, Shibindji?'

Shibindji said nothing. The question was not intended to be answered. It was simply chat. He took the flare and held it ready, wondering whether his captain would drink the coffee or launch the operation.

He did both. He took the flare, undid the safety wrapping, held it out and tugged the ignition tape. It took off with a *swoosh* into the whitening sky. Then he swallowed the coffee. 'Good stuff.'

Shibindji shrugged his tired frame loose from his heavy issue greatcoat, and hefted his heavy issue FN rifle. Everything issued to a cop was calculated to outlive that cop. He heard Dent work the breech mechanism of his lovely sporting Winchester, shovelling one of those special lead-tipped hunting rounds into the chamber. He did not do the same. He would fire when and where his captain told him so to do.

Dent said, 'Our boys have seen the flare, Shibindji – they've begun.' And it was so.

In the drought-grey shade in the valley of kwaIsingogo, like aimless fireflies, little lights were flitting here and there. They were not fireflies though, neither were they moving without aim. It was Mzabele and his Pondos, and they were working exactly to plan. They were setting alight the upwind fringes of the kwaIsingogo thicket.

It wasn't long before gouts of orange flame were leaping from the high dry grass, hungry for the trees.

'Look, Shibindji.'

The fires were spreading quickly, joining into one long barrier of unbreachable flame. Dent was smiling. It was a happy smile.

'What did I tell you Shibindji? It couldn't be better. Anyone who doesn't want his arse roasted is going to have to make a break for this end of the valley. And we'll be here, won't we Sergeant Shibindji? We'll be waiting for them.'

Another question that did not need an answer. Mzabele's arsonists were doing their job as though they'd been born to it. The forest was all but encircled by flame now, fanned by the predicted south-west wind. The only area that had not been torched was the northernmost boundary of the woods. That was the escape route from the flames. But anyone lucky enough to find it would then run right into Dent's chosen killing ground, wide and open, and well lit now by the morning sun.

'Give me the second flare,' Dent said. 'It's time to signal phase two.'

Shibindji had been anticipating the order. Phase two had been planned to commence once the fire wall was established. That time had definitely arrived.

Phase two signalled the beginning of the slaughter. Some of Mzabele's boys were to begin then, hurtling dynamite sticks into the flames. 'To panic 'em. Get 'em running.'

The main body of Pondos was to regroup in the killing ground to take on the fleeing Zulus. It was to be a time of revenge – for the Pondos – Dent had said. But Shibindji wondered who it was that was really seeking revenge.

The flame hissed upwards, and, even before the smoke trail had blown away, the ground was quaking with the thunder of high explosive. As though some monstrous bellows was being pumped, the flame would snuff beneath the blasts, then roar up red and angry and many times more savage than before. And they did panic, they did come running.

Three Zulus burst into the killing ground – one had a fighting stick, the others were unarmed. All stopped short when they saw the waiting Pondos. All died fighting.

There was no method to the Pondo attack - no tactics. There were nearly fifty of them, with that many different weapons pangas, spears, axes and kieries, all brandished high. They rushed in, in a whooping, hacking blood lust, each man intent on his strike for flesh.

It was all over very quickly for the three Zulus. Two Pondos were dragging themselves painfully away. The rest of them milled around expectantly. They wanted more: more blood, more revenge. kwaIsingogo gave them that.

The north side of kwaIsingogo forest was violently ablaze now; the roar of resin-dried trees exploding into flame quarrelling with the blast of high explosive. Eddies of stinging hot smoke and smut were swirling in a wind that knew no direction. And suddenly more Zulus were bursting from the woods, many more.

These men did not look confused or panicked. They looked angry. They looked prepared. Each man held a kierie and an assegai. And most importantly, they had a leader – a tall induna, full of pride and shouted drill. He formed them up. He advanced them. Then he died.

Dent's rifle crashed and the induna dropped. That shook them. So did the next shot and the next. Every shot took down a man and Dent fired as fast as the action of his rifle would allow. Then the two groups closed and Pondos too began to crumple and fall.

The Zulus were doing well and they would have done better, but for the bullets from Mawamabi hill. But, the forest fire, their enemy, had become their ally too. The smoke was thickening, widening; drawing in a harsh, grey curtain between Dent and those he had come to kill.

Shibindji knew exactly what was going to happen next. Next, Dent was going to turn and beckon to him to follow him down the hill. And so he did.

'Come on Shibindji! Can't see a fucking thing any more from here.'

They were going to climb down to the killing ground and carry on shooting Zulus from there.

'Move it Shibindji!'

He cocked his rifle and followed.

* * *

Where there should have been quiet, there was noise. Not much noise, just a murmur of voices. But the level of sound outside the *indlunkulu* hut was unimportant. That Uhlanga's paramount zone of silence had been trespassed upon at all, *that* was important.

It was serious enough to lift Uhlanga from her work; to set her face in anger. It was an outrage that only the *imikhovu* slayers would know how to deal with.

'Go . . . treat jackals like jackals.'

They went, but whatever action they took, it was not enough. The ill-mannered mutter continued. To Mvulaba it seemed as though the volume was increasing. There was an urgency emerging from the sound. Uhlanga must have sensed it.

'Mvulaba.' Her frown was gone, her eyebrows were raised in question. 'What is happening?'

The noise makers alone could supply that answer. So it was to them that Mvulaba went.

'Fire!' they said. 'Fire!'

'Where?'

'At the forest edge. Look over there. You can see the glow.'

He *could* see the glow. Much of the skyline was touched by the dawn-like hue, but this dawn had nothing to do with the breaking of a new day. This was the work of arsonists.

The voices of the officers could be heard: 'To the south, towards Mawamabi hill. Form up the regiment. Be quick! Be ready to fight.'

Mvulaba was quick – as quick as a civet. He sprinted to his *indlu*. There beneath the leaves he found the diary. Even as he was stuffing it into the girdle of his *uMutsha*, he was running for the *indlunkulu*. There was only one remaining thing in that whole forest that he wanted.

He lifted it from the hearth stones, it burned him but he did not care. He did not see Uhlanga there until she said:

'I thought you'd come for it. You've wanted it so badly, for so long, haven't you Mvulaba?'

'I thought you'd gone,' he said. 'You'd better be quick Uhlanga. We are being attacked.'

'Yes, I know.'

She nodded. 'You had better be careful with that, Mvulaba. That pot will break like eggshell.'

'I'll take care. You too must take care.'

As though a giant had stamped in anger, earth and *indlu* shook then – the air was filled with rumble and boom – again, then again.

'They will not beat us you know,' Uhlanga said. 'By attacking us they make us stronger.' She turned at the door of the *indlunkulu* with one final warning. 'You must hurry now, Mvulaba. Fire is your special enemy – you know that don't you? Fire is the element *you* of all people must fear the most. Remember Ulundi, Mvulaba. Remember what happened to your spirit father there.' Then she was gone.

He was alone in the *indlunkulu* with its tunnel of grey morning light; but not quite alone; with him was one Zulu *madala*, to do with as he pleased.

They had left Mancoba propped against a centre pole, but he did not remain in that position for long. The punch of the next explosion was so close that the whole hut shook. Bits of chaff and binding were falling. Mancoba flopped sideways like a drunk.

The problem was one of choices. His escape depended on speed and agility. Carrying the fragile earthen vessel and nothing else, he would be quick. Carrying nothing but the frail-boned Zulu, he would be equally as quick. Carrying both the Zulu and the sontekile vessel would present an impossible task. He chose sontekile. He cradled it to his chest. He ran.

Whatever it was that stopped him in his flight, and turned him back towards the Abanzanzi kraal, occurred when he was well into the maze of kwaIsingogo. Somewhere in the scramble through those thorn sharp tunnels he remade his decision. There was no noble cause to it, no flush of virtuous warmth came up to bolster him. If there was new found strength in him, then, it was fuelled by a vast and growing bitterness. By the time he reached the kraal again it had corroded deeper. It was hate.

A rage of hate, molten in him, rising, pushing – a whole volcano of it roaring up. And all of it directed at one thing – one man. This loathful little Zulu who had tried to stop him all along; who, even now, lying half conscious, sprawled upon the *indlunkulu* floor, had summoned the power to draw him back.

Brute roaring flames had reached the kraal and wrapped it in a barrier of heat. He rushed it. But it was a mighty thing. It scorched and singed him. It flung him back in pain. He crouched and ran at it again. The furnace closed around him and he was in it.

Inside the *indlunkulu* there was less heat, there was air there that didn't sear like swallowed acid. Mancoba lay where he had fallen – one limp arm outstretched, as though begging for rescue. That was the wrist that Mvulaba grasped. He dragged him by it like a child drags at a stubborn doll. And that was how he hauled him from the *indlunkulu*, and into the forest, cursing and jerking at his burden as he fled.

His movement was too slow. The ground was burning – the sky was burning. Bright fire was passing them, striking tree and bush left and right; fire, his special enemy, berserk in its desire to have him.

His thighs and calves were buckling. Shoulder to wrist his strength was melting. 'Pull,' he commanded. Lame arms and legs obeyed – 'Pull,' and the burden shifted on.

But the fire had leapt ahead of him; out-manoeuvred him. There was no direction that did not lead to flame; no space that was not agony. He was choking. Still he held on; still he pulled. Mancoba looked dead. His head was lolling, twisted, wide-jawed in the dragging sand.

'Pull.'

Now there was more smoke than he had encountered before. Thick acrid stuff that blinded and ran like knotted rope into the chest. It was terrible but not as terrible as the flame – and now there was less flame.

'Pull.'

There was not another pace in him when he reached the forest verge. His retching chest was doubling him. His eyes were stung closed – a seam of vision was obtainable, no more. But he could hear.

'uSuthu! uSuthu! uSuthu!'

He was in time to partake of the madness.

'Intlaba mkosi!' The Pondos answered the Zulu battle cry.

There was no distinguishing between the sound of the dying. Zulu and Pondo, animal agony shaped their throats alike.

He discovered that he had rescued a corpse. Mancoba was dead; crumpled and burned and very dead.

And then he heard a sound that made a puny thing of war cries: The rampant trip-hammer crash of automatic weapons. God help Abanzanzi if that was the enemy.

More rifle blasts – closer – louder. He had to get away.

Once more that day his effort was insufficient.

The men with the guns caught him, not five faltering steps from the body of Mancoba.

There were two of them, and he heard them before he saw them.

'There's the bastard, Shibindji. Watch it, he's going to run. Get around in front there and cut him off.'

It was too easy for them. Running was something Mvulaba did not even contemplate. He clutched the sontekile to his chest and stood there.

Shibindji had been badly affected by the smoke. The man's every breath, it seemed, was concluded in a desperate hacking fight for air. Despite that, he did what was asked of him. He emerged from the drifting smoke squarely in front of his quarry. He was a policeman, a tall, thin, blue-uniformed policeman with an automatic rifle.

'I've got him,' Shibindji coughed. 'Over here, Captain.'

The captain's arrival was a quieter affair. He was as broad as Shibindji was spare. He wore the camouflage and shoulder rank of a captain in the South African Police. For all his size he moved with the practice of a hunter.

'Well done, Shibindji.'

A hunting rifle looked natural in his hands. The barrel of it pressed heavily on Mvulaba's shoulder, forcing him to kneel.

'Montague Law . . . On the seventh day he arose again.'

The foresight moved sharp beneath his chin now. The pressure insistent. His head was tilted backwards to its limit.

'Look at me, Monty Law, you white-skinned kaffir. I want you to get a good look at me before I end your miserable fucking life, for real. Hey! Look at me!'

Mvulaba forced his swollen blinking lids to stay apart. His focus progressed to the rifle nozzle; along the barrel to the big and competent hands. Onwards.

'Dent.'

The name-tag on the chest he read aloud. And Dent's face was tight with hate. Why? He knew this policeman vaguely, but had never given him any reason for such hate. Dent must have sensed his puzzlement; he said:

'People like you, who turn against their own, shouldn't be allowed to live.'

Was that his reason? Was that how he saw it?

'You . . . don't . . . understand.' The words came with difficulty.

'I'm not even going to try,' Dent said. 'You see, I also have reasons that you wouldn't accept, or understand. That doesn't alter the situation. In my world you have no excuse to exist. And you happen to be in my world.'

'Listen . . . please . . .'

The man with the rifle. The man who owned the world – he had to understand. There *was* an excuse. Clasped right there in his blistered hands was his reason to exist. A little earthen pot, eloquent with reason.

'I'm listening,' Dent prompted.

But what was there to tell this man – the secret of secrets?

The policeman was right – in his world Mvulaba's absence would not be missed. The message that Mvulaba bore was not for them. So he said nothing.

'That's it then,' Dent made it sound very final. 'I'm glad you didn't beg for your life, Law. I would have killed you anyway.'

Why didn't he do it then? Shibindji was coughing again. The smoke was rolling thickly by. Mvulaba closed his eyes, fearful that it would hurt. God! There had been enough hurt.

He heard the explosion. He fell backwards. And it did not hurt. It didn't hurt because it was not Dent's rifle that had fired.

It was Shibindji's FN that was hammering. His target was a spearman pounding downhill at full stretch.

The warrior was hit. He staggered, grunted like a wounded buffalo, and came on. Another bullet ripped into him. But his momentum and his stubborn Zulu heart took him all the way.

The impact was a brutal thing – loud with death: the smack of impalement and Shibindji's scream. At last he heard the blast of Dent's own rifle.

One well placed shot from the master. That was all it took to kill the Zulu, to bring him stumbling, tumbling down.

Mvulaba, prone upon the ground, was far too slow to avoid the falling man. His dead weight struck him with the force of a lopped tree, smashing the breath from him, then plunging on.

The little earthen crock was shattered. The fine black powder of sontekile had burst across Mvulaba's chest. Frantic fingers brushed at it, but that just spread it further. His body, his hands, were sticky. There was nothing to be done.

Dent was puzzled as to how a man in Law's predicament could in any way be amused. Yet there it was. One side of the man's face was burned raw. He must have been in shocking pain. But through the soot; the mess of his blistered skin, and the agony, the man was smiling.

Law's ribcage was quaking with soundless mirth. There was no mistaking that.

Captain Dent could not understand it. But Captain Dent had never been exposed to the capricious justice of the wise spirits of

Uhlanga the sangoma.

It was hard to kill a man who had been hit so hard, yet had it in him yet to smile . . .

*   *   *

The fire became a lesser thing. It swallowed the forest of kwaIsingogo and struck out across the shale and mountain grass. But there was little to sustain it on those goat-cropped slopes. It crackled and crept, and flared where it could, but its heat was vague; its smoke no longer bundled out the sky.

And through that sky Dent's helicopter came. First, the sound – the clap of blades, the whirr of turbines. Then the flashing red nav-lights; the down-turned faces, and the invisible power of the prop wash.

Men arrived; men with stretchers and compassion in their voices. They lifted him. They carried him. A stranger, looking intently into his eyes. Perspex above, glinting in the sun. Then, that same face again. It smiled. It said something, but the engine roar was greater.

'Hold on!' Was that it? He held on.

'You're going to be fine.'

They didn't know. How could they know? Their knowledge was a hundred years behind. They were fussing with him.

'Vein. Find a vein.'

Wonderful, wonderful cool water washing past his lips.

'Drink.'

His stretcher was being clipped down next to another man's. A black man in camouflage with a blotched red bandage around his chest. It was the man called Shibindji. A door slid closed, and suddenly he realised that they were taking him away from there. Out of reach of fire and destruction. And, out of reach of the only person who could save him.

'Let me go.' A whisper that was lost before it passed his lips. 'Mustn't take me away.' He tried to raise himself, but there were straps to hold him safe. They smiled, the strangers; how were they to know?

The roar built up and up. The twin blades whirled, then scattered to a blur. They rose into a shining sky of blue. And even as that happened he felt the sontekile grip.

The world, and everything the world contained was slowing, slowing, slowing, a gramophone record groaning beneath the drag of some relentless spoiling finger, labouring leadenly on but always slowing. And he was part of it. He was the pivot of this paralysis of sound. It seemed the oddest way to die.

But he did not die. The metronome of life swung back. The torpid mush of visual things firmed into perspex and rivets and faces – no longer grinning confidently. Now the faces were creased with great concern. He lip-read: 'You OK?'

How could such a question be so seriously phrased? He nodded to reassure the man.

'Hold on, we're nearly there.'

God, how long had he been gone?

A long time it seemed, for they *were* nearly there.

Air Force chopper Mike November Pappa logged in at its destination dead on ETA – 13.20 hours. Addington Hospital's trauma unit opened its doors to one more case.

* * *

'A strange case,' said Sister Richards.

'A most unusual case.' Doctors Whitaker and Secker both concurred with the charge sister's comment, but for different reasons.

'He was wearing animal skins,' said Sister Richards.

'He has respiratory tract burns,' said Whitaker, 'combined with second degree, bordering on third degree, burns to a few areas. About forty per cent of his total surface area is affected. One side of his face will require skin grafting. He must have suffered severe plasma protein and electrolyte losses and shock, right?'

'Right,' said Secker.

'*Wrong*,' said Whitaker. 'This man's haemocrit levels are just about normal. His blood flow is unimpaired. There is no sign of hyponatremia or acidosis, so what do you make of all that?'

'It's not possible.' That was what Doctor Secker made of it. 'Are you sure we're discussing the same patient?'

Whitaker handed the lab printout he was holding to his colleague. 'Hot from Pathology. Read it yourself.'

'He's quite conscious,' an apologetic Sister Richards said, 'but just refuses to give us his name. See – there's a blank there on the Path report where the name should be. That's all we wanted from him – just his name.'

'Most unusual.' Secker shook his head. He pointedly turned his back on the sister from Trauma. How Whitaker could stand the bitch he did not know. 'I mean even if Path had it screwed up, there's his cardiac response. *That's* all wrong. His blood pressure is down – sure: But his heart and respiratory rates are way down too. It just doesn't make sense. I've seen burn patients, I've seen many burn patients. But I've never seen anything like this. Is this man from the planet Earth?'

'Thought you'd be interested,' Whitaker said. 'Well, I've got him on plasmalite and penicillin I.V., and oxygen. I've dressed him with Xeroform. I don't know what else I can do.'

'Sure.' Secker bent to the patient for the first time. Behind the pressure dressing a pair of deep onyx, very intelligent eyes took him in. 'Can you hear me?' Both eyes closed in a slow and calculated blink. 'You're going to be up and about in no time.'

But Doctor Secker had never made a more unwarranted prognosis. The man in the Xeroform mask knew that. Secker's words dawdled to him vaguely like sounds heard underwater. He felt the power of sontekile pushing him under once again. This time it was so much stronger . . . swooning inwards and outwards . . . ever slowing, never ending. It was sucking him brutally down, down, down.

He made no sense of Whitaker's shouted words – 'Damn it . . . respiratory arrest . . . defibrillator! . . . Sister, *move it!* His heart is going to stop!'

And it did. But the patient beneath the defibrillator paddles neither observed the scramble that took place, nor felt the slam of 250 watts per second as it jolted through his chest.

'*Now!* . . . . . *Now!*'

'I think he's slipping,' said Sister Richards. 'We're losing him.'

'Shut up, Sister!' Whitaker was sweating like a miler as he held fast the kicking shock paddles. 'Give me three hundred joules this time. *Now!*'

* * *

'He wasn't in pain, Miss Law.' That was the kindest thing that Doctor Gray Whitaker could think of to say. 'If we had known his identity, we could have reached you while he was still conscious.'

'I came as soon as I got the news. You say he was conscious then, when they brought him here?'

'Oh yes,' Whitaker tightened his jaw against the yawn that was stretching in him. Thirteen hours of duty, and it was something to midnight. But never to yawn in the face of the bereaved. Especially a face as beautiful as this. 'Kirsten, if I may call you Kirsten. Your brother was admitted at one thirty yesterday afternoon, with forty per cent second to third degree burns. He was conscious. He died of his injuries late this afternoon.'

In Whitaker's book there had always been two categories of next of kin who stalked the corridors outside the trauma ward. Those to be held together with valium and euphemisms when the mortuary trolley squeaked past. And those who could absorb words such as dead – died – death like a well-sprung punch bag. Kirsten Law did not conform. She was drawn and ashen, and her voice, he suspected, would run a key lower on a better day. But that just added to her appeal. This woman was proud and dignified . . . *and* a stunner.

'Could you use a cup of coffee?' He hoped she would say yes. 'I'd like to talk to you.'

She said, 'Yes.'

'Do you have anyone with you?' To that question he hoped for a negative.

She obliged. 'No.'

'I'm going off duty right now.' And that was what he did.

The staff cafeteria at that hour was a fully automated affair – all chrome and plastic tables with a bank of garish slot machines that digested multiples of 50 cent pieces, and passed food or cigarettes or beverages, with change and all. The coffee was free.

'Sugar? Milk?'

'Both.'

'It's not very good.' He smiled. 'But it's hot.'

'You said you wanted to say something to me.'

'Yes,' Whitaker sucked the steam off the brim of his polystyrene cup. His eyes were focused on the sorrowful, beautiful face of the woman who sat opposite him. He said, 'You know your brother's case was . . . well, it was strange.'

'Oh?'

'Do you feel strong enough to talk about this, Kirsten?'

'Go on.'

'Look, your brother suffered burns. Serious burns. But I honestly didn't expect him to die, certainly not the way he did.'

'Why? What do you mean by that?'

'I mean that in medicine, especially in trauma management, there are certain cause and effect rules which are consistent – the same for every patient. For instance when someone suffers burns, like your brother's, then there is a massive body-fluid loss, and with it a dangerous change in body chemistry and function. It's always the same, *always*.'

Whitaker took a sip of coffee. He needed the pause as much as he needed the beverage. He was saying too much. His explanation to this woman was skidding way beyond the demands of protocol. All he was obliged to tell her was – Montague Law is dead. Because of certain factors, a post mortem examination will be called for. You will be advised of the District Surgeon's findings – I'm sorry – good night. And perhaps that was all she wanted to hear.

'Look,' he said. 'You're probably tired. It's probably a bad time for this kind of discussion. Why don't we . . .'

'Why don't we what?' A sudden flare of anger. 'Look *yourself*, Doctor Whitaker, just go on. I am tired. It *is* a bad time, but just go on, will you?'

He did as she asked him. 'I told you that I thought your brother's case was strange. You see, despite his severe trauma, his body chemistry was as near normal as matters. He was well-hydrated. He showed no signs of shock, no air hunger. In fact, his respiratory rate, and his heart rate were very, very slow. I can't better describe it than to tell you of an experience I had when I was a kid. I was brought up in England, in Cornwall. One of my brothers gave me a hedgehog for a pet. I called him Percy. Anyway, Percy was my best thing. We were great friends. Where I went, Percy went. And then one day, one early winter's day, I went down to the shed at the bottom of the garden where Percy slept, and, found him dead, rolled up into a ball, cold, dead. I cried all that morning and well into the afternoon. And then my eldest brother came home from school and explained to me about hibernation. Percy, he told me, was hibernating. He would be up and about next summer. Kirsten, it was as though your brother was going into hibernation. It's a dumb explanation, I know and highly unprofessional. But that was honestly what it seemed like. Of course humans don't hibernate. Some time later your brother's heart stopped altogether. We tried everything we knew; nothing helped. There was nothing we could do.'

'*Hibernating!*' Kirsten invested the word with a bright-eyed expectation it had no right to.

'Yes.' Whitaker realised his mistake. '*No*. It was a poor explanation, I told you that.'

'No, it wasn't.'

Christ, the woman was overwrought. And it was totally his fault.

'I can't explain to you, Doctor Whitaker. It's too long a story. But let's say you are right. In a way my brother is *hibernating*.'

And she was serious. She was addressing him with the reverence deserved of a Pasteur or Lister – Doctor Graham Whitaker, discoverer of Percy's Syndrome.

'Where is my brother?'

It was time for reality.

'Your brother's body was removed from the ward and taken to the Police Mortuary.'

'God, no!'

'Possibly a post mortem examination has already been done, but it is more likely that this will take place in the morning.'

'No! That must not happen!'

'It has to happen. Kirsten, that's the law.'

'To hell with the law.'

Whitaker reached a hand across the table, firm with sympathy and reassurance. She dodged it – left it stranded like a beached porpoise.

'If any of those bloody bastards in butchers' aprons and gumboots comes near my brother, God help them.'

'OK.' Whitaker found himself repressing a smile. Her summary of mortuary technicians was apt. He rescued his hand and sat back in the chair. 'So what do you want me to do?'

'Firstly you can stop being so bloody patronising. Then you can listen to me; really listen to me . . . *please*. A few minutes ago I said I can't explain this thing to you. But what you've just told me leaves me no option but to try. Listen to me.'

'I'm listening,' he said. And, as tired as he was, it was the truth.

'My brother was – *is* – a botanical scientist, a man obsessed in the search for something that you as a doctor, might understand, a cure for the incurable.'

She spoke for nearly an hour. And during that time he did not question or interrupt her once. In pure scientific terms she had little to offer. Her emotional appeal, however, was irresistible. Words tumbled from her in a jumbled spate. As though the more she said, the more was the likelihood of him being picked up and swept along. And he was – by the depth of her sincerity; her desperation; her hope. He saw Kirsten Law with her defences lowered. And what he saw he liked; liked it so much, that when she appealed to him:

'Will you help me then?'

He said, 'It's a long shot, but I'm going to try. Something you said gives me a bit of hope.'

'That's wonderful.'

'Kirsten can you operate a telex machine?'

'Sure, but . . .'

'It's one thirty in South Africa now. What time does that make it in California?'

'Somewhere in the early afternoon, I think.'

'Come,' he said. 'We've got an office to break into, and then, a telex to send to Stanford University. Have you ever heard the word *tetradotoxin*?'

'Spell it for me.'

'T-e-t-r-a-d-o-t-o-x-i-n. I'll tell you about it as we walk.'

Whitaker – very gallant – held Kirsten's arm, that she should not fall or falter as they shuttled through the labyrinth of disinfected passage ways. The feel of her was also very good. They walked until they reached a door marked HOSPITAL ADMINISTRATION: NO ENTRY. Of course that sign did not apply to senior physicians who were so much a part of the iatric furniture of that place. Such staffers knew of the existence of a side hatch through which papers and conversation of administrative nature passed during office hours; through which anyone with average agility could pass at any other time.

That was how they gained access to the office block and the telex machine. Kirsten flushed with excitement, certain that this man, who knew of things like tetradotoxin, was the key to her brother's survival. Whitaker, aware that he had called to the limit, was ready to play his hand out to the limit. And if the prize was Kirsten Law, he would go all the way.

* * *

Warrant Officer 'Vleis' Visagie yawned deeply of the 15 degrees centigrade coolth inside the main cutting room of the Police Medico-Legal Laboratory. The mish-mash odour of gammy meat and formalin dismayed him not a bit. Had he *not* been standing where he was, had he been inclined to yawn anywhere else in Durban on that sweltering summer morning, he would have to have inhaled air that was a dismal 20 degrees hotter. Thermal bliss was just one of the benefits that came the way of a Durban mortuary cop.

Other nice things were the conditions of employment. The hours were easy. If you started early enough, as he was doing that morning, the afternoon was yours to do with as you wished. It was an undemanding job, largely because of the restful nature of those citizens who passed through that place – nobody ever complained about the treatment they got at the MLL. Visagie was happy in his work.

He lifted his plastic apron from a row of like plastic aprons that hung along one white-tiled wall, and tied the strings. He took up a portable electric reciprocating saw, test revved it for a burst. All was as it should be. It was time to commence work. For his attention, on that morning's roster: one brain removal; one female genital complete; one combined brain, spinal cord and internal organs – that one had come in the previous evening.

Visagie was an efficient man – a skilled technician. The chief pathologist, Professor Sanderson, relied on him where the delicate touch was required, like the brain job that he was about to begin.

The first thing to do was to part the hair. Not the normal parting, this path had to run from ear to ear, good and straight. The longer the hair the better it fell. Next came the incision.

Visagie applied just the right pressure to do the job in one continuous cut – right along the path he had just created – right down to the calvarium. If you did that properly (and Visagie always did), a gentle push and a snip or two would see the skin flap open – the skull exposed.

Nothing too difficult about that. Visagie sometimes imagined he was taking Professor Şanderson's pathology students.

'Great care for the next stage if you please!' He addressed his imaginary class. 'Now, if the calvarium is sawed correctly, one flip of the skull key will lift the skull cap, no need for hammer and chisel. That's for amateurs.'

He could almost feel the phantom presence of his phantom class as they watched him rev the buzz saw. Steady now . . . and if you've set the blade depth properly, there's hardly any spray. The sound will tell you if you're doing it right. OK, now in with the key, a sharp twist, and off she comes. Excellent. See, no damage to the dura whatsoever.'

Nothing short of the truth. The parietal lobe, a convoluted marbled grey cabbage, lay intact, waiting for the arrival of the real-life professor and his real-life students. To be plucked out 'neatly now' and off to the dissecting sink.

It was at that moment that Visagie became aware that besides himself and his trio of cadavers, there were others present in the cutting room. It was not the professor, nor was it any of the post-grads.

Stark against one white-tiled wall, just beyond the brightness of the neon, a group of men were standing, watching him intently: four Zulus who had no right whatsoever to be where they were.

'The viewing room is back there,' sternly. 'You can't come in here. *No* one is allowed in here.'

Perhaps they didn't understand. They didn't look like town kaffirs. Despite their assortment of tatty clothing they were shoeless. They wore bits and pieces of charms and beading and carried big clubbed fighting sticks. Visagie had been a rural cop in his early days. He knew the type. He knew how to handle them.

'*Suka!* Go on – piss off!' All with the appropriate arm gestures. And, with his blood-stained scalpel still grasped, there could be no doubt – they were meant to go.

But they did not go. They advanced. Speaking a fluid Zulu, he had no hope of making sense of, they came on towards the cutting tables. Visagie should not have reacted as he did.

Amongst the essential instruments of the post mortem technician is a knife, very sharp and long, used to section lungs and liver. He picked it up. He shook it at them.

It stopped them for a moment, only to bring about a change of tactics: they separated, and came at him from different angles.

Visagie sensed that this invasion had more to do with what lay upon the marble slabs than himself, but everything was happening very quickly. His instinct was to defend; that was wrong, but it was too late to change – too late to question:

'What do you want?'

The first stick whistled, close enough to tip his nose, but just a feint, just a ploy to draw him out. To measure his ability. He had no ability – he was still reacting to the feint when the same club struck him – neck, elbow and ribs – hard and laming.

The man danced back watching him, bobbing like a mongoose before a cobra. But Visagie was no cobra. His reactions were dull – he had dealt too long with the dead. All he had going for him was courage. He advanced, lunged out at the stick fighter, missed him widely, then swung again. It was exactly what he should not have done.

He had been decoyed. The big marble cutting tables had offered some protection. Now he was in the open, and the kieries were swinging fast, and from all sides. Now the blows were dreadful.

They hammered him down in seconds. They broke his arms, then smashed him to his knees. The final fraction of Visagie's life – a scream of pain and terror – ended with a brutal blow to the head. It came from full stretch and crushed his skull as though it were eggshell.

They laid Visagie on a cutting table; exchanged him for its previous occupant, a man whose single item of dress was one cardboard baggage label attached to one big toe. It read: Addington admittance 114687 T W: Identity unknown.

But the Zulus knew who he was. They lifted him reverently and carried him to a rickshaw waiting in the hearse lot outside the old brick building. There they covered him with a blanket.

There was one other person who knew him too; one other early morning visitor to the Police Medico-Legal Laboratory. She caught a partial glimpse of the blanketed man's features as the rickshaw rattled past her in the parking lot. That was enough. His hair was singed, his skin abraded and raw with burns. But she knew who it was.

'Stop! . . . My God . . . *Stop! Yima wena!*'

She darted after the rickshaw, and would have caught it too. But the alley that led out to the street was narrow, and men were blocking it. Four big Zulus who jostled her; who spun her rudely around and shoved her stumbling back.

Whitaker moved to help. He had no idea why Kirsten had hurtled from his Mercedes before he had even killed the engine. He was astonished that she should wish to take on four very big, very angry Zulus. However, he had once been junior middle boxing champion of his house. He knew what he had to do, even if he did not know why. Fists up, heart pounding, he came down the alley at a run. He did not even see the whirling kierie that knocked him cold.

6

Graham Whitaker lifted his rather straight blond fringe (thatching, someone had once called it) laying bare an area of scalp that was woefully contused. He pulled a wry face at the sight of it. 'Shit,' he said to the bathroom mirror.

Consoling him was the fact that once the hair had fallen back into place, very little of the damage was apparent. He had good regular features and deep blue eyes, any or all of which could have been permanently wrecked by a blow of greater savagery. In a paradoxical way he had been lucky. He said as much to his reflection: 'It could have been worse, fella.'

He might have said more, and continued his examination further but this was not his mirror, nor his bathroom. He was more than seventy kilometres from his own penthouse bathroom. This was the guest house at Prospect Hall, and unfortunately he was not the only guest.

There was the cop from the Lebombo mountains. He was huge. He had a tan that formed a V sharply below his neck, and cut halfway across his bicep. A mess of centipede-like scars crawled the whiteness of the remainder of him. It was a body that had, off and on, known considerable pain. That it was still intact after such abuse, was evidence of a robust constitution and a quick mind. Dent did everything in an unmeasured, careless way that made sharing with him a chore.

The doorhandle of the bathroom turned; Whitaker had not seen the necessity of locking it merely to urinate. The door opened, admitting a blare of TV sound, and Patrick Dent.

'Sorry.'

'You're welcome.'

Neither man meant either word.

Dent crossed to the toilet bowl, he too wished to urinate. He did not wait for Whitaker to depart. He let it go in a thick horselike stream from a thick horselike penis. He farted loudly, grinned, and shook the prehensile thing all over the place.

'Aah!'

Whitaker backed off into the guest lounge. The television set was full on there. He turned the volume down and paused. A glumfaced newscaster said 'good evening' and began to read the early news. The lead item was the fight at Mawamabi hill. A colour contour map filled up the screen. A little flashing red arrow pointed to the location of Mawamabi.

'Here in the Lebombo mountains at a hill called Mawamabi, one of the bloodiest faction fights of the decade has taken place.'

A still of peaceful mountains with even more peaceful kraals in the foreground.

'At a press interview in Durban today a police spokesman said that the white man who was killed in this action has been positively identified as Doctor Montague Law, a botanical scientist who went missing and was subsequently presumed dead, more than a year ago.'

A close shot of the police spokesman, panning backwards to reveal a roomful of press reporters and some other policemen.

'Look,' Dent shoved his finger against the screen. 'That's me . . . see?'

Indeed it was Captain Dent – a smug-looking Captain Dent in the uniform of the South African Police.

'Faction fights are a fact of life in kwaZulu,' the policeman explained somewhat condescendingly to the assembled reporters. 'Here we had a situation where a faction of Zulus erroneously blamed a gang of Pondo dam workers for a bushfire that had destroyed their homes. The Zulus attacked these innocent men. We have seen the result. An even greater bloodbath was prevented by the swift and efficient action of the police commander in the area.'

A quick shot of a somewhat guarded-looking Dent.

'A police sergeant was wounded in his endeavours to keep the factions apart. We are pleased to say that he is recovering well.'

A reporter asked: 'Have any arrests been made?'

'Investigations are continuing,' said the spokesman.

'Bloody right they are,' said Dent in the flesh.

A hike in the price of fuel energy was the next item to be

covered.

'They didn't say a thing about the policeman who was killed at the morgue,' Whitaker said. 'Not a word.'

'It's a sensitive matter,' Dent said. 'It wouldn't go down well with the general public. The cops will release that story in their own good time. While we're on that subject; how's your head?'

It was painful. 'It's fine,' Whitaker said.

Dent looked amused. 'You don't expect a mortuary cop to get wasted. OK, a cop on the beat or tracking rustlers can expect to get knocked about. Ask me, I know.'

Whitaker was not much interested in the violent world of policemen. He saw the results of violence every day of his life. The subject held no appeal for him.

'I'm going down to the tennis court,' he said. 'Are you coming?'

'Nah,' Dent sat down. 'I reckon there'll be better sport on television. Anyway, I've got a meeting with Mark Ingram. Are you having a game with Kirsten?'

'Yes.'

'She's quite something, isn't she?'

'How do you mean?'

'Well look at it. Her brother, who was supposed to be dead, resurrects himself only to kick the bucket one day later. Then the stiff gets nicked by a squad of body snatchers, probably to hack up for *muthi*, and one day later it's – anyone for tennis? Quite a bit tougher than the girls I'm used to . . . Death is one thing. But hey! Having your nearest's body hijacked off the mortuary table – that would upset me.'

Whitaker doubted that. He said, 'You've got to understand that Kirsten has not as yet been able to accept her brother's death. In your own words, Monty resurrected himself once. Right now she doesn't know what to believe. She's confused. She's angry. She's probably feeling guilty too. She's trying to act as normally as possible. I think she's got a lot of guts.'

Dent went back into the bathroom. Over the sound of running taps he continued to converse: 'So you couldn't save her brother?'

'We did all we could.'

'Did you know much about him?'

'Just what Kirsten told me.'

'He was a weird bugger all right; lived in the Lebombos like a kaffir witchdoctor. Can you believe it? I mean just look around you. Would you leave all this for a loincloth and a wattle hut?'

'He must have had his reasons.'

'No reason . . .' Dent passed from the bathroom to his bedroom, towelling his face and hair '. . . Just went off his bloody head. I know; I'm station commander in that area.'

'How the hell did Law manage to hide for a whole year from an efficient cop like you, Patrick? That's the question I would have asked had I been one of those reporters.'

'Would you?' Dent sounded piqued. 'You should come up there one day and see just how impossible an area I've got to police.'

'That a fact?'

Whitaker allowed his tone to hold a yawning lack of interest in the manifold problems of Captain Dent. He hoped to end the conversation. Dent came through a few minutes later smartly dressed in an open shirt and slacks; smelling of aftershave.

'Well,' he smiled at Whitaker. 'Business before pleasure.'

Graham Whitaker could not help but wonder where a dam builder and a policeman from the Lebombo mountains would find common cause.

'Enjoy the game,' Dent went on. 'You're right in what you say you know – she is *one helluva* woman.'

Whitaker had no answer for such an inventive misquote. Patrick Dent walked away.

*   *   *

The windows of the library of Prospect Hall were sash design with fitted seats and pelmet curtains. They presented a view of the western terrace and the tennis court, and of course, in the distance the ubiquitous cane fields. The bookshelves that covered two sides of the room from plinth to ceiling were heavy with leather, gilded volumes. Marble bust statues of the pioneer Laws gazed out from the corners; proud-jawed, deep-eyed. It was a room of erudition and dignity. It was the room in which Mark Ingram received Captain Patrick Dent; gestured to him to sit.

'It's good of you to come, Captain.'

A leather chair creaked comfortably as it absorbed the policeman's weight. Dent said:

'I'm grateful for the invitation.'

It was in fact at Dent's instigation that this meeting was taking place.

'How did the enquiry go?' Ingram asked. 'It was this morning, wasn't it?'

'Yes, it was.' Dent reflected on the events of that morning; the sceptical reception his version of the action had received from his superiors; the ensuing press conference. He hated such shows. He could see no merit in the dictum of public accountability. 'It made the television news,' Dent said. 'Didn't you see it?'

Ingram shook his head negatively. 'Sad business, Kirsten's brother's death. Damn shame.'

'Yes.'

'She's taken it well.'

'Yes.' Dent did not let his amusement show. This was the same man who, not one week previously had been clamouring for the head of Montague Law. It was obvious that Ingram did not want to be party to any details regarding the demise of the late Montague Law, or the Pondo affair. That suited Dent equally as well. There was nothing to be gained by reminding Ingram of his complicity. Dent said:

'The man wasn't exactly on your side.'

'There's that to it,' Ingram gave. 'He caused me a lot of problems, cost me dearly.'

'He did. But it doesn't end there. You see Law was a member of a secret Zulu organisation called Abanzanzi. Abanzanzi stands for everything that *you* are opposed to. And Abanzanzi is still very much alive. I expect more trouble from them.'

Ingram raised his eyebrows reprovingly. 'Can't you deal with these thugs?'

'Oh yes,' Dent said. 'I understand their philosophy. I know where to hit them. Abanzanzi is fundamentally weak in two areas. Firstly leadership. There is one woman sangoma – a witchdoctor in your language – who is holding the entire structure together. Get her and you've cut off their head. The body will flop around and cause a bit of indiscriminate damage. But if there is no rallying point, Abanzanzi will die. Their rallying point, now, that's their second area of weakness. Like Mau Mau, there are certain totems that play an essential cohesive role in their organisation. With the Mau Mau it was the *githathi* stone, and the seven oaths of *batuni* . . . With Abanzanzi it's the Inkatha of Shaka Zulu. It's a python skin, wrapped around some doctored straw. That's all I know about it, other than that Abanzanzi have been searching for it, long and hard. Their very foundation is based around this Inkatha. The search for it has been their inspiration.'

Ingram said, 'And no one knows where it is?'

'Someone knows where it is.'

'Do you know who that someone is?'

'Yes I do. It's Kirsten Law. She's got it.'

'Kirsten!' Ingram shook his head in disbelief. 'Why should she have such a thing?'

'I don't know,' Dent said. 'But she has. She knew exactly where the cave was where it was hidden. The story she gave you about having fallen on the mountain was only half the truth, I'm afraid. She might have fallen but it was while she was making her way to the cave where the Inkatha was hidden.'

'That's incredible.'

'It's the truth. The Inkatha is contained in a big rush basket. I think you've seen that basket.'

'Good God!' Ingram turned to face the windows. The white clad figures of Kirsten and Whitaker were visible; walking towards the courts. Ingram pointed: 'I'm sure she had that thing, that basket, on my helicopter.'

'I know she did.'

'She must have brought it here; to Prospect Hall. I'm going to find out what the hell she's up to.'

'I don't think that would be wise. Look, I know how you feel, Kirsten has lied to you; you're bloody annoyed about it and I don't blame you. I'd feel the same if I was you. But what have you got to gain by confronting her?'

Ingram nodded thoughtfully. Dent went on.

'It's obvious that Kirsten doesn't want you to know anything about it or she would have told you. So what? That suits our purpose perfectly.'

'It would suit me better if I knew where she'd hidden it; and why . . . You don't suppose it has anything to do with her brother do you? She thinks that Monty Law is still alive. Did you know that? She actually wants to go back to the Lebombos to look for him.'

'She's confused,' Dent said. 'She's angry. Maybe she feels guilty. Let her go. What she believes doesn't affect things in any way. As *you* said, what's important now is to discover where Kirsten has hidden the thing. What I want to do, and what I'm sure you want me to do, is to put an end to the Zulu–Pondo faction fighting. To do that I need the Inkatha.'

'It should never have happened in the first place,' Ingram said accusingly. 'But of course you're right. That business hit us hard.'

'I know.'

Ingram glanced towards the tennis players. 'Is there no alternative?' he said. 'Do you have to have this thing?'

'I don't like deception any more than you do.' Dent wondered what more he could say to ease Ingram's conscience. 'It's your money that's involved.'

'I think I know where she would have hidden such a thing,' Ingram said. 'But we'd better be quick.'

'As quick as you like.'

'What exactly are you going to do with the Inkatha when we do find it?'

'For the moment,' Dent said, 'I am going to leave it exactly where it is.'

* * *

It was not a very competitive game of tennis. Whitaker was anxious to show his skill; just as anxious not to make it obvious. He played a basic game from back of the court. He did not serve a single ace. Kirsten too seemed content to place her returns within easy reach; stretching now and then to drive angrily and accurately. Both of them tried just hard enough to maintain the illusion that they were out there with winning on their minds. Both of them saw through the sham. They duelled for a few badly scored, delightfully enjoyable sets. Then made their way to the thatched gazebo. There was iced water with cut lemon floating in it, on a table. Whitaker preferred his water from the tap and detested lemon. He poured, two huge tumblers, to the brim.

'Down the hatch!'

The chairs were punitive wrought-iron things with foam cushions, that were less effective than a layer of whipped cream.

'Aah . . .' He sank back – a man at ease.

Kirsten sat opposite him abstractedly twirling her tennis racquet. Her forehead was halved by a towelling sweatband that smoothed her long black hair and gave her the look of a Cherokee squaw. A very lovely Indian squaw. Her dress was fashionably short, one of those outfits that come with matching knickers, and he could see those knickers – white and tight above her long tanned legs. He couldn't bear to look, and he couldn't bear not to look.

'It was really nice of you to be my guest. How are you feeling now?'

'I'm fine, Kirsten, fine. How are *you* feeling?'

'You're the one that took the bump on the head, remember. I won't ever forget what you did for me.'

'What I tried to do.'

'OK, what you tried to do. It's nice to know that people like you still exist.'

'I wish I could have got a reply to our telex earlier. Who knows, we might have got there in time. We might have been able to do something with the information on tetradotoxin, though God knows, the Yanks for all their technology know little enough themselves. I'm sorry Kirsten, I shouldn't be talking like this. What's happened, has happened.'

'And what *has* happened, Gray?'

'Don't you think we should leave it alone?'

It seemed that the answer was – no. She did not want to leave it alone. She said: 'Tell me what *you* think this is all about . . . come.' She stood. He stood to join her. She took his arm, and, together, they walked. She seemed to have a destination in mind.

'What I think', Gray Whitaker said, 'is that a brilliant and dedicated scientist has tragically died. I honestly believe now that he was on the verge of a medical breakthrough that would have shaken the world. I believe that same world should know of this man's sacrifice, if only that his work may be continued.'

Whitaker was acutely aware that Kirsten had tightened her grip on his arm. They continued their journey. Their direction was westwards, past the stables, towards the sharp red setting sun.

He said, 'I think that it's awful that but for us and a handful of Zulus, no one knows of the greatness of your brother. It was those same Zulus who came for the body of the man they revered. Rightly or wrongly they took him. And, *that* is what I think.'

A row of fire-eyed ponies watched them from atop their stable doors. They walked across the paddock and into the cane lands. Rows of lofty, leafy cane as straight as guardsmen closed ranks around them. Confined now, and hidden, they walked on.

The ground began to incline. Baked hard into it were the memories of rain; the gouging of a tractor tyre, a single footprint. It seemed such a private journey. There was the ground, the flanking hedges of cane, the darkening sky, and the two of them, walking in silence now.

The place was on the top of that hill; a virgin tract of tufty Guinea grass bordered by cane on all sides. There were a few twisted Enkeldoring trees, and some shrub; an acre in all, perhaps a pace or two more. It was hard to judge in the fading light.

Standing there, he could see the old stone building that was Prospect Hall, its windows glinting redly across the distance. There were some trees and some roads – a railway line and a siding. And everywhere else the sugar-cane.

Fields that were cutting and fields that were growing. Highlands, dips and plains all fused into a geometry of greenness that seemed fundamental and complete. As though God had wedged it all together like that. Away to the south-east the sky and the sea met in a wash of total blue.

'Peaceful, isn't it?' Kirsten broke the silence.

'It really is.'

'It's a lovely view, but that's not why I brought you here. Come.' They turned back to the open knoll. 'I want to show you something. Hold my hand.'

There was no pathway. They walked together, the long grass brushing at their calves, crunchy underfoot, and dry smelling. Towards the centre a fallen thorn tree lay, decaying, one branch stretched upwards like a supplicative arm. That was where they stopped.

'Look.'

He could not make out what it was that Kirsten wanted him to see.

'Look around you. You're standing where once a Zulu *indlu* used to stand. And over here,' she guided him a few paces more, 'another hut. See.'

Yes. Now he could see what she meant. They were standing within a circle; an area where the ground beneath was smoother, the grass more profuse, and of a different species. He picked a stem.

'The Zulus call it imBubu grass,' Kirsten said. 'It grows wherever kraal sites used to stand. My workers believe that this is a place where, during the Zulu wars, a chief's son was executed for turning against his father. They won't come near this hilltop. They call it Bulalana – put an end to the heavy heart.'

'That was a hundred years ago,' Whitaker said. 'They still remember that?'

'They're amazing story tellers, and those campfire stories were just as much a part of Monty's childhood as they were of any little Zulu *umntwana*. He spent many a winter's evening, snuggled with the other Zulu kids at the feet of the local storytellers, listening to their tales. I was a girl so I was never allowed to be there. But he would tell me all the stories. We used to climb up here and talk for hours. We felt superior to the Zulus up here. They were scared of the place and we weren't. Monty used to say that he felt as if this place dragged at him, as if lead weights were tied to him, to prevent him from leaving here. But he was never afraid of Bulalana. Never.'

'And you, Kirsten,' Whitaker prompted, 'were you afraid of Bulalana?'

She hesitated. 'This is the saddest place I've ever known. I am dejected to my soul to come here now.'

'Then why *do* you come here now? Haven't you gone through enough trauma without this?'

'I don't know. I felt I wanted to share it with you. You see this is the place where Monty and I first came to terms with death. One day when we were sitting up here, he said to me: "People die you know, just like horses or butterflies – something happens to them and they cross to another place and you never see them again." I'll never forget that. Up to then I had somehow imagined that I was the only person really alive, and that everything else was there when I could see it. When I couldn't see it, if I closed my eyes, or turned my back, or went into another room, then things simply did not exist any more. Then Monty said, "*people die you know*". And those days were over. It was here on Bulalana hill that I first realised that one day I would die; Monty would die. Just like the horses and the butterflies. I came here yesterday, Gray. I sat here, thinking; meditating. When I left this hill I knew that my brother was not dead.'

'*Kirsten!* For God's sake.'

'No. Don't say any more, Gray.' She pressed a finger to his lips. 'I don't expect you to understand. You've been very good to me Gray, and I love you for it. You're a special person. I just wanted to share this place with you. And now it's getting late and we must go.'

'Please Kirsten, leave this business alone,' Whitaker said. 'There is no hope for Monty. Go home, and let time heal your wounds.'

'I'm going back to the Lebombos.' She began to walk away. 'I'm leaving on Monday.'

Graham Whitaker had never felt such a sense of loss.

7

'You can go free.'

September Mabutane opened his eyes, lifted himself stiffly onto his elbows, and looked up at the big police induna who had said those words. The cell light was shining from the wall behind, expanding the man's silhouette to nightmare proportions, but this was no dream.

'Here are your clothes.'

Yes, they were his clothes. The trousers and shirt that had been stripped from him the day they had brought him to that dreadful place and locked him in.

'Thank you.'

Before he dressed he folded his blanket, squared it neatly, and placed it in the corner of the cell.

'Thank you,' he said again. That time in acknowledgement for the blanket that the police induna had provided for him. And the food and water too, though he had taken very little of that. The trousers hung on him as though they belonged to another man, a bigger man. He pulled the belt in tight.

'Your money and your sheath knife.'

The policeman tipped out a little canvas bag.

'Your cigarettes, your snuff box . . .'

One by one he handed the items over until the bag was empty.

'Is that everything, Mabutane?'

It was all that Dent could give him. Some things were lost forever.

'Yes,' Mabutane said. 'It is everything.'

The police captain walked with him out of the cell and down the passage way. He had more he wanted to say.

'Abanzanzi is finished, wiped out. There was a big fight in the hills at Mawamabi and Abanzanzi was beaten. Your people will tell you all about it. That's why I'm letting you free. There is no need to punish you any longer. Those who needed to be stood on have been stood on. Yes, and now I hear that I am being blamed by your people for these deaths. But what could I do? I am a policeman. It was my job to try to stop that fight, and I did try. I had to shoot to stop them fighting. But can a man be blamed for doing his duty?'

They entered the Charge Office. Dent steered Mabutane's arm, still talking. 'You remember Mancoba, don't you? He died in that fight. A lot of people died, mostly Abanzanzi warriors.'

Outside the police station it was dark. Faintly in the moonglow Mabutane could see the mesh and barbed-wire perimeter fence. A dog appeared out of the shadows and trotted next to him, sniffing suspiciously at his ankles. Dent walked with him to the gate. There Dent said:

'Even Mvulaba died.'

September Mabutane faltered at the news. He could not believe all this. But worse was to come.

'But Mvulaba betrayed Abanzanzi you know. He was entrusted with the job of finding the Inkatha of Shaka Zulu; of bringing it back to your people. Did you know that, Mabutane? I know that because he wrote down everything he did, and everything he was going to do, in a diary. Yes, and I have got the diary. I know all about him now. He found the Inkatha, but instead of returning it to Abanzanzi, he had it taken to a place where Abanzanzi would *never* find it. A place far away from here. But I found that place. I can get the Inkatha any time I want it.'

They reached the gate. There was no sentry that Mabutane could see. Dent and his dog stopped there.

'Well, good luck, Mabutane. I don't hold anything against you. I told Warden Reynolds I was releasing you. Your job is waiting for you. Go back to your kraal in the valley, your wives have been crying for you there. Be a man to them.'

Could he ever be a man again? He would go back to his home in the valley – to his wives. But there was no heat in him.

Dent spoke on, 'Abanzanzi is finished but some of their ideals were good ideals. For instance, I also believe that the Inkatha should be returned to the Zulu people. Perhaps you are the man for that job Mabutane. It would make you a man of importance, a big man. *That* would put things right for you with the spirits.'

Dent patted him on the back as he would have his dog. It was more than Mabutane could stand. He brushed the ingratiating hand from his shoulder.

'What do you want from me, uDende? That I should say *thank you, inkosi*? You are a great *induna*? You'll never hear such words from me. In the time that you have kept me here I've observed your ways, uDende. I've seen how capable you are of blending lies and truth, like mud and water, until they seem inseparable.'

'Inseparable?' Dent laughed. 'How do you think I know about Mvulaba – the eyes of Abanzanzi? He's dead, Mabutane. Well, I tried to help you.'

'I was a fool to think that you were a man of destiny, uDende; a big man. I'll suffer for that mistake, but I won't repeat it. Please don't pretend that you tried to help me, in any way, at any time.'

'You'll see,' Dent said. 'You'll see.'

Mabutane turned away and walked into the darkness. When he was sure he was out of sight he began to open his stride. He knew exactly what he had to do. He had to make a sacrifice, a big sacrifice. Sontela, the black ox with the twisted horn; nothing less would do. Surely the spirits would look favourably on such an offering. And when they had licked their share and were well inclined to listen, he would explain to them all that he had done. But more importantly, he would beg their blessing for all he had still to do. He would find Uhlanga the sangoma. He would confess to her, and tell her all he knew. uDende was mad if he thought one lost battle meant the end of Abanzanzi.

September Mabutane began to run; to stretch his limbs; to feel the heat rise up in him once more. And he began to think of home. Five thatched huts and a wattled wooden cattle kraal within the sound of the Suthu River. Twelve fat cattle and two fat wives. Four girl children who would one day bring in a fine *lobola* – bride price. No one could call him a poor man.

He had been away a long time from his women. That was bad. But now that was over. His wives, Lulele and Vuloyi would be moist with longing for him. And he would be a man to them.

With that delicious thought in mind Mabutane arrived at the path that skirted his mealie patch and led down to the river. There were weeds to be seen, but nothing that a scolded wife would not cope with in a single morning.

But before wives, before anything, he had to bathe away the sour clinging smell of prison from his skin. He would have to be very wary though. He was totally vulnerable: he had as yet not made contact with his ancestors. He had no protection from the sorcerers who spent their time in wait for such as he. They would be lying coolly in the river in the form of crocodiles. That was how clever those *umthakathi* were.

The only crocodile to be seen was a small inGwenya, dozing, mouth wide, on the opposite bank. Still he took no chances – he scanned around as he sank down in the shallow brown water, looking for ripples or bubbles, or any other warning sign. He rubbed himself with river grit then spilled off. When he emerged he was smelling of water – as a man should smell. He felt his vulnerability however, felt it acutely. It was as though a thousand spiteful eyes were watching him at his toilet. They followed him all along the pathway to his kraal.

The kraal of September Mabutane was a blessed kraal. It lay downstream from the Suthu dam and would thus be unaffected by the waters once they rose. His huts were hard against the game-proof fence of the western boundary of the Ndumu Game Reserve. He had water and he had grazing. He had employment that did not admit him to a life of jack-hammers, stoop and sweat at the dam site or in the gold mines of Johannesburg, a thousand miles from there. It was a kraal where there had never been a shortage of meat or *amasi*-milk – or until recently, laughter.

The coming home of September Mabutane should have brought the return of that precious sound. Yet he was not even smiling as he smelt the animal goodness of his herd, listened to the drop of early morning dung and the cackle of hens.

He would have to be quick to make his sacrifice. There was a heaviness all around. He could feel it. Even his dog could sense it. He stood guarded and distant, scare-tailed and yapping, as if his master was some creeping thief. Vuloyi his left-hand wife responded to the noise.

Rubbing the night from her eyes she pulled back the door to her hut. She smiled delightedly to find him there.

'Father of my daughter,' she greeted him properly. She was a handsome woman with hips and breasts that were bursting with love. Her smile, her song, made it a brighter place. 'We were lesser, we had tears. Now the great bull of the herd has come – we rejoice . . . we . . .'

'Yes, yes,' Mabutane cut her short – on any other morning but that. 'Get back inside, Vuloyi, and listen to me from behind the closed door.'

The door crashed shut.

'Is Lulele with you?'

Lulele answered that she was indeed there. 'I am here with Vuloyi, husband of mine for whom I long.'

'Stay inside, both of you,' Mabutane warned. 'Do not so much as peep. Strengthen yourself with the *umkhondo* leaves, and do not stir until I call to you again. I can smell the pollution of sorcerers. The air is heavy with it. I must make things right before I see you again.'

It was then that Mabutane heard the drone of an approaching vehicle. He listened for a while nodding his head at the familiarity of it. He knew the pattern of that sound down to the last gear change. It had to be the Land Rover of Warden Robert 'Raba' Reynolds. With 'Raba' himself driving as slowly and methodically as ever.

'Raba' was Reynolds' Zulu name. An extremely rude name for an extremely good man. Then, the Zulus were not known for reverence when it came to naming the white people in their lives. The better the person, sometimes, the worse the name. 'Raba' Reynolds was adored by the people who secretly used that name. To his face however they called him Umnumzane – the headman. It *was* Reynolds. He drove up to the kraal and waved.

'*Saubona* September. It's good to see you. I came to tell you that the animals at Ndumu signed a petition for your release from the prison. I did not want you back, but what could I do? The rhinos are sulking, the crocodiles refuse to come up for the tourists. You better hop in and come back with me to save the place.'

'Umnumzane, I can't.'

'Can't?' Reynolds frowned.

'Umnumzane, there are big things I must do.'

Reynolds switched off the engine; looked around. He took in for the first time the frightened look on the face of Mabutane; the absence of Lulele and Vuloyi. Mabutane's four pretty daughters who normally mobbed him when he visited, were skulking behind the cattle kraal.

'Something *is* wrong. Where does this heaviness come from, September?'

That was a question Mabutane was not prepared to answer. What he said was: 'I must make a big sacrifice.'

'I often helped your father Ndawonye do such things when he was alive. He will remember me fondly,' Reynolds said. 'I will drive down to the river and wait for you. I've got troubles at the reserve, September. I need every man I've got on the job.'

So Mabutane took his ancestral assegai and killed the big black ox with the twisted horn. He strapped its horns with thong to a pole in the wall of the cattle kraal. And when the beast was fast, he began to *gya*, to dance and stab at the imaginary enemies – now in front, now behind – he dispersed with them. And when that was done he turned and stabbed his sacrifice to the heart. And the ox bellowed loudly, which was good, and he worked the wound and it bellowed louder – the spirits speaking their acceptance. And he spoke to them in turn. To his father he said:

'Father who has crossed over and resides below . . .
You are mighty . . . Your deeds on earth are remembered.
People tremble still at the mention of your name.
The whole nation remembers you.
Whatever you say to me this day
I will do . . . as one day I will
also answer to my sons – your son's sons.
I have done things in my stupidity
for which only you can intercede.
I broke promises that I had sworn, in your name, to keep.
I have offended you and all who reside below.
But it was not with arrogance,
rather with the mind of a child
I am sorry for this Ndawonye
Please do not be harsh . . .
Now, there are things that have been told
to me by the police induna, uDende . . .
There is a way for me to make amends to
those I must serve. Please help me in this task.
Please clear the way . . . I am your son –

*your oldest son. If I am struck down,
and am no more, and that is the way it must be,
then I will accept it . . .
But if that happens who will be left to worship you?
Is there any other of your line who attends to your welfare
with more diligence than I?'*

Mabutane twisted the assegai again but Sontela, the black ox with the twisted horn, had given its last bellow. It was past pain.

*'See, I have given you Sontela
the ox for you to eat,
. . . All I ask is that you lift your
mighty shield. That all my enemies . . .
even the most powerful of umthakathi may fall
back afraid . . . That is all I ask of you.
Would you summons now Hanjwa, your father,
my deeply respected grandfather, so that I
can praise him too . . . so that he too can eat.
For Hanjwa was a warrior . . .'*

As Warden Reynolds had promised, he was waiting at the riverside. September felt exhausted, totally drained. Spiritual contact was a debilitating experience.

He sank down next to the warden, dipped his hands into the water and let the river wash away the blood.

'The heaviness, is it gone?' Reynolds asked.

'It is gone.'

Robert Reynolds spent the rest of that morning assisting his game guard in the restoration of his spiritual well-being. It was time well spent however. By midday, when at last the big steel mesh gates at the western end of the park swung closed behind him, September Mabutane was once more in balance with his world. Ndumu had gained by it.

Warden Robert Reynolds' game park occupied a mere 10,000 hectares of the surface of the continent of Africa. It was long and narrow; its northern boundary was the Suthu River, in the south its game fence ran along the Ingwavuma plains and up into the Lebombos. It had a camp for visitors that consisted of seven huts – twenty-one visitors, that was its capacity. No Kruger or Mala-Mala this. Then neither was its warden provided with the resources that the giants of the business enjoyed. Reynolds' staff consisted of three assistant rangers and thirty-six game guards.

What that meant in geographical terms was that every man had an area of nearly 300 hectares to patrol. In real terms, it meant that the war against poachers was incessant and tough.

It was time for Game Guard Mabutane to render service once again. There were problems in the thickly wooded kuMahemane area in the centre of the reserve.

'Poachers,' Reynolds said. 'A whole gang of them. Thonga tribesmen from Mozambique, I think. But they aren't operating like your everyday baRonga fence-cutter.'

Reynolds took on a shockingly rutted section of tract – all grunt and bicep against a flailing steering wheel. There was no breath for conversation until the road improved.

'These bastards aren't working the fringes of the park like they usually do. They've come right into Ndumu, right into the middle of the Ogonyweni bush. I've seen their spoor.'

'Have you found snares?' Mabutane asked. 'Have they dogs with them?'

'That's the strange part about it. All I've found is spoor, barefoot man spoor. And that was quite by accident. There was an important white man here last week who wanted to see the old burial sites at Ogonyweni. You know the ones? It took us two hours to locate the graves. And it was while I was walking in that area that I found the man tracks. There were three separate sets of spoor. All barefoot; all headed in approximately the same direction.'

Ahead lay the thatched and timber homesteads of the game guards. Matendini – the place at the bottom. It was sited on the verge of the seasonal flood plains. They drew up there.

'Get your rifle,' Reynolds instructed. 'And change into uniform.'

Standard issue for game guards on the volatile Mozambique border was the FN 7.62 assault rifle. His weapon lay on his bed – cleaned and oiled. He changed from his civilian clothes into khaki shirt and shorts; high brown combat boots, which someone else had taken a brush to that very day, and a weathered felt hat. The old brass badge of the Natal Parks Board – crown and wildebeest – was smooth polished, gleaming from two generations of

Mabutane pride.

The warden inspected him; back and front; hat to heel to handcuffs. There was no fault to be found. He issued ammunition. 'You've got good friends I see.'

'Indeed, Umnumzane. They looked after my things.'

'Have you had anything to eat or drink?'

'No, Umnumzane.'

'Sort yourself out then. There's food in the cookhouse. Then let's go.'

The road to Ogonyweni skirted what, in a wet summer, would have been the high water mark of the Suthu River floor plain. Now it was a sun-wrinkled, hard-baked pan; the grasses yellow; the inyala and impala herds sunk-eyed and slow on their legs.

'Here.' Reynolds switched the motor off. 'It was near here that I found spoor.' He turned off the track and coasted into the shade of a spreading umKhulu mahogany. He checked his rifle and slung it. 'I'll take you too to the spoor.'

The forest was thick there, leafy with umPhofu, wild coffee shrub and green-barked unHlofunga trees. And muddling everything, tangling everything, ropes of hairy umBoya creeper. There were not three straight paces to be taken in that part of the forest.

Reynolds found the trail. Without a wasted step he took them to the place. 'There.'

He was clever for a white man this Reynolds. 'I see it, Umnumzane.'

Pressed fresh into the dust and fallen leaves, a trail of barefoot prints. Unhurried, unburdened prints, leading towards the distant Suthu River. These men were far from the grounds preferred by the poaching gangs from Mozambique. And, were they baRonga, heading home, they would have been heavy with the weight of carcasses.

'I don't have to show you where I found the other spoor,' Reynolds said. 'You know this forest better than anyone.'

'*Yebo*. I will find them.'

'I want these men brought in, Mabutane.'

'*Yebo*, Umnumzane.'

'Do you need help?'

'No, Umnumzane.'

'Good. I'll pick you up at the old umKhulu tree.'

Reynolds turned away then. For a white man he walked very softly. Soon the only sounds to be heard were the scree of the cicadas, and the dreary toot-oot-to-to-to complaint of the ever moping *isibhela* dove.

Mabutane sat there for a while, touched by the sounds of freedom; wondering what cleverness it was that had caused these men to change their old, and usually successful tactics. He thought he knew every poacher in the Lebombo hills, where they came from, and all of their tricks. Apparently not.

He would start his patrol by the river, for if these men were still in Ndumu, and if they were paddling their own dugout, then that craft would certainly still be hidden somewhere amongst the reeds on the Ndumu bank of the Suthu. Trodden mud at a river's edge could not keep a secret.

Hau! But they *had* been clever. Where the rocks were big and smooth, and gathered in the shallows like fat black hippos, they had landed. A rock won't show a footprint, but it will show a smudge of mud. They had hauled their dugout ashore there and hidden it somewhere in the long river reeds.

It was a place of danger. The reeds were a maze of crocodile tunnels, and sudden sandy beachlets. But Mabutane moved slowly, watching, listening for the nesting female who would unhesitatingly attack. The crocs were in the water. What was on the bank was an old, plank, fisherman's dinghy. And something had been unloaded from that dinghy – something that had left marks, square and heavy on the river sand – some crates perhaps, longer than they were wide.

Three men had unloaded that dinghy; had then sat on the bank and smoked cigarettes. Then, had done the strangest thing, they had all removed their footwear – six boots of almost identical appearance were tied by their laces to a branch of a young umVubu tree. The barefoot spoor did not belong to poachers. Poachers did not come into Ndumu bearing crates.

Game Guard Mabutane followed the tracks through the reeds to a point where they joined a well-worn game trail. There they had been trodden under by inyala and other buck. Clever, but not as clever as the man who was tracking them.

They had made several journeys from the dinghy into Ogonyweni, and each time their load had differed. Mabutane trod carefully, leaving the spoor undisturbed, keeping just off the game trail, he followed.

Where the forest opened into the wooded grasslands, there he shared the cover with the sleepy rhinos. He moved so close to them he could have tossed his hat onto their horns. Still they did not sense his presence. Neither did the men.

Mabutane heard them. A distant thump-thump sound; someone cutting wood . . . or someone digging. Yes, that was it, someone digging into hard dry ground near the Mahemane tourist road. It was not long before he could hear the murmur of human voices. He lowered himself to the ground.

Now he moved on them, sliding like a mamba, and like the mamba he could feel through his belly the tremor of the ground as the spade bit in. A car rumbled past, all pop music and chatter – tourists. They would not see much game that way. Still they served a purpose: the spade man doubled his efforts for a while. Then the covering sound faded and he returned to his steady soft rhythm. He was singing quietly in tempo with the falling blade.

'Ba ni shani – *sa!*

Ba ka hi hlu – *pha!*

Ba nwa ma kho – *fi!*

Ba nga hi nyi – *ki!*'

The words were sad – the song of a Djonga mine boy, who craved a little coffee and a little kindness, and got neither from the white boss. Mabutane slid yet closer.

There were two of them. The spade man, sweating, shirtless, waist-deep in the hole he was excavating. His comrade seated in the shade of a leaning umKhamba tree, was smoking a cigarette rolled from newspaper. The man's seat was interesting; an olive painted, rope handled, wooden case. Stencilled in yellow lettering along one side was the message:

МАГНИТНАЯ МИНА ВЕЩЕСТВО

LIMPET MINES. EXPLOSIVE. Words that were meaningless to Mabutane. What meant more to him were the rifles that they had propped against the spiny umKhamba tree. He knew exactly what they were. They were Russian-made Kalashnikovs – AKMs. Reynolds had pinned to the cookhouse door a photograph of just such a weapon. The bearers of such rifles, he had warned all the game guards, are dangerous men – killers – if you see them, shoot them, and shoot to kill.

They did not look dangerous these two. The digger, the singer of the Djonga lament, had a pleasant babyish face and the voice of innocence. His companion was some years older, bearded, but he did not look fierce either. Mabutane could not recall having seen either of these men before.

'Is it finished? Is it deep enough?'

The Djonga added this new verse to his song.

The bearded one stood up, stretched what must have been an aching back, and ambled from the shade.

'A bit more I think.' He jumped into the hole, gauged it critically. 'Yes, a bit more. Here, Nukwe, give me the spade.'

Mabutane eased his rifle forward, slowly propped himself onto his elbows. They were the easiest of targets those two. Nukwe's young sweaty face sat plumply in his back sight. Both men were standing in the hole, both rifles were well out of reach against the tree. There was just one problem – where was killer number three?

Game Guard Mabutane watched the two men complete the digging; watched them lift five olive green cases, (they were heavy those cases), and lower them carefully into the hole . . . Still the third man was nowhere to be seen.

They filled in the hole and tramped it down, mindful to match the topsoil and replant the dry veld grass. To complete the camouflage, Nukwe dragged a fallen thorn branch into place. What cleverness. The remnant subsoil they scattered at the entrance of a nearby ant bear burrow. It was done.

Another car droned past. The tourist roads of Ndumu were quiet at that time of day. The visitors were resting on their deck chairs back at the rest camp – limp with beer and braised meat; sweating in the heat. *ukuSiesta* was a custom the white man followed diligently. Very wise.

The two men made little effort to hide, merely stooping slightly at the height of the sound. Then they returned to the shade and rolled cigarettes. They shared a tin of pilchards; opening it with a bayonet and scooping out the contents with their fingers. And all the time they kept glancing around as though expecting someone to arrive.

September lay where he was. There was no point in moving. His position was perfect. They were obviously waiting for the arrival of the owner of the third pair of boots. And when he did come, he, September Mabutane, would stand up and arrest them all. In the meantime, to amuse him, an active little impi of army ants was on parade. They emerged from a hole, an arm's reach from where he lay, marched in one tight short column along the ground, then down another hole not far away. Only to re-emerge and countermarch to their first home. What discipline. They kept at it for ages, up and down, up and down. At whose command? That drillmaster had no pity.

The two men at the tree could have learnt much from those little black insects – they were becoming impatient. They argued:

'It's better that we go now.'

'No.'

'I'll go and see if he's at the river then.'

'No. He said he'd come back here.'

'Maybe he can't find us.'

'That's stupid.'

It really was stupid. It was a simple place to find. Anyway, the river was an hour's walk from there: two hours there and back, and already the shadows were lengthening.

'We stay here.'

The bearded one had more sense.

'I'm thirsty,' Nukwe whined. 'I did all the digging.'

'Shut up.'

The bearded man had heard something. He cocked his head – tight-faced with concentration. The squeal of brakes – not an unusual sound in a game reserve. Just a tourist who had seen a sudden buck. Then came a sound that was totally foreign to Ndumu. They did not hear it, Mabutane did: the metal on metal clatter of a skating pistol slide. Mabutane stiffened.

'Hello, September.'

The hardness of a pistol barrel in his neck – but no explosion, no impact in his spine.

'Relax, Mabutane. I wouldn't shoot an old friend in the back. No don't turn around, not with that rifle in your hands. I trust you, but not that much.'

The man knew him, and he knew that mocking voice . . . from where?

'Gebeza . . . Peter Gebeza?'

'Eh! What a memory! What a man!' Gebeza called to his companions. 'Over here. Look what I found.'

Nukwe and the bearded man came at a run.

'He's been watching you two baboons dig for the last hour and you didn't even know it. That's what I call good tracking.'

'A game guard!'

'Yes,' Gebeza mocked. 'So it is.'

'Fuck you, white man's stooge,' Beardface shoved himself close and spat the English hate words on his tinned pilchards breath: 'Fuck you, white man's stooge. You're going to get it.'

Mabutane had no doubt about that – how he was going to get it was the only question. That would be for Peter Gebeza to decide. He was obviously the leader of these men. It was Nukwe's turn to vilify him:

'White shit!'

He possessed neither the fervour nor the command of English of his comrade. His breath was less offensive too. Gebeza seemed to find all this very amusing.

'Forgive them, Mabutane. You see Comrade Nukwe and Comrade Dlamini don't know you as well as I do. They don't know, for example, that you have just come out of prison. They don't know that you are a member of Abanzanzi, and that you were tortured by the police because of that.'

September Mabutane's jaw slackened in amazement.

'They don't know that you and I, that ANC and Abanzanzi, are blue bucks of one forest. How could they possibly know that?'

Indeed, how could they know that? He, September Mabutane, did not even know that. All he knew was, that as little as five minutes ago, he had thought himself to be firmly in charge of his own destiny. But even then he had been at the mercy of Peter Gebeza, the same Peter Gebeza who had been dismissed as a game guard and sent to prison for poaching, not three years past. And who was it who had been responsible for catching him? Who was it who had testified against him?

'Game Guard September Mabutane. They know nothing about you. But I know everything about you. Don't I, September?

We're old friends; aren't we, September?'

'Yes.' Mabutane shook his head, wondering at all these lies. Where was this trail of honey leading to? At least Nukwe, and the one called Dlamini, seemed happier about his right to survive. Peter Gebeza was speaking for him. And Peter Gebeza was in charge.

'How are your wives September? Vuloyi. Eh! there is a fine woman. And the beautiful Lulele. It's time you planted your seed again there, Mabutane. Four girls is not enough for a bull like you. Eh! What a happy household . . . May it stay that way, Mabutane.'

'Indeed, may it stay that way.'

'I need your help, Mabutane.'

There it was. The reason why he was not lying there feeding the army ants. The threat. Now the demand.

'You *will* help me, Mabutane?'

'Yes. If I can.'

'Oh, you can. Yes, you definitely can. It will be very simple for you to help me. You see, I need to meet with Uhlanga the sangoma. You are one of her councillors. So you will be able to take me to her.'

'Why do you wish to meet her?'

'Eh! Mabutane. I would have thought you might have guessed that. I need to hold a big *indaba* with her. ANC and Abanzanzi must work as one. Our objectives are the same. We are the left and the right arm in the battle. What is the good of the one without the other – the shield without the assegai?'

'Or, the guns without the people.'

'So right, Mabutane. You are as sharp as ever. Yes, you'll do.'

'Uhlanga may not see it your way. She may not even want to meet you.'

'Oh she will, Mabutane. She has just learnt a very important, very hard lesson about modern warfare, about guns and explosives. She'll receive me well. You just get me to her, that is all *you* have to worry about.'

'It will take me time to find her. I have a job to do here at Ndumu. I will only be able to look for her at night.'

'The nights are the best times to find such a person, Mabutane, especially when the moon has turned its face away. I will meet you at your kraal, five nights from tonight. I hope you will have arranged the *indaba* by then.'

'I will try.'

'Of course you will. We are going now, Mabutane. Five nights, remember, and no tricks. Think of your family.'

'What must I tell Warden Reynolds? He saw your spoor.'

Gebeza laughed. 'I'll leave that to you, Mabutane. You always were a good liar.' He turned and walked away.

Mabutane watched the three men until they had disappeared into the thick Ogonyweni bush. He *was* thinking of his family, of Vuloyi and Lulele; of his children that were and his children to be. Let nothing happen to them of his causing. He would die before he brought them harm. And Gebeza and his men were capable of any evil. They smelt of evil those three.

Raba Reynolds was waiting for him at the rendezvous under the big umKhulu tree – smiling.

'Well?'

'They were poachers from Mozambique. I tracked them to the water's edge, but they had already gone. They took some impala, that's all.'

'Well, we tried.'

'*Yebo*, Umnumzane. We tried.'

Peter Gebeza was right: he always had been a good liar.

*   *   *

September Mabutane did not find the sangoma Uhlanga. It was she who sent for him.

A meeting was to be held – an important *indaba*. All senior Abanzanzi were to attend.

Mabutane had seized his chance. He knew of powerful men, he had told the courier; men who had serious matters to discuss with the Abanzanzi leader. Could a meeting be arranged for them?

The answer came on the evening of the fifth of his allotted five nights. 'Yes. Bring them with you, September Mabutane. They must understand that there are things that they will not be allowed to hear. But if these men have something important for the ears of Uhlanga, and if you trust them, bring them tonight.'

What could he do? He brought them; Gebeza, Nukwe and Dlamini.

They gathered, with others, at a place in the Suthu River gorge, upstream from the whiteness of the floodlit wall – so close, you could feel the tremble of the ground as the roaring metal-mouthed machines took it piece by piece.

The courier met them there; then led them through a reedy marsh, and along the river bank. They climbed a massive ridge of water-worn rock. The river sound filled the hollowness of the air there, rushing past blackly somewhere down below.

The place was called Amandlamanzi – mighty water. Mabutane had played there as a child. Not often – only on days of daring. On days when the inner voice had said: are you a man, can you do things a man can do?

Well, now he was a man, and every day he did things a man could do. But there were new doubts to taunt him that night on the way to Amandlamanzi.

Eh! It was black. *Nkata wa hweti* – the moon and its husband star were no one's friends that night. No one excepting those who did business with the darkness.

Uhlanga was waiting for them at a bend in the river where the cliff was hollowed and gaping like the mouth of *imVubu* the hippopotamus. The path dipped downwards to a sandy beach, to be swallowed by the cavern. There were torches burning, and stern faced warriors half hidden behind their big hide shields. No one was talking, no one was moving. A man came and took the ANC men to a place in front. There they sat; Peter Gebeza the only one even trying to look confident. They wore uniforms of faded green. This time they wore their boots, but they had not brought their guns; they had had the sense to leave their rifles elsewhere.

Uhlanga the diviner, the high priestess of Abanzanzi sat upon a raised, mat-strewn rock. Her neophytes to her left. Her head held low, her brows severe. She was the child of the thunder. A man would need to talk with a prudent tongue that night.

Mabamba, the most senior induna, was the first to speak. Uhlanga nodded to him. He stood, fierce in his leopard tail *uMutsha*. He raised his spear. He called:

'Who are we?'

'*Abanzanzi! Abanzanzi! Abanzanzi!*'

'Where do we come from?'

'From the place where amathongo dwell!'
'Where is it that we go?'
'Upwards on the river of time.'
'Who leads us there?'
'The sangoma with the eyes of rain.'
'Where is she?'
'There is she! There is she! There is she!'

Mabamba raised his hand – a demand for silence. They gave him silence. But for the whisper of the Sutho waters, there was no sound at all.

Uhlanga lifted her head; looked slowly up as though, for the first time, aware of those assembled there. How sad her words:

'Are there tears enough in this world to wash away the sadness from my heart? So many dead, *so* many dead. They came and took us in the night. Like jackals they bit the flesh and ran. But here we are. We are scarred. The flesh was torn from us. But are we less because of it? No! We are wiser. We know the enemy. We know his lair. We hunt it. We stab it. Yes!'

'Siya Vuma! Siya Vuma!' They roared out their agreement. This was what they wanted to hear. This was what they wanted to shout. *'Siya Zabalaza!'* Let them come! Let them come! We stand strong! They filled the cavern with their sound.

Once more Mabamba's governing hand – once more silence. Uhlanga went on:

'There are those with us tonight who have come from a distance so that we should hear what they have to say. It is right therefore that we hear them.'

September Mabutane, from his position, had a clear view of Peter Gebeza. The man's tongue was darting like a lizard's to moisten his nervous lips. Not the same Gebeza who had strutted back into his life five days ago. Mabutane enjoyed watching the ANC man's discomfort.

'It's true. I have come from far, and, it is just as true that I am your neighbour. Many of you know me here.'

He told them he had been to kwaRashiya – the land of the Russian people. He had learned many things there. Things about war. About guns and explosives. He spoke softly at first; tremulously. But as he continued, so the swagger returned. He sensed their mood, and he tried to tap into it.

'I don't have to tell you of the power of such things. You yourselves have felt it in your fight at Mawamabi hill. What I have to say to you is that you too can have such power. Yes, guns and ammunition, for *you*. I can arrange this. Think of it. Think how this hyena, this policeman uDende, could then be beaten. *Hau*! What a day that would be. uDende, who comes at night to burn and shoot and who is protected by the white man's law; who is, himself, the upholder of this law, is he not the enemy of both African National Congress and Abanzanzi? Does brother stand back when brother is attacked? No, he comes forward to help. Just as I have come to you, my brothers.'

Rousing words. Too rousing it seemed. Uhlanga spoke into the ear of the induna Mabamba. Mabamba spoke into the ear of Gebeza, and Gebeza sat down without saying another word. He looked stung, and angry.

'Gebeza,' Uhlanga said. 'Do you think we Abanzanzi are like those who stand staring viciously at the mist? Do you think that we are unable to recognise our enemies? Do you think that oratory will make you allies here? Now, tell me about these wonderful guns of yours. Tell me, in what way will these weapons benefit my people?'

Peter Gebeza conferred quickly with the bearded one, the one called Dlamini. When he spoke again his voice was strained:

'They have guns, you must have guns. Surely you saw that at Mawamabi hill?'

'You did not answer my question,' Uhlanga said. 'How will this benefit my people?'

'How?' Gebeza spread his hands – frustrated. 'You want power, guns are therefore essential.'

'So where is all the power of the ANC? You have been fighting with guns and bombs for more than twenty years. Yet you still have to sneak across the border at night into your own country. Do you call that power?'

'We are fighting,' Gebeza said. 'At least we are fighting.'

'But you are fighting wrongly. Bring your guns, and the white man will bring a hundred to your every one. What does that gain our people? And supposing we accepted these weapons of yours. At whose command would Abanzanzi march? We would be nothing more than the soldiers of kwaRashiya; doing what those from another land told us to do. This is not the way of the Zulus.'

'You will never beat the white man your way, Uhlanga.'

Strong words; Gebeza whatever his faults, was no coward. He went on:

'You and those before you have been fighting with nothing but a stick in your hands for over two hundred years. And what has *that* gained our people? The Boers have carved up the country and taken the best for themselves. They pay us nothing. They give us less. They humiliate us at every step. We bleed. Yes, but we fight! Let them bring a hundred guns to our one – we will still fight.'

'So you will fight,' Uhlanga shook her head at the insanity of it. 'And you will lose your fight. You will learn by a hot wind, Gebeza, that your way is a foreign way. It is not guns that will win this country back.'

'What is it then?'

'It is the spirit of the nation. There is no other way to greatness. There is no other way for the Zulu. And the Zulu it is, who will lead this country and *all* its tribes.'

'Show me this spirit. Where is this spirit? The Boers have locked it in their prisons. That is what happened to the spirit of the nation.'

'You are quite wrong,' Uhlanga smiled. 'You are talking of *this* man and *that* man. I am talking of a *nation*. You are talking about men who now hold ideals that are foreign to our people. These are not leaders, nor do they deserve to be followed. You are talking about a single drop of dew. I am talking about a mighty river. Where is this prison that can hold my river?'

'Words!'

'Yes, but the truth. The Zulus will get their leader when the time is right. The *amathongo* spirits have promised this.'

'And while you wait Uhlanga – while you talk and throw your bones and invoke the ancestor spirits; while you do these things, the white man continues to steal what is yours. Look around you, Uhlanga. In the shadow of your own kraal they are building a monster dam. For who? For the Thonga-Zulu people who rightfully own this water? I don't think so. *No!* The profit will end up in the pockets of the government gangsters of Pretoria, Ulundi and Manzini. What are you doing about *that* Uhlanga?'

'Things are happening here. Things that your mind has lost the ability to grasp, Peter Gebeza from kwaRashiya. Stop playing at being a Russian, Peter Gebeza. Stop for a moment and see what is happening here. Be an African – be a Zulu. Don't be ashamed of what is yours. These things are our greatness, Peter Gebeza. Must we become little clay model Russians, or Americans? What is there to be gained by that? Listen to me, Peter Gebeza. Eternity is an ever turning circle. Our place in time has come again. The custodians have told us that. Be the Zulu that you are or go away to what you are not. It doesn't matter to us. We are strong – *we* are Zulu.'

'You are a thousand years behind the times, Uhlanga. Let us see how well your magic works against a million tons of concrete. But ANC won't be waiting for you, Uhlanga. We are men of action. We have things to do here in Ingwavuma, and in the Lebombo mountains.'

'Have you said all you came to say Peter Gebeza?'

'Yes.'

'We have heard you then. Now go. There is nothing here for you or those you serve.'

They left. But not through a friendly gate. Peter Gebeza's eyes ranged hard and hostile over those seated in the light of the tallow torches. September Mabutane took the stare and returned it – threat for threat. *He* was part of Uhlanga's mighty river. Let Gebeza not forget it.

There was tension in the grotto for some time after the ANC men had gone. There were those who looked at September Mabutane with blame in their eyes. Uhlanga and her indunas conversed; bent sombrely together. Of the others, those seated left and right of Mabutane seemed disinclined to speak. Perhaps they realised it was not the time for old friends and idle memories. Perhaps they knew of the grave reason for this *indaba*. Mabamba held up his arms for absolute silence. Uhlanga began to speak again.

'They think *we* are clinging to the old dreams. My country is screaming in its pain. My country cries out for a healer – the spirits say that such a one will come soon. I hear you thinking – how soon? How long must we endure the nose ring of the Whites? I hear you say – "Mother it is hard – the corn is being carried off by the wind." To those I say – be patient a while longer. Okhethiwe!

He is coming.'

There was a murmur of excitement that Mabamba stilled once more.

'Even the fowls who scratch on the floor know that there can be only one leader – the buck in the forest know it. It is a law of nature. Only it seems the white man does not know it. He sits with a dozen chiefs in a single *indlu*, all of them enemies, and expects to have government. This is not our way. An enemy is an enemy to the death. We will not be trapped into such an arrangement. Our leader is coming.

'We have enemies, yes, powerful enemies. We have seen how they attack us and destroy our places with fire and bombs. But don't they know that we are like the moon in the sky – to be killed by the sun only to rise again and again. You councillors and elders of Abanzanzi, don't you know this?'

'*Siya Vuma!*' The cave rumbled with the sound of agreement. Uhlanga nodded.

'We died at kwaIsingogo to rise again in the Swazi valley of Manshanja. That is where the warriors now sharpen their spears. They cannot kill us.'

'*Manshanja*' – September Mabutane knew that valley well. It lay in the remote Lubemba hills; the northmost hills of the Lebombos. North even of the Swazi border.

'uDende,' Uhlanga went on. 'That hyena that bites the sleeping face. He will never find that place. He will never do again what he did at kwaIsingogo. We bled at kwaIsingogo – precious blood. No blood that was shed there was more precious than that of Mvulaba. Mvulaba of the eyes. Mvulaba who came back in the spirit to disclose the hiding place of the Inkatha of the Kings of Zulu. But did they think they could kill such a spirit?'

Now a man was stepping from the concealment of the shadows. A man whose body was a twisted horrid mass of livid scarring – on one side. On the other side . . . '*Mvulaba!*'

How could they help but shout the name? What joy Mabutane felt, yet what remorse. He, September Mabutane, was he the man who had caused this terrible thing to happen? What a fool he had been. He had broken his vow of secrecy; he had trusted uDende, and look at the result. uDende had done this. uDende was a thief: he had stolen the Inkatha of Shaka Zulu. uDende was a murderer:

he had killed those Abanzanzi and done this to Mvulaba. uDende, conceived of the semen of a snake . . .

'A curse on those who did this terrible thing,' Uhlanga cried out. 'A curse on *all* of them – their guns and their concrete and their hearts. *A curse!*'

* * *

As certain to Kirsten Law as her sense of sight or taste, was her sense of intuition. Intuitively, at that moment, she knew that she was being watched. Since her return to the Lebombos this awareness had occurred to her on several occasions. But never had she felt the feather touch gaze of the watcher in the night as acutely as she felt it then.

She stood up from her seat on the verandah of the cottage, allowing the slanting moonlight to catch her face. She peered this way and that into the darkness. Whoever was there, she wanted him to know that she was aware, and not afraid. She was in consent.

So compelling was the presence of the watcher that she wanted to call into the darkness. But what words would she call? Here I am? Please come to me? *Please* take me to my brother?

She said nothing. She stood there in the grey-white moonlight and waited. And as it had happened in the past, so the contact waned, then ceased.

'Please . . .' she said. But that was all she said. The word had no carry, and no effect. She too turned away.

Inside the cottage few lights were burning. Kirsten walked from the lounge to the kitchen and stooped at the refrigerator. As she opened the door the motor switched on with a whirr. The sound startled her for a moment. It was so, so quiet in the cottage. She poured herself some milk. She thought about eating and rejected the idea. Then, as she stood in the light of the refrigerator, she sensed the gaze of the watcher once again. The kitchen windows were open, the curtains undrawn. The gentlest of night breezes caressed the chintzy fabric, then was gone. And at that moment Kirsten wondered if her instinct had not become a liar to her; a liar in the service of her cause. What *had* she but the flimsiest of evidence to subsidise her hope? Was she then calling in the phantoms to see her through?

'It can't be.' In the darkness the whisper sounded very loud. 'It can't be.'

Despite those words the doubts remained.

She had intended to return to the verandah; to enjoy the evening coolness a while longer. But now she wanted no further association with the night. She went to the bedroom and snatched the curtains there tightly shut. To hell with the heat. She stripped and lay upon the bed and turned her mind to places beyond the Lebombos. She thought about her life.

She thought about the man who had been part of that life since college days. Mark Ingram, a person she never had wanted to hurt and constantly seemed to do so. Mark, who wanted children by her, and she couldn't face the commitment. Dear Mark . . . God, in all the years she had known him those two words had qualified the level of her endearment . . . *Dear Mark*. Never darling, or my dearest, or any cute pet name, just *Dear Mark*. Like the first two words on a letter to anyone. And he had never demanded more.

Dear Mark, I don't know how to break this to you, but I honestly believe that we have grown apart.

No. She did not honestly believe that. What she honestly believed was that a life of children and liftclubs and five-thirty cocktails would dry her to the marrow. And what of sex?

The helicopter was Mark Ingram's aphrodisiac. The more hectic the flight, the more hectic was his need. It energised him, that machine. He'd hangar it and burst from it like a supercharged thing, with but a single destination on his mind – the bedroom. But once there, the most amazing of transformations could overtake him. He could become the college boy once again; muttering his love needs like a virgin. Fumbling like a teenager. She didn't mind. In fact she liked to dominate. But sex in whatever form that it came in was not enough. It did not compensate. When the bedroom games were over, there was very little left. And what *was* left was being eroded still further by his undying antagonism towards her brother. How could Mark Ingram hate so fervently a man whom he believed to be dead?

And that brought Kirsten back to the subject that she was so studiously avoiding. She tried to go to sleep then, but Monty would not have it so. The kindness of sleep would not be hers for many hours yet.

8

By the end of April the rains still had not come. The nights were becoming colder but the days were as hot as ever. Those tribesmen who were still looking to the sky, were looking with dull, hate-filled eyes. Even amongst the fools, there was no hope left. They turned their cattle loose on the shrivel-stalked *amaBele* fields, and sweated. They carried their stick-legged children to the clinics, and sweated, and hungered and shivered through the lengthening nights. And who was to blame for this most terrible of catastrophes?

At the dam, that month, the volume of concrete poured shot to an all time high – 56,000 cubic metres. They celebrated: bonuses and crates of Antinor wine for the Italian concrete technicians. Davis set a new monthly target – 58,000 cubic metres of concrete.

Morale was high, production levels excellent. The minimum crest elevation level required for the next rainy season was reached and passed, months ahead of schedule. Diversion channels, built to carry the flood waters that had never come, were now holding back progress. The decision was taken to build across them. There was no chance of heavy rain in May.

The clients were happy. The engineers were confident. The artisans were flush, and the wall grew apace. 50 metres thick at its foundation, they raised it and formed it. Five metres at a time – six weeks between lifts.

They could not work any faster. The concrete had to cure and it had to cure for a certain time at a certain temperature. That concrete held an aggregate, fifteen centimetres in diameter – stone chips the size of cannon balls in its mix. In the massive way they were working, massive problems presented. The hardening concrete had to be kept refrigerated or its temperature would rise above 50 degrees centigrade – a thousand ton block would crack like porcelain. The colder early winter nights were a bonus, but they were not enough.

The colossal refrigeration plants were pumping coolth, at a measured rate of 200 tons of ice per hour – their maximum – into the wall.

Quarrying and stone crushing continued at maximum production. The batch plants were unable to produce a single cubic metre of concrete more than they were.

So the wall rose up – five metres every six weeks. They kept up that production ratio until the end of August.

Progress underground, at 70 metres a month, was equally good. The machine hall cavern had been completely excavated. Over 97,000 cubic metres of solid rock had been removed to create a place for the giant turbine generators that were to come. They had completed the major penstock tunnels that would feed in water to the turbines. Tunnels so big that fifteen-ton face loaders could turn there in their own tracks. Here too they too were ahead of schedule, so more bonuses, this time with beer and *amasi* for the Pondos. It was South Africans who were doing all the excavating. Theirs was not an envied task. There were unique problems to be faced underground.

The Suthu River gorge, in fact the entire Lebombo range, was made up of volcanic rock, dacite being the main constituent. Dacite is strong and hard, but brittle too. In mass formations it is not too difficult to work with. It is when dykes are encountered of palaeolithic molten magma, breccia, bad things happen.

Breccia is deformable and weak, like a rotten cavity in a tooth. If you don't clean it out and fill it up, the surrounding material will crumble.

Unlike a rotten tooth you don't always know that you have got it – no warning twinge. It may lie treacherously behind a few centimetres of the most solid looking dacite – waiting to spew out by the mega-ton.

So far they had been lucky; one mud rush had occurred during a shift change. It had carried a loaded dump truck half a hundred metres down that tunnel. There had been a lot of running, a lot of yelling. But when they had counted heads, they had all been there.

A bulkhead had been built. Some exploratory drilling done. A new direction taken.

And now they had completed that section, and the machine hall cavern too. The Italians were moving in with their shotcrete and mesh.

The South Africans tunnelled on. There was a 70 metre high surge chamber to be excavated, the river flow outlets, and the remainder of the turbine tail-race section. Another four months' worth of sweat and dust and nitrite fumes ahead. Drill and blast – drill and blast.

> *Tshwala muhle – hamba pansi*
> *Puza futhi, stelek muthi*
> *Puza baba, unga saba*
> *Tshwala muhle – hamba pansi*
> *Tshetsha!*
> *Tshetsha!*
> *Tshisa holo – BOOM!*

> *Don't be afraid,*
> *Drink strong beer father*
> *And go underground.*
> *Be quick!*
> *Be quick!*
> *Drill the blast hole – BOOM!*

Even the Italians loved to sing that Fanagalo verse. If they made opera from it, it did not matter. All men are the same colour underground – the colour of rock dust. And all men speak the same language – Fanagalo. The communication bridge between a dozen African languages – the lingua franca of the underground.

When Mark Ingram next visited the Suthu River dam site it was to inspect the walls of the huge machine hall cavern after blasting operations had been completed. His engineers had done a fine job; working from the vault downwards they had blasted from solid rock a cavern that was near on 50 metres high. Standing in the well where the number one turbine would be housed, Ingram peered upwards, the dome looked dim and distant. It was the equivalent of looking to the top of a ten-storey building. The walls were sheer raw dacite, fractured by dynagel and dotted with rock bolts – dark umber where water trickled from the faults. His inspection was a formality. He had a team of experts who would have informed him long ago if anything was seriously wrong.

Ingram swung himself onto the ladder that led deeper into the turbine well. Aware of the many observers of his progress, he grabbed the metal rope hand-holds with an agility and confidence that was a sham. He was a hopeless victim of vertigo, but none of the watchers would guess it. The ordeal of those hundred slippery rungs was as intense as it was private.

He thought about his ability as a pilot. He flew for the fun of it, for the hell of it; flew like a kestrel in the sky – but the malady persisted.

Ground at last; he reached the bottom of the shaft. The tunnel along which he wished to travel sloped mildly upwards now. It was long and straight and lit by a progression of glowing lamps buttoned to the roof. Water was dripping, and the floor, in sections, was awash. There were thick pipes there to pump water out, and thicker pipes pumping concrete in. There were pipes to blow air, and pipes to suck air, and pipes to carry power – the arteries of mining. They had created a new metabolism in the innards of that mountain.

Someone had been hurt down there. At the face of the tunnel a rescue team was waiting. A Pondo was lying on a stretcher and Doctor Tyrell, unfamiliar in his gumboots and hard hat was attending to him – fitting an inflatable splint to a very obviously broken leg. No one noticed Ingram until he said:

'How did it happen?'

It had happened while they were mucking out blasted rock. It was one of those accidents that invariably occur when man and machine are confined so closely. The worker had tried to squeeze between the 'Jumbo' drill rig and a reversing front end loader.

'Got hit by the shovel, Mister Ingram,' the driver said. 'I didn't see him until it was too late.'

'Temporal concussion and fractured femur,' Tyrell stood from his patient. 'Get him to the clinic . . . Hello, Mark.'

Tyrell was sweating heavily. He lifted his hard hat and mopped his brow with his sleeve. He neatly repacked his medical kit. 'Didn't know you were on site.'

The multiple head 'Jumbo' drill started up. Six compressed air drill-heads began to batter at the rock. Conversation was suddenly a mouth to ear affair – all gesture and lungs. Tyrell said something but Ingram only made out the words: 'Kirsten didn't . . .' He signalled that he had not heard; that he was going back up the tunnel. The two men walked together from the work-face.

'I said that I didn't think Kirsten knew you were coming up.'

'That's quite possible.'

'She invited me for supper tonight.'

'Oh? Well that's fine.'

They reached the turbine well. An access tunnel there led to the surface. They took it.

'I hate coming underground,' Tyrell confessed. 'It's so bloody hot down here, and where all the water comes from I'll never fathom. Up there there's a drought that's entered its fifth year and down here there's enough water to float a battleship. Where does it all come from?'

They reached the surface.

'I'll see you later on,' Ingram said. 'We can talk about the hydrologic cycle then, if you like.'

He did not see Tyrell wince.

*   *   *

'The interesting thing about water, on a global scale, Ernie, is that it can be neither destroyed, nor generated. The amount God gave us is the amount available, no more and no less. Isn't that interesting?'

Tyrell said, 'Yes.' He hoped his insincerity was apparent.

'The whole hydrologic cycle is fascinating.'

'Yes.'

'Yes. Water evaporates from the oceans and forms into clouds. The clouds move inland. They condense and we get rain. The land channels the water into rivers and into subsurface phreatic zones. But in the end it all drains back into the sea, no more and no less.'

'Yes.' Tyrell swirled the ice cubes in his empty glass. This signal too went unnoticed.

'You asked about subsurface water. Drought makes very little difference to it. Once it has percolated down to those levels . . .'

'You're boring the doctor.' The screen door squeaked as Kirsten Law came onto the verandah. 'All this talk about water and you haven't even refilled Ernie's glass. *Really*, Mark.' She bore with her the fine aroma of well-cooked food.

'By Jove, Kirsten.' Tyrell sighed. 'Where were you when I was at the marrying age?'

Ingram poured for all of them and a half measure for himself. He had not eaten since early that morning.

'So what draws you to Ingwavuma, Kirsten?' Tyrell asked. 'Tell me. I'm eaten up with curiosity.'

Now *that* was a question that would provoke an interesting answer. Ingram waited, amused by Kirsten's discomfort. He would enjoy his role in whatever lie she decided upon.

She did not lie though. She said, 'I came here the first time because I believed that my brother Monty was not dead, as reported and, in the event, I was proved right. Ironically, I had no sooner found him than he was involved in the fight at Mawamabi hill. He was supposed to have been killed there too. But I don't believe that either.'

Kirsten took her drink and sat down. Neither man passed a word in comment.

'Mark was kind enough to indulge me, on both occasions. Weren't you, Mark?'

'Yes,' Ingram said, 'but . . .'

'But you didn't really believe he *was* alive. He still doesn't believe it, Ernie, but that's the nice part about being a woman — their silliness is forgiven by the men who adore them.'

Tyrell gave a polite little laugh — never to be accused of missing the joke. But their expressions told him that this was no joke. He said:

'I recall your brother's . . . er . . . death, Kirsten. It was assumed that he had fallen victim to a crocodile. Reynolds from Nduma gave evidence. Naturally I've heard the news — the tragic business at Mawamabi hill. You're telling me *those* reports are false too? It didn't happen?'

'That's what I'm telling you, Doctor Tyrell. It didn't happen.'

'What did happen?'

Tyrell had not missed the term of address Kirsten had just used. He was the professional now — the man to be trusted with a delicate confidence. Trying to display a clinical detachment was difficult though. *This* was sensational stuff.

'I don't know all the facts,' Kirsten said. 'But this I do know. My brother was alive last month. I saw him. I spoke to him.'

'And this month?'

'As I said, he was involved in the fight at Mawamabi hill. He was *supposed* to have died as a result of the burns he suffered.'

'I remember the incident, of course,' Tyrell said. 'We provided beds at the clinic for many of the injured. At the time I didn't know your brother was involved. I didn't even know he was alive.'

'Can I say something?' Ingram stood; agitated. He began to pace the verandah. '*Some* of what Kirsten says is the truth.'

'Who are you to judge what . . .'

'Don't interrupt me, Kirsten.' Ingram was angry now. 'The truth is that Montague Law *was* alive last month. Yes, I didn't know that either. That was Kirsten's secret until recently. He *was* involved at Mawamabi hill. There was a huge bushfire there as we all know. He was burned. He died of his burns. A death certificate was issued in the name of Montague Law. I believe that the doctors at Addington Hospital are competent to know when someone is dead. Montague Law was certified by them as being dead. Now, I don't know what possessed you to bring all this up in front of Ernie, Kirsten, but as you have, and as he is not just a friend, but a doctor too, can we ask him for his professional opinion. Ernie, can this man possibly be alive?'

'I don't see how he can be. Unless it was a case of mistaken identity.'

'No mistake.' Ingram shook his head emphatically. 'Patrick Dent knew Law. He did the ID of the body.'

'Then I think we must accept that he . . .' Tyrell broke off – embarrassed. 'I'm sorry, Kirsten.'

'You see,' Ingram said. 'No one believes this . . . this madness.'

'I didn't ask you to believe me,' Kirsten said. 'There *are* professional people who agree that Monty's case is not unique, but that's beside the point. You asked me what had brought me to Ingwavuma, and I told you. What you care to believe doesn't affect the issue. Since I've been here I've been seeing a lot of people and asking a lot of questions. And do you know what? I'm more convinced than ever that Monty is *not* dead.'

'For crissake!' Ingram raised beseeching arms. 'Tell her to stop this Ernie.'

Tyrell was appalled. Why this vehemence? Why this obsession by Ingram? And this naivety by Kirsten? Could guilt be the common denominator? He said:

'Sometimes Mark, it is very hard to accept the loss of one who is very dear. We feel robbed, as though the whole thing was unfair. There should have been more – we look back in anguish at the lost opportunities. The times when we could have done more, and did less, the times when we acted unfairly. Perhaps . . .'

Kirsten put her arms around Tyrell; kissed him softly on the cheek.

'You are a darling, Ernie. What you say is true.'

'Haven't I said that a thousand times?' Ingram had misinterpreted her meaning, perhaps deliberately. Kirsten had the good sense to let it ride. She said:

'Yes Mark, you have, haven't you. Why don't we talk about something else?'

'Like supper,' Ingram said, grateful for the reprieve. 'Whatever it is you're cooking up, the aroma is driving me crazy. Let's go eat.' He hooked an arm into her waist. She turned and smiled at him – very stiff.

'I hope you like warthog roast,' Kirsten said to Tyrell. 'Warden Reynolds from Ndumu gave me a leg.'

It was delicious. Crisp-skinned and succulent, with a side plate of asparagus and avocado, and a fine cold Riesling to spark it. That was pursued by coffee (black for Tyrell) and rare old brandy.

'I've still got rounds to do,' Tyrell stayed the brandy bottle. 'The chappie at the hospital. Got to drop in there. Never trust a temporal concussion – dangerous injury. They can pop off like that if they're not managed right.' He snapped his fingers. 'Just like that.'

'Can we give you a lift then?' Kirsten sounded concerned. Tyrell looked a little unsteady. 'I thought you'd be going straight home.'

'Oh! I'm fine. Thanks for the offer but I can drive myself. My car's at my house. It's a short walk and the air will do me good.'

'It's bloody dark tonight,' Ingram said. 'At least let me lend you a torch.'

'If you insist.'

'Can't afford to lose our doctor, can we? Here, the switch is a bit wonky. Keep it pressed forward and it works fine.'

'Thanks. Good night, Kirsten.'

He kissed her lightly on the cheek, then walked away. He hoped that he had been able to do some good that night. Mark deserved a better deal than he was getting from Kirsten lately.

The doctor's house lay on the eastern slope of the plateau. It enjoyed a lesser view than Ingram's house, but otherwise it was practically identical. If he took a straight route, across the centre of the oval, two minutes' brisk walk would bring him to it. If he kept to the ring road – five minutes. It was a glorious night, an astrologer's dream.

He would stroll along the ring road; swing his arms a bit. Get rid of some of the hurt that was knotted into his shoulders. Someone was on the ring road with him. There it was again, closer this time, the sound of movement – of footsteps.

The torch worked at the third try. He played its beam along the road; through the foliage that lined the outer walk-way, along the walls of the adjacent cottages. Nothing.

There was no reason for this mischievous fear churning cold and low inside him. No reason to do anything but continue with his walk. The stars, however, had lost their attraction. He held the flashlight switch hard forward and quickened his pace; the pallid circle of light probed comfortingly ahead . . .

There is a time to obey instinct, and a time to heed reason. Tyrell should have run for his life then. Every instinct screamed it. Instead he did what any reasonable and intelligent man would do: a man who refused to be panicked by no more than a feeling of imminent danger. He continued to walk.

*   *   *

Mark Ingram sat deep in his chair, brooding on the events of the evening. Kirsten, in saying what she had said, had embarrassed him. But he could hardly tax her for having told the truth. Justification for his mood, however, did exist. It would require a measure of contrivance. He would need to be less than honest with himself. But he was hurting, and his hurt needed salve. Bitterly he said:

'You lied to me Kirsten.'

She was drawing the blinds. She hesitated momentarily, then said: 'I did, and I'm sorry.' She completed the chore. 'I should have told you the first time I came here what Mancoba had told me about Monty. I didn't. It was a hard time for me. I'm sure you can appreciate that. Anyway, now you know everything.'

He kept at it. 'I can't understand why you had to lie to me. Why didn't you tell me from day one that you knew that Monty was alive?'

'I wasn't sure myself Mark. It wasn't a lack of trust in you. If anything, I didn't trust Mancoba. I didn't know what to believe.'

She made a helpless little gesture that touched him, but he knew that this was not the real Kirsten – and this was not a time for leniency. A weak spot in this most imperturbable of creatures had been presented. This was a time to enter and exploit. A time for questioning: questions that would draw her.

'Did you know Mancoba was dead?'

'God no! I had no idea what had happened to him. How do you know he's dead?'

'Dent told me. He thinks your brother might have been implicated. Do you think so?'

'Of course not.' She whitened with the words. 'How could Dent say such a thing? How could you believe him?'

'He saw them quarrelling once.'

'Dent's a liar. I don't trust him.'

'Who do you trust Kirsten? For God's sake, even after you had spoken to your brother, even when you *knew* he was alive you didn't trust *me* enough to confide in me. How the hell do you think I feel?'

'I told you Mark. I was confused.'

'OK, granted. But even now you're holding back on me. I can sense it.' Ingram sensed no such thing. It was sheer factiousness, but the results were startling. Kirsten looked shaken.

'Oh?'

'Yes,' Ingram realised his sudden advantage. 'How can I possibly help you if I don't know in which direction you're pointed? You've got to square with me, Kirsten.'

'What do you want to know?'

That was the trouble; he did not really know the answer to that question. He said:

'Why don't you tell me what Monty was really up to in these mountains?'

'He was doing research. I don't know much about it. All I know is that it concerns a remedy that the sangomas here have been using for hundreds of years.'

'And did he find it?'

'I'm not sure. There are so many things I'm not sure about, Mark.'

'You can be sure of one thing, Kirsten. And that is that I'm on your side all the way. You do know that, don't you?'

She did not know that. She looked into the eyes of this man who professed such support and saw not a flicker of trust. He stood, he opened his arms to her forgivingly, but where there had once stood a champion, stood now an empty space. She said:

'I am certain of this: my brother is alive, and one day I will find him.'

'Crap!'

The word was out and spilt like some obscene and indelible stain, never to be removed from the damask of their relationship. In anger Kirsten stiffened; pushed herself from this most careless of men.

'How dare you!'

'Kirsten . . .' He tried to repair things and made them worse. 'How can you believe . . .?'

'No!'

The hands she held up to him were trembling with emotion. 'No, don't say anything more, Mark. I've been listening to your questions and wondering why they were so pointed, so painful, not just tonight. It's as though some inner poison has been eating at you Mark, and now it's surfaced, now it's visible. It's done terrible things to you, and now you're touching me with it. You've changed so much. What's happened to you?'

'Kirsten, I don't want to see you hurt.'

'No,' she shook her head. 'No, it's not that. You're the one who is touching off the pain.'

'I didn't mean to.'

'Of course you meant to. The only question is: why?'

'Damn it, Kirsten. You know why.'

'No, I don't Mark. Oh! I can understand you being angry with me. But this thing runs deeper than that. We've coped with anger, you and I, many times in the past. Anger creates a clean and open wound. What is it that's brought about this festering, dirty thing? It's as though you hated Monty; you wished him dead. Why?'

'I'm sorry,' he said.

It was not an apology for anything he had done or said. It was a statement relating to the plight of their relationship. 'I didn't want this.'

'And neither did I, Mark.'

'Can't we just forget it?'

'Is that your answer to this: let's forget it and it will all go away?'

Ingram shrugged. 'Won't it?'

'I don't know Mark. I'm going to continue in my search for my brother. I believe that the certification of his death was a mistake. It wouldn't be the first time such a mistake had been made. If that is going to cause such anger in you then I'll . . .'

'Kirsten,' Ingram interrupted. 'Go on looking for your brother. Go on using my cottage as your base. I won't say another word.'

'It's more fundamental than that, Mark.'

'Let's not think that.'

He held his arms out. She moved back stiffly into his embrace. He could not help himself; he tightened his arms and drew her body in, and thoughts of retribution faded with that touch. He felt the heat of her hard girl-like breasts. His hands were artful and practised. He lowered them and subverted the hostility of her hips and brought them hard against him. He knew of the surface-deep lust in this woman and he knew how to exploit it. Sex was what they needed. Sex would cure them. His fingers searched and clothing fell away.

'Kirsten wait,' he pleaded.

But this was just part of the game; words to quicken her breath and push her over the edge.

'Kirsten!'

He played the little boy. Wanting, yet afraid of this seduction. He hovered at her nipples. 'Ah!' He suckled. He had done it right. Her eyes were all pupil – black with the lust of the gypsy. Tawny skinned. Raven haired. *Strong*.

'Na. Na,' he whimpered.

He dropped submissively to his knees; subservient to that springy, musky fleece. In search of oral pleasure; of suffocative flavour. She danced herself against him, and he followed. This slave, this vaginal scullion.

She lowered herself – bent back and opened like a limbo stick dancer . . . wide and pink and vibratile.

And *he*. He was explosive. He was the phallic rocket. He stood proud of the size of him; wanting her admiration. 'Look.' She looked.

He bent to her. He lunged, arched and lunged. She matched him thrust for thrust.

When Ingram slept, he dreamed he was on a sunny sandy beach, and there was a canoe – a canoe in the form of a human corpse. He launched it and straddled it and paddled across a friendly sea. But the sea became wild, and as black as ink, and the corpse rolled terribly beneath him. There was a wall, his wall – his dam. It was high and white, and shaking from the pounding of the ink-black water. Splits were forming. He tried to cement them over, tried and tried. But it was no good. The wall crashed down, pinning him, crushing him.

He awoke, gasping, sweating, the sheet beneath him wet and twisted. He sat up, disoriented; shuddering at the recollection of his nightmare. The echo of a scream was lingering in his ears: not his scream, not Kirsten's scream. She lay there breathing nasally, sleeping peacefully.

A white half-moon was framed in the open window. It was 3.00 a.m. And something was terribly wrong. Something bad had happened. He did not know what. Then he remembered the nightmare; the human corpse; the storm and the breaking wall. The mystery of his mood explained, he began to relax again.

At some time during the heat of the night Kirsten had stripped off her nightie. Her arms lay flung above her like a baby's, one breast lay exposed, so beautiful. Like a thief he stole the remnant sheet from her – downwards to the deeper shadowed valleys. He reached for a cigarette – his lighter. Amazingly bright, that little flickering flame. How perfect the woman in the light of it. How intimate the moment.

The lighter burned his thumb. He snapped it shut and tossed the unlit cigarette aside. With the voyeur moon to witness his act of sex, he reached for her.

*   *   *

When Kirsten felt the sheet being slowly drawn away she knew what was to come. She lay there, maintaining the rhythm of the breath of sleep. She watched through hooded lids as Ingram inspected her with his little flame. She did not want him.

She moved mechanically to accommodate him. Her eyes she kept closed and her face turned rigidly away. There was no joy. She lay awake for the rest of that night, listening to his trickling little snores; avoiding his spread-eagled satisfied limbs. In the half-light of dawn she crept to the bathroom and thoroughly removed every trace of sex from her body. She washed herself as one does who wishes to be rid of something adherent and unpleasant. Then she went to the verandah.

The sun was a mellow thing, squeezing itself from the east hills. Kirsten watched it until it was too bright to look at. For her it was a troubled dawn.

She had seen things that night that she had not seen before. She had obtained a glimpse of the real posture of the wearer of the golden breastplate of Mark Ingram. The man did not fill out the armour. She had touched on deceit and she hated deceit. But instead of disowning it, she had drawn it to her. She had slept with this lesser man because it was expedient to do so. She needed to stay under this roof because it was here that brother Monty had reached her once before. It was a place of hope.

So the sun lit up that morning a new-found whore. But who would not forgive her?

* * *

Ernie Tyrell was a creature of habit, and one of his habits was to lunch in the company canteen on Wednesdays and Fridays. Every Wednesday and every Friday, come 1300, he would take the same seat at the same table with the same group of men. It was rumoured that, after lunch, they sneaked away to some place unknown for a rubber or two of bridge. No one was sure of that however.

That Wednesday Tyrell did not arrive for lunch. He was not at his house, nor at the clinic. In fact, according to the night sister, he had not arrived the previous night to visit the injured Pondo, as he had said he was going to. Kirsten and Ingram had been the last to see him.

An intensive search of the dam site was undertaken. Neither the doctor nor his vehicle was found.

At 1500 Captain Dent was informed about the missing man.

Kirsten Law heard about it at exactly the same time. She was sitting in Warden Reynolds' cluttered office when the news was transmitted by radio. Reynolds turned up his volume control.

'Did you hear that?' he asked Kirsten.

'Yes. I wonder what could have happened to him.'

'Hey! Did you hear that, September?' Reynolds shouted towards his open window.

A game guard, who had been waiting on the verandah outside the office, appeared at the window.

'Yes, I heard it too, Umnumzane.' He spoke English and he wanted Kirsten Law to know it. 'I know Doctor Tyrell. He is a good man.'

'He is indeed,' Kirsten agreed. 'He's a very close friend of my fiancé. In fact we had him over for dinner last night. I hope nothing is wrong.'

'Something's wrong,' Reynolds said authoritatively. 'You can bet on it.'

Another transmission came through. They heard Dent say that a routine police patrol had discovered the doctor's Land Rover on the banks of Lake Mandlankunzi. Then Ingram's voice: 'I'll meet you at the Lake, Patrick. Give me exact co-ordinates.'

Dent again. 'At the old cattle dip. Do you know it?'

'I'll find it,' Ingram said.

'Well I'll be . . .' Reynolds stood up; crossed to a map covering one entire wall of his office. He traced a calloused finger along the southern border of his game reserve. 'Look, Kirsten. That's Mandlankunzi right here.'

She joined him at the map.

'Here,' he stabbed at a large light blue blob. 'That's not more than a few kilometres outside our gates. I'm going to drive across there, see if I can do anything.'

'I'll come with you; if that's all right.'

'Come by all means,' Reynolds slung his rifle across his shoulder. 'You know Kirsten, this business is so similar to your brother's tragedy – the vehicle at the lake, the missing driver. I hope that at the end of the day we're not faced with another croc disaster. Every time someone gets taken, there's pressure to cull. I hate shooting crocs for sheer retribution.'

They walked from the administration rondavel to Reynolds' Land Rover. The game guard called September was waiting there for them.

'Do a patrol of the perimeter of the rest camp,' Reynolds instructed. He started the engine. 'I'll be back before you're finished.'

But the Zulu did not want to do a patrol of the rest camp fence. He wanted to come with them. He trotted next to the now moving vehicle.

'Umnumzane will need me.'

'No, I won't.'

'What if you require a tracker?'

Reynolds applied brakes. 'He's got a point,' he said to Kirsten. To September he said, 'OK, Mabutane. Oh! great tracker of trackers. *Gibela*, let's go.'

Mabutane's smile came very naturally. It was broad and enduring and lasted as long as it took him to clamber to a rear seat; to say:

'*Ngiyabonga* Umnumzane – I praise you. Don't stop doing kind deeds – even tomorrow.'

He sat there, clasping the canopy post, his rifle wedged between his thighs, and did not say another word. But he was listening, listening intently. There was a keenness in his expression that told of that. Kirsten was constantly aware of him.

'I shouldn't have spoken like I did about the crocs and that,' Reynolds leaned closer – the better to be heard. 'It was insensitive of me, and I'm sorry.'

'No need for apologies, honestly. In fact I agree with your sentiments.'

'Your brother was a fine man, Kirsten. He used to come up to Ndumu quite often. He loved the tranquillity of the place. I think he was a lonely man though. He was hard to get near to, but when you got to know him, as I think I did, you got to appreciate him. I think it was this desire for solitude that caused him to fake his death. I can't think of any other reason.'

'Thanks for talking to me,' Kirsten said. 'You've been a great help.'

'I hope I have. I can understand your need to find out what caused him to turn away from people. You know, you look a lot like your brother; same eyes. I can still see those eyes – he'd turn them on you, quickly and hold you, as if for a moment he'd found you out.'

'And I've got those eyes?'

'It wasn't a lack of trust. You got to know that when you knew him. It was just his way. Yes, you're a bit like that too, Kirsten.' Reynolds half turned and addressed his rear passenger. 'Do you remember Doctor Law, September?'

'Indeed,' Mabutane said. 'It is as Umnumzane says, they share the eyes that stab. It was a bad thing that happened at Mawamabi hill. That day was a day of tears for all who knew your brother.'

'All my game guards liked your brother,' Reynolds added. 'Still, I doubt whether any of them could tell you anything more than I have. He had a manservant though. A little old Zulu from Southern Natal. I only saw him once or twice and I forget his name.'

'Mancoba,' Kirsten said.

'Yes, that's right, Mancoba. He's the man you should be speaking to.'

'He's dead,' Kirsten said. 'He too died at the fight at Mawamabi hill.' 'I didn't know that,' Reynolds said in mitigation. 'He *was* old. There's the lake up ahead.'

Mandlankunzi – the lake with the strength of the bull. It was a mirror of golden sun and blue, blue sky, flocked white with squabbling pelicans. Where the ribs of the old dead trees emerged, the spread-winged cormorants perched, loving the afternoon heat. A peaceful place. Not a place of sudden death. Yet somewhere amongst that beauty and serenity – sharp-toothed, keen-eyed, the crocodiles lurked.

'Look,' Reynolds pointed to a group of Thonga women, thigh deep, scooping water into cans. 'Sooner or later one of them is going to get taken. For a week after that happens they're careful. Then they go back to their old habits. Incredible isn't it?' He waved and they waved cheerfully back.

'There's Ernie's Land Rover,' Kirsten was the first to spot the abandoned vehicle.

'I see it. Good God. If I'm not mistaken, he's run it right into the shallows.'

Reynolds was not mistaken. The tracks of the Land Rover ran straight across the wide drought rim of sun-crusted mud and reeds that skirted Mandlankunzi, then onwards. Onwards, right into the lake.

A bored looking black constable was seated on the back seat of the bogged-down Land Rover. He turned; lazily regarding the approaching vehicle.

Reynolds drove wide of Tyrell's tracks. Where the crust started to break beneath the tyres, and the mud oozed up, he stopped. 'Well look at that.' He spoke to Mabutane. 'If there are any tracks out there, then they're under water.'

Reynolds took off his shoes and socks and waded out towards the vehicle. If he was any more wary than the Thonga waterfetchers, it was not noticeable. He stood there, the lake waves lapping at his thighs, chatting to the constable. Kirsten watched them for a while. Then she too stepped down from Reynolds' vehicle. There was shade to be had under some nearby fever trees. She walked towards them. Mabutane, it seemed, preferred the shade as well. After a while he came and sat there with her – politely distanced, close enough to talk.

'It's very hot.' Mabutane sat gazing at the lake. He lifted his arm and pointed. 'That's where the crocodiles lie.' He pointed to a distant marsh bank. 'I can see one there . . . Look, can you see it?'

She could not. She stared at the marsh bank Mabutane had pointed out. Finally she admitted: 'No.'

'Your eyes are not up to the search, Inkosikazi.' The rebuke was delivered with the utmost tact, the highest degree of respect. Mabutane had addressed her as: *Inkosikazi* – wife of the chief. He went on: 'It's a road of thorns that you have chosen, Inkosikazi. I heard the questions you put to Umnumzane; and I heard more than questions.'

And she had heard more than a sentence of censure for her poor eyesight. She had heard a few words that had touched her like flint sparks. Dear God, she was so kindled with hope, don't let it be extinguished once again. She said:

'I didn't see the crocodile. I think I am seeing something far bigger than a mere crocodile. Tell me straight, Mabutane; do you know things about my brother?'

'Yes. The Zulus call him Mvulaba.'

'Then he's alive!'

'As alive as you are Inkosikazi. And yet not so alive.'

'You lift me! Then you drop me. What kind of talk is this? I asked you to be straight with me, Zulu.'

'Don't be angry.' Mabutane spread his hands earnestly. 'You know, I shouldn't have even told you as much as I have told you. Once before I trusted a white person and he betrayed me. He used the knowledge I had given him to attack my people.'

'Not all whites are the same, Mabutane.'

'True.'

'Don't judge all people by the bull that gores. It was not me who wounded you. Can't you see Mabutane? Here is someone who has just emerged from a long dark journey. I feel light and wonderful. My brother is alive. I want to shout the words, and yet I know that they mustn't even be said in a whisper in some places. Don't be afraid, Mabutane. I understand.'

'I hope you do, Inkosikazi.'

'I want you to take me to my brother.'

'I can't,' September Mabutane said unhappily. 'I was afraid you would ask me to do that. Even though you are the sister of Mvulaba it would be an impertinence for me to assume that he wanted to see you. You must understand that.'

She did understand. She had half expected that reply. She said:

'Will you at least take my words to him? Will you tell him that I beg to see him?'

'I'll do that.'

'Tell him not to be afraid.'

'Is that all?'

'Yes.'

Mabutane nodded. 'I hope he sees you, Inkosikazi. I suffer with you, Inkosikazi. But there are things you do not understand about your brother. He is perhaps not the same man you once knew. Things have happened to him – things that would have killed a lesser person.'

'I know he was burned.'

'Yes, most terribly. And those scars are not just of the skin. But the change runs even deeper than that. I will take your message to

Mvulaba. I will do it tonight. But more than that I cannot do.'

'I understand and I'm grateful. Will you promise to bring me his reply?'

'Yes, Inkosikazi. I promise that too.'

'I too have suffered, Mabutane.'

A vehicle was approaching. A dusty beige Landcruiser with an aerial like a lashing stockwhip.

'uDende,' Mabutane nodded towards the vehicle. 'Do you know that man, Inkosikazi?' A change had come over September Mabutane. Standing beside Kirsten now was a bitter, resentful man.

She said: 'You sound as though you know him better than I do.'

'There,' Mabutane pointed to the huge man exiting from the Landcruiser, 'there, is the enemy of your brother. There is the bull you spoke of. The bull with the blood on its horns.'

'*Mabutane*,' Reynolds called from the lakeside. '*Yiza wena* – come.'

'Wait.' Kirsten's gesture of restraint was hesitant, and ignored by Mabutane.

'I must go now, Inkosikazi.'

'You must tell me what uDende did. Why is he my brother's enemy? I must know.'

'There's no time now, Inkosikazi. Be careful when you are with uDende. That's all I can say.'

'I'm not afraid.'

'*Be* afraid. Do not trust him.'

Mabutane began to walk towards the grouped men. Kirsten kept pace with him. Dent stood, hands on hips, head tilted – imperiously; inquisitive. He watched them approach.

'Tell me why.' At the risk of being overheard by Dent, Kirsten persevered. 'Why mustn't I trust him?'

'Haven't you understood? Have I not made myself clear? That man is the one who all but killed your brother.'

Perhaps she had understood, but she was weary of innuendo; tired of grasping at shadows. She wanted the truth. And she wanted it in twenty paces.

'Tell me,' she said, 'exactly what he did. Are you absolutely sure it was Dent?'

They were too close. It was too late for the answers she wanted, or it would have been had not a flock of raucous Hadeda ibis winged suddenly by. All blare and startle and beaten air. Mabutane could have shouted, had he so wished.

'He stole from a man whom he thought was dying. He stole Mvulaba's diary. If you must have proof. Does that not prove his guilt?'

Did it prove his guilt? When the ibises were gone, and the only sound was the wash of the lake, and the murmur of the men, Kirsten thought about that question. There could be no answer until she possessed her brother's diary. Reading that document would be like reading the mind of the man the Zulus called Mvulaba. And God knows she needed that insight.

Dent broke into her reverie. 'Hello, Kirsten. I heard you were back in Ingwavuma.' He nodded to Mabutane. 'I see you've met the celebrated September Mabutane.'

They ran a winch line from Reynolds' Land Rover to the abandoned vehicle.

'This reminds me of something,' Dent said. 'Seems that we've done all this before.'

The winch whined; the cable tautened – and Tyrell's vehicle rolled back to shore. Dent climbed into the driver's seat and turned the ignition key. The starter motor kicked but the engine did not respond. They opened the bonnet; dried and wiped and blew on things electrical. It still would not start.

Dent shrugged, 'No spark. I'll have to tow it.'

He began to search the vehicle. He cleaned the dash tray and peered under the seats. 'Nothing.'

He opened the storage bins and examined their contents. Old medical equipment – a broken manometer and some used syringes, a few half-full ampoules.

Kirsten watched him as he worked. Not everyone was given an opportunity to study a potential adversary, and so closely. Here was an efficient man, methodical, strong, quick hands with shrewd eyes that took in everything the first time. Not the sort of man who would do something without good reason.

So, Kirsten dear, what good reason can you think of for Dent having done all that September Mabutane has accused him of doing? She looked around for Mabutane, but the game guard was not in sight. It came to Kirsten that she had not seen him for some time.

'Want to try the ignition again?' Reynolds called from under the open bonnet of the Land Rover.

'Sure,' Dent slipped into the driver's seat and turned the key. The engine coughed, faltered, then roared into life. Reynolds slammed the bonnet down.

'You're a genius,' Dent said.

When Ingram came, it was by helicopter. Fast and low, he swept across the lake – a predator of monstrous proportions. The water fowl panicked helter-skelter for the sky.

He circled the vehicles, hung gracefully for a moment, then set his machine down a short walk away. Even his dark glasses could not conceal the concern in his eyes.

'Hello, Kirsten.' He seemed surprised to find her there. 'Patrick . . . Reynolds,' he nodded in greeting to the men. 'Found anything yet?'

'Not yet,' Dent said.

But that was not true. Mabutane had found something. He was standing at the edge of a reed bed, not two hundred metres away. He was gesturing – big urgent gestures for them to come. Kirsten saw him. And at that moment she knew that Ernie Tyrell was dead.

'*Umnumzane*,' the Zulu cupped his hands to his mouth, 'over here!'

They all saw him then, and all but Kirsten began to run in the direction of the game guard. She walked. She would have preferred not to have gone there at all. She would have liked to remember Ernie Tyrell the way he was. Dear Ernie who had preferred club blazers and other people's liquor – dapper Ernie, cheerful Ernie. The healer who had understood the limitations of the script pad; who had preferred the infinite power that flowed from kindness and consideration. Someone had killed that lovely man. Please God don't let it have to do with ritual murder. Please, please, *please not that*.

The ground was soggy towards the water's edge. Squelching and sucking at her lifting feet. Even where it looked grassy and dry there was no substance. The reeds just bent and sank, and beneath them, the ooze rose up, black and stinking. Mandlankunzi was showing its other face. It had become an ugly place.

At a place where some water fig had set down roots, a little islet had formed. The weaver birds had come there in their thousands to flit, and woo, and make that place their own. That was where September Mabutane brought them. Beneath that multitude of little woven homes the intruding men were standing.

They were talking, looking down occasionally to the sprawled and muddied dead thing lying there. But no one looked for long.

'No, Kirsten, don't come closer.' Ingram saw her, held up a forbidding hand; shook his head, his features grey and shocked.

'Go back . . . *please*.'

But she had to see. She had to know. She hauled herself onto the enclave. And she saw. And she knew.

She turned away and retched until she buckled. And somewhere in the numbness of her mind a voice was saying: let this not be the doing of this man called Mvulaba. For whoever has done this terrible thing must answer for it.

'Zwit-zwit-zwit,' agreed the citizens of the water fig trees.

9

Mark Ingram's private office at the Sutho River site was more utilitarian by far than his suite at the Ingram Associates head office in Durban.

It had functional metal windows and a functional panelite door. It was identical in dimension to any of a score of other offices that were situated along the northern face of the big prefab office complex. It was littered with trade journals, glorifying big yellow-painted machines that hauled or pushed or dug, or carried out some other monstrous engineering function.

The view from his window was of the huge, and ever rising concrete wall – the dusty construction site, and machines, big and yellow-painted, that hauled, pushed, and dug and all with a considerable amount of noise.

Kirsten closed the windows and the sound abated.

'That's better.' She returned to her moulded plastic chair and her cup of coffee. 'So Ernie's patient haemorrhaged and died. Now the Pondos won't go underground because they believe the dam has been bewitched. You want me to talk to them?'

'Just the leader,' Mark Ingram said. 'His name is Mzabele. I had him brought to the site office this morning.'

'Is he here now?'

'Yes.'

'You know, Mark, you haven't got a doctor on site any more. Supposing I do persuade Mzabele to take his Pondos back underground. And supposing that there's another accident. You don't even have someone here who's competent to set a broken leg.'

'Don't think it hasn't occurred to me.'

'It would make your position even worse if something like that happened again.'

'I know. But what the hell am I supposed to do about it? There are medical facilities at Mkuzi but that's four hours' drive from here. That's one reason why I want to get this thing settled; so that I can fly back to Durban and get a replacement for Ernie Tyrell sorted out.'

Kirsten said: 'Why don't you talk to Gray Whitaker?', then wondered why she felt so sheepish about that suggestion. 'He is a doctor.' The unnecessary rationalisation only heightened her embarrassment.

'Good idea.'

Ingram had not noticed her difficulty. More confidently she went on: 'He works for the Provincial Administration so I don't suppose he's paid a fortune.'

'He wouldn't be interested,' Ingram said. 'He's over-qualified for the job. But he might be able to recommend someone else.'

'Try him anyway.'

'I will. I certainly will.' Ingram made a brief note in his diary, then stood up. 'Now let's see if we can get this Pondo fiasco sorted out this morning. It's costing me . . . Come on.'

He walked slightly ahead of his fiancée – the better to guide her through the monotony of like-walled, like-lit passageways of the site office. He spoke as they walked.

'These Pondos are nothing but trouble. I was on the point of firing a few ringleaders once before. If we can't persuade them to go underground, I might have to do something like that.'

'I wouldn't,' Kirsten said. 'Not unless you want a full scale strike. They're not the type to be intimidated.'

They reached a door, distinguished from all other doors by the bold word 'PRIVATE!' They stopped there. Ingram opened it.

'I'm relying on you to do a deal, Kirsten. This dam is fast approaching its final phase. We're ahead of schedule and I'd dearly like to keep it that way.'

They entered.

Filling this room was a long, wooden boardroom-type table. It had fourteen satellite chairs – thirteen of them unoccupied. Mzabele, overalled and gumbooted, sat at the head. Impassively he watched them enter.

'Good morning.' Ingram started shuffling chairs, unsure where to place himself – flustered by this Pondo's impudent grasp of the initiative.

'Sit at the other end,' Kirsten instructed. 'I'll sit here.' She drew out a chair for herself in the middle zone of the table.

'Well . . .' Ingram began polishing his palms – a display of great enthusiasm. 'Right.' He looked at Mzabele, and Mzabele looked back, unsure how to react to all this energy.

'Greet him,' Kirsten prompted. 'You're the senior man. Sit down and greet him.'

'What must I say?'

'Tell him you welcome him . . . Oh, just say anything. I'll sort it out.'

'Good morning,' Ingram smiled down the table. 'I . . . er. It's very good of you to . . .'

'*Iti Nkosi* – the chief says that you, *owezemvuba* – son of the milk sack cattle, are welcome in his modest house.'

Ingram nodded. The Pondo smiled back, delighted to be addressed in the idiom of his homeland. He said:

'Nkosi's hand is beautiful. He has often been wetted by the rain. I am as a son of the great house.'

Kirsten turned to Ingram. 'He says you are generous. You are wise. What else can he do but be obedient to his father.'

'Great,' Ingram mistook traditional Pondo politeness for servility – a mistake. 'So now we can get down to the nitty-gritty then. Tell him I want this issue sorted out chop-chop. I want his men back on the job in the morning. He has the influence. He must use it, or else.'

'*Iti Nkosi*,' Kirsten breathed some sensitivity into her fiancé's cause, 'so senior does he consider you – Mzabele, that he has brought me, his right-hand wife, to this meeting. He wishes that when we leave here today that we will be of one mind.'

'Tell him,' Ingram went on, 'I don't hold with this voodoo rubbish, and I don't expect my men to.'

'The chief says that he understands that the finger of witchcraft has been pointed towards your people. He says that he has done things that will bend the finger backwards – we need have no more fear.'

Mzabele looked unconvinced. He said:

'I think Inkosi Ingram is promising something beyond his powers. Are we to believe that he can protect us when it is clear that he is unable to protect his own people?'

'What did he say,' Ingram demanded.

'He's not happy, Mark. I've told him that you've taken steps to ensure the safety of the Pondos. But they know about the death of Ernie Tyrell. They obviously saw Tyrell as a powerful man; a man who was capable of making potent *muthi*. Can you see what I'm getting at? The opposition must be even more powerful. They're frightened, Mark. They don't see you as being able to protect them.'

'All right,' Ingram said, 'tell him that we know who committed that murder. Captain Dent is going to arrest the people responsible. Tell him that.'

'I don't think that will impress him.'

'They're scared of Dent. Go on tell him that. See if that will satisfy him.'

Kirsten shrugged. '*Iti Nkosi* – the chief says that he understands your fear. He says that the branch of guilt has been laid at the door of the one who has done these terrible things. The police captain uDende, who knows everything; he will end the matter soon.'

'uDende?' Mzabele looked anxiously at Ingram. 'We want no more to do with that man. We are still bleeding from the kindness of uDende. To call on his protection is to call on the protection of inGwenya the crocodile.'

'Why?' Kirsten was intrigued. 'How so?'

'We trusted him at Mawamabi hill.' Mzabele nodded, certain that that sentence; that gesture told it all. Perhaps it would have, to those who had been there.

Kirsten was hard put to mute her rising excitement, 'It would be good if we put our mouths together about uDende, about the happenings at Mawamabi hill. Let today be the day we put an end to dissension.'

'Mawamabi,' Mzabele said, 'was the place where the army of the witch Uhlanga hid. uDende took us there to burn them out. To kill the grey-eyed witch and the white wizard too. But these things you know.'

'Yes,' Kirsten said, 'of course. And he killed neither of them – they escaped.'

'Quite so. And how many Pondos died, and for what cause? We Pondos have little reason to trust uDende any more.'

'Forgive my ignorance, but you say the Inkosi here knew about all this?'

'Yes. uDende told us that Inkosi Ingram had given the order for the attack.'

'You were never given that order by Inkosi in person – you were told by uDende?'

'Yes.'

Mzabele was telling the truth; there was no guile in the Pondo. Kirsten was sure of it. She was equally as certain that Mark Ingram would never have given such an order. Why should he?

'Well?'

Kirsten found herself staring into the hard, ambitious eyes of the dam builder.

'*Well?*' Ingram said again, 'what are you two babbling about? Do we have a deal or don't we?'

Such an effort to draw herself back to the reluctant Pondo; the boardroom table, the deal.

'We don't,' she said. 'But I think we're close. I think an offering of some cattle might swing it. Can I make an offer?'

'As many as they want,' Ingram said. 'Go for it.'

'*Iti Nkosi* – the chief greatly regrets the trouble you have had, specially with the policeman uDende. He asks, however, that you look at the ashes of your own fireplace. Perhaps your own ancestral spirits are denying you the protection that you require from evil influences. Perhaps a big sacrifice would cause them to look favourably once more, towards you.'

'Indeed,' Mzabele nodded – a thought worth considering. 'It is difficult for us to keep with tradition. We are so far from home.'

'*Iti Nkosi* – Bawu Ingram understands. He is prepared to provide the finest animals to open the way.'

'Inkosi's hand is beautiful.'

'What does he say?'

'He wants twenty oxen.'

'Done . . . and then will they go underground?'

'Oh, yes,' said the right-hand wife.

'*Yinkwanekwa!*' said Mzabele the Pondo – we are not afraid.

Ingram walked Mzabele to the door – all amiability now that he had what he wanted. They grasped hands and the Pondo departed. Ingram leaned against the closed door for a moment, collecting his thoughts.

'Twenty oxen,' he said to Kirsten. '*You* are some negotiator. I feel like I could eat one of those oxen all on my own. Come on, it's nearly lunch time.'

'Not for me,' Kirsten declined; she shook her head. 'I've got things to attend to.'

'To think,' he said bitterly, 'that I could have forgotten.'

A flicker of annoyance touched Ingram. Like the shadow of a scudding cloud on a sunny day, she might have paid it no attention previously. Now, the slightest emotion of Mark Ingram would be noted, would be evaluated.

'I forgot, you're still engaged in this . . . quest of yours. I wish I could convince you of the futility of it. But I suppose I can't. It's your problem, Kirsten. I just don't want to see you hurt.'

'That's kind of you Mark. Now I must go.'

'Be careful,' Ingram grasped her arm. 'I'm going back to Durban. I'd prefer it if you came back with me, but I know your mind is made up to stay here. Just be careful, OK? I don't want you out after dark – not after what happened last night.'

The warning was superfluous. The horror slaying of Ernie Tyrell had been dominant in Kirsten's mind since her flight back from Mandlankunzi the previous evening. The thought of it was still with her as she drove her borrowed Land Rover away from the site office and turned onto the dirt road that would take her to Ndumu Game Reserve.

There were differences, however, between her doctrine of trust, and that of the late Doctor Tyrell; Ernie Tyrell had been a person who had believed that violence, like lightning, could be conducted safely away from oneself. A harmless dreamer, certain in the knowledge that goodness conquered all. And when, at times, it did not, there was always the amnesia of alcohol. *That* was 100% infallible.

Kirsten held certain myths too. But she was far from harmless. She had a gun. Beneath the denim jacket that she wore was a customised leather holster. And in that holster rested a big Colt .45 auto. And in that she trusted.

The gates of Ndumu came up. It was at the gates that Kirsten received her first setback of that day.

'September Mabutane? No. You won't find him here. He was taken away by uDende's men this morning.'

'Are you sure?' she asked the gate guard.

'Very sure. I was on duty when uDende's men drove in, and I was here too when they drove away with him. He was handcuffed, Inkosikazi. They've locked him up for sure.'

* * *

The gatekeeper was right. September Mabutane was in the cells of the Abercorn Drift police station. 'In the president's suite' – Dent's joke. Dent was standing alone in the Charge Office when Kirsten arrived. He had swapped his usual camouflage for blue fatigues. Solid colours made him look even broader. He lowered himself until his elbows and palms were resting on the Charge Office counter; his face discourteously close to hers.

'Sure you can see him,' he said. 'But not now, Kirsten. I'm investigating a murder. I want a statement from him. Then you're at liberty to speak to him. OK?'

'I want to speak to you too, Patrick.'

'Well that will have to wait too, Kirsten. I'm really busy. Look, why don't you come back tomorrow? I'll have more time then.'

She almost left it at that. Dent was a formidable man, and he had said that she could speak to Mabutane tomorrow. Perhaps it was impatience with all the promised tomorrows that never seemed to arrive that caused her to say: 'No. That won't do. I want to see him, *now*.'

'It's going to have to do, lassie.' Dent was annoyed. He dragged his fingers into a fist. 'Now you run on.'

'No.' Quietly and determinedly.

She had not wanted this confrontation. She was not, as yet, prepared. This was a runaway thing, and God knows where it would end. 'No,' she said again. 'There are things that have to be spoken about, *now*.'

'You've overstepped the mark,' Dent said. 'You're trying to pressure me, and that is not on. Don't you understand, Kirsten? I'm in total charge here. I don't give a damn who you are, or how much money you've got, or who your friends are. It doesn't mean a thing to me.'

'You're very certain of yourself, Captain Dent.'

'And you are being very annoying, Kirsten Law.'

'What would make you give a damn, Patrick? A complaint against you?'

Yes, that would cause him consternation. That was obvious in his reply.

'What complaint?'

A man who had mired himself in such a marsh of illegalities might be drawn by such a question. He asked again: 'What complaint?'

'Wouldn't your office be a better place to talk?'

'All right,' Dent said coolly. 'This way.'

A very limited victory: she was invited to say what she had to say. It was but a short walk from the Charge Office to the rear of the police station and Dent's office. It did not allow Kirsten very much time to prepare her strategy.

'Sit down.'

She sat down.

'I'm listening.'

'Monty Law, my brother, was a scientist and he had a burning ambition. He believed there existed amongst the Zulu sangomas, the knowledge of a cure for the disease multiple sclerosis. He wanted to find that cure, no matter what it cost him. In the event, it cost him his life. Did you know these things about Doctor Law, Patrick?'

'Look Kirsten,' Dent sat back in his chair; widened his arms, papally forgivingly. 'I'm sorry about your brother. You've gone through hell, and I can understand your bitterness. Please forgive me.'

'Forgive you – for what?'

'For not getting to Mawamabi hill in time to do something about stopping that faction fight. Perhaps thus saving your brother. Isn't that what you're upset about?'

'No it isn't, and I think you know that.'

The man was in retreat; throwing up little defences to test her strength. She was gaining.

'Scientists keep records of their work, Captain. Monty kept records. He kept a diary. Before he lapsed into coma, he told Doctor Whitaker about his diary. Do you know what he told him?'

'How could I, Kirsten?'

'He told Gray Whitaker that you had that precious document. That *you* had *taken* it from him.'

'That's a lie.'

It was a lie. But it was a very skilful, very deserving lie. It could almost stand up on its own, but she knew how to develop it into the perfect fiction: indistinguishable from the real thing.

'Yes, Gray Whitaker was a bit sceptical too. Monty had been partially delirious. So he told me about it, and we decided to take the matter no further. Then, what do you know, I come up to Ingwavuma and get told the identical story from a completely different source.'

'What story?'

'You can't be that unintelligent, Captain. The story that you took a dying man's diary. Why did you do that?'

'For chrissake, I tried to save him. Who do you think called in the rescue helicopter if it wasn't me? All right, I tried to do a cover up. I admit it. But do you know why? Let me tell you why. I recognised that man as being Monty Law. I got the shock of my life I can tell you – Doctor Montague Law dressed like a raving mad *Laka Inyanga* in the middle of a faction fight. Can you imagine how the newspapers would have loved that one? But it didn't get to the newspapers did it? Because I didn't want Mark Ingram or you to be embarrassed in that way. As for the diary; I read it. It represented the scribblings of a psychopath. There's enough evidence in those pages to incriminate your brother on a dozen charges of accessory to murder. That's why I took it. You want it, lassie? It's yours.'

Dent stood; walked swiftly to a rather bulky old fashioned safe. It was not locked. 'Here. Take it. But let me make a prediction. Let me predict that you are going to wish that you never heard about this bloody little book. The man who wrote it is dead, and I think after you have read this book you will want to bury his memory too.'

She held the book – black cardboard covers with a peeling red rib binding. From the outside it looked very ordinary: a school boy's fourth term exercise book, dog-eared and thumbed. Kirsten let it fall open where it would – the script flowing and rounded was unmistakably from the hand of her brother. She read at random.

'*To date I have experimented with 193 botanic specimens, all toxic, all curative when administered correctly. Some it seems, are capable of killing in the most minute of doses. I think I must be half-way through my education in Zulu toxicology.'*

She snapped it shut. Dent was studying her. The faintest smile was pulling at his lips. He said:

'Don't worry Kirsten, you *can* touch the pages, insanity is not infectious.'

It was a loathsome thing to say. She allowed her expression to tell him so. Dent felt no pain. He had more to say:

'If you still want to register a complaint against my conduct, you're welcome. I'll provide you with the required stationery. If you don't, then it's time for you to go.'

It was time to leave. An early winter dusk was drawing in, darkening Dent's office. She had the diary. She had extracted a promise that she would be allowed to speak to September Mabutane. She had achieved all she had set out to achieve; and suddenly that was not enough. Now she wanted to hurt this most excellent of liars.

'You're not the saint of Mawamabi hill you'd have everyone believe, are you, Patrick? It didn't all happen the way you said it happened. Did it?'

It was a puerile comment to have made. It had gained her nothing. In fact it had lost to her a most valuable initiative. Her anger however would not be muted.

'You're a bad man, Captain Dent.'

And *now* it *was* time to go. She walked from the office.

'The fact that you don't approve of my actions doesn't make them wrong.' Dent followed her. 'Anyway *you* are not the one to judge, Kirsten. Go read the diary and see what I was up against. You are blinded by a family loyalty to a man whom you remember as a decent clean living boy. Read it, and see how he changed. It wasn't your brother Monty who died, Kirsten. It was a madman who believed his name was Mvulaba. I tell you, Kirsten, I'm glad he's dead. It was the most merciful thing that could have happened.'

He held the door of the Land Rover while she climbed into the cab.

'One last thing,' he closed her in, then leaned against the step plate. 'Your name is mentioned in the diary, Kirsten. You'll find it towards the end. Something about you having taken the Inkatha of Shaka Zulu from the Suthu River gorge. Now I know that's true because I saw you do it. I was watching you on the mountain that day, and I saw everything you did. God knows what you want with the thing. But that's your business. What I have to say to you is, be careful. Be very careful. There are people who would kill you if they knew what you had done. Do you understand what I'm saying, Kirsten?'

'I think I do,' she started the engine. 'I think you're telling me that you are in an unassailable position. Is that right?'

'You're quick,' Dent said. 'Maybe we'll be allies yet.'

'The hell we will!'

She grated the first gear and jolted the clutch – in too much of a hurry to be away.

'I'll see you tomorrow,' Dent waved. As though looking forward to her return.

Kirsten drove slowly, the setting sun central in her windscreen. If there was such a thing as rush hour at Ingwavuma, it was then. Slow-footed cattle were being driven unwillingly along the road. Abantwana herd boys, hardly as tall as the sticks they wielded, opened a way for her; waved and smiled. There were donkeys, home bound with their precious water barrels, to be bullied to one side. But she was not in a hurry. Mark Ingram had returned to Durban. No one was waiting for her at the bungalow. She had time to think.

The meeting with Dent had been a viperous, vicious affair; a weaving and feinting, a spitting out of venom. Yet neither of them had been really hurt. In fact, in some twisted and perverse way an understanding had been reached. She could accept or reject his account of the events at Mawamabi hill. He did not care. His indemnity was her brother's reputation. He in turn, would say nothing of the robbing of Umzeze's cave. It was a trade-off that was venal in its appeal. Allies? More a mating of snakes. Perhaps, though, some good would come of it.

As it became darker, so the road cleared, and she could increase her speed. Her thoughts reverted to the other man at Abercorn Drift police station – September Mabutane. Dent had taken him in for questioning in connection with the murder of Ernie Tyrell. That could mean that the police knew of Mabutane's Abanzanzi affiliation. The question that Dent would have to ask himself was: would September Mabutane be so insane as to take actions that would lead to his own arrest? The game guard had led them to the mutilated body of Ernie Tyrell. Was that not proof enough that Abanzanzi were not involved? In Kirsten's mind it was. She would return to Abercorn Drift in the morning. She would see to it that Mabutane was released. He had to be freed. September Mabutane was the only link that existed between herself and her brother. She reached across for the diary she had placed upon the passenger seat; riffled a dog-eared corner with her thumbnail. Suddenly she felt very tired; very alone.

* * *

Mabutane was due for release long before the dawn. It had never been Dent's intention to imprison the game guard for longer than a few hours . . . Kirsten had actually delayed the man's release.

Dent watched the departing Land Rover as it wound slowly along the river road and up into the hills. His cautious smile expanded now – the compère of his mood. He had reason to be pleased. His meeting with Kirsten had gone better than he could have hoped for. There would be no further trouble from her. Now he had another interview to conclude. But before he did that, there were some preparations to be made. Briskly he walked back to his office.

Firstly, logistics. He unlocked his arms cabinet and stood quietly and studiously examining his array of weapons. Not for him his favourite hunting rifle with its mounted weaver scope. Its accuracy was negated by its slow rate of fire. The 12 bore Browning pump action was too indiscriminate a weapon. The 7.62 FN too cumbersome. From its felt-lined niche he took a recent acquisition: an R4 Assault rifle. The SA equivalent of the Israeli *Galill*: perfect. Light and hard hitting, its mechanism mint gunmetal blue and, like all his weapons, spotless. He stripped the R4 and checked it through. Finding no fault he reassembled it, but for the breech block cover. A slight modification was required. He reached for a small dovetailed wooden box marked: *Single point 231. Nitrogen collimator combat sight*. He took the system from its moulded box and fitted it to the R4. It would provide this weapon with an owl-like first hit capability.

More magic – more *Made in Britain* nocturnal wizardry. A hand-held bioptic nightscope no larger than the zoom lens of a camera – and totally undetectable. The latest in tristage intensifying optics, this. When held to the human eye the darkest night could hold no secrets. The most discriminating of night snipers could not have wanted for more, or better equipment.

The last thing Dent did before leaving his office was to fill his canteen to the brim with coffee and condensed milk – sustenance for the hunter. All his equipment he left lying on his desk. Now it was time to meet with Kirsten Law's dear Zulu friend; September Mabutane.

September Mabutane was pacing his cell when Dent arrived. When he looked at his gaoler it was with the eyes of the captive leopard, savage and hating. Dent had expected it. It neither disturbed nor deterred him. He unlocked the heavy barred door and entered.

'Sit down,' Dent instructed, 'on the floor. Now listen to me.'

Mabutane lowered himself – still the leopard, crouched, ready to spring. He listened.

'All of us make mistakes, Mabutane. My mistake was believing that Abanzanzi had been trampled on sufficiently, at Mawamabi hill, to cause them to change their ways. Your mistake, Mabutane, was not staying away from trouble. Abanzanzi murdered a white man. *That* was *their* mistake. They saw old Doctor Tyrell as a wizard. Another *umthakathi* to be done away with. Am I right? Is that why they killed him Mabutane? Was his *muthi* more powerful than Uhlanga's? Was he interfering with her magic?'

Not for a second did Mabutane take his eyes from his gaoler. He said nothing. There was no point in denying anything, or admitting anything. uDende had not come to judge him. uDende had come to provoke him into saying things that he would be able to use against Abanzanzi. The game was violence. The rules had been modified for the occasion, but uDende could never change; he was set and unalterable like a clay figurine, and in a way just as brittle. The violence would come.

'Typical of Abanzanzi,' Dent went on. 'They needed *muthi imbengo* – really powerful stuff – to make the men invincible. Doctor Tyrell's body had the thyroid taken from it, didn't it? You saw for yourself, September. Were *you* doctored with that *muthi*? Eh? Have you got the power of the doctor now, Mabutane? Do you feel any different? Eh boy?'

Yes, he felt different. But it had nothing to do with *muthi imbengo*. It had to do with the anguish of a human being – a white woman who was searching for her brother. It had to do with the mask of horror that he had caused to fall upon her lovely face. It had to do with what could happen to that woman when she drew aside the awesome curtain of magic that Abanzanzi had hung. He had brought her a little distance. He could not desert her now. She thought she was strong, but in the place where she was going she would be broken like a twig. He, September Mabutane, would be her shield. Yes, he felt different. *He felt afraid*. But the fear was not for himself.

uDende was talking. He should be listening. For in the place where he was now, this man was God. He listened.

'I know what you're thinking,' Dent said. 'You think I've got no proof. And you're right. But don't think I couldn't hold you here if I wanted to. I could hold you here until the flesh rotted on your bones. But I don't want to do that, Mabutane. Punishing you would not be punishing Abanzanzi. I've thought of a better way. I'm going to do what the British Redcoats tried, and failed to do a hundred years ago. I am going to take the Inkatha of Shaka Zulu, and I'm going to burn it.'

'No!' Mabutane broke his promise of silence.

'Ah! So you do have a tongue, and a mind. I thought I had a zombie with me tonight; one of Uhlanga's *imikhovu*. Tell me why I should not burn that piece of old rubbish, Mabutane?'

'Abanzanzi would kill you if you did.'

'Hmm,' Dent stroked his chin as if to think about that. It was a mockery of course. He took a pace forward then crouched face to face with his prisoner. He was massive. 'They'd kill me?' He pretended to cry, then pretended to laugh. Mabutane braced himself for the blow that had to follow.

'You!' He said to Dent. And that was all he said. Where Dent's hand had been empty, now it held a truncheon, black and wickedly fast it cracked against the forehead of the prisoner.

He had begun to say: You have no right to punish Abanzanzi. Whatever they have done wrong you have done a thousand times worse. The words were still there, in amongst the dazzling shock and pain. He rose up to defend himself, but Dent was quicker by far. 'No right – No right – No right,' he held on to that thought as the terrible blows came fast.

Still Mabutane reached his feet. His only chance was to smother the deadly black truncheon. He threw himself at Dent. The move had been anticipated. Dent swivelled back, drove hard to Mabutane's throat – staggered him – did not stop him. Once, twice, three times Dent hooked him to the belly. Blows that dug in, knuckle and fist. *That* stopped him. In a spew of gag and vomit, Mabutane buckled. He dropped to the stone cold floor.

Dent was sweating. His chest was heaving. The ecstasy of sadism burst in him. A storm. A dervish fury that drove Dent forward to inflict more pain; to explode with pleasure. It brought his boot within a raging inch of Mabutane's skull. And there it stopped. He needed this man.

'Get out!' Dent slowed his breathing. The madness slipped away. 'Get out. The door is open. Run Mabutane. Run, before I kill you.'

Mabutane could only crawl. So he crawled, from the cell to the passage way. But the damage to his body did not endure. By the time he had reached the Charge Office, it was starting to repair. He could stand. Clutching for the support of walls and chairs and whatever was at hand, he staggered to the outer door. From there on he ran.

It took Dent seconds to buckle into his gear, then follow.

It was very dark. The moon would rise late that night and set with the sunrise – *ihlekwe izinyoni* – laughed at by the birds.

The ground underfoot was black, shadowless and deceptive. But that was September Mabutane's disability; and Dent had planned it to be so. Dent could see well, and he needed that advantage. In order not to be detected, he would have to remain at least 50 silent metres behind his quarry.

He slung his rifle, shrugged the strap until the weight was comfortably balanced, then jogged to the perimeter gate. There he unsheathed the nightscope. The landscape of the hunting cat unfolded. Grass and trees and swooping bats all painted luminous green. Mabutane was standing at the roadside about 100 metres from the gate. He was bending and stretching, and rubbing the beating from his throat and gut. Good, that had taken the youth out of him.

When Mabutane walked on, Dent followed. His present course would bring him within a short time to a junction in the road, where a footpath crossed it. If he turned east there, his heading would then be in the direction of Nkonjane – his home kraal. Dent had followed him once before to Nkonjane, and that had been a fruitless exercise. He was expecting Mabutane to follow the western track. That would lead him into the mountains. Hopefully the sangoma Uhlanga was in those mountains. Mabutane had an important message to deliver. Dent had something for her too.

Still without any resolution to his step Mabutane reached the junction, and there he paused, seemingly undecided. Perhaps he was unsure of his location. He squatted, peering around, trying to make something of the amorphous blackness – trying to gain the silhouettes that would orientate him exactly. Then he stood up. He turned right. He did what Dent wanted him to do and headed westwards along the footpath that led off to the mountains.

Dent released the breath he had been holding in expectation. 'Perfect.' He started forward again. The track was winding and narrow, and deeply scored into the ground. It was a simple matter to follow it as it crept into the foothills, the Zimpisini valley. Then onwards towards the true Lebombos.

Dent would not have had a chance without the scope. He used it frequently to check his bearings. And even with that phosphorescent stare to guide him on, the terrain appeared foreign and sinister. Now and then a gleam of eyes would seem to follow him from some adjacent kraal. But it was just an illusion. Those humans there were blind. It would have taken the eyes of a jackal to mark his progress in those moonless hills, and he was the only one who had such eyes.

Another turn-off in the track, this, curving to the north. Dent made certain that Mabutane passed it by; he also checked his front and back before lowering the scope. There were no other travellers. The route was clear. He could walk on.

Not twenty paces further on he knew he had made a bad mistake. He heard the sound of someone close ahead – and approaching. He lifted the bioptic scope and stared into the face of September Mabutane. Dent dived off the track. His rifle butt clattered on a rock. From a nearby kraal a dog began to bark.

Dent crawled into a little gulley and waited. And Mabutane waited . . . Then from the kraal came the sound of voices raised in argument. A kicked dog yelped. The source of the night sounds now resolved, Mabutane continued along the track.

He had either missed the northern turn-off in the dark, or had reconsidered his route. Either way the man was now pointed north. Warier now, Dent was back in pursuit. The search for Uhlanga, the sangoma with the eyes of rain, pressed on. Slower now, because the track had narrowed and steepened.

Dent thought they had reached their destination. At a place called kwaMabona, Mabutane turned aside. Set amongst the mountain aloes were four huts and a well-kept cattle kraal. A door opened and quickly closed and the game guard was gone.

He was gone for less time than it took Dent to suck a mouthful of cold sweet coffee from his canteen, unzip his fly and empty his bladder. When Mabutane reappeared he was not alone. His new companion wore a blanket tossed high across one shoulder in the fashion of the mountain people. They stood there for a while, intently close, talking.

So, Mabutane did not know how to find the sangoma Uhlanga. The way to her lay through one, or more, link men – neurons as it were, in the physiology of Abanzanzi. People employed to decide on the priority of the messages she received. Dent hoped that the message that Mabutane carried was painful enough to work its way swiftly up to the head.

Apparently it was. The men ceased talking. The blanketed courier, with Mabutane at his heels set off northwards once more, and fast.

It was not the first time that that tribesman had travelled those mountains on a moonless night. He had the instinctive ability of a mountain buck. Had he not been hindered by the slower moving Mabutane, Dent would not have been able to keep up at all.

They pulled away from him – 200 metres – more. The footpath dwindled and disappeared. The underfoot became rockier; looser. The thorn shrub closed. Dent's thighs burned and ached. Sweat, more than he could wipe away, was trickling over his eyelids – stinging, obscuring the rear lens of the scope. It was getting harder to spot them all the time.

There they were. They had crested kwaMabona and were moving westwards along the mountain ridge. Dent struggled upwards to the heights; stood there gasping for air; his legs wobbling unsupportively beneath him.

Quickly he lifted his binoculars and swept the ensuing valley. It was as he had predicted – they were out of sight. The ground was undulating, in places patched thick with thorns. Hopeless! He had tried – he had failed. He had not been able to last the pace.

Further along the ridge he observed an outcrop of rock; a ledge that overhung the valley that would make a perfect observation point. If the men continued at their present course and speed, before long they would be climbing the opposite slope. From the ledge he would have a good chance of picking them up again.

It was not to be. Despite the advantageous view; despite the thoroughness of his search, Mabutane and the man from kwaMabona were not to be seen.

Dent's patience however, his positioning and his technology, were rewarded. At the western end of the valley he saw a campfire burning. The flame was obscured, but he knew it was there because the foliage above and around was a surrealist dream of soft luminous frondescence.

There were some excellent reasons for disregarding that distant glow: herd boys out searching for strays lit fires; Amadoda on beer drinks would sip the night away around such fires. The blacksmith's flame was never allowed to die. It was midnight, it was cold, and he was tired.

Dent lifted himself though, and began the long walk towards that fire. Because Abanzanzi, too, might light just such a fire.

So Dent began the climb that would take him down that most treacherous of loose-rocked slopes. Every step was a risk, and every handhold was a branch of thorns. The valley was called maKhathi – the space between heaven and earth – a most appropriate name.

Whoever was master of that fire had chosen to burn rare Ironwood; an extravagant man indeed. The unmistakeable honey-sweet smell of Ironwood smoke was drifting on the downward breeze.

What made this man even more unusual was, that he was not there to enjoy the heat and golden aroma. Dent made absolutely sure of that. At a prudent distance from the fire he halted. There, using the nightscope, he did a thorough reconnaissance of the site.

The fire was in a clearing at a bend in the valley. There was nothing especially notable about the place – there were no huts or beer drinkers; no wandering herd boys – no human beings of any calling.

The place was deserted, and that was strange, because spontaneous combustion was something that did not happen to midnight piles of Ironwood logs.

Dent unslung his rifle and approached, initially to the edge of the clearing. Then, when he had probed the deepest shadows once more, onwards into the circle of fire light.

The downwind smoke of this fire was nothing to be avoided. It slipped past the nostrils and into the chest in the most conducive of ways.

There was no call for hurry now. A bright moon had risen, the hunt was over. He knew that if he followed the maKhathi valley southwards for a further four or five kilometres, it would spill him out in the Suthu River gorge, a short distance downstream from the dam wall, and in good time to reach Abercorn Drift for breakfast. In the meantime he had an hour to idle, and a splendid Ironwood fire at which to idle it. He took his metal canteen and placed it on some embers. He felt disappointed, but relaxed, very relaxed.

'uDende.'

... Quite tranquil in fact ... The fragrant flame was lulling him with its amiable warmth.

'uDende.'

Yes, he was uDende. Someone was calling him; someone with the persistence of a buzzfly on a sleepy afternoon.

'*Saubona* uDende. Look over here and you will see something that will surprise you.'

A rather impudent request. He looked anyway, more puzzled than surprised at what he saw.

'It's you, Law. Where were you hiding? I didn't see you.'

'Mvulaba ... Mvulaba is my name.'

'Oh yes. It's a strange name, for a white man I mean. What do you want?'

'Perhaps I should be asking you that question. You're a long way from home, uDende. What brings you into the hills? Did you come to kill me, uDende? Did you come to do what you could not do at Mawamabi hill?'

'No. I didn't come to kill you, Mvulaba. I didn't even know you were alive. Kirsten said you were alive but I didn't believe it. I thought you were dead.'

'You thought I was dead? Well you've got a rifle. Wouldn't you like to use it, to make up for your past mistake?'

He did have a rifle; loaded; in fact pointed at the chest of the man standing there.

'Go on, uDende. Pull the trigger.'

Pull the trigger? What an incredible request. It shattered the quiescence of the moment; set his mind excitedly in search for reasons, reasons for hate, reasons for a rifle shot. They were there, he knew it, lying submerged, not far beneath the surface. But just too deep; too scattered to find. 'I can't do it,' he said. 'I don't want to kill you.'

And the turbulence receded. The waters became smooth and reflective once again. He looked at the rifle in his hands – a weapon without a master.

Mvulaba came towards him. He did not face Dent. He squatted, facing the fire. He spoke very softly.

'How do I appear to you, uDende? How do you see me?'

'As if I am being deceived by my senses, Mvulaba. As if you are something at a distance which if I examine it closer may turn out to be something quite different.'

'Does this alarm you, uDende?'

'It only amazes me.'

'I'm quite real, uDende. I want you to be sure of that.'

'I am sure. What do you want?'

'Mabutane told me that you have the Inkatha of Shaka Zulu. Is that true, uDende?'

'I know where it is.'

'Knowing where it is and having it are two different things. Where is it?'

Where was it? Was that not his secret?

'It's right that you tell me.'

Of course. It *was* right that Mvulaba should know.

'Kirsten has hidden it in the cellar at Prospect Hall.'

'You saw it there?'

'Yes.'

'Mmm. Do you know, uDende, how precious an article that Inkatha is?'

'Yes. I think I do.'

'Many people have died for that Inkatha. Others are ready to die for it. Are you ready to die for it, uDende?'

'No.'

'I think that you should know that you have put your life in danger. If anything should happen to that Inkatha; if it were damaged or destroyed or even put in jeopardy; then your life would be the minimum payment that would be extracted.'

'It's hard to understand this whole thing. I read your diary, Mvulaba. I don't understand what you are trying to prove. Reading what you wrote was like seeing the thoughts of two totally opposed men within a single body. Who are you? What are you?'

'I was confused. I was lost. You saved me, uDende. You did what had to be done.'

'But how?'

'That day on Mawamabi hill, uDende. How well do you remember it?'

'Very well.'

'Do you remember a little pot of ashes that was crushed against my chest?'

'I think so. Yes.'

'That was the sontekile, uDende. I was trying to get away from Abanzanzi that day. I had what I wanted in my hands, in that little pot, a miracle. I had the formula and I had a sample. I was ready to go back. I wanted to be Montague Law again. Montague Law the bringer of botanical miracles; Montague Law the sugar baron of Prospect Hall. I wanted to play polo and claim my seat at the Cane Growers' Club. I wanted to make love with blonde white women, perfumed and groomed. You changed all that, uDende.'

A momentary urge seemed to move Mvulaba to turn then – to face Dent. A transient weakness. He averted it. Staring into the fire as though his audience was the dancing flame, he spoke on: 'I was burned; horribly burned. You thought that I would die. I thought I was dead. But I revived because of the miracle of sontekile, and the love and care of a Zulu sangoma.'

'Uhlanga?'

'Yes, Uhlanga of the eyes of rain. She saved my charred and blistered body. But she did more than that. She saved my mind. She made me understand who I am. So you see I have to be thankful to you, uDende. You tried to destroy me but instead you were the instrument of my salvation. I am Mvulaba. Montague Law died in Addington Hospital. His body was my stepping stone. There *is* no more confusion.'

'And sontekile? What happened to Law's obsession with that? What if that overpowers you once again? Would that not drive you to return to your own people?'

'The Zulus are my people. Sontekile belongs only to them. My work belongs to them. You must return the diary, uDende.'

'I don't have it any more. Kirsten wanted it. I gave it to her.'

'That too belongs to Abanzanzi.'

'And you Mvulaba. Do you belong to Abanzanzi?'

'You know I do.'

'But you're a white man. A civilised man.'

'Am I?'

'Look at you.'

'Yes, do that, uDende. I wanted to show you the mind of me before I showed you the body of me. Now you've seen my mind let me show you what your fire did.'

Mvulaba stood. 'Look.' He slowly turned. 'Look. Your handiwork, uDende. How do you think your civilised world would take it? How would the blonde and perfumed ladies react to me? . . . Don't turn your eyes from me, uDende.'

The other side of Mvulaba, the side he had been so careful to keep hidden was now displayed.

'Look.'

He spun slowly, the better to show the hideousness of his latter side. His fingers ran delicately from scar to scar; emphasising his liquescent grotesqueness as though it was the finest fashion.

'Look!'

But Dent had seen it all by then. He could look no longer.

'Don't be upset, uDende. I'm not.'

But that was mockery. The man was crying. His face was wet with tears.

'Which side of me do you think I should present first to our civilised friends? Or should I hold myself sideways forever? Or even better learn to pirouette so fast that I was constantly just a blur. Oh! uDende. uDende, what have you done to me?'

'I saved your life.'

'Yes, you saved my life. Would it not have been more humane, more civilised, to have pulled that trigger? No, you don't have to answer. I think you had no choice in doing what you did. My spirit is that of Mvulaba. My mind required to be shown it. Your actions were dictated. You had no choice.'

No choice? Was this a form of forgiveness, an acknowledgement of man's illusive will? An appealing concept to one who had mutilated thus the substance of God. Once more in mitigation: 'I saved your life.'

'And now I am going to save yours. No, not because of any debt of gratitude, uDende. Please don't think that there is any gratitude in me. I am doing this because your actions were no more voluntary than the stone that is lifted and thrown at someone in anger. Can that stone be punished? Stand up now, uDende.'

He stood as meekly as the prisoner in the dock – a role he had seen rehearsed a thousand times.

'You are a murderer, uDende. You came into the mountains tonight to do more murder. Admit it.'

The prisoner nodded. 'Yes.'

'Uhlanga was to be your victim.'

'Yes. I came to kill Uhlanga.'

'You have been condemned to death by the full council of Abanzanzi, uDende, and by the voices of the higher ones. Every hand was against you. But I pleaded for you. I told them of my belief, and because of that it was agreed that you would be given a chance, one last chance. And this is it: This persecution of Abanzanzi must stop. All interference in Abanzanzi affairs must stop. You must leave the Inkatha. Dismiss it from your mind. We do not wish you as a friend, uDende, but neither do we want you as an enemy. You have been destructive beyond words, uDende. This must stop. If it does not stop then we will kill you. It will be easy to kill you. As easily as you were trapped tonight we could trap you again. As easily as I could kill you now, I could kill you at another time. Do you believe me, uDende, do you believe what I say?'

'Yes.'

'Giving to you, uDende, is like hand-feeding the hungry crocodile. But there it is. I have done it. What must happen now must happen . . .'

'Yes. What will happen to me now?'

'You are in no immediate danger, uDende. Do everything just as I have told you and you will be safe. Go now. Hurry.'

The maKhathi valley was lightening along its rim. The fire was dying. Dent turned away and walked towards the dawn.

'Remember, uDende, it would be easy to kill you.'

Incredibly, the warning was followed by the sound of laughter. Silly and wild, and ascending like the giggle of a hyena. The echo of it seemed to follow him all the way back to Abercorn Drift.

As he had predicted, he arrived in time to smell breakfast cooking. He was a sick man by then, however. To him it was a cesspool odour.

He reached his room. He grappled the door open. His skull exploded. His vision shattered. An axe-blow concussion pitched him forward.

They were waiting for him there: a crucible of hideous, melting, dancing men – giggling in a parody of mirth. They caught him as he fell.

* * *

Sergeant Shibindji was faithful to his captain for many reasons. One of them was that he disliked change. He did not want uDende to be replaced by a younger, perhaps more sober, certainly more troublesome, commanding officer.

That was why he lied to the tired-eyed woman standing before him. 'He's out.'

'But his truck is here.' Kirsten's night with the diary had been very long. Her patience was bubble thin. 'Where could he possibly have gone without his truck?'

Shibindji shrugged.

'If you're lying to me Shibindji, your legs will swell up. You will suffer forever the uMankunkunku.'

Now *that* was a consequence Shibindji was not prepared to risk. Not even for uDende. This woman with the pointing finger looked capable of such mischief.

'He's in his room.'

'I want to see him. Where is his room?'

It was at the rear of the police station. A twin rondavel structure neatly thatched and painted. Its entrance, an archway of purple flamed bougainvillea. An old and much scarred bull terrier bitch lay on the cool verandah floor, thumping a lethargic but welcoming tail. This did not look like the lair of the Ogre of Ingwavuma.

Shibindji held the screen door open. She and the bull terrier struggled for priority.

'This way.'

She didn't have to be shown any further. There were only two rooms in the bungalow and from one of them a low, distressful moaning was coming.

'He's sick.'

'Drunk,' Shibindji corrected. 'He does that sometimes, madam; when he is sad about the past I think. The Captain is a very sad man. When he is like this it is better just to leave him.'

'You can't just leave him, Shibindji.'

'It's better that way.'

'I suppose so. I really came to speak to September Mabutane. The captain said I could, last night.'

'He's gone.'

'Gone!'

Kirsten shoved open Dent's bedroom door. The bull terrier beat her once more into the room. It took the bed in a single wheezy bound and began to lick the face of its master.

If Dent was hung over, then it was the most evil hangover Kirsten had ever seen. He did not even have the strength to turn from this avalanche of love. He looked dead. His skin had the colour of a cadaver and at his lips and nose little purple veins were branching. She tugged the terrier off the bed.

'Get that dog out of here, Shibindji.'

She shook Dent lightly and he moaned.

'Captain Dent . . . Patrick.'

His lips were moving but she could make no sense of the tongueless throat sounds. There was a faint acetone-like smell about him and the room smelled of vomit, but the sickly-sour odour of yesterday's liquor was absent. Heart attack – that was

Kirsten's diagnosis.

'Shibindji!' she called. 'Come and help me. Find some extra cushions – quickly.'

Together they struggled to prop him up. Now what?

'Water, Shibindji.'

She tilted the glass to his lips. His adam's apple bobbed reflexively.

'Good. I'm going to radio for a doctor, Shibindji. Where's your radio room?'

'No doctor . . .' from Dent, a whispered yet definite refusal of such aid. His fingers were clawing – a gesture for Kirsten to bend closer.

'I'm OK . . . bit too much of the local stuff. Just need to rest.' His breath was rationed; his words slow in coming; dull. He sat up slowly. 'What are . . . you doing here, Kirsten?'

'I came to speak to September Mabutane.'

'Oh yes. I let him go.'

'Why? You promised me I could speak to him this morning.'

'You sound cross that I let him out Kirsten. What's the matter, did you want me to keep the poor bugger locked up all night just for your benefit? If you want to speak to him go and find him. Now get out of my bedroom.'

'It was just that you promised,' she said. It was not a very triumphant exit line. The trouble was that Dent had made a perfect analysis of her emotions. He could, however, have no idea as to the justification of her annoyance: the man who could possibly bear for her a vital message was *gone*.

The bull terrier, it seemed, had become attached to her. It accompanied her back to the sunlit yard. She patted it and it oinked with pleasure like a pig. A friend in need.

More friends; the rumble of an approaching vehicle. A dusty light green Land Rover with the Natal Parks Board emblem on its doors drew up in the yard. Reynolds was the driver. He looked surprised to see her.

'Hi, Kirsten. What are you doing here?' He climbed out.

'I came to see Captain Dent. Actually I came to speak to September Mabutane.'

'And did you speak to him?'

'Apparently Dent let him out last night.'

A Zulu constable appeared on the police station verandah. Reynolds addressed him curtly:

'Where is September Mabutane?'

'He is not here, Umnumzane.'

'Dent let him go,' Kirsten said. 'He told me.'

'Well he did not report for work this morning.' Reynolds looked annoyed. 'I think I'd better have a chat with our captain friend.'

'He's sick, Rob. I've just come from him.'

'Hung over, more like it.'

'Maybe Mabutane is on his way back,' Kirsten said. 'I'll follow you back to Ndumu. I'd like to speak to your game guard, if you don't mind.'

'You're welcome, Kirsten.' Reynolds glanced at his wristwatch. 'But aren't you cutting it a bit fine?'

'Cutting what a bit fine? I don't understand.'

'Well, you obviously didn't receive your radio message then.'

'What message? From whom?'

'Hmm.' Reynolds fingered his chin reflectively, never wanting to be accused of eavesdropping. 'Let me see if I can remember. Ah yes. It was from Ingram. He wanted you to meet the helicopter. A Doctor someone or other.'

'Whitaker?' Kirsten suggested.

'Yes. That's it. Doctor Whitaker is on board. You were supposed to meet him.'

'At what time?'

'At 1100,' Reynolds said. 'You've got half an hour to get back to the helipad. Tell me, is he a medical doctor?'

'The best. Thanks for the message, Rob.'

'Is he going to take over at the dam clinic?'

Kirsten heard Reynolds' shouted question as she was running towards her Land Rover.

'I hope so,' she called over her shoulder. 'I really do.'

Her tiredness was suddenly a trivial thing. Her hope had been rewarded; her day enhanced. For the first time she noticed the radio, set into the dashboard of the Land Rover. She found a station that was playing hits from the sixties: Bacharach's

'What the world needs now is love sweet love:
Love's the only thing there's just too little of.'

How lovely the words, how sadly true . . . She drove as quickly as the dirt road would allow.

Reynolds shook his head. He did not approve of extremes. Such a driving style would end in disaster. He wondered what Kirsten's interest was in his truant game guard, September Mabutane, who had lied to him about a certain day's tracking and about a barefoot trail that ended at a buried arms cache.

Hung over or not, Dent had to be informed immediately of that most startling and disturbing of discoveries.

*   *   *

Had Gray Whitaker been tuned to the same broadcast as Kirsten, he would have been in wholehearted accord with her sentiments.

He, however, was engaged with a static-plagued conversation with the Ingram Associates company pilot.

'There's the dam,' the man said. 'The hospital is there in the valley, near the compound. See it?'

'I don't know. I think so.'

The pilot did another circuit.

'It's the white-painted building. It's got an asbestos canopy in front of it. Look, you can see an ambulance parked there. See it now?'

He saw it. He saw the dam wall; the site office; a hundred crawling, dust-smothered mechanical things. He scanned a thousand upturned faces. But the face he wanted to see he did not see.

'The strip is in the next valley,' he was told. 'I'm going to let down now.'

Then he saw it: the open-top Land Rover, dragging a mile-long dust plume – the driver with the streaming raven hair. She looked up and waved and he waved back.

'The boss's missus,' he was informed.

The ground floated up to meet them. The Landy and the Bell Jet Ranger reached the helipad at almost the same time.

'Mind the rotors.'

That was the last message Whitaker got before removing the headphones. He gave the pilot a thumbs up; collected his carry bag and clambered out.

The chopper was airborne before he reached the Land Rover. He shouted through the noise. 'Hi!' He waited for the sound to diminish; the dust to settle. 'It's good to see you, Kirsten.'

'You too, Gray. I nearly didn't make it in time. I didn't get Mark's message when I should have. Hop in.'

He slung his gear onto the back seat. A dashboard radio that was belting out rock 'n roll she subdued.

'Hop in,' she said again. 'Are you taking the job?'

'I don't know,' he said. 'It depends, I guess.'

'On what?'

'Well I'll sniff around a bit and see how I like it.'

'Oh you'll like it,' Kirsten laughed. She reached across and touched his hand. She smiled: the quick and poignant smile of emotions hidden. Then her hand flew from his grasp like a bird.

'Where to?' she said.

'I was going to ask you that. I've got to get to visit the hospital, but there's no crisis. We can dawdle a bit: take the long road. Find somewhere quiet. There are a few things I want to talk to you about.'

'I know just the place.'

It was a high place; a hilltop lay-by with a view of three countries: 'Mozambique and Swaziland over there. And behind us, *ons land Suid Afrika*.'

With the engine switched off there was no remaining sound, but that from the mouth of the dry north wind. It spoke of drought and hunger. But the view was filling them up and they did not hear it. They climbed a little koppie of tumbled rock and sat there; humbled by this infinite perspective of earth and sky.

'Beautiful, isn't it?' She expanded her arms up to the sky; drew in a deep breath. 'I've come here often over the past months. It's been a trying time for me. But this place has never failed to give me courage. But what am I going on about? You said you wanted to talk.'

'You haven't found your brother, have you?'

'No. But I *was* right you know. He *is* alive. I met a Zulu game guard who knows how to reach him. I've sent a message to him. I'll just have to be patient now.' She stood up and walked a little way from him; paced there agitatedly. 'Is it Monty you wanted to talk about, Gray?'

'Yes, and other things.'

'I'm feeling a bit sensitive about my brother at the moment. Is it vital that we do?'

'It is important.'

'OK Gray . . . OK.'

'Kirsten. You know that when your brother was at Addington Hospital we drew blood for analysis.'

'That's standard practice isn't it?'

'Pretty much so. The results weren't standard though. Monty was badly burned – so badly burned that I wouldn't have been surprised had he died of the consequences.'

'We've *been* over this haven't we?'

'Kirsten, bear with me. Hear what I have to say.'

She nodded, sighed. 'I'm sorry. I told you, I'm edgy. I'll explain it to you later. Just go on.'

'Well, your brother had forty per cent burns. In those circumstances he should have suffered marked fluid loss, and severe shock. He suffered neither. His haematocrit levels remained normal. There was no sign of hyponatremia or acidosis. His bloodflow was almost normal. Instead of his heart and respiratory rates increasing, they decreased. I couldn't understand it. A senior colleague of mine was just as puzzled. We drew another blood sample, in case the lab had somehow got it wrong. But before we could submit it. Well, you know what happened. Your brother went into a decline and . . . died.'

'But *didn't* die.'

'Yes. That's when I met you, Kirsten. And you told me about your brother and his work.'

'And you told me about Percy, the hibernating hedgehog.'

'You remember that!'

Her laughter was quick to spill and overbright; like a palmful of mercury. Yet the laughter did some good. He felt he could go on safely.

'What I wanted to tell you is the story of that second phial of blood. I sent it to Stanford University, to Professor Beard. You remember, the man we sent the telex off to, the American toxicologist doing research on tetradotoxin as an immunological catalyst in the human system.'

'Of course I remember.'

'Sure. Well last week I heard from the professor. He telephoned me from Stanford. He was excited, I can tell you. He told me that they had run extensive comparison tests on that sample. He said he had isolated a totally unique alkaloid containing a class of heterocyclic nitrogen atoms, that he considers to be an even more potent somatic motor neuron blocker than tetradotoxin, and in this case with an even greater potential for the enhancement of the human immune system. Well you can imagine the excitement at Stanford. The professor wanted to know where I obtained the sample. How it came to be administered. And most importantly, of course, the source and availability of this new compound. Beard himself suggested he fly out here to meet with me. Kirsten, can you understand the significance of this?'

'Tell me.'

'Well, here are our Americans. They have been engaged for how many years in research which they believe is totally unique, and vital. They have only just after all this time managed to establish the immune interactive qualities of tetradotoxin. Then *presto!* From the other end of the world a sample of an even better, even more potent compound of a similar molecular structure arrives by mail, from some never-heard-of doctor in darkest Africa. They want *in*. Their immunologists have been involved since 1979 in trying to discover a drug to combat the killer immune deficiency disease AIDS. They've spent millions of dollars and, to put in Beard's own words, "they've gotten nowhere". Now they believe that there is more than an even chance that we have got what they're looking for. Is that, or is that not, exciting news?'

She did not answer. She stood now with her back turned to him, tossing little pebbles at some imaginary target. He went on.

'So, that's how important it is that we find Monty.' And even as he was saying it he knew that his words had been ill chosen. He stood and swiftly walked towards her. He had not meant it like that, and he wanted to tell her so. He never got the chance.

'You!' She turned. She pointed an accusatory finger. 'I never expected to hear that from *you*.'

'Kirsten . . . Kirsten wait.'

'No. You wait, Doctor Graham Whitaker. I've got something to tell you now. I sometimes make a mistake in judging somebody, but not often. I'm not much on immune systems, but I'm usually a bloody good judge of human nature. Now, you had me fooled for a while. I really believed you that day when you said . . . what was it now . . . Ah! yes: "The world should know of this man's sacrifice; a brilliant and dedicated scientist has tragically died." That was all for my benefit wasn't it, Gray? What you really want is a free ride to medical stardom.'

'Stop it Kirsten! For chrissake that's not so!'

'Oh no? You could have fooled me, Gray. Not one word of compassion. Not one word of hope. Just "*let's go get 'im*". You talk about this as a project. You've turned the tragedy of my brother into some kind of scientific glory hunt. God, that's despicable. You make me angry, Gray. But more than anything you make me sad.'

'You have misunderstood me,' Whitaker said. 'It's not like that at all. Yes, I do want to see this discovery brought into a scientific environment. There's a suffering world out there, and I'm a doctor. But I'm not involved in a glory hunt. I don't want any bloody glory. I don't want a cent out of this. I'm sorry if I gave you that impression. I can't take back any words, all I can do is apologise. Kirsten, you are the last person I would want to hurt.'

She was not hearing him any longer. She was striding towards the Land Rover. He was not going to let this happen. He shouted: 'Kirsten. What I said at Prospect Hall I meant. I stand by those words. I also said that the world should know about your brother's sacrifice. Remember that. You never told me then how despicable that thought was then. What the hell has changed?'

She slammed the driver's door; started the big V8 engine. She was going to drive away. By Christ she was going to leave him there. Anger moved *him* now. It moved him to sprint, to reach a rocky gap, past which even a Land Rover could not drive unless it crushed him from its path. There he stood, legs wide and braced – daring her to try.

She switched the motor off. There was no more anger in her. She was pale and her eyes were damp. Very gently his fingers linked with hers. Willingly, her hands released the steering wheel; this time there was no flight. Quietly she said:

'I'm sorry.'

He shook his head. 'No, I deserved it.'

That quicksilver laugh of hers again. When it was gone he said: 'It was not just your brother that I wanted to talk about, Kirsten. I wanted to talk about you and me. You see I believe there are things that relate to us that should be spoken about. Am I right, Kirsten?'

'Yes.'

'I think you've sensed how I feel about you, Kirsten. I think *you* know that the reason why I'm here now is because of you. I want to be here, Kirsten. I want to be where you are. I want to help you. Oh! It's more than that, but that's enough about how I feel. The point is that I don't want to make life any more difficult than it already is, for you, or for me.'

'I hear what you're saying, Gray. My answer is that I want you to come to the Lebombos.'

'Even if it complicates things?'

'You sound like you're warning me.'

'I am. Kirsten, what I'm saying to you is that I love you. I don't know when it happened, or how. But that's how things stand with me. Do you still want me to come up here?'

'Yes.'

She turned her face up to him then and kissed him hard. But if there was passion in it, it was the passion of desperation.

'I want you here.' She spaced the words fervently. 'I *need* your help. I need it desperately. Some terrible things have happened recently, and I think that Monty may have been involved. I'm frightened Gray. I'm frightened that if I don't get to my brother soon, and get him out of here, then it will be the end of him.'

'I'll help you Kirsten.'

'Then read this.' She thrust a notebook into his hands. 'It's his diary, Gray. Once you've read it you'll understand things better.'

10

The diary of the man called Mvulaba was the most intriguing document that Gray Whitaker had ever read. It was the first-hand record of the progressive deterioration of a schizoid reaction personality; a word picture every bit as eloquent as the art of Vincent van Gogh.

The initial precipitating factor; the easel, upon which the Mvulaba canvas rested, was the death of the fiancée of Montgomery Law. From that traumatic moment the conduct of the writer had centred on self blame. As a highly trained scientist Law had been well equipped to understand the cause and consequence of her sickness. She had not just died of some mortal disease of which only the medical doctors had some knowledge. He had known what was happening to her, every insidious inch of the way. Every diffuse neurological sign, every smiling remission, and every exacerbation, he would have anticipated with hopeless dread. He had watched her beauty fade and waste. He had seen the hand of death beckon her from him. And like an impotent lover he had lost her, then blamed himself.

He had had no defence. His genetic grooming had defeated him. His brilliant introspective personality had precipitated him into the morbid sunless dreamscape that was the vision of the schizoid.

Then into the story came clever little Mancoba, with his dusty manuscript, and obsession for travel to distant misty mountains. Just the place for one whose old familiar world had been destroyed. Just the place for this lonely fugitive from reality. With a soul that was an ache of guilt; with the manuscript and Mancoba he had set off to find sanctuary – and possibly, just possibly, redemption: the cure for the disease that had killed his beloved woman. Would that not bring redemption?

He had found instead Uhlanga, the sangoma. Or had she found

him?

'I have been waiting for you. You have arrived on chameleon's legs.'

She had looked into those brooding eyes and seen the brilliant shattered mind that lay behind. And in her way she had saved him. Her psychology in its very primitiveness had been effective.

'You are not who you think you are. You did not come to me, you were called. I was chosen to be your teacher; and you my pupil.'

She had developed the required emotional bond between herself and Law.

'You are the eyes. I am the skin.'

She had not tried to reason him from his guilt. She had simply transferred it. She had grafted a new personality to the schizoid mainstem of the mind of Montague Law; a personality that like a strangler fig would ultimately twine down and choke the life out of its host. How diabolically clever was the sangoma Uhlanga. How educated was her methodology; her usage of hallucinogenic compounds to nurture the growth of the id of Mvulaba; her mastery of the symbolism of death and born again.

She had conducted Law's thoughts through a world that differed utterly from ordinary experience. He had walked through strange dimensions and in a different time. And therein he had found forgiveness . . . almost. Uhlanga had denied him one thing: the knowledge that he had come to seek – the sontekile. In the conflict of his mind, that need had remained constant. The will of Montague Law had somehow endured in desperate existence. It had always been there to be reckoned with, by the man, and by the sangoma.

'There is little time. Uhlanga returns today . . . I will have to demand it. I can not continue.'

The last entry read:

'It is hard to think clearly with everything closing on me as it does. It feels as though my mind is about to snap – and nothing achieved.'

And then in a page-wide scrawl:

'Fire   I have it   Uhla . . .' The pencilhead had snapped in the writing of those final exciting words. *I have it*, certainly meant that Monty Law had obtained the formula of the sontekile. There was no knowing how the sentence had ended: Uhlanga is dead? Uhlanga is gone? *Uhla . . .?*

The fate of the sangoma Uhlanga was of no great concern to Graham Whitaker. What concerned him was the present locality of the man who knew that incredible formula.

Whitaker laid the diary down and tiredly pressed his forehead against his knuckles. His fatigue, however, was just a physical thing – burning eyes and aching spine. Mentally he was quick. He felt stimulated, excited. Since he had come to the Lebombos, so many things had happened, and so rapidly, that it was hard to keep a balance. Like a novice skater he was up and going and feeling good – and at the same time apprehensive. There was more to this than he had had time to learn. His movements had yet to become easy.

It was lightening now. There was a new day to be thought about. Kirsten had said that she would call for him at 7.30, and in an hour it would be 7.30. His chin was rough with stubble, and the eyes that looked back at him from Tyrell's bathroom mirror were veined.

'Not good enough,' he lectured the image there. 'I want you shipshape in sixty minutes, pal.'

And he was. In less time than that in fact he was dressed and groomed, and poised to answer her knock.

Kirsten drove him to the clinic. As they drove they discussed the contingencies of their circumstances and planned their future actions. What if Monty did not respond to the message that she had sent to him via Game Guard Mabutane?

'Why shouldn't he?' Whitaker wanted to be encouraging. 'There is hardly a page in his diary where you can't sense, or read of his desire to return to his old life. His whole purpose in doing what he did was to discover the formula for this sontekile, and bring it back.'

'It was something that Mabutane said to me. He said that my brother has changed. He wasn't convinced that Monty would even see me. I trust Mabutane, I believe him.'

She sensed that he was staring at her.

'What is it, Gray?' She glanced curiously at him.

'I think what I've got to say might upset you. I don't want that.'

'Say it anyway.'

He told her what he could of the state of mind of Montague Law, as he saw it. He explained how brilliantly Uhlanga had applied her primitive psychology.

'Your brother was easy prey to her. He was ravaged with guilt, and she transposed that guilt onto the shoulders of a personality more resilient than the battered Montague Law. He fought her but it is not clear from what he wrote, what the outcome was, or who is out there now, Monty Law or Mvulaba.'

'I'm not upset, Gray. I read the diary too, and I'm not a fool. You think Monty is schizophrenic, don't you? You think he's gone off his head.'

'I'm not a psychiatrist Kirsten. I'm a physician. But I've always had a deep interest in mental disease. I would say your brother has a schizoid reaction-type personality.'

'Which,' she interrupted, 'is as near as saying schizophrenic as matters.'

'I'm just guessing, Kirsten.'

'Well I think you're right, Mister Physician. But I happen to know that people are cured of mental illness every day – schizophrenics included. I want Monty back. And I want him cured.'

They drove on in silence down the valley road. The compound came into sight: an unredeemingly intrusive sprawl of prefabricated asbestos.

'It's sited just below the dam's ultimate high water mark,' Kirsten said in mitigation. 'It will all be pulled down once the civil construction project has been concluded.' She pointed out other features around the site. Then they drew up next to a twin-stretcher Land Rover ambulance, parked in a port that extended outwards from the clinic admittance doors. It was there that Kirsten voiced her real fear about her brother's mental condition.

'Gray, am I right in being so optimistic about Monty's return to health? I know that psychiatry has come a long way, but will he ever be totally normal again?'

Whitaker was so, so careful about his answer.

'That would depend on how fully developed his illness was; how far the process of mind disintegration had advanced. How far he has turned away from reality, and how much insight he has into his problem. You see, Uhlanga could have steered him in any one of a number of directions. I don't know what she's done. I don't know what you can expect. Did Mabutane not tell you more?'

'No,' Kirsten shook her head, 'Mabutane just said he'd changed. I think his exact words were: "He is not the same man that you knew. His scars are not just of the skin." '

'That doesn't sound promising.'

'No it doesn't. The fact that a simple man like Mabutane was able to observe such a change. Shall we go inside now?'

Whitaker had never met his predecessor, nor had he been able to assess him in any way. The bungalow in which Whitaker had been billeted had been cleansed of any memory of the murdered man. It was just a shell. From the moment he set foot in the reception room of the clinic, however, the old doctor's personality smiled through.

Everything was spruce. The walls were decorated with pictorial warnings of the hazards of working without a hard-hat, or dozing beneath the big-wheeled trucks. All very eloquent. What was supposed to be polished was polished, what should have been laundered was laundered.

Sister Lubemba was clean and starched and buxom – very Zulu and very efficient. She shook Whitaker's hand and curtsied.

'Welcome, Doctor Whitaker.' She smiled at Kirsten: 'Inkosikazi.'

She conducted them on a tour of the clinic. The ward: twenty-two beds. Four of them filled. All of them uniformly made up and squared. The occupants were in excellent hands. Two traumas – clean and perfectly bandaged. One bilharzia – for observation and tests. One falciparum malaria – lying in febrile anxiety. Whitaker read the spiking fever chart. Chloroquine phosphate therapy was being administered, and the patient was responding.

'Well done, Sister. Very good.'

Sister Lubemba grew by inches. 'This way please, Doctor.' There was a smaller two-bed ward for female patients. It was empty. 'We don't get many women.'

'I should imagine so,' Whitaker said as they walked towards a pair of swing doors marked 'STRICTLY NO ENTRY' – 'The theatre.'

Small but adequate; there were good halogen lamps and a multi-adjustable table. A complete set of instruments was laid out. In one corner a small portable X-ray plant stood ready. Whitaker opened the resuscitator kit and checked the contents. There was no fault to be found.

From the theatre they walked to a well stocked, well registered dispensary. Whitaker spent a little time reading through the drug inventory. Then they moved on.

'Your office, Doctor. Would you like some tea?'

He said he would love some tea and Sister Lubemba bustled off.

'It looks as though she's decided on you,' Kirsten spread her arms expansively – "Your office, Doctor". Seriously though, how do you like it?'

He liked it. He had in mind a few minor changes in surgical equipment and standard drug requisites. But those were of a preferential nature. In addition he would order Chlorpromazine and Trifluroperazine: two highly specialised antihallucinatory drugs. Medicine to calm the psychotic frenzy. He said:

'It's perfect.' He sat at the desk. A rather antiquated binaural stethoscope lay before him. The only totally personal item of his predecessor's that he had as yet come across. 'He was a good man, Tyrell. He ran an efficient operation.'

'Yes,' Kirsten agreed. 'He was a humanitarian. Everyone liked him.'

Sister Lubemba brought the tea tray and set it down. She wanted to know if there was anything further 'the Doctor' would like to see.

Whitaker shook his head and smiled. 'Not for the moment. If I think of anything, I'll call you.'

'We'll make you very happy here,' said Sister Lubemba. Then, if a Zulu could blush, she blushed. She clapped a hand to her loquacious mouth, and fled.

'She likes you.' Kirsten poured the tea. 'I think you'd better go easy on that smile of yours.'

'When I'm happy, I smile.'

'Like Sister Lubemba,' Kirsten said. 'I'll work at it.'

More than anything Whitaker liked it when Kirsten laughed. She laughed then. But it was a quickly censored mirth; a trespass on the seriousness of the moment.

'So what if Monty doesn't respond to my message?' She reverted suddenly and solemnly to the subject of Montague Law: 'What if his illness is fully developed, and . . . and he's taken on the personality of Mvulaba; what then? Would he respond to me? Would he even recognise me?'

It was a question that even a Freud or a Jung would have shuddered away from. His answer was inadequate but it was the best he could do.

'Kirsten, we must not jump to any conclusions about Monty's state of mind. So very little is understood about this subject. I don't think your brother was a fully developed schizophrenic up to the time of his final entry. His writing was too lucid. But it's hard to judge just from that factor. You may not like what I've got to say Kirsten, but I . . . *our* best course of action would be to forget about searching for Monty.' He waved down her interjection. 'Just listen to me. Whatever the state of your brother's mind, the sangoma Uhlanga has some control over it. Ethically, if ethics apply in this case, it would be right to approach *her* and try to get her on your side. Another factor is that Monty is hiding from you. You've been searching for him for months without getting much closer. But as yet you haven't made sufficient effort to find the sangoma Uhlanga. Maybe she'll be easier to locate. I see her as the key piece to this whole enigma. Find her and a whole new field of possibilities opens up. Without her help, you've got much less chance of success. Give it some thought.'

She did think about it. She sat. She took Tyrell's old stethoscope and stared at it as though it was some meditative object.

'There must be some way of influencing her,' Whitaker went on, 'some inducement that would cause her to co-operate with you.'

'You know, Gray,' Kirsten said thoughtfully, 'there is the Inkatha factor. Monty begged me to give him the Inkatha a few days after I had taken it from the cave. I refused. Often I've wondered whether that was the right decision. I told him it was his lifeline. And in the light of your suggestion, it looks as though I was right. The Inkatha's hidden in the cellar at Prospect Hall. That's where I took it. It was the only safe place that I could think of. I don't want to move it until the time is right. That will be when we have located Uhlanga. If she wants it as badly as it seems she does, then she'll *have* to come to terms. I'm not convinced that she is going to be any easier to find than Monty. But it's certainly worth a try.'

She kissed him; lightly; quickly – very disconcertingly.

'You're damn smart, Doctor Whitaker. That's just one of the

things I love about you.'

He hoped her assessment of him was correct. In his silence there existed terrible doubts as to the wisdom of trying to interfere in any way in the life of this poor demented man. Kirsten wanted it this way; she wanted her brother back. She wanted, returned to hearth and home, the Monty whom, she had known and loved – and she had a moral right to want such a thing. This commitment of hers however, could lead to destructive consequences. In a psychiatric sense it was quite possibly the wrong course of action for this man to be cut off from the mental nutrition that Uhlanga was providing. Such a detachment could well prove traumatic – precipitating Law into a deeper and less accessible stage of schizophrenia. At worst he could become totally catatonic – a vegetable, unable to perform the simplest daily task. The mind was not an organ that could be prodded and auscultated to obtain an exact diagnosis. It was easy to make a misdiagnosis in mental illnesses. Often, trained psychiatrists were guilty of that, with mortal repercussions.

These things could happen. Graham Whitaker knew how easily they could happen. Yet here he was aiding and abetting Kirsten in her course of action. Because she demanded it, and he would do anything for her? Because locked into the disordered mind of brother Monty was a secret that could revolutionise the world of medicine?

These doubts were in the silence of him, and that was where they were destined to remain. Words that were prompted by such delicate emotions were best left unsaid. He was going to help her, and that was all that mattered for the present. The truth would have its day.

'Doctor Whitaker,' Sister Lubemba was back. 'There's a patient here who I think you should examine, if you have time, a pregnant woman.'

'Of course,' Whitaker said. 'Have you taken a urine sample, Sister?'

She had taken urine; she had weighed the patient, she said, and prepared her for examination.

'I won't be long,' Whitaker told Kirsten. 'Only a few minutes.'

He followed Sister Lubemba to the women's ward. 'You'll have to translate for me,' he told her. 'I'm afraid I don't speak Zulu.'

'We'll teach you,' she said. 'But don't learn Fanagalo like all the others here, it's a bastard language. True Zulus are offended by it. Here we are.'

The patient looked rather warily up at him. Her name, Sister Lubemba told him, was Vuloyi.

'Vuloyi,' Whitaker said. 'That's a pretty name.'

'Your first Zulu lesson: it actually means witchcraft.'

'Really?'

'Yes. It's common for mothers to name their children defiantly. In this case it was obviously a challenge to some witchdoctor to do his worst.'

'Ask Vuloyi to raise her legs, please Sister. Ask her if she's felt any movement yet.'

Vuloyi said that she had indeed felt the stirrings of her child. Whitaker's examinations gave her to be more than twenty weeks into her pregnancy.

'There's softening of the cervicouterine junction, Sister, and the fundus is very enlarged. Everything seems to be fine . . . Has she any complaints?'

'Severe backache,' Sister said. 'Worse than she had with her other child. She says she's hurting right into her legs.'

'Is that so?' Whitaker pondered on the advice he could offer this suffering woman. 'Tell her to mind her posture: to walk tall, tummy in, buttocks tight. That generally helps.'

Sister Lubemba did not tell her a thing. She was regarding him in a rather puzzled way. 'How will she do that and still work with a hoe in the fields, and, at the end of the day, carry on her head a full load of firewood back to the kraal? If I tell her that, she might not come back to you again.'

'Oh,' Whitaker felt rather foolish. His advice came straight from the textbook. There were other equally irrelevant offerings: wear low heels, do daily exercises, a good firm mattress.

'She already knows the reason for her pain,' Sister Lubemba went on. 'She's had advice from her witchdoctor. What she wants from you is medicine.'

'You mean this patient was referred to me by some local witchdoctor?'

'You could say that, I suppose.'

Good God! This was a whole new world. 'Did Doctor Tyrell get patients that were sent to him by witchdoctors?'

'Yes, occasionally.'

'And what would Doctor Tyrell have prescribed for our lady here?'

'Carisoprodol tablets, four times daily . . . *Very* effective.'

'Then give her Carisoprodol, Sister.'

Vuloyi thanked Doctor Whitaker effusively. Singing happily she almost skipped away.

'She's singing about you,' Sister Lubemba said. 'She's made up a little song in praise of you. She says you are a great Inyanga; that you have been wetted by the rain.'

'Oh.' Whitaker felt himself colouring.

'You're going to have lots of outside patients, Doctor Whitaker.'

'Lots of referrals, eh? By the way, did Vuloyi tell you what the witchdoctor's diagnosis was?'

'Yes, she did. Her ancestors felt offended by her husband. He's a game guard at Ndumu and was recently in trouble with the police. Her ancestor spirits were entreated to help in the matter of his release. He, it seems, was not grateful enough.'

'So they are punishing her?'

'Yes, and him, through his seed.'

Whitaker shook his head. 'Does she believe *that*. Do you believe that?'

Sister Lubemba grinned and shrugged. 'Don't rush into judgement before you have come to know these people, Doctor Whitaker. They don't judge whites as being crazy when they sprinkle holy water on their children's heads, and make the sign of the cross to protect them from the devil, or swallow some pieces of bread, and wine. Don't be hasty in your judgement of the Mabutanes of Ingwavuma. They are good people.'

'The Mabutanes of Ingwavuma . . .' Whitaker looked for the first time at the patient's admittance chart he held. 'Vuloyi is the wife of September Mabutane.'

'That's right, Doctor.'

'And she was sent to me by a witchdoctor – a sangoma?'

'Yes.'

'What was the name of the sangoma, did she tell you that?'

'I believe it was old Ngodini from Lake Mandlankunzi.'

'Is she well known?'

'He, Ngodini, is a man. He divines with the use of bones, and is indeed well known.'

'Have you ever heard of a sangoma called Uhlanga?'

'The sangoma with the eyes of rain. Yes, I've heard of her, but I've never seen her. I don't know of anyone who has actually seen her. She is a diviner priestess umLozi. The most powerful of all sangomas. Many, many spirits speak through her. Why are you so interested in isangoma, Doctor Whitaker?'

He ignored the question. 'Say I wished to speak to this Uhlanga, how would I find her?'

'You wouldn't simply find her. You would have to consult a lesser sangoma first. If that sangoma felt incompetent to deal with your problem, he or she might enlist the aid of a higher sangoma, and so on. Eventually, if Uhlanga deemed your case as being worthy of her, she might send for you.' Sister Lubemba chuckled. 'You sound like you might be interested in such a consultation, Doctor Whitaker.'

'Not quite, Sister Lubemba. But if I'm to work here, then it might be wise to pay my respects to any fellow practitioners. Don't you think so?'

She did not say what she thought. She regarded the new doctor from beneath a pair of quizzically rucked eyebrows.

'This Ngodini,' Whitaker went on, 'where could I find him for a start?'

'His home is on the southern shores of Lake Mandlankunzi. In fact, if you're that keen I can show you the way later on this afternoon.'

He was keen. Oh yes, he was very keen. He said, 'Miss Law will drive us there. I know she'd be fascinated to meet the sangoma Ngodini.'

But they did not go to the kraal of the sangoma Ngodini that afternoon. That afternoon Mark Ingram arrived. They had scheduled the final blast at the Number 2 tail-race outlet, and he wanted to be there. And he wanted Kirsten at his side. They were thirty days ahead of schedule. A celebration was in order.

They gathered at the canteen that afternoon; blasters and geologists and underground engineers. Men who bore the pigment of dynamite and mine dust. Men whose ears had been dulled, and whose mouths had been loudened by a lifetime of clamour and blast. They were harder than the rock against which they did head-on battle.

Ingram was the master of it. He laughed as hard as they did, and he drank them stupid. And beautiful Kirsten stayed at his side. And Graham Whitaker could only watch, and be jealous; and bitter. He stood alone skulking against a far wall, with an untouched drink, and the mortified spirit of a kicked mongrel.

'Welcome aboard, Graham.' The good host Ingram came to stand with him. 'Kirsten tells me you've made your decision.'

Whitaker said: 'Yes.'

'I hear you've visited the clinic. I hope everything was to your satisfaction?'

'Yes, perfect.'

'Well if you need anything just let me know. I visit the dam site once a week for site meetings. If you require anything urgently, use the radio telephone to reach me.'

'I can't think of a thing I'll need,' Whitaker said. 'The clinic is well equipped; well stocked.'

Ingram shrugged. 'You never know . . . By the way you can fly back with me tomorrow to get the rest of your personal kit. I'll pick you up at the cottage at zero seven hundred. All right by you?'

'Fine by me.'

'Kirsten's made this place her home from home.' Ingram spoke to the woman at his side. 'Haven't you Kirsten? She'll take good care of you until you find your feet.'

'Fine,' said Graham Whitaker. 'Thank you.' He did not know what else to say.

A man called Davis appeared. He was introduced to Whitaker as the resident engineer. 'The man who really bosses up this operation.' He had deep intelligent eyes and a friendly easy going manner. On any other day Whitaker would have enjoyed the man's company. At that minute all he was capable of was pretence. He pretended to be listening. He pretended to be answering. In truth Whitaker was where his eyes were, and they were on Kirsten Law. Her eyes, her dark, sad, searching eyes caught Whitaker's for a moment. He gave her nothing. He looked away and pretended he had not noticed; pretended to be enjoying himself. And when he looked up again it was Ingram who was scrutinising him, a lisp of a smile was stirring the edge of his mouth. He raised his glass to his new employee in silent salute, and the new employee responded alike.

The toast was a satire. They were antagonists, and both of them knew it.

'They make a lovely couple don't they?' It was Dent. Whitaker did not have difficulty in placing that mocking voice. 'I hear you're joining our happy band.'

'Hello, Patrick.' He turned to find the policeman at his side. 'Yes, I'm coming to Ingwavuma. You sound surprised.'

'I am a little. You're somewhat over-qualified for the job aren't you? Your predecessor was a GP.'

'The job interests me.'

'Something must interest you.' Dent rolled his eyes to where Kirsten was standing with Ingram.

'You've got a dirty little mind, Captain Dent.'

Dent shrugged. 'Cynical,' he corrected. 'While I'm on the subject of your predecessor: you did know that he died a somewhat bizarre death, didn't you?'

'He was murdered.'

'Yes. In a rather gruesome way. That's what I want to talk to you about. Ernie Tyrell was a good man, a pacifist, and like most such men he had a conviction that violence would never touch him. He used to drive that ambulance of his up and down the mountains, at any time of the day or night. He thought that the bright red crosses painted on the sides provided him with some kind of divine protection. Well they didn't. I tried to get him to carry a firearm, but he wouldn't have it. I hope you're not going to be that stupid, Doctor Whitaker.'

'I don't like firearms.'

'Neither did Tyrell.'

'I don't have one.'

'Neither did Tyrell. But I offered to provide him with one, and to show him how to use it. I'm making the same offer to you.'

'All right. If you think it's absolutely necessary.'

'I never waste my time doing things that are unnecessary. You'll learn that in due course. I'm going to the bar – can I get you a refill? You look as though you could use a drink.'

'I could.'

Whitaker stepped closer to an adjacent conversation.

'At the rate we're going,' someone said, 'we'll be able to sign over the civil works to our clients in three months, maybe even less.'

Three months. A quarter of a year of this. Kirsten was right to fear for the survival of such an interminably enmeshed relationship as theirs!

'With the weather and the workers on our side, we'll make it,' Davis said.

And Montague Law and the Inkatha of Shaka Zulu? For Graham Whitaker, the equation was unsolvable without the inclusion of those two factors.

The Inkatha was in the cellar of Prospect Hall, but where was Montague Law?

* * *

'That's the spot,' Warden Robert Reynolds slowed down his Land Rover, 'there by the leaning Paperbark.' He pointed out the tree for the benefit of his lone passenger. 'Can you see it?'

The passenger was Patrick Dent. 'I can see the tree,' he said. 'Drive a little further down the road, Rob. We'll walk from there.'

Reynolds felt irked. He did not like Patrick Dent. He did not like the idea of having to bring this heavy-handed policeman into Ndumu. More than anything he hated receiving superfluous instructions. He drove on for about five hundred metres, then pulled well off the road.

'That'll do,' Dent said. 'We're well hidden here.'

Dent took with him his rifle and a web sidepack; Reynolds slung his rifle. In his hand he held a shovel. They followed a game trail that wandered well clear of the road. To avoid conversation, Reynolds kept a few paces ahead. A good tactic. They did not talk again until they had reached the Paperbark tree.

'Where?' Dent asked dourly.

Reynolds indicated with a nod. 'The arms cache is buried under that dry thorn branch. I covered it up again.'

'Good.'

Dent dragged the branch away, spat on his palms and began to dig. Rather accusingly he said: 'I'm surprised you didn't come to me with this information earlier. I would have got something out of Mabutane for sure. Now the bastard's disappeared.'

'I told you, September Mabutane was one of my most trusted men. When he told me that the tracks were the spoor of poachers, I had no reason to doubt him. His father and his grandfather were both employed as game guards here. Recently I discovered more spoor, and followed it up. I got the shock of my life when I found this stuff.'

'It just goes to show.'

Dent did not say what it went to show. Were all Reynolds born stupid, or Zulus, untrustworthy? He leaned into his work, shovelling hard. The sun was low, nevertheless Dent's camouflaged shirt was soon sweat-blotched. He was a tough one this Dent, and stubborn too. He did not look well. Once or twice he staggered slightly as he dug. Despite that, or perhaps because of it, he bluntly refused Reynolds' offer of assistance.

'I can do it.'

Reynolds sat down leisurely, the more to emphasise the digging man's discomfort. He said:

'You're damn lucky that it didn't rain in the interim, my friend. That spoor is almost as fresh as if they'd made it yesterday.'

The cut of the spade sounded different that time: it did not ring as it did against the rocky earth. It gave off a muffled hollow *thunk*.

'Ah – ha!'

Dent backhanded the spade; scraped it across the drab-coloured plank he had just exposed. 'Well, what have we here?'

What they had was a box; an olive-painted, yellow-stencilled wooden box: магнитная мина вешество Such Slavonic articulation was beyond Dent but his translation was succinct enough: 'Limpet mines. A whole fucking boxful. Fuses and all.'

And next to that box, another like-stencilled box. Dent said: 'There's probably more under these.'

'Why don't we look and see?' Reynolds peered over the edge of the pit. 'I suppose a cigarette is not indicated at the moment.'

'It wouldn't matter if you smoked, Rob. But the fact of the matter is, that I don't want you standing around here any longer.'

'They're not going to go up are they?'

'Chance in a million, Rob. But it's a chance I can't take. Sorry, but you'll have to go back to the truck and stay there.'

'And what are *you* going to do?'

'Police business, old buddy.'

What Dent did was to open up his side pack and take out a camera. He photographed the pit and the surroundings from a few angles. Then, taking it by its rope handles, he lugged a box out of the pit, opened the lid, and photographed the contents. He did that again, and again, until five opened boxes lay on the veld. Then, in reverse order, he went through the same procedure, almost the same procedure. The contents of the last remaining box seemed to interest him more than any of the others. He busied himself therein with a small pair of pliers and a screwdriver, and a little red cylinder that came from his satchel. He worked with the precise concentration of a watchmaker. When he had finished he carefully closed the lid and lowered the crate back into the hole. Finally he took up the shovel and gingerly shovelled back the earth. He smoothed over the spoor with the thorn branch then walked back to the truck.

'What now?' Reynolds asked.

'Now we drive away, as quietly as we came.'

'Do you want me to put a watch on the place?'

'No.'

'How will you know if they dig the stuff up?'

'I'll know,' Dent said shortly. 'I don't want you or any of your patrols poking around here. That would just fuck up everything. Do you read me, Rob?' Dent massaged his temples as he spoke – a man in the grip of a violent headache. 'I've done everything that has to be done. Your superiors have been informed, my superiors have been informed. Everything is under control.'

Reynolds nodded. 'You should see a doctor, Patrick. You don't look yourself. They've got a new one at the dam you know. He flew up from Durban this morning. Whitaker, that's his name.'

Reynolds could feel his passenger's eyes on him as he drove towards the road.

'Maybe I'll do that,' Dent said.

It was dusk by the time they reached the main camp. Sergeant Shibindji, as he had been instructed to do, was standing, rifle in hand, guarding the police Landcruiser. Dent said:

'If you see Mabutane or hear of his whereabouts, I want to know about it immediately. I don't care how many years his family has been in service at Ndumu, or how trusted he was, he's dangerous now. Things have changed here at Ingwavuma, Rob. I think you appreciate that too. If I had my way I'd close up Ndumu until things were straightened out, but Parks Board don't want that, so be bloody careful. Be observant and don't take any chances. Report anything to me, *anything* that appears out of the ordinary. The people that we're dealing with are ruthless and very, very clever. Be on your guard, old buddy, and stay in contact.'

Dent let Shibindji drive him back to Abercorn Drift. 'I want to think,' he told the Zulu. But he did not want to think. He did not want to do anything more that day but close his eyes and rest. He felt sick. His mind was clamped into a vice-like grip of pain that tightened with every jolt. And the road was full of jolts. He contemplated continuing along the river road towards the dam, and Graham Whitaker. But the thought of those extra few kilometres was more than he could contemplate. Not tonight. He would see Whitaker in the morning.

He needed rest. He had read in forensic medicine reports about the type of drug that had been used on him by Law; some form of narcotic that rendered the victim so passive that sections could be carved from his living body without a murmur of protest. Somehow that poison had been administered to him. The Zulus were past masters at that sort of thing. But Law had made a bad error of judgement. That madman had thought that such a display of *muthi*-magic would terrify him into leaving Abanzanzi unhindered; into dismissing the Inkatha from his mind. They had overestimated their power. It was time for the war on Abanzanzi to be intensified. This time on his terms.

'*I'll kill him.*'

The words came in a hiss of pain. As noisy as the inside of the Landcruiser cab was, Shibindji heard him.

'Was the Captain speaking to me?'

'I said, some people misjudge others, Shibindji. Some one tried to frighten me, Shibindji.'

'A bad mistake, Captain.'

'Yes. I'm going away for a day or two, Shibindji. I want to fetch something that belongs to me.'

'*Yebo*, Captain.'

'For chrissake, Shibindji, are you aiming to hit every bloody pothole from here to Abercorn Drift? Move this bloody thing will you?'

'*Yebo*, Captain.'

He willingly complied. There was nothing Shibindji liked better than driving flat out. He wondered who this man was whose life uDende had decided to put an end to. He had better run, that man. He had better run with his shield held across his back. Because nothing frightened uDende . . . except perhaps those memories of Kenya.

*   *   *

Uhlanga the grey-eyed sangoma was walking near a brown and turgid river. It was raining – storming. The skies were black and the wind was roaring across the land. She called him and he walked towards her. But he could not seem to get closer. Walk as he did, she remained as distant as ever. She was pointing to the ground and gesturing for him to hurry. It seemed that she had found something. But the more he hurried the slower and more tortuous his progress became. There was danger all around. He could not see where or what it was, but the feeling was so strong. And all the while there was this voice telling him to hurry, *hurry*.

At last he arrived at the place where Uhlanga was. But when he arrived she was no longer standing. She was lying in a muddy place, her legs were parted, her vagina was open and her face was creased in agony. He bent to her and she told him to insert his hand into her; to help her with the birth.

He did as she instructed. He slid his hand into her vagina – then deeper. He could feel the baby writhing to be free. He pulled, but it was not a baby, it was a snake; a python that coiled its tail to his arm and drew him, resisting, inwards. Not into her vagina, but into the depths of a cave, a deep black cave. And there he heard the salute of kings:

Bayede! Bayede! Bayede!

It seemed as though a million voices were raised in royal salutation. He knew it was not for him. And yet who else was there? In the darkness of the grotto he was alone.

Mvulaba awoke confused, and apprehensive that the darkness

around him was the darkness of his dream grotto. But it was not. He was within the smoky confines of his *indlu*; curled and warm beneath his sleeping kaross. He tried to go back to sleep again. To join with the dream again. But his mind had had enough of that.

The light of dawn was not far off. He took the shimmering remnant of his dream and began to retexture the pictures in his consciousness. It was not a difficult task – the dream almost in its entirety had occurred to him before. The swift flowing river, Uhlanga's painful labouring at birth, and the grasping coiling python. This dream had departed from its usual course, in that Uhlanga had laid upon a bed of mud. He was sure that was how he had seen it – mud, oozing black mud, as you find it at the mouth of a tidal river.

This dream had a lingering urgency; a portentousness that made him feel uneasy. He reached out his arm and shook the heavy shoulder of the woman at his side. Uhlanga awoke with a start. Her tongue was thick with sleep.

'What is it, my Mvulaba?'

'I had the dream.'

'The dream of me at childbirth? The dream of the river and the uMonya snake?' She sat up and sighed sleepily.

'The same one.'

'Did you hear the royal salute repeated three times?'

'Yes, it was all the same, excepting for one thing. When I came to you Uhlanga, you were lying on a bank of sucking river mud. But the dream ended in the same way as ever – in the cave.'

'A dream has no end, my Mvulaba. Nor does it have a beginning. A dream is a circle with the dreamer as its centre. That is how the spirits give them to us. When you have dreamed it more than once it is a sign that the circle is complete and the spirits wish urgently to communicate something. You are not an ordinary person, Mvulaba, you are the eyes, therefore the message will not be ordinary. We can expect to hear great and important things. Eh! I feel it, my Mvulaba. Do you feel it? Do you see it?'

Oh yes. He saw it now. A small light, now purple, now white, now soft, now fierce. It was coming to him out of the darkness as it always did when Uhlanga felt it near. Oh yes! He was frightened and he wanted to tell Uhlanga that. But his lips were saying other things.

He wanted to reach out and be reached out for. He stretched his arms but as he did it they changed, they became huge muddled things that belonged to someone else, he did not know who. And the light of his mind flashed purple; flashed white – grew bigger and bigger. Blink as he would, turn as he would it increased its stabbing fierceness. It became like a fireball, an incendiary thing that would burn out his mind and leave him a shell – just a blackened brainless shell. There was a smell of burning, him burning. The lights exploded. Inside himself he screamed, and on the flight of that scream he escaped from the pain. He left the burned man lying there and moved away to another place. He had been there before and he knew where he was. This was the place of the higher beings: the place of the souls – the *amathongo* – *amakhosi* of the royal chiefs of Zulu. It was a place as black as night. He was addressed there by the one he knew only as uKhozi the eagle.

'You've come back Mvulaba . . . was it difficult this time?'

'Just the initial pain. It gets easier every time.'

'Ask about the dream,' said the voice of the Guide from the inner place. 'We must know what is meant by that.'

'I've come to ask about the dream.'

'What dream?' shouted uKhozi, stretching huge black wings as wide as the night.

'Uhlanga at the river. The birth.'

'I know that dream.' inGwenya the crocodile crawled up from the swamp bed. 'That comes as a message from Unkulunkulu the god of gods. It is for the grey-eyed sangoma Uhlanga. The time is near for the arrival of Okhethiwe, the chosen one. As the dream is yours Mvulaba, so the pain will be yours. Your eyes will be the eyes that find the child, and your arms the arms that carry it to Abanzanzi.'

'The chosen one. My arms will carry it to Abanzanzi,' he repeated.

'Yes,' snapped inGwenya.

'Ask for a sign,' came the voice of the Guide. 'Ask quickly. You know inGwenya never stays for long.'

But inGwenya had dived back under.

'He's gone already,' he reported.

'He's very quick,' screamed uKhozi.

'A sign,' pleaded the Guide from the inner place.

'Do you know what the sign will be?' he asked uKhozi.

But it was uMamba the black snake who hissed the answer:

'A new-born child, listen for the crying of the new-born child. Look for him at the *indlu* by the river. Wait for the time when the storm winds blow.'

'You must listen for the cry of a new-born child,' he passed on the message. 'Look for the child at the *indlu* by the river. Wait for the time when the storm winds blow.'

'What sacrifice would be sufficient?' The Guide from the inner place. 'You must ask first what sacrifice must be offered.'

He asked on behalf of the Guide: 'What is the sacrifice that would please you?'

'Ha!' screamed uKhozi swooping down. 'Ha! Did we ask for the heart of the man who builds against the Suthu River – the one who destroys the sacred burial grounds? Did we ask for that before?'

'Yes.'

'And did we get it Mvulaba?'

'A man was killed in error. It was dark that night. Must we try again?'

'No, he is *not* the one we want now.' His great wings were beating, lifting him away. 'You must wait. Be assured you will be told who it is who we want in good time.'

'Did he tell you?' asked the Guide. 'Who is it to be?'

'We must wait. They have not yet decided,' he said. 'Can I come back now?'

'You can come back,' said the Guide. 'Come,' said the Guide. 'Come back to me now.'

Like a falling feather, he wafted down so gently, so comfortably, into the arms of the Guide of the inner place; the tutor of his mind. 'Come to me,' said Uhlanga, cradling him to her bosom, rocking him gently in her arms, smiling down at the traveller of the eyes.

'My Mvulaba, my honey of the comb, come to me now.'

He smiled up at her, he reached up for her. 'I am here,' he said. 'I am here, Uhlanga.'

'You are beautiful, my Mvulaba. I open myself to you my assegai of love.'

They arose from the sleeping mat in time to greet the rising sun. The seven stars of isiLimela – the heralds of the season of cultivation – were still visible in the lightening sky. They had arrived with iKhwezi the morning star that very dawn.

'See them,' Uhlanga pointed. 'Look. That is the sign of the coming of Nomkubulwana, the princess of heaven. Soon she will visit us, enshrouded in the mists of spring. If she feels welcome, she will grant us rain. If she frowns . . . but this time she will not frown. The *amathongo* spirits have prophesied rain; and more than that. They have told us that the chosen one – the one we have waited for, for so long, he who will grow to be chief of chiefs, and as mighty as the great Shaka Zulu – he will come hand in hand with Nomkubulwana. We must prepare for this wondrous event. Call the *imikhovu* to me, Mvulaba, and call uMabutane. I have instructions for him. This season Nomkubulwana will smile as she has never smiled before.'

*   *   *

Meteorologists of a more scientific bent have a different name for this whimsical deity of global weather. They call it El Nino – the Christ child. A misnomer perpetuated since the days of Cortez. El Nino is wild and unpredictable and most ungodlike. It is the product of the relationship between the Pacific Ocean and the sky above it. The sky is genetically more responsible because *it* has to do with the shift in normal pressure systems that lie above the mother ocean.

It happens every few years, for no known reason, that the high pressure system natural to the eastern Pacific starts to weaken. From far off Indonesia a low pressure system is sucked away towards this hiatus. The trade winds falter, then reverse, and in sympathy with the wind, the warm surface currents of the Pacific turn around. The weather pattern of a quarter of the globe is given to the child, and monstrously abused. The cycle can last for years on end.

This El Nino brought cyclones to Polynesia and massive floods to Peru and Ecuador. It condemned Australia to raging bush fires and dust storms – 80,000 square miles of billowing silt choked that country. San Francisco suffered tidal waves and floods. Half a dozen tempests hammered little Tahiti in that many months.

To Southern Africa El Nino brought drought – five years of pitiless, bone-bleaching drought. It was the most disastrous climatic event the country had been called upon to face in living memory.

But now El Nino's strength was waning. Even as Uhlanga the sangoma was watching that late September morning sky, meteorologists, world wide, were predicting the demise of that destructive infant. By the new year, they said, it would be dead. But how was Uhlanga the sangoma to know that?

To those born rural; to those who knew the constellation of the Seven Sisters as isiLimela, it made good sense to look to the princess of heaven, Nomkubulwana, to bring back the fat times.

They would have to be patient those Zulus. The princess of heaven was not to be hurried. The first summer mists that enshrouded her, that told of her presence, did not appear that September.

It would be imprudent to worship her before her arrival. So they waited. October, the month of the dripping moon, would surely unite her with her needy subjects.

With Zulu optimism they watched for the prophets of the princess of heaven.

uThekwane the Hammerkop bird was just such a prophet. For those curious about rain, or lakes, or the flow of rivers, then the nesting Hammerkop Heron had a headful of wisdom to impart. Where it laboriously piled and wove its reeds and sticks, there the water would never reach. If it abandoned a previous nest and sought to build on higher ground – beware. The waters would rise and cover the place where once it had nested. There would be floods that season.

In the Lebombo valleys that October the Hammerkop Herons began to build sturdy new nests. They sought out sites high up on the riverine cliffs. And the Zulus then knew that there was to be an end to the drought of a million deaths. But when? '*Ngangimuhle, Thekwane, ngoniwa yiloku naloku,*' was all that that cryptic bird was prepared to say as it admired its reflection in the mud – 'Look here and look there. It's lovely to play where the river bends.'

Thirsting, with eyes upturned to the spiteful sun, the Zulus waited for the arrival of Nomkubulwana, the princess of heaven.

11

The mid-November site meeting at the Suthu River dam site was peopled by smug-faced engineers and toned with optimism.

By now the wall contained more than a million tons of concrete. Moulded into a graceful double curvature, 100 metres from foundation to crest, and arching some 780 metres from bank to bank, it spanned the Suthu River valley from kwaZulu to Swaziland.

'In fact, gentlemen,' Mark Ingram swept his pointer across a pinned up blueprint, 'this stage of the structure is now complete, a month ahead of schedule.'

This was not news to any of the engineers. There were, however, senior representatives of the client present at that meeting. Collectively, they nodded their heads in approval.

Ingram continued: 'The spillway is complete. Besides the spillway, for the discharge of flood waters, we have these four chutes each fifteen metres by nine metres. The gates to control these outlets are being fitted now.' He tapped the blueprint again. 'They're radial gates and they weigh about sixty tons each – reckon on another two weeks' work per gate.'

'Eight weeks,' Mr Meleka was very black which made his smile very white. He scribbled his deduction into a wirebound notebook. 'Eight weeks . . . very good Mister Ingram. Now without being over-technical, would you describe your progress underground? We had some bad luck there in the past. Have you had any more problems in that area?'

Ingram lit a cigarette before replying. 'It's always harder to make judgements and predictions when it comes to underground works. We have completed the machine hall cavern, as you know. That was the single biggest underground project. We had to shift ninety-seven thousand cubic metres of rock in order to complete that job. The turbines can be placed in position soon, in fact the number one spiral turbine housing is on the way; it is on the road right at this minute. There's a lot more work to be done on the underground power station though. The tail-race sections – the tunnels through which the water exits, once its energy has been extracted by the turbines – still have to be completed. We're blasting them, and simultaneously the final two river outlet tunnels . . .' To bear witness to Ingram's statement, a muted explosion shook the conference room – then another.

'Most timely,' Mr Meleka commented. 'You're quite a showman, Mister Ingram.' There was some laughter.

'We're on schedule with our underground works,' Ingram continued. 'We are dealing with some unique geological formations, Mister Meleka. Let's hope we don't encounter problems. But you asked me about our underground progress. The fact is that we are now in a position to close the silt outlets and impound the Suthu River. All we need is your government's authorisation to do this.'

'I am empowered to grant that authority, Mister Ingram,' Meleka said. 'The areas that will be affected have already been evacuated. The Swazi government is most anxious to move ahead. All we need now is rain, and lots of it. November must surely bring it.'

* * *

The month of November saw the arrival in the Lebombos of the biggest mechanical machines of all. They rolled and rumbled along on a hundred slowly turning wheels. The bellow of their exhausts preceded them by hours, and hours after they had passed the frightened earth was still atremble.

There were two of them: 700 hp MAN diesels, bright with flashing lights and flags and busy vehicles of escort. They carried a massive load.

Along the route the villagers turned out to watch, and point, and clap their hands in awe. From the oldest, sagest greybeard, to the youngest toddler, dragging at his mother's hem, they made their way to the roadside to watch the growling, grumbling northwards trek of these two metal monsters.

'Look at that; there's room for them alone along the road today.

Hau! What can they be bringing that can be so very big?'

Peter Gebeza was one of those who observed the cavalcade of the giants. He too went down to the roadside, but not through simple curiosity. He knew exactly what it was that those transporters bore. They were the casings, and turbine runner shaft for the number one turbine – the guts of the Suthu River hydroelectric scheme. He wished to view them from the closest possible position, because one day, soon, he would be expected to place charges against that massive spiral casing, and hopefully destroy it. Now *that* would be a setback for the Boers.

Anonymously blanketed, he raised an arm in laconic salute, and the driver, high in his cab of metal and glass, waved back. Another blanketed tribesman came and stood next to Gebeza. The man said:

'He would be more inclined to shoot you than wave to you if he knew what was on your mind, comrade fighter.'

'Yes – both of us, Nukwe.'

'When are you going to do it, Peter?'

'There's no hurry.' The first low-loader was immediately opposite them now. Gebeza shouted above the row: 'We'll give it a few more days, let them get to the dam. That will cause them even more inconvenience.'

He waited until the two low-loaders and their attendant vehicles had passed before he spoke again.

'What we've got to do now, is to return to Ndumu and unearth the limpet mines. Without them we can't do a thing. Go back to my father's kraal now and fetch the pick-up, Nukwe, and the spade. We are going to be tourists at the game reserve this afternoon, my friend.'

'Will Dlamini have to come with us?'

'Why not? Don't you like Dlamini?'

'You know I don't. He's a loud mouth and a bully when you're not around, Peter.'

'I'll be there, Nukwe,' Gebeza patted the younger man's shoulder affectionately. 'I'll keep him in his place. You don't want to have to do all the digging on your own do you?'

'As long as you're there, Peter,' Nukwe smiled. He had a tender smile that boy – his lips were soft in everything they did.

Nukwe sang all the way on the drive towards Ndumu. Happy in

that he was sharing the cab with Peter Gebeza, and Dlamini was alone under the fibreglass canopy at the back. He sang as they exited from the pick-up; he sang as he took his turn at the spade – his digging song.

'Ba ni shani – *sa!*
Ba ka hihlu – *pha!*
Ba nwa ma kho-*fi!*
Ba nga hi nyi-*ki!*'

Peter Gebeza sat in the shade of the unKhamba tree and watched the play of the back muscles of this handsome slender boy. Even at labour, Nukwe moved with the grace and harmony of a dancer.

The boy must have sensed he was being appreciated; he turned to smile at his admirer. Then he died. There was a flash – a harsh hot concussion that fisted Peter Gebeza and flung him whirling through the air. His face was screwed into a scream but he could not hear it. He jolted to a stop against a tree trunk.

Where Nukwe had been digging there was nothing but a blackened smoking crater, and the lower half of Dlamini's body. Now he could hear the scream that was tearing up through the numbness of him.

Peter Gebeza ran. Where he was running to, he did not know. He knew he had to get away from there and hide. He knew he had been betrayed. September Mabutane had done it.

He did not stop running until he had reached the south bank of the Suthu River. There, like a noonday animal, he kneeled and sucked at the muddy water until his thirst was gone. Only then could he once more think coherently. Revenge was what he thought of. And the thought was as reviving as the water.

Revenge for his betrayal. Revenge for the stilling of the lovely voice of Nukwe. '*Eh! Mabutane you will curse the womb that gave you birth. I swear it.*'

* * *

They heard the explosion from as far away as Lake Mandlankunzi.

Kirsten Law was there, at the shady shore-side kraal of Ngodini the sangoma. She was seated on a rush mat with the grey-haired

Ngodini watching him at his craft. She was intrigued by the mastery of this old man of his *Bula* divinatory bones.

'It was a death sound.'

'I don't think so,' Kirsten argued. 'Every day they make such explosions at the dam.'

'The breath of a spirit passed me by,' Ngodini said with finality. 'It was a death sound. Anyway it is of no consequence to us. You say that Vuloyi the wife of September Mabutane spoke of me. Eh! That heifer has a gate for a mouth, a gate that can't be closed. She will have a boy child. Did she tell you that? I predicted it and it will be so. But is it age that makes me ramble on so? Give me something of your household so that my *Bula* will know who they now speak for. Let us get on with it.'

Kirsten gave him the signet ring she wore. It bore the staghead and oakleaves of the family Law.

'It is old,' Ngodini said. 'That is good – your *nsila* will be strong upon it. My *Bula* will carry your smell to the spirits.'

He cast the ring amongst a few of his bones. '*Yingwe*, claw it, leopard. *Malumbi*, smell it antelope of the night. Lick it *Djuma* the cowrie, lick it with your open mouth. Take her *nsila* my *Bula* and let us only hear the truth.'

He gestured to Kirsten to take back her ring. Then taking his entire set of *Bula* in his cupped hands he breathed on them an incantation: '*Ukulahla amahloni*!' Then he scattered them to the mat. 'Your trouble is of the spirit, not of the body.'

'*Ngiya vuma*,' Kirsten agreed.

'You are a searcher in the land of mists, a wanderer in the land of sadness.'

'*Ngiya vuma*.'

He gathered up the Bula; cupped them; whispered to them. Then spilt them again.

'The sadness will get worse,' the *Bula* predicted. 'The tears of the past are nothing compared to those that the future will bring. The bond of the past that you wish to retie has no hope of ever being retied.' He stopped; frowning he looked up from his *Bula*. 'Do you wish to hear more?'

'I do,' she said.

He did as she asked. The *Bula* scattered and he reported. She was awaiting a guide – someone who would lead her towards the thing she had lost. The time was near for the arrival of such a person. But beware. 'See, you will walk with him.' He pointed out the she-impala's astragalas. 'But look where he takes you, this guide of yours. The black crocodile stone is your journey's end. Death and tragedy ... such tragedy ... Eh!'

He threw again. 'Lady, Inkosikazi, go home. You have been wading in waters that tomorrow will suck you under. Listen to my warning, Inkosikazi. There is no doubt about the truth of it. The *Bula* with your *nsila* show this in their posture with every fall. There is an angry and powerful spirit that is set against you. *This* is the cause of your trouble. You are in great danger. That is all that my *Bula* can tell you.'

'I hear what you have to tell me, Ngodini.'

'But you will go your own way,' Ngodini sighed. 'At least I have opened your eyes to what lies ahead. As to your question concerning Uhlanga the sangoma – the *Bula* disagree in their fall. Or is it that the question on your tongue was not the question on your heart? No, no.' He held up his hand to stay her protest. 'It is of no consequence. I have told you everything. You will at last see the face you seek. It will happen soon, very soon.'

Ngodini gathered up his *Bula*: 'They must rest now.' His astragalus and cowries, his claw of the eagle, his tortoiseshell chip; he removed them all from the divining mat. The last item to be deposited in his basket of the eyes was his black stone from the belly of the crocodile; the *uhlolo* of death and tragedy. 'You will need courage.' He raised himself stiffly from the rush mat. 'I have an amulet for you to wear. Wait for me here, I will bring it, Inkosikazi.'

It was a tiny snakeskin purse on a string of woven grass. She showed it to Sister Lubemba and Whitaker when she returned to the Land Rover.

'My *muthi* – for strength and courage,' she told them light-heartedly. But her flippancy was of the tongue, not of the heart. The amulet remained where old Ngodini had tied it – firmly to her neck.

'Incredible,' Graham Whitaker chuckled as they drove away. 'To know this sort of thing still exists. He's a fascinating old scoundrel, isn't he? What amazes me is that for all his bone throwing and divining and the like, he's still enlightened enough to send the odd patient down to the clinic for treatment. You'd think he'd be dead set against modern medicine.'

'It's not so amazing,' Sister Lubemba said. 'Look at it from his point of view. He realises that much of what you have to offer is good. He knows that his patients know that too. So he's decided to work with you rather than against you. Most probably one of the bones in his *Bula* set relates to you Doctor Whitaker. If the patient's *nsila* affects the fall in such a way, he may decide that you should be consulted too.'

'If you can't beat 'em – join 'em,' Whitaker chuckled. 'Old Ngodini is a pragmatist of the first water.'

'Pragmatist?' Sister Lubemba was a stranger to the word but not the sentiment. 'He judges which patients are suffering from illness caused by a natural breakdown in health like mumps and measles in children, and colds when the seasons change, and which diseases are caused by the malice of the ancestors or wizards, or some insult by the patient to his surroundings. Then he treats his patient accordingly. Does that make him a pragmatist?'

'Why do you think he sent Vuloyi to me?' Whitaker asked. 'You told me that Vuloyi was suffering because her husband had scorned her ancestors.'

'She was also suffering from severe pain. He gave her advice on both counts. He treated the cause – he left you to take care of the symptoms.'

'*That*,' Whitaker said, 'is pragmatism, Sister Lubemba, and that's your English lesson for the day.' He turned to Kirsten. 'By the way, did you hear that bang, while you were with old Ngodini? It didn't seem to come from the direction of the dam.'

'A death sound,' Kirsten said softly, so softly that the words were submerged beneath the engine noise.

A few kilometres further along the road she made herself amply heard.

'Stop!'

'Stop?' A startled Graham Whitaker slowed the Land Rover. 'Why?'

'Go back,' Kirsten instructed. 'Turn around, and go back.'

'OK . . . but why?'

'I think I saw September Mabutane.'

But it was not September Mabutane. It was a much younger man who stared at those who drove up and down the road – and could not make up their minds in which direction to go . . . Kirsten said no more on the drive back to the clinic.

Mabutane came that night.

* * *

Gray Whitaker and Kirsten had grown to love the darkness. The darkness emancipated them. It nurtured them. Like creatures of the nocturne, their landscape was the night. Together in the darkness they discovered a magnificent gem. They found love and they were rich with it. But love made misers of them – liars too. At the coming of each dawn they hid this lovely shiny thing from the eyes of others. For there were considerations that far outweighed the right for the possession of joy for those two people.

That night they dined together. Doing that had become part of their loving ritual. They sipped from a bottle of vintage Cabernet, absorbing its warming richness. Then, to complete their contentment, they stepped from the verandah to meet their indulgent friend, the darkness.

Mabutane was there.

'Inkosikazi; over here. *Alone* Inkosikazi. This man cannot come with you.'

The summons had come at last. The summons that they had awaited, and spoken of, so earnestly for so long was at hand. Kirsten was about to go, armed only with her trust and her will, on a journey that held an awesome potential for tragedy. It was Gray Whitaker's duty to send her off without hindrance or foreboding; without a single word of doubt. This he knew. But he was weak with doubt, and he found his duty beyond him.

'Kirsten . . . *wait*.'

She was ready for this. 'I'm in good hands.' She kissed him firmly. 'Get the Inkatha from Prospect Hall now, Gray. Keep it safe until you hear from me.'

'I will, but . . .'

'No "buts", Gray.' She silenced him, pressed a finger to his mouth. 'We've spoken this out a hundred times. I know the risks. I'm as prepared as I'll ever be. This is what I wanted, remember?

It's the only chance I've got.'

'You must come now,' Mabutane called urgently. 'Follow me now.'

She did as she was instructed. She followed the voice of September Mabutane into the night – into the leafy gloom of the Lebombo forests. The pathway climbed and dipped and twisted towards the north, then to the east. At midnight the moon came out to show a bright river. They forded it and met another forest. There were inky moon-patched glades. There were tunnels of black emptiness where every step was placed in hope. Connected to nothing but the voice of the man ahead, she followed.

Where the morning shadows started, there the forest ended. Above them there were jagged rocky kranzes mellowing in the dawn light. Below, still deeply shaded were valleys of vertiginous depth. They skirted a jutting cliff that bottomed in a flowing river. Hollowly, from the depths of the gorge she heard the rush of running water. There was a kraal down there.

'Is that it?' Kirsten pointed. 'Is that where Abanzanzi moved to after the burning of kwaIsingogo?'

'Yes, Inkosikazi . . . Your brother is there.'

'Thank you, Mabutane.'

'Thanks are not due. It is only because he wants to see you that I brought you here.'

'I know, but it's what I wanted too.'

'I hope it brings you joy to see Mvulaba. I know that you love him very much.'

'I do, Mabutane. How is my brother?'

She asked the question as they picked their way down a narrow, precipitous pathway that cut the cliff. It seemed, however, that Mabutane had said all he was going to say. Perversely she persisted with her words.

'I'm glad we're climbing down this pathway in the daylight, Mabutane. One wrong step and over you'd go. I met your wife Vuloyi, you know. She was at the clinic. What a pretty heifer that one. *Hau*! And fat with calf. You are a bull of a man she says.'

That reached him. A silly, bashful grin spread wide across his face. He stopped and turned to face her.

'She said that, Inkosikazi?'

'*Yebo*, September. That was what she told Sister Lubemba.

You must forgive her, she is very proud of you. Very happy to be the mother of your child.'

'Why was she at the clinic?'

'She had very bad backache. Old Ngodini decided she should see the doctor there.'

'I am glad she went there. Ngodini knows I trust the medicine from the clinic.' He turned as though to continue down the mountain, then hesitated. 'Your brother: it is dark with him, Inkosikazi. But you will see soon enough for yourself. Come.'

It was cool in the ravine. The shadows looked deep and permanent. The trees had broad sun-seeking leaves, and were tangled with green vines. A little river, more noise than water, slid shallowly through its rocky throat.

'Where are we? What's that river's name?'

She did not expect Mabutane to answer those questions – nor did he. He pointed ahead. They had arrived.

It was an unusual kraal. Its very location was odd. Zulus by tradition build on high ground. The induna who had selected this site could not have found a deeper ravine in all of Africa. The huts were of a type of *indlu* that the Zulus had favoured a century ago. It was very neat and clean. And *very* well guarded.

Kirsten had noticed them since sun-up: sentries posted at vantage points, high up on the kranzes along the route. Tall, proud-shouldered warriors who bore war shields and long bladed assegais. There were two such men at the gate of the kraal.

'Wait here, Inkosikazi,' Mabutane indicated a spot under a sycamore tree. He saluted the gate sentries as he passed them. Presently a drum began to throb. Mute and dismal, the sound reached out for those within that dark, sepulchral gorge. The hands that played that vellum had no joy to report. For Mvulaba a visitor had arrived. Dragging at her were the pendant emotions of despondency and apprehension. Not quite the pilgrim fulfilment she had anticipated.

'Come, Inkosikazi. Your brother will see you.' Mabutane had returned. He had stripped off the blanket he had worn earlier. Now, he could have exchanged places with any one of those stern-faced sentries.

'Come.'

*   *   *

The curse of waking up had come again for Mvulaba. A monotonous and ugly routine that varied only by degree in the infliction of its lashes. It was a time for the acknowledgment of his half-burned, deformed body. It was a time for clenching the jawbone tight until the teeth were locked and holding back cold inner terrors. It was a time for the outwards-turning of the eyes, to seek the terrors of the not-self. And of those, there were many.

It was morning. But this was not just to be any morning. This was the day when he was to see his sister Kirsten. He did not want that. He was afraid of that. Kirsten would bring love with her, and love was an emotion that was too different and too strong to be looked at. She was the summer-time and he was the winter, never to come to the same place at the same time. She was different. She would injure him with her sunniness and not even know it.

Inside him a gust of arctic wind arose, it eddied and blew angrily against the pictured face of Kirsten, as clearly as if she was already there. Then it was still.

'A warning wind,' he said aloud. Hoping that she might hear and stay away. But it was Uhlanga who heard him.

'Where were you?' she asked. 'Were you with me, or were you in a higher place?'

'I was with you here. I do not want to see her, Uhlanga.'

She handed him his *muthi* gourd. 'Drink. It is better that you see her.'

'She shines dangerously.'

'I will not let her do harm. Drink.'

The bitter burning liquid was part of his every-morning taste. There was more of it by a swallow that time. And that was all he thought about it.

'I will see her alone then.'

Uhlanga nodded. 'Mabutane has brought her.' She looked purposely at him. 'Are you ready?'

'Yes,' he said. And he knew the lie was safe, because without the help of the higher ones, not even she could get inside him. 'Bring her to me.'

Two sentries brought her. Firstly in shadow. '*Ngena*,' they instructed. And the shadow at his door became the head and shoulders of his sister. She shone with beauty as he had known she would. Memories, like that many bees, began to stir and swarm. But where to focus? They were all too quick and frenzied. He stared at her, glad of the advantage that the darkness of the *indlu* gave him; aware that soon her vision would be equal to his, and she would see him. Before that could happen he said:

'Why do you come looking for a dead man?'

'Monty?' She peered towards his voice. 'Is that you Monty?'

'Monty's dead.'

'Is it you?'

She came towards him hesitantly. He turned his good side towards her – a vain and puerile gesture for which he scorned himself. Her fingers reached out to touch his cheek.

'It *is* you.'

Don't let her burn you. Her fingers will burn you.

He jerked back sharply. On an inwards-drawn breath he hissed, 'No!'

'*No!*' Startled by his vehemence, she copied him.

The smell of burning flesh subsided. With her incendiary fingers withdrawn, and the rules of no touch established, they sat there silently looking at each other. She unsure how to proceed; he welcoming the uncertainty. Finally he said:

'Montague Law was burned to death. Mvulaba survived.'

'And you are Mvulaba?'

'Yes.'

'Am I your sister?' she asked hesitantly.

The woman is a fire trap.

'You are the sister of a dead man.'

'Then let me speak to him. Let me speak to the man that you, Mvulaba, answer for.'

Suddenly with a swoosh and a beating of wings uKhosi the eagle was there. 'You don't listen Mvulaba. I warned you but you didn't listen.'

'I listened . . . I did.'

'Yes, she's very clever,' uKhosi said, 'and very dangerous. She wants to drag you back to that world of hers. Show her the scars that her world gave you.'

'Look.' He followed uKhosi's instruction. He turned the other side of his face towards her, the burned and grotesque side of him.

'Look.'

She did not gasp, or throw her hands in horror across her eyes. She did not run away. She said:

'So that is my brother. I see him. I love him.'

'*Sorceress!*' screamed uKhosi. 'Don't listen to her, she wants to trap you. Call the *imikhovu*, they will know how to deal with her.'

'I . . . can't . . . do it.'

'Don't you think I know what's right for you?' uKhosi screamed. 'Do as I tell you. There's no end to the tricks of that world of hers.'

He shook his head – a violent judder that quivered his cheeks and tongue. It also momentarily dislodged uKhosi. uKhosi the black eagle was the only high one who could cross over at will from the place of the spirits. Now he was gone again; there was a respite from the bedlam of screamed demands.

'You can talk to me now,' he told his sister. 'Tell me what I am to you. I'm puzzled. Why is it that you've sought me out?'

'I want you to come with me. I care for you. I want to help you.'

'I'm burned inside and out. There's nothing left to salvage.'

'I'm so sorry. It's wicked what happened.'

'Your pity would kill me. Your sorrow is my poison. If I have become your punishment then the fault lies with you. Walk out of here and forget me. It would be best for all of us.'

'No . . . please, please listen to me. It's time to forget about the past now. You've got a whole life ahead of you. You can't live it out like this.'

'We *are* our pasts, little sister. That is the stuff that our minds are made of. That is a law of nature. We are the puppets of our histories. There is no escape.' And to prove that statement the tumult of uKhosi was suddenly with him again. '*She must go. She must go,*' screamed the eagle beak.

But he had spoken to little sister and he had not been burned. He had discovered affection, growing like a single bloomed berg flower – so hard to find, so beautiful once found. And the talons of uKhosi were tearing at the fragile petalled thing.

'You must go,' he said. But she did not hear the desperation in his voice. She could not see what he could see.

'Why won't you let me help you?' She reached out for him. He tried to pull away but was too slow. Where she touched him his flesh sizzled and smoked. In agony he screamed.

'*I warned you Mvulaba!*' uKhosi screeched.

She tried to touch him again.

'*Look out. She's going to kill you.*'

His scream had brought Uhlanga – and behind her the *imikhovu*. They seized her, they thrust her from his *indlu*. He screamed again. 'Don't! Don't! *Don't!*'

Then Uhlanga was cradling him. Cooing to him, softly, soothingly, the pacific liquid words of the mother of the fevered child.

'It will pass. It will pass, my Mvulaba. Did she hurt my Mvulaba? Did the evil woman hurt you my dove, my honeycomb? What will we do with the evil thing? What will we do to make her suffer as she made you suffer?'

He curled into her healing warmth. He wondered if anyone could ever suffer as the world had made him suffer. He closed his eyes, exhausted.

'Can I sleep now?'

'Sleep, eyes of mine, sleep. Sleep now and see what you have to see. They are waiting for you in the little death. They have things to tell you, those *amathongo*-spirits. Go to them. Go to sleep . . . Go to sleep.'

'*Come with me*,' said uKhosi, and his great black wings unfolded.

* * *

At midday the sun reached down into the gorge of kuManshanja and touched on the dome-thatched *isindlu* of Abanzanzi. Its visit was transient, its effect was little. The shadows of that place prevailed. The morning dew remained undried.

In front of the main hut there was an open place. It was there that Mabutane led the sister of Mvulaba. Uhlanga received her there; offered her *amasi*.

'Sit and be comfortable. Drink, it will refresh you. You have come a long way and I can see by your face that you are confused and tired. You have come about your brother. You wish him to go back with you?'

'Yes.'

Both of them drank from the *amasi* gourd. It *was* refreshing.

Uhlanga filled it and passed it to her again; she said:

'Let me explain something to you, sister. The crocodile's strength is the water.' The sangoma spread her arms out territorially. 'This place – this *umuZi* is the water of Mvulaba. Take him from here and he dies. We are his people; his river and his reeds.'

'He is *already* dying, Uhlanga. I knew him as he was, now I see him as he is. I am his sister. I know.'

Uhlanga shook her head. 'You mistake the state of his mind. Such a possession of one spirit by another is not a sickness. It is something to rejoice in. He is on a pathway that few are selected to travel. He is a gifted person. I am his guide and his teacher, but already he has passed me in certain talents. His vision knows no barriers. He has the ability to converse with the godspirits that even I cannot reach. Be glad for him. Stay with us, sister of Mvulaba, if that is what you want. Make this place your place. Be a part of this great and wonderful thing that is happening to our nation.'

'Uhlanga, I want only one thing. I want my brother, the man you call Mvulaba. How can one man, a man who is not even a Zulu, be so important to you and the dreams that you have for your nation? Let him go Uhlanga, I beg you. I don't come empty-handed to you, Uhlanga. Perhaps you already know this Uhlanga, I have in my possession the Inkatha of Shaka Zulu. I found it and I took it away from here. I've kept it safe. That is my contribution to you. I hope it makes my voice a favoured voice in this valley of yours.'

'It makes your voice that of the thief in the night, who comes in the morning with soothing words to hide his guilt.' Uhlanga pointed to her *imikhovu* bodyguards. 'They know how to deal with thieves.'

It would have taken but the click of a finger to have brought the *imikhovu* running. Kirsten felt fear then, but she kept it from her bearing and her throat.

'Your suggestion is less than worthy of you, Uhlanga. I have come to appeal to you for my brother's release. No matter how gifted you think he is, or unique his talents, he is suffering terribly. You know it and I know it. It is wrong for you to hold him. It is also wrong for me to possess what is rightfully yours.'

'So you wish to trade?' Uhlanga said. 'Is that what I hear? The Inkatha for Mvulaba. Sister, I find your suggestion to be immoral. The Inkatha is not a bag of seed. Mvulaba is not a hoe, to be swapped for it. If he wants to go with you then there is nothing to stop him. There's his *indlu*. Go and tell him that you've come to take him away from here.'

'You know he wouldn't come with me, Uhlanga.'

'I know it. But you don't seem to know it.'

'Oh I know it. That is why I'm here. I know I can't do a single thing to help my brother without your support and guidance.'

'Sister, from me he has all the help, all the guidance and all the love he needs. Your motives are based on the ignorance of your race. You see your brother as being sick. That is quite wrong. See him rather as being blessed. See him as the visionary that he is. But I see that my words drop short. Your culture has made you what you are, sister. I understand your pain but have no cure to offer. Mvulaba stays.'

'Please Uhlanga . . . please.'

'Sister, look at me. What do you see?'

'I see a great sangoma.'

'No. No. Look at me. Look into my eyes. They are strange eyes for a Zulu, are they not?'

'You have the eyes of rain.'

'Yes. Let me tell you about these eyes. Once they could not see.'

'You were blind?'

'In a sense I was blind. Then Mvulaba came and where there was darkness, suddenly there was light. He brought me vision. He cleared the mists of destiny. He steers me on the river of time. Eh! The things that I see now that I could not see before. And you, sister; you come to me and say: Uhlanga, let me put out your eyes. What answer do you expect from me?'

'Your eyes suffer, Uhlanga. They are in shocking pain.'

'No . . . No.' The sangoma shook her head. 'It is only you who makes Mvulaba suffer. I should not even have allowed you to see him.'

'Then why did you, Uhlanga? You must have known what I wanted. Why did you let me come at all?'

Kirsten Law held fast to the stare of the extraordinary grey eyes of the sangoma Uhlanga. Against the frowning darkness of her face they *were* like rain – cold and penetrative. They were also quite unmoved by Kirsten's anguish.

'Sister,' she said again, 'it is you, with your mistaken ideas, who have caused the suffering.' She stood up and tossed back her kaross, and Kirsten saw her fully for the first time. The woman was huge; ponderously breasted, paunched, and heavy-limbed. Yet she carried herself easily. She loomed over the sister of Mvulaba.

'Your biggest mistake, sister, was to believe that the destiny of the Inkatha of Shaka Zulu could be determined in any way by yourself. The spirits control the destiny of the Inkatha, sister, not you. All you have done is to bring yourself into conflict with them: that is a dangerous game. I hope the spirits consider that when they reckon with you.' She beckoned to Mabutane to come closer. 'This man will attend to your needs. Now I must go.'

She walked away.

'She didn't answer my question,' Kirsten turned to Mabutane. 'Tell me Mabutane, why *did* she allow me to come here?'

But he had no answer for her either. 'Come,' he said kindly. 'You must be very tired. An *indlu* has been prepared for you so that you can sleep. Perhaps when you wake up you will see things more clearly. Come.'

She spoke to him as they walked, and the wretchedness of her spirit was suddenly more than she could hide. 'Oh! Mabutane. Why won't she let him go? What is the reason for all this? My brother is sick. His mind is gone. How can she use him like this? She's killing him, Mabutane.'

'She believes he is a gifted prophet, Inkosikazi.'

'How can she, Mabutane? My brother is living in a cruel fantasy world. He mutters sentences that make no sense at all. Is this the wonderful vision that Uhlanga bases her plans on? She must be as mad as . . . as . . .'

'You mustn't even think what you are thinking, Inkosikazi. The sangoma knows your thoughts. Mvulaba and Uhlanga are both great isangoma.'

They stopped outside a hut.

'Here is your *indlu*, Inkosikazi.' He gestured for her to enter – then momentarily stayed her progress. 'Don't despair, Inkosikazi. It is black for your brother. I have known it for a while

'. . . Sleep now, Inkosikazi. I will watch your *indlu*. Do not be afraid.'

'I am not afraid for myself Mabutane. Don't you see?'

'I see a tired woman.' Mabutane ushered her through the door. 'We will talk again when you are rested.'

Kirsten *was* tired. She was leaden with fatigue. Her sadness, however, was a greater thing than that. She dropped her face into her hands, and the wetness of her tears ran past her wrists. She saw her brother's tortured face and heard his tortured words.

She slept until aroused by the urgent whisper of September Mabutane.

'Inkosikazi . . . Inkosikazi.'

It was time to be up again. It would be dark in a short while, he told her. If she wished it he would take her to the river and stand guard while she attended to her toilet.

'There is a deep pool there where you can bathe. I'll show you where it is. You'll like it.'

It was beneath a flowing waterfall; circled by green ferns and guarded by huge, lichened boulders. Kirsten found a nook where she could strip. She folded her pants and shirt, and placed them with her shoes, socks and panties, on a rock.

The water was as pure as a mountain spring can be, and as cold. It shocked the breath from her. It was deep enough to submerge in, even at full stretch. So that was what she did. She tumbled head over heels under water until the cold began to numb her. Then she clambered out, feeling so much fresher in body and spirit.

Where she had undressed and left her clothing, another set of garments lay: an *isidwaba* buckskin skirt, and *usu* cloak. She did not even bother to search for her own clothes. They would not be there. Mabutane had been told to get her clothed in Zulu garments, and that was how he had done it. She drew on the *isidwaba*; that was adequate; soft and comfortable. The *usu* cloak however did not cover her breasts. It was not made to.

Mabutane appeared from the riverine forest as she walked back towards the *umuZi* – the kraal of Uhlanga the sangoma.

'You tricked me, Mabutane.'

'In the nicest way, Inkosikazi.' Bashfully, keeping his eyes averted, he took his place at her side. 'You would not have exchanged your garments for these would you?'

'No.'

'It had to be done. Uhlanga wanted it. The white people's clothes offend her.'

'Do they offend you too, Mabutane?'

He took a long time in answering. 'You look lovely like this, Inkosikazi. With the greatest respect I tell you that.'

'Thank you, September Mabutane. I did enjoy the swim.'

'I told you that you would.'

'Indeed you did. What you didn't tell me is what river it was that I was swimming in when you tricked me into this state of Zulu maidenhood.'

Mabutane hung back a little, as though distance might free him from the reach of her inquisitiveness. It was not to be.

'Come, Mabutane. I think you owe me an answer.'

He shook his head. He said, '*Hau!*' So she would know just how big a thing she was asking. Then he said: 'It is the Manshanja.'

'But that's not in kwaZulu. That's across the border in Swaziland.'

'Yes. That is where we are. Not far from here the Manshanja flows into Mozambique, where it joins eventually into the Suthu River, or the Maputo as they call it there. Do you know where you are now, Inkosikazi?'

'Yes. Thank you for telling me Mabutane. I know you weren't supposed to tell me.'

'No, I wasn't. This is where Abanzanzi came after the burning of kwaIsingogo.'

'Are you sorry that you told me?'

'No . . . I'm glad. I trust you, Inkosikazi.'

And so, in a few simple sentences a bond of faith had been cemented between the two of them.

'I trust you too, September Mabutane. Do you know that old Ngodini's *Bula* predicted that I would soon be seeing my brother?'

'What else did they predict?'

'He said that there was an angry and powerful spirit that was set against me, and that I was going towards great danger.'

'I hope you heard him, Inkosikazi.'

'Oh I heard him. Do you know what else he said Mabutane? It

concerns you.'

'Tell me.'

'He said that Vuloyi would soon give birth to a son.'

'Did he really say that?'

'Of course. Are you pleased?'

'Eh! A boy! At last. I am a *king*.'

'So *King* Mabutane, will you be there at the birth?'

'Can anything keep the buffalo from its water?'

'Don't blame Ngodini if he's wrong.'

'He's *never* wrong.' September Mabutane was suddenly embarrassed by his joy. 'I fear he is never wrong,' he apologised. 'His *Bula* never lie.'

They had reached the kraal – the *umuZi* of the sangoma with the eyes of rain. The place of the black crocodile stone of Ngodini – who was never wrong. September Mabutane stopped her before they entered.

'Inkosikazi, you remember the day we first spoke about your brother. The day of the tragedy of Doctor Tyrell?'

'Yes, perfectly.'

'You told me to take a message to your brother. You said you just wanted to see him. That was all. Now you have seen him. You have seen how it is with him. Don't you think you should leave now? Don't you think you should go away from here?'

'I came to take him away with me, Mabutane.'

'That was not the message I was told to bring.'

'I know. There wasn't much time to talk that day, especially after uDende arrived.'

'Eh . . . that hyena. But let's not talk about that foul thing. This mission of yours, Inkosikazi; my advice to you is to abandon it. There are things that you don't understand, Inkosikazi.'

'And there are things that you too don't understand, Mabutane. I won't leave without him.'

'I admire your courage, Inkosikazi. Like an assegai in your hand I hope it is not turned by a stronger arm to bring you down. You know it was no accident that you were called to see Ngodini. No one is ever delivered into the presence of an Inyanga or a sangoma by accident. Vuloyi was the pathway that brought you to Ngodini, and Vuloyi is my wife. In some way therefore, you and I, Inkosikazi, are linked by the *Bula* of Ngodini.'

Kirsten was acutely aware of the stares of the men who watched her as she walked into the kraal. The evening air was cool and no matter how she hung the *usu* cloak, one anguished nipple would peep. At the door of her *indlu* Mabutane said:

'I am going to ask permission to go and visit my wife, Vuloyi. I must find out how it goes with her. So you may not see me for some days. Please Inkosikazi, close the gate on any dangerous thoughts while I am gone.'

'I promise,' she said quietly. 'Mabutane?'

He halted. '*Yebo*, Inkosikazi?'

'Will you do something for me, if you *do* go. Will you get a message to Graham Whitaker. Tell him not to worry about me. Tell him everything is all right.'

That night September Mabutane was gone. A bigger, sterner, coldly taciturn attendant came to take his place outside her *indlu*. His name, he said, was 'Zimuka' – the one who moves ponderously – and the name suited him. There was to be dancing that night, he told her:

'The regiment is to perform. You will watch. You will come with me.'

'Another night, Zimuka. I am very tired.'

'Uhlanga says you will come.'

She went with him. And there was dancing that night, and on the night that followed, and on every night during the November moon of umKhosi weGade – because although the food was little, it was right to be grateful. On some nights they trod in a unisoned swirling frenzy that shook the earth, and their demands were many and shouted. On other nights the movements were more tamed – the words more coercive. Always they moved with the grace of nature.

So the men of the regiment performed, and the harmony, as weightless as the wind, swept through the valley, and upwards to the ears of heaven.

You could not listen and not be moved by it. Kirsten was amongst the listeners drawn there every night. Often during the day hours she would find some cryptic line hovering in her consciousness:

'*Come Nomkubulwana, come,*
The dry black earth is broken – come.'

But the summons that Kirsten herself was listening for was never voiced.

She saw her brother at the dancing, and only there, seated next to Uhlanga. And he saw her. Every time she looked at him he was watching her. Never did he seem to take his eyes from her. But her presence went unacknowledged, her smile ignored.

She would move her lips for him to read: 'Please Monty . . . I want to help you . . . I've come to help you . . . Please see me.' She looked into his half-handsome, half-grotesque face and mouthed her desperate pleading words. But the only life his eyes displayed was the orange glint of the firelight. He just stared and stared.

Every night the certainty in her grew stronger that she had lost her brother, that Mvulaba had gained his suffering body and mind. But with every dawn her hope returned. She knew there would come a day when her resolve would take her no further. She was determined that it should endure until the return of September Mabutane.

One morning she awoke to find that the valley of Manshanja was white with rolling mist – *Inkosazana yase zulwini*. The princess of heaven Nomkubulwana had finally arrived, and the land was clothed in the dampness of her garment. In the valley of Manshanja there was rejoicing.

'And now we will sacrifice,' Zimuka said. 'Today it will be told to us what it is that will please the *amathongo* spirits. Today Mvulaba will take us to where his eyes have been. *Hau!* A great sacrifice will be asked for, have no doubt, Inkosikazi.'

It was the most that Kirsten had ever heard Zimuka say. Kirsten replied to him, 'Perhaps Nomkubulwana will grant us rain.' She would have said more had someone not suddenly screamed. It was the throat sound of a mind in anguish, the cry of a man in the torment of a nightmare, and it came from the *indlu* of the man called Mvulaba. The features of the sister of Mvulaba drew sharply back in reflexive pain. And the scream came again.

*   *   *

Where Mvulaba was, there was fire and brutal unbearable heat that came from all sides. It seared him. It burned its way brightly through his eyes and into his skull. And there it caught the pages of his memory. Leaf by leaf they blackened and curled and charred. Memories in weightless white smuts rose up from the heat, but they were too delicate to hold. They powdered to the touch. He had to have them though. He reached out left and right and tried to catch the flimsy fragments.

There was a place by a river, a mossy wall of tumbled bricks, some age-rusted sugar milling plant . . . Kirsten, a very young sister Kirsten, smiling, chasing, tickling – laughter. Then pain. Flames, flames, and the memory blackened, ashened, lifted away into neverness.

There she was again, older now with pleading eyes and arms that reached out for him protectively. The inferno of him took this Kirsten too – torched her – whirled her away until she was just a scream. Then that too burned. 'Come back,' he tried to call her, but the heat consumed his very words. 'Help me,' he pleaded. 'I'm burning. *I'm on fire.*'

And then, as it always happened, he found he could step away from the furnace of that place. The agony was suddenly totally controllable. It was simply a matter of abandoning his wish to observe past things. The past was his torture – his pyre.

There was a kinder place waiting only a little distance away. A place of rock, barren, black and cold, it stretched to the horizon. There were pools there of black water, and a sky of night. It was a place where he could distance himself from pain; a place without heat. He turned to it. A voice was waiting for him there.

'I'm glad you're back.' It was the Guide. 'I warned you not to walk away from me, but you didn't listen. Was it painful there, Mvulaba?'

'It was awful. I'll never go back.'

'Is uKhosi the eagle with you? Or any of the others?'

'No. I feel so bad, so very bad.'

'Wait for them. Stay where you are and wait. They will arrive soon.'

The Guide was seldom wrong. Presently he felt the rush of beaten air. uKhosi swooped down.

'So there you are, Mvulaba. I was looking for you.' He settled nearby and began to preen.

'I went to the place of fire; the place of the past.'

'Unwise, Mvulaba,' the eagle reprimanded. 'Very unwise.'

'Who is with you?' asked the Guide from the inner place. 'Who has come? Tell me who you are talking to.'

'uKhosi is here with me.'

'And any of the other creatures of the soul?'

'Just uKhosi.'

'Good. Ask uKhosi what news he has for us.'

He did as the Guide had requested. 'What news, uKhosi? What news from the spirits of the high ones?'

'They are angry,' uKhosi twisted his mobile head. 'You have been slow to sacrifice.'

Mvulaba reported this to the Guide.

'There is confusion here, uKhosi,' he came back with the Guide's reply. 'We were not told what it was that would satisfy Nomkubulwana. We were instructed to be patient. Now we see that Nomkubulwana has arrived in our valley and still we wait.'

'Wait no longer;' inGwenya the crocodile had climbed out from the black swamp. 'It is she.'

'Yes,' screeched uKhosi, 'inGwenya is right. It is she who they want.'

'But who?'

'The woman who dared to come out of the past and cause you such pain. Her!'

'My sister?'

'*Yes! Yes! Yes!*' uKhosi and inGwenya chorused. 'She is to be the one. Nothing else will satisfy.'

'No!' Mvulaba shouted. He saw the face of the woman they wanted. And suddenly he was burning again.

'*Fool*,' screamed uKhosi. '*You walked back. You must never walk back.*' He swooped and lifted him from the place of fire.

'It must be her,' inGwenya croaked from below.

'What is it?' called the Guide from the inner place. 'What do they say? Tell me Mvulaba.'

But Mvulaba could not tell her. There was no throat room for anything but his screams. Then uKhosi set him down and the screams changed to sobs.

'Is it her?' asked the Guide. 'Is the sister to be the one?'

'She's the one,' said Mvulaba.

'Yes, she's the one,' agreed the creatures of the high place.

Then they were gone. With a beating of wings uKhosi flapped away, inGwenya disappeared without a ripple. There was no one but him in the place of souls.

'They're gone,' Mvulaba said. 'Can I come back now?'

'No, not just yet,' the Guide replied. 'I sense there is more that the *amathongo* wish to communicate. Be patient, Mvulaba. You've done well.'

He was patient. He did as the Guide had instructed. Finally it was uMamba who coiled his way up to the dark place to meet him.

uMamba greeted with his darting blue tongue. 'It is well that you waited for me.' Mvulaba took the words of the black snake as they were spoken and repeated them to the Guide.

'The one you have waited for for so long is almost with you. Where the river flows, where the storm winds blow, seek him there and greet him with the royal salute, because he will lead the Zulus; and his spear will be the spear of Dingaan, and his hearth stones the hearth stones of Cetchwayo. The Inkatha of Shaka Zulu is his seat, and the nation will bond to him, and it will become mighty. Be ready you Zulus. Your task has only just begun.'

Then in his silent sullen way uMamba slipped away.

'He's gone,' Mvulaba said, 'can I come back now?'

'Have you seen everything; heard everything? Have you reported it all to me?'

'Yes.'

'Then you may come. Yes, you may come. You are free of the spirits, Mvulaba. Follow the pathway. You know it well. No, don't look back . . . come . . . come . . . come.'

Drawn by the soft words – cushioned by the soft flesh, he settled slowly in the waiting arms of the Guide of the inner place, the sangoma Uhlanga of the eyes of rain. 'Come Mvulaba, my imPindisa flower. My warrior. My eyes.'

'Can I rest now?' Mvulaba winced in tiredness. 'Can I sleep?'

'No.' Uhlanga stood. She raised him with her. 'No, the time for rest is over. You must be fortified, Mvulaba. You must be ready to fulfil your life's task. Today you must find the hyena uDende. You must take from him the Inkatha of Shaka Zulu. There can be no more rest for us. Abanzanzi have been called upon. Take whichever *imikhovu* you might need to help you in your task Mvulaba, go, and do what must be done. The ancestor spirits are with us, Mvulaba. Our cause is just. Our day has come.'

* * *

Kirsten Law realised that morning that she had failed – she could not carry on. She had held against a head wind of bitter frustration, for how many days? The struggle was futile. It was time to let go.

It was the screams of her brother that had finally caused this realisation. She had dashed out into the mist and ran towards the *indlu* of Mvulaba. Of course, her entrance had been barred. But she had stood there refusing to be shoved away; waiting, sick with anxiety, waiting. And then he had emerged. He had seen her standing in the mist. With eyes as dead as the *imikhovu* zombies that had flanked him, her brother had looked at her. She had called out 'Monty, Monty,' and then stopped. This was *not* Monty. This was not *anyone* she knew. There were no words in *her* vocabulary that this man would respond to. He was the living dead, he kept company with the living dead. She had watched him walk away then with his *imikhovu* bodyguards. There had been something final about that moment.

She had seen the face of Uhlanga in the darkened doorway – *her* eyes were very much alive. They were quick and they were sharp. And they were victorious.

She had lost. She turned away, and with Zimuka escorting her as though she were some criminal, she returned to her *indlu*.

She would wait no longer. As soon as the mist rose from the valley she would take polite leave of the sangoma Uhlanga, and go. It would serve no purpose to wait for September Mabutane. There was nothing to hold her now. Her mind was made up. And then she heard the cheerful voice of September Mabutane outside her *indlu*.

'*Saubona* uZimuka.'

'*Saubona* uMabutane. *Unjani?*'

He was well, he told Zimuka, and was it not a wonderful sight, these the mists of Nomkubulwana. 'I've come to take over from you uZimuka. You can stand down now.'

'Eeh . . .' Zimuka ground that information through the slow mill of his mind . . . 'I was not told you were coming to relieve me, uMabutane.'

'Well, I haven't been back long. I reported to the induna Mabamba and he posted me here. Go on. You can go now.'

'Eeh.'

When next Kirsten heard Zimuka's voice it was some distance from the *indlu*:

'She's not allowed out,' he called. 'Do you know that?'

'I know all about it,' Mabutane confirmed. 'Mabamba told me everything.'

And before Kirsten could react to the implications of this discussion, September Mabutane came scrambling on hands and knees into the *indlu*.

'Forgive my rudeness, Inkosikazi.'

'Mabutane.'

He shook his head quickly. He held up his hand. Urgent gestures. She was not to speak. She was to listen.

'There is no time, Inkosikazi. Before the mists lift you must be out of here. You are in terrible danger.'

'But Mabutane what's happened? Why . . . why this urgency?'

'You must have heard what Zimuka said to me.'

'Of course I heard it. I can explain that. I was upset this morning by something that happened here. In the process I upset Uhlanga. I suppose this is just her way of retaliating.'

'No. No, Inkosikazi. There is much more to it than that. Believe me, Inkosikazi. I know what is about to happen here. Things are bad for you.'

'Oh come on, Mabutane. We've known all along of the dangers. Look, I've decided to leave here anyway. There's nothing I can do to help my brother. But I'm not going to slink off with my tail between my legs. No, there are a few things I still want to say to Uhlanga.'

'Don't do that, Inkosikazi.'

'I must, Mabutane. But there is no cause for you to worry. Only uWhitaker and I know where the sacred Inkatha is hidden. Uhlanga wouldn't dare harm me. Surely you can see that.'

'Is *that* what you believe?'

'Of course. It's the truth.'

'If only it was, Inkosikazi. We've all had dreams about the Inkatha of Shaka Zulu, even myself. I believed once that I would be the one destined to return that to the nation. Do you know who promised I could have it? uDende.'

'He couldn't have. He's never had it. He doesn't even know where it is.'

'Ah! Inkosikazi. You are so wrong. uDende is the liar of all liars, and that is the least of his evils. But this time he was telling the truth. He has got the Inkatha. The whole of Ingwavuma knows it.'

'I don't believe it.'

'It's the truth, Inkosikazi. Even your friend the doctor knows it. I went to see him, just as you asked me to. I gave him your message. And he in turn gave me a message for you.'

'Let me have it, Mabutane.'

'Inkosikazi, do you see any pockets in the clothing I wear? The only safe place for your message is in my head. But we're wasting precious time, we must go. I will talk to you when we are safely away from this place.'

'Tell me what he said, Mabutane. I must know now.'

'Eh!' Mabutane shook his head – this obdurate woman. 'uWhitaker said that he went to Prospect Hall. That is your home isn't it? He said that he searched everywhere. The Inkatha was not there.'

'That's terrible news, terrible.'

'You had to know if I was telling the truth?'

'Yes. I hope you understand.'

'I understand this, Inkosikazi. You don't hold the power that the possession of the Inkatha would have given you. You are in more danger than you could possibly realise. In a very short time now the mist is going to lift. In that time we must get past the gate sentries and into the mountains. Or it will end for you. You must trust me totally.'

'I have always trusted you.'

'Then listen to me. We must go *now*.'

'*I* must go. I can do this alone. And I must.'

'Yes I believe you could, Inkosikazi. But you would have a better chance with me to guide you.'

'No, you've done enough.'

'I have something else for you that uWhitaker made me bring – your gun, Inkosikazi. Like your message, it was not something to be borne in the hand past the induna Mabamba and his sentries at the gate. At least let me give you that. Let me take you to that place, *then* you can continue on your own.'

'Is it far?'

'No.'

'And you promise that you'll leave me after that?'

'I promise.'

Mabutane bent down to exit from the *indlu*, then hesitated. 'Stay within a pace of me,' he warned. 'Be silent and be quick.'

In the valley of Manshanja the mist lay still and heavy.

12

The day's work was done. In the cottage at Abercorn Drift Captain Patrick Dent sat quietly in his favourite easy chair; his chin resting in the palm of one hand. His other arm dangled idly – his fingers moving occasionally to wander across the head and tattered ears of his sole companion. Bess, the bull terrier bitch, breathed in stentorian ecstasy. If the hand remained still for too long it would be nudged. Its reward was to be licked. They had an understanding. It was a subliminal response process that interfered not at all with the evening thoughts of man or beast.

Dent was gazing at a largish woven basket that lay several paces from him on the carpet – Fana's *iquthu* basket. He was thinking about its contents. The sacred Inkatha of the Kings of Zulu. He remembered the passages in the diary of Monty Law that described the history of this most potent item of royal Zulu regalia.

He bent to his knees and shuffled closer to it. What masterful weaving. Fana had had fingers to rival the shuttle of the loom. It began, at its base, with a fine coil of *umchobozi* rush and rose up in a single tightly stitched spiral to form a sphere. The stitching was of *Ilala* palm leaf-blades, and it held the basket so tightly that it could have been used to carry water. In fact the Zulus of Fana's era had used such baskets as water receptacles. This *iquthu* however had never carried anything but its present contents. It had been woven around the Inkatha and there was no way of removing the Inkatha, intact, without first destroying the basket.

There was a neck on the *iquthu*, to which a woven cap was fitted. Dent prised loose the cap. He could not see inside the basket without a torch, but did not consider stirring to fetch one. He had observed the contents of Fana's *iquthu* a dozen times already: a rather aged-looking, stuffed python skin coil the size of a small car inner tube that lay at its base, nothing more spectacular than that.

Bess sniffed at the basket, sneezed, poked her head into the neck and growled. Dent pulled her away. 'No my girl.' He took the *iquthu* and placed it on his desk. Bess sneezed again, then wandered out of the room. Dent heard the screen door squeak, then bang and another distant sneeze.

There was a bottle of Napoleon on the desk. He poured a measure; checked his wristwatch, then settled back into the easy chair. A portable radio was at hand. He switched it on and adjusted the volume low. The well modulated, studied voice of the announcer (Dent imagined he must be a thin man with a thin moustache) read out the predicted weather bulletin. It was the only programme that Dent listened to regularly with attention. '*A low pressure trough extends northwards over the central interior. Moist air is in circulation.*' Good news at least for the Free State mealie-boers. '*Conditions elsewhere will generally be fine.*' What a misnomer was that word fine, what was so fine about dying of drought. '*Tropical cyclone Dorinda is moving slowly southwards down the Mozambique channel causing cloudy weather over the south-eastern coastal regions . . .*' Now *that* was interesting. Cyclone Dorinda had looked at one stage as though it might rear off northwards. Would it be too much to ask for Dorinda to continue southwards, perhaps even south-westwards? God knows they could use the rain. The thin man spoke for a while more, then announced the news. Dent removed him from his living room.

Now it was totally dark and – but for occasional downwind sounds from the dam site – totally quiet. This was a favourite time for Dent. It was a time to sit outside and feel the ground surrender its heat to the cool dark air. It was a time to let the good brandy sink in benevolently. That night, however, he did not carry his bottle to the stoep. The hand that was usually thus occupied held something totally different – a 12 gauge Browning automatic loaded with heavy SSG cartridges. Some called it a riot gun. This change of habit was forced, but Dent was philosophical about it. When what had to be done was done, he would enjoy his liquor the more for it.

He was a patient man, a dedicated man – the attributes of a good hunter. He also knew a lot about his enemy. He knew that they enjoyed the darkness. He knew who it was who would lead them, and that they were totally ruthless and committed.

He knew that they were experts in the use of toxic substances.

Knowing these things, he had formulated his plans accordingly. He became largely nocturnal; sleeping as often as he could during the day; watching through the dark hours. He did not handle anything he was not familiar with. Sergeant Shibindji prepared his food. He was never unarmed. He had planned for every contingency.

So he cradled his shotgun, and he sipped his ration of liquor. He stared through his nightscope into the gloom, and hoped that *that* night would be the night that they came.

Bess returned from her nightly ratting expedition at the rubbish dump. She never caught anything, she was too old now, and too slow for the scurrying brown rats. But she had memories to sustain her, and the doggedness of her breed. Dent watched her amble towards him, bright-eyed and luminous in the image intensifier. And behold, she had a rat, a very smelly and long-dead rat. Dent prised it from her reluctant jaws and tossed it far away. 'Yech! Bad girl. Stay.' She leaned companionably against his leg and nudged his elbow; proud of her achievement. He stroked her head, and waited.

Shortly before midnight Dent realised that Abanzanzi had got to him in the most diabolical; the most brutal of ways.

Bess began to retch and gag; her belly buckling inwards into spasm; thick mucous ropes spilling from her open mouth.

'The dead rat!'

Oh God! The bastards had poisoned her with the rat. He bent to her. He lifted her shivering retching body, surprised by its heaviness. No, not her heaviness – his weakness. He had handled the rat – only momentarily, but that had been enough, quite enough. The *umthakathi* toxin had been designed for him. Poor Bess had been the means of conveyance. So clever. So vile.

'Bess . . . they're not going to get you, Bess.' But his voice was trembling with the lie. He tried to lock his front door behind him, but was not sure whether he had managed that. The bolt felt so stiff, his fingers so powerless and clumsy. He knew what he had to do. In his medicine chest there was a syringe, and a little glass ampoule of Bemegride.

'Come on, old girl.'

He remembered Whitaker's instructions: 'Give yourself half, then wait and see. It's a CNS stimulant and it might be useful. I don't know for sure, because I don't know what drug it has to counteract. It's all I can suggest. If they poison you again, please don't wait until a week's gone past before you consult me. Bang in the Bemegride and get hold of me immediately.'

'Will do.'

The identical words he had used that day with Whitaker. But it was not that easy. The walk to the bathroom was like a drowning man's struggle against the tide. Somewhere in the darkness of the passageway he felt the shotgun slip away and clatter to the floor. Then he was at the bathroom door and fumbling for the light switch.

'Will do.'

He set Bess down and reached for the little mirrored cabinet; fighting desperately the lethargy that was dragging at him, weakening, drifting into apathy. The same deadly tranquillity he had felt that night on the mountain was overtaking him now.

'We're going to make it, girl.'

Did he say that? 'Trust me girl.'

His voice . . . But Bess did not need the reassurance. She was as still as a darted beast. Her eyes still followed Dent alone; her ugly little piggy eyes, and they were uncritical and totally certain. She gave him strength.

He fumbled with the Bemegride ampoule. The delicate neck of the little glass vessel broke as he was sawing it. The phial tilted and spilled a drop of its precious liquid. It always looked so easy when a doctor did it . . . needle in ampoule . . . lift the plunger . . . the barrel filled, one cc. He looked down to where Bess lay. God, she was still.

'This one's for me, girl.'

The needle stung his bicep and he pressed the fluid in . . . 'Now you girl.' God he hoped it was going to work. It had to work! '"I hope you never have to put it to the test",' Whitaker again. '"But if it is going to do something you'll know it within a few minutes."' How long had it been now?

'How long?'

Does it matter? Does it really matter?

'Yes it matters, damn it.'

He cursed the toxic apathy sucking at his will. He fought against it. Hate was his ally. He looked down at poor Bess and his ally was with him. He forced himself to focus on his watch face – nearly midnight. How many minutes? How long had he got before his resolve was drained and gone? How long could he continue the fight?

He heard the screen door squeak, then the rattle of the front door bolt – he *had* managed to lock it. It would not hold them back for long. He reached up and switched off the bathroom light. Had that come easier?

The front door was creaking, giving under a pressure it had never been designed to withstand.

As shakily as a newly crawling infant he hauled himself into the passageway, fumbling for the shotgun that was lying somewhere in the dark.

He found it. It felt as heavy and as unwieldy as a tree trunk. He trained it, belly high, in the direction of the door and took up the trigger slack. He fought the lassitude of his fingers. He fostered the hate. The lock burst apart, the door smashed back against the wall. He fired.

The muzzle-blast flash-lit the passageway, and in that firebright instant he saw his enemy. Two Zulus, all sinew and bared teeth and assegais up ready. Monty Law at the doorway, his arms upraised as if feeling his way. Dent fired again, then again. The noise was massive; the jolting shotgun almost too much for him. A jerky Kinematic sequence of pictures presented: a Zulu clutching at the red mess of his belly with one hand, his spear arm sprung. A Zulu crawling, pain faced, reaching for the muzzle flash that was killing him. Dent fired. A hand was tugging at the barrel. The shotgun fired in reflex the hand was no more. He fired. The spearman was toppling. He fired again and again. And the lead tore the flesh and the bone and the life from the Zulus. Then the weapon was empty. Law could have escaped then. He was not hurt and the killing machine was spent. He should have taken the Inkatha and run, but he did not.

He did not move. Even when Shibindji arrived, breathless and wide-eyed, and switched on all the lights, he did not move. Monty Law stood where he had stood from the beginning – his arms and fingers outstretched as though stiffened by death. His mouth was open, his lips fixed back, but if he was screaming, then only he could hear it.

'Lock . . . him . . . up,' Dent whispered. 'Lock the bastard . . .' Then all his senses dimmed into blackness.

*   *   *

Graham Whitaker's clinical experience was extensive. He had witnessed, often and intimately, the results of violence on the human anatomy. He had an elementary knowledge of ballistics, and knew how frail was flesh and bone in the path of a firearm trajectile. Simply put: he was a hardened man. What awaited him in the entrance hall of Patrick Dent's little bungalow, however, caused him to revalue his previous education. Simply put: he had never seen anything like it. It was horrific.

There were only two bodies, which was not a lot in trauma ward terms. It was the state of those bodies that was so unbelievable. It was the reconstruction of the slaying that caused Whitaker to look at Sergeant Shibindji and shake his head in disbelief.

Both of Dent's assailants had been shot within a single pace of the front door; the door and the adjacent wall were spattered with blood and tissue. That had not stopped them. One man had fallen and stretched a bloodied hand against the wall, there was an ongoing trail of blood for a few metres, then he had been hit twice again – more tissue splattered against the whitewash. Incredibly he had still succeeded in hurtling his spear – and very hard. It had split a bookend within inches of where Dent's head must have been then and gone on to penetrate a thick Encyclopaedia.

The second assailant had been equally hard to kill. He had crawled along on his gutted belly for some metres. One side of his skull and one hand had been shot away, in what order Whitaker could not be sure. He had come even closer to killing the police captain. His spear, still firmly handheld, was buried in the skirting at the base of Dent's bookcase – its blade was bloodied. Dent's blood. The Zulus were beyond medical attention.

'The white man', said Shibindji, 'is in the cells.'

'Yes. You told me. We'll go there now.'

Whitaker wanted to examine Dent once more before he left the cottage. The defender of Abercorn Drift lay on his bed, where Shibindji and his colleagues had laid him. His condition seemed to be stable. He had been nicked by the spear in his thigh, but the wound was superficial. His pupils reacted normally to torchlight. His respiratory action was slow, his blood pressure still low. No further clinical evaluation was possible until the man was hospitalised. It appeared that some kind of sedative-hypnotic was responsible for Dent's condition. He would do urine tests at the clinic.

'You did get hold of my night staff, Shibindji?' He had already asked the policeman that question. Shibindji was good enough to reply without rancour.

'Sister Lubemba is bringing the ambulance. She should be here soon.'

'Of course.'

'Will the Captain be all right?'

It was Shibindji who was now being repetitive.

'He'll be fine. Don't look so worried, Shibindji.' Graham Whitaker lifted his stethoscope from the slow, somnambulant rib cage of Patrick Dent. 'Your captain is as strong as a horse. He'll sleep for a while longer. He'll have a headache when he comes around; be a bit disorientated that's all. You did the right thing, Shibindji. He'll thank you for phoning me.'

'I thought he was dying,' Sergeant Shibindji spread his palms apologetically. 'That's why I phoned. Then there's the other white man. The one I locked in the cells. I'm sure he needs a doctor badly. I've never seen anything like it before. I'm sure you should see the man straight away.'

Whitaker returned his manometer and stethoscope to his medical bag. He gestured to Shibindji to lead on.

'A white man?' Whitaker feigned a mild and benign interest. 'And dressed like a Zulu sangoma you say. How surprising. Do you know his name?'

'No I don't. Not his real name. There are stories about him. I think the local Zulus call him Mvulaba. I've seen him before, at Mawamabi hill. He and the Captain are enemies for sure. But even so uDende called in a helicopter to casivac him when he was injured there. So I'm sure he would have wanted me to call you this time.'

'Of course, Shibindji. You've acted very responsibly.'

'The Captain is a good man.'

'I'm sure,' said Whitaker.

They had reached the outer cell door; a medieval dungeon-like barrier of steel and rivets, with a drop bolt as thick as an arm. Shibindji slid back a little flange to expose an observation hole.

'Look.'

He had known that the man he would see would be Montague Law, a burned and demented Montague Law. That knowledge however had been insufficient to prepare him for the shock that followed Shibindji's offer.

'Here. Look.'

'Sweet Jesus.' The mutilation of Montague Law had gone much deeper than his skin.

'Can you help him?'

'I don't know, Shibindji. I'm going to try. Open up.'

He was dressed in animal skins and seated crosslegged on a folded grey blanket. His mouth was fixed open; his lips drawn back like a man who tastes pure acid. His chin was wet with drool.

'You see,' said Shibindji. He closed the solid door behind them. There was another, barred, door but this had been left ajar. 'Is *he* going to die?'

That in fact, was a question that had already troubled Graham Whitaker. It was the first time he had ever considered the merits of euthanasia.

'No,' Whitaker knelt next to the catatonic man. 'No, he won't die.'

He could not do it. Not even to spare Kirsten this pitiful sight could he do it. He did what he could do. He opened his case. He took out a syringe and filled it from an ampoule of Chlorpromazine – 200 mg.

'Will that make him better?' Shibindji stood well clear of the hypodermic tip.

'Oh yes,' Whitaker assured. 'Oh yes.'

It took three injections – 600 milligrams – of Chlorpromazine to make him better, manageable, psychiatrists would term it. His rigid acerbic features began to soften and remould. His body slumped. As though seeing them for the first time, he dragged his gaze from Whitaker to Shibindji and back.

'I was sent by uKhosi,' he said. 'Is this the place where they keep *it*?'

'Keep what?' Whitaker asked.

'Are you one of them. Are you a godspirit?'

'No, I'm just a doctor. I'm here to help you.'

'You say that. Then you force march me.'

'I'm here to help you,' Whitaker repeated. 'I want you to trust me. No harm will come to you. I'm going to take you to a place where you can rest.'

'Rest . . . rest.' Law smiled with the half of his face that could still smile. 'I'd value it if you could see to my rest.'

'I will. I want you to know that I respect you. I am a doctor and I understand what you have been trying to do. I know what you've been through.'

Law turned his fish-cold empty eyes on him. Whitaker so much wanted him to hear what he had to say. He tried again:

'I know that everything is very cloudy. I don't know how much of what I'm telling you you can hear, or comprehend. But let me say this: your work could soon receive recognition. The knowledge that you have is vital. I'm going to make you better so that you can impart that knowledge to the world. You want that don't you?'

'Don't know . . .' The burned man shook his head lazily. 'I don't know. It depends on uKhosi I suppose.'

'I don't know who uKhosi is,' Whitaker spoke slowly, giving his words the gravity that he hoped would cause them to filter through the layer of schizophrenic sludge that was covering this man's intellect. 'Your sister loves you. She cares for you. She wants you to come away from here.'

'I want to come away,' Law said. And for a moment it seemed as though he was focusing and alive. He looked at Whitaker as sharply as a bird. He said:

'Kirsten's dead.'

'I don't believe it.'

'No, well it's the truth.' He drew a deep breath as if a thousand words were waiting for liberation. 'She,' was all he said. Then he smiled that half-lipped smile and slipped with his breath, and his unsaid words, beneath his muddy sensorium of madness.

'She's not dead,' Whitaker said. 'You wouldn't let that happen to your sister.' But his voice did not have the same degree of control any longer, and he knew it was not reaching the man.

From the yard of the police station came the squeal of car brakes

– a bustle of slamming doors and hurrying heels. Whitaker stood up.

'I don't believe it,' he said again. 'She can't be dead.' He shook his head and looked at Shibindji. And Shibindji shook his head in accord. He was good that way.

'The ambulance is here,' the sergeant informed him. 'We had better go get uDende into it.'

But they did not have to go and get uDende, because at that moment the solid metal cell door rammed open and Dent was there. He was ashen; his massive chest was heaving and he was staggering like a drunk. His disabilities, however, were far from sufficient to incapacitate him. He reached Montague Law a few paces later than it would normally have taken him. His fist was dead on target. Hammerhard it caught the temple of the seated man – jolted him sideways, sprawling. The surprise of the whole thing cost Whitaker his defensive potential. Too late he threw himself at Dent – but he need not have done so. That single vicious blow had vented the anger of Patrick Dent.

'He killed Bess.'

Dent was shaking, and the emotion that was moving him was sadness. 'Shibindji, the bastard killed my Bess.'

Montague Law smiled on. His nose was bleeding and bubbling red. His forehead was beginning to swell. But if he felt pain, he showed no sign of it. He shrugged himself back up onto his elbows. 'Dead . . . she's dead.' He grinned through the rivules of blood.

'No.' Whitaker grabbed Dent's stiffening forearms. 'Damn it Patrick, you're acting like an animal. Can't you see what's going on?'

Dent shook his wrists loose from Whitaker's grasp. Despite his ordeal there was an awesome power in this man.

'OK. I won't touch him. It's over.'

'He's sick,' Whitaker kneeled to attend to Montague Law. 'He's not responsible for anything he does. God knows what further damage you might have done by hitting him like that. I want him out of here, Patrick. This man is my patient, and for that matter, so are you. You should be at the clinic, Patrick. You need treatment.'

'Not so fast, Doctor Whitaker. I saw your ambulance outside, and I appreciate your concern. But you can send it back now, empty. I'm dead right.'

'I'm sure you are,' Whitaker condescended. 'That's why you have to hold onto the bars for support. And Law, he's fine too. Look at him, Patrick. He's a picture of health isn't he?'

'He's not going anywhere, Gray. I don't care if he is your patient, he is my prisoner. I'm charging him with murder. The only way he will get out of police custody is if the court decides he's not fit to plead. I know you want him, Gray, and I know why. But I want him too. So that's it I guess.'

'No.' Whitaker ignored Dent's gestured invitation to depart. 'No, Patrick. You can't leave this man in a cell like this. He's capable of harming himself.'

'And you think that would be a bad thing?'

'What is it with you, Patrick? That wasn't the comment of a law man. Is it revenge that you want? If it is, you can forget it. Monty Law is not capable of feeling pain, or remorse, or any emotion that might satisfy your needs. He's beyond you, Patrick. Don't you understand?'

'You'd better go now,' Dent said quietly. 'It's been a long hard night for me. I think I've been very patient.'

But Whitaker declined again. He shook his head. 'I've been patient too, Patrick. And my patience isn't endless either. You wouldn't even be standing if I hadn't done what I did for you. I did you a favour with the Bemegride, now I want a favour in return. I want you to listen to me. Just listen to me, OK?'

'I'm listening.'

'Thank you.' Whitaker's mind felt clumsy. He began to pace in a feeble attempt to find space where there was none. 'I get the impression that you think I'm into some kind of ego trip, Patrick. Maybe you think I'm in this to impress Kirsten. If you do, you're wrong. I think you know how I feel about Kirsten Law. But this matter goes way beyond any personal feelings of mine. You read Monty Law's diary, so you know he was engaged in some very – if you like – *bizarre* research.'

'I like the word,' Dent nodded. '*Murderous* is another good word.'

'Yes. I'm not denying that that's how it seems. But let's for a moment forget what the man did. Let's look at what he achieved.'

'You mean, apart from the death of Ernie Tyrell and a few dozen others?'

Whitaker refused to be drawn. 'I mean his discovery. This compound that the Zulus know as sontekile. It's similar to something that western medical researchers have been investigating, but more potent, far more potent, yet paradoxically, more manageable in terms of human compatibility. He did some pretty bad things, sure, but he didn't invent ritual murder. He simply used it as a vehicle for his experiments. I'm not trying to excuse his behaviour, I'm just trying to explain to you the consequence of his discovery. He was carried away by the thing. Law was looking for a cure for multiple sclerosis, but it looks as though this drug could modify the course of many diseases that affect the human immune system. I'm talking about cancer, transplant rejection syndrome. I'm talking about Acquired Immune Deficiency Syndrome - AIDS - the deadly HTLV III virus - OK? That's the magnitude of the discovery that Law made. Or should I say that that is the magnitude of the knowledge contained in the mind of the man you just attacked.'

'The answer is no.'

'Do you want to kill this defenceless man, Patrick? Is that it? Is that why you want to hold him?'

'Don't try that with me. I didn't try and kill him and you know it.'

'I don't know any such thing,' Whitaker stopped his pacing and turned, suddenly very hostile. 'I just witnessed a deadly assault. Not the first of such assaults you have made on this man.'

'You don't know what you're talking about.'

'Yes I do. There's a Pondo underground worker up at the dam called Mzabele. Ah! I can see by your face that you remember him. Well, you confused that poor man terribly, Patrick. You told him that Inkosi Ingram had sanctioned the attack at Mawamabi hill. Mzabele took it that it was all in the day's work. The silly man went and spoke to Kirsten about what had happened. You like the word "murderous", Patrick? It's a good word to describe what happened that day on Mawamabi hill, don't you think?'

'I think you're bluffing,' Dent said. But there was no conviction in the words.

'I'm not,' Whitaker said. 'I can get an order for Law to be taken for psychiatric observation, and you know it. But I don't want that. That would destroy him, *and* what I'm trying to achieve. Besides that it would take time, and time is something I can't afford to waste. Force me to and I'll do it. But I'll destroy you too Patrick, so help me.'

'I believe you would Doctor Whitaker.'

'Please do.'

'You're not doing this for Kirsten or Law. I can see that. You're doing this for yourself. What do you want from me, Whitaker?'

'I want Law.'

'I can't do it.'

'You can Patrick, and you will. You run Ingwavuma like a feudal barony. You always have. This should be a simple matter for you. Now I want something else from you, Patrick. Kirsten could be in trouble. She went into the hills a week ago. A Zulu called September Mabutane came to take her to her brother. Well we now know where her brother is. So . . .'

'So where the hell is *she*? Is that what you're trying to say?'

Whitaker nodded. 'Yes.'

'Wait a minute,' Dent said. 'Let me get this straight. Are you saying you actually stood by while she wandered off with a criminal like Mabutane? And then did nothing, said nothing for a whole week? Does Mark Ingram know about this?'

'No. She wanted it that way. You know Kirsten. I was against it. I tried to talk her out of it. But her mind was made up. She was desperate to find her brother.'

'And so were you, ol' buddy. Is that why you allowed her to put her life on the line. But you *are* one callous bastard, Doctor Whitaker.'

'That's rubbish, Patrick. I don't control Kirsten. No one tells her what to do, and you know it.'

'I know this, ol' buddy. Mark Ingram will be here in a few hours' time, and Mark Ingram is going to ask you why you waited for a whole week before you reported Kirsten missing. You might have a little trouble answering that question. Something else that may bother you is that there's a cyclone heading for Swaziland. You'd better start praying that it doesn't come further south.'

'You know,' Whitaker said quietly, 'I think you're enjoying this. Human misery is your stock-in-trade, Patrick Dent. You don't care about anyone. You couldn't give a damn whether Kirsten was alive or dead.'

'*Kirsten dead,*' came the voice of the burned man. But whether he was confirming that fact, or questioning it was any man's guess.

'Christ.' Dent pointed. 'Look.'

Montague Law, his head up-tilted, his arms beatifically outstretched, addressed the ceiling light.

'uKhosi is here,' he smiled, then lowered his gaze to his audience. Whitaker went to his side. 'Are you a godspirit too? Did you arrive with the lights?' Law asked.

'I'm just a doctor. I care for you. I have come to take you away from here. Will you come with me?'

'Not towards the fire.'

'No never towards the fire.'

'You look safe. You don't shine.'

'I'm safe.'

'uKhosi is here. Can you hear him?'

'No. What does he say?'

'The chosen one is almost with us.'

'Who is the chosen one?'

'The one who we will serve. The one who will lead us all. Look for the new born child, look where the storm winds blow.'

'What else does he say? Does he say anything about your sister Kirsten?'

'inGwenya is here.' Law's voice tailed to a whimper of exhaustion. 'And now he's gone. He never stays for long.'

'Do uKhosi and inGwenya know where Kirsten is?'

'Kirsten brought the fire . . . Kirsten dead . . . I need rest now. Can I rest now?'

'You can rest. Yes, you can rest.'

The burned man sagged. As though gnawed by some terrible inner pain he drew in his limbs until he lay crumpled like an aborted foetus on the dirty grey blanket.

'It was *you* and *your* fire that did this.' Whitaker turned accusingly towards Dent. 'It was . . .'

He did not complete his sentence, because the object of his censure was no longer in the cell. Dent was gone. Shibindji was gone. The studded metal door stood wide and invitingly open. The night had passed.

There was not a policeman on hand to witness the removal of Montague Law from the cells at Abercorn Drift. Whitaker and Sister Lubemba and the stretcher that they transported, passed silently from the cells to the Charge Office, to the ambulance, without hindrance, or help – without contact of any sort with the constabulary of Ingwavuma. Perhaps they were somewhere out there, standing hostile and hidden in the belly of the early morning mists.

It was the second morning that they had seen such mist. Vaporous and drifting, it came down on them as though it were a living thing.

'Go,' Whitaker instructed Sister Lubemba, 'take him to the clinic. I won't be long. I still haven't done everything I have to do here.'

As he turned towards Dent's bloody cottage a shiver passed through Whitaker – cold, deep and enduring. Involuntarily he clenched his teeth and caught back at his breath.

He did what he had to do. He gathered the *iquthu* basket of Fana and drove with it from that place.

The night had drained Whitaker and the coming dawn carried with it no promise of relief. Dent was a bastard but Dent was right. If Kirsten Law was in trouble then he, Graham Whitaker was largely to blame. He should have reported Kirsten's situation to Dent long ago. He had thought about it, and he had rejected the idea. That might have been the worst decision of his life.

In a few hours' time Mark Ingram would land his helicopter in Ingwavuma. He would have to meet that helicopter and he would have to explain many things to Mark Ingram. He would have to tell Ingram that he agreed with Dent – Kirsten was now in mortal danger: a danger that was increasing by the minute.

Graham Whitaker drove on in an agony of apprehension.

* * *

It was seven miles on the wings of the crow from the valley of Manshanja to the kwaZulu border and September Mabutane's kraal; not much further to the Police Station at Abercorn Drift. In pedestrian terms, the twisting, humpback trails that ambled through that rolling Swazi landscape doubled the distance to be travelled. Still, under normal conditions, two fit people should have been able to hike those fourteen miles at a whistle.

Conditions were not normal. The two people were being hunted. They were being chased and cut off, hemmed in and tracked down like animals. And like animals they ran. They had tried to outdistance their pursuers, but you cannot outrun the call of a mountaintop sentry. They had come within a glancing spear of being killed. So they had resorted to stealth, breath-holding, elbow-scraping stealth. But for all their cunning they had not been able to reach the place where Mabutane had cached the pistol. The Abanzanzi cordon had beaten them past that spot. Mabutane could thus happily break his promise. He could not leave her now, could he? She did not have the firearm after all, did she? He could not go back anyway. He was compromised. He was now as much the fugitive as she.

On the second morning of their flight, the mists of Nomkubulwana came again. Kirsten and September Mabutane took to the grey valley like the children of the mother.

Kirsten was exhausted. Their diet during the duration of their flight had consisted of a few shared handfuls of berries. Of drinkable water they had tasted none. She was in pain. Her *isidwaba* and *usu* cloak protected her shoulders and hips quite adequately, but her legs and arms, her face and her chest were scratched and wealed with thorn splinters – but all that could be easily endured. Her feet were seriously damaged. From toe to heel both soles were an agony of bruises; the ball of her right foot was cut to the extent that she was leaving a messy blood trail.

September Mabutane watched her bully her feet forward. He shook his head.

'It's no use trying to hide your pain, Inkosikazi. Let me see that wound.'

They stopped. Kirsten sat down where she was. She cocked her foot back and they examined the cut. The area was black with blood and dirt. She spat onto her palms, wiped at the mess, then splayed the edges of the wound with the pressure of her fingers. It was very deep.

Mabutane frowned – concerned. 'We can't go on like this.'

'How far do we still have to go, September?'

He thought about it. 'In distance, not far. If we could continue from here along the footpaths, we would be across the border and at my kraal within a few hours. With Abanzanzi blocking the footpaths and tracking us through the valleys – who can tell.'

'How many of them are there, September? One hundred – two hundred? That's not enough to have sealed off every last game trail in these mountains.'

'It's enough.'

'Then how are we ever going to get back?'

'We must continue this way – in the dark of the night and in the valley mists. I know how they think, Inkosikazi. The tracks will all be guarded because they will be expecting you to break. You see, they don't know you like I know you . . . And now I must attend to your feet, Inkosikazi, or we will never leave these mountains. Wait here for me, woman. Don't move from here.'

Mabutane brought leaves – '*ujoyi*'. He ground them with the butt of his spear against a rock. 'Pull back the edges of the wound.' He pressed the green paste in. It burned, and then soothed. 'It's taking away the pain.'

'Of course. When we reach my kraal Lulele will attend to your feet properly.'

'You're a great Inyanga, September Mabutane.'

He grinned at the compliment. 'Let's see now how great a shoemaker I am before we say any more.'

He was not a great shoemaker. The sandals he cut from his *uhutsha* kilt were vellum-thin and every pebble pressed through. The thongs that held them to her feet were adequate only when cuttingly overtight. She laughed at his anxious expressions.

'Not bad, not bad at all.'

'Can you walk now, Inkosikazi?'

'I can run,' lied Kirsten Law. 'Let's go.'

The repair of Kirsten's feet had cost them an hour. Within a hundred paces the wound began to bleed again, but the pain was not crippling any longer. They continued through the mist. And even when the mist began to rise they still pressed on – 'Just a little further.' It was a mistake.

A sudden gust of wind, and the mist lifted away. They found themselves in a steeply eroded, earthen-walled ravine – a barren place. There was nowhere to hide there. The choice was simple – advance, or go back. To the south the ravine continued to wind, innocently empty for as far as they could see. To their rear lay the well-bushed mountain they had just traversed, already shimmering in the late morning heat.

Thirst had a lot to do with their decision. Somewhere to the south the Suthu River ran. Suddenly another day on a dry mountain slope seemed too much to endure. Mutually, and without comment, they turned and walked towards the water . . . and the Abanzanzi ambush.

There were two of them, they were crouching at a sharp bend in the ravine. As Kirsten and Mabutane passed that place they stood up and came at a run, shields high, spear arms balanced and swaying. The attack was sudden, soundless and brutal – thudding feet and hard hissed breathing. Just a grunt of alarm from Mabutane as he turned to face them. '*God!*' – a single word from Kirsten. Then a shield battered her, smashed her back against the ravine wall. It came on to crush her, smother her. Nothing but shield, faceless humanless grinding ox-hide shield. She was under it and the weight was killing. She could not breathe. She was weakening fast.

Blindly she reached for some weapon – anything. A hand grasped her wrist. She twisted and bit down desperately on it. The awful pressure eased. She drew breath and clamped down even harder. A violent jerk thrashed her head sideways. Still she held fast. It was all she could think of to do.

Incredibly the suffocative pressure eased. The hand grew weaker as it jerked and jerked again. She would not relent. It flopped between her jaws now like a beached and dying fish. Still she held on. Her vision went blue . . . then crimson. Blue for the colour of the sky above. Crimson for the lifeblood that was spilling over the shield and onto her face. It came from her attacker's severed neck. She let go of the dead thing in her mouth.

September Mabutane stood there – framed in crimson and blue. He pulled the body of the man he had killed off her, and lifted the shield away. She stood; she felt sick with the horror of it.

The dust of combat had not yet settled in the startled dry ravine. It held passively in the air, and waited for the peace that was natural to that place. It would not be long in coming.

Kirsten's assailant was dead. The other man was dying, pinned down, it seemed, like a specimen insect by Mabutane's spear. His mouth was moving and straining, but the sounds were all gag and bubble – pink-dyed with the fluid of his lungs.

Still Mabutane listened to him. He kneeled and placed his ear at the dying man's mouth. Then he nodded in understanding. The battle axe rose and fell and the sound stopped for ever.

The ambush was over. The victory was joyless. 'They were once my friends.' Mabutane stood, bowed, looking incredulously at the slain men who had once been friends. Then he turned away from them. 'Now we must hurry, Inkosikazi. Before long they will be after us again. You must be safe by then.'

Abercorn Drift with its high fence and armed policemen – for her, that was the closest place of safety. What of Mabutane? Where would he ever find refuge?

'We'll see,' he replied to that question. 'Before anything I must consider my family. My baby boy is due to be born. I want to be with Vuloyi when that happens. I'm going home. That's all that seems important to me at the moment.'

'You can come away with me. You and Vuloyi and Lulele, the children – all of you.'

'You're dawdling like an old woman, Inkosikazi.'

'But you must think about it. You can never go back to Abanzanzi now. I don't think you really expected this to happen, September. Shall I tell you something else? I don't think you ever intended to leave me even if we did manage to find my pistol. You lied to me about that. You were going to stay with me no matter what. Weren't you?'

'You have the eyes of the sangoma, Inkosikazi.'

'You're a brave man, September Mabutane. I'm glad you're my friend. I'll stand by you too one day when you need me.'

'*Ngiyabonga* Inkosikazi,' Mabutane thanked her. 'And now we must move on. We must think about nothing else but reaching Ingwavuma. Come. Faster, Inkosikazi.'

She tried to move faster. She wanted to move faster. Her legs, however, were irresolute things – feeble-kneed and obstructive. The pain in her feet once more was crippling. And it was hot. The sun ascended punishingly and the ground beneath it cringed and shimmered.

'One more hill,' promised September Mabutane.

It was called Comane, and they climbed it because the valley of

Comane would have led them off to the east. On any other day it would have been a small hill, a gentle slope – a pleasant climb. Comane grew beneath them into a monster in that midday heat; fortified with boulders, and studded with hindering spike-armed aloe that grew from every fissure. For all that they climbed it.

And Comane, for all its cruelty, worked magic too. For when they reached the crest and lay there febrile and praying for water – they saw water. In the valley that sloped from there the Suthu River ran.

'Look, Inkosikazi,' September Mabutane pointed, 'you can see my home from here.'

Kirsten peered over his levelled arm.

'Yess,' she stretched the word uncertainly. On the far bank, amongst a clump of river trees, a glimpse of grey that could have been thatch. 'I think I see it.'

'The light is bad.'

It *was* bad, and it was getting progressively worse. Kirsten had vaguely sensed a change of spectrum in the course of their climb. She had wondered if she was imagining it. She was not.

'The sun is dulling.'

What Mabutane said was true. This was no visual cosmetic – no biological kindness for those about to dry up and die. The high sun had dimmed as though reaching the point of sunset. The sky was yellowing too. A hazy dusk-like cupola was drawing down on the midday hills of northern Lebombo. Mabutane thought he knew what was causing it.

'*isiPhepho!*' he said. 'It's coming, Inkosikazi. It's going to be a big one – a wild one, this storm. We mustn't be caught in the open when it strikes.'

'If it's rain that's coming, then let it come,' Kirsten said. 'I can swallow everything that God can provide.'

'Look!' September Mabutane was pointing northwards now – alarm in his voice, Kirsten thought he had spotted their pursuers. But it was not that. On the northern horizon some small dark clouds were building – fluffy unpretentious stuff. Kirsten noted happily that they seemed to be coming in their direction.

'It won't rain much,' she predicted. 'You can see that it won't rain much.'

September Mabutane did not comment. He took her hand like a

father with a stubborn child. 'Lean on me,' he told her. 'We'll be able to move more quickly if you do.'

And as reluctant as she was to do it, she did lean on September Mabutane. The descent of Comane seemed an even more tyrannical exercise than the climb. Or was she weakening, constantly weakening? The river did not seem to get much closer – the distant splotch of grey remained just that.

The south breeze that had licked their sweat all morning died somewhere on that slope. The air seemed to bank up and thicken. The topaz sun became hazier. The cloud bank was changing too.

At every opportunity Kirsten turned to observe its progress. It was not so fluffy any more, or innocent looking. It was advancing towards the south, refusing to remain hidden behind the hill they were descending. And it was growing – darkening and distending and tumbling in the sulphureous sky. Still, she had no fear of it.

Perhaps she was too tired to care, or too ignorant. September Mabutane was frightened. His eyes, when he observed the sky were wide with apprehension. The arm supporting her grew more demanding.

'I'm going as fast as I can, September.'

But she was not really. If it rained on them right then, she would stop and throw her face back to the sky, and let the water wash away the rind of blood on her skin and the smell of death still in her nostrils. But more than anything she would gulp and she would drink until her belly was awash. She welcomed the thought of the cloud overtaking them as one who awaits the columns of an army of relief.

Before the sky and the sun were completely conquered the east wind came. It blew softly at first, coolly – whispering good things about the change that was to come. Then it strengthened so that not only the leaves and the grass were bothered by it, but the dry sand lifted and stung, and big tree branches thrashed and twisted. Her buckskin *usu* cloak flapped out. And Kirsten, who was used to estimating windspeeds gave this blow thirty knots. She tightened her grip on Mabutane's shoulder.

They reached the valley of the Suthu. They were about 500 metres from the river when the cloud fringe charged by overhead. It brought darkness and the clean smell of rain.

At first a few drops – plump, cold and stinging. Kirsten felt their strike and trickle and loved it. She watched them pat into the unexpectant ground and jump up muddied – and loved it. For an amiable minute this gentleness endured. Then suddenly, violently, the mood of the black sky altered. Rowdy savage water rushed to earth.

The sheer down-shoving power of it was a shocking thing. It caught the travellers and stopped them short. Kirsten gasped. Then she did what she had promised herself she would do. She closed her eyes, tilted up her face and opened her mouth to the storm. Mabutane was shouting at her; tugging at her.

'The river, Inkosikazi . . . we must cross . . . quickly.'

She pushed him off and kneeled bare breasted to the storm. She cupped her hands up to her lips and drank. Her palms overflowed and the water gushed and choked, still she drank. And when she opened her eyes again she saw that Mabutane was doing the same thing.

They drank until their thirst was just a memory. Then together they ran – they hobbled and splashed through the quickly forming rivulets and ponds, and across the steaming earth.

13

El Nino's final tantrum cost the people of South Eastern Africa as dearly as the drought that had preceded it. Cyclone Dorinda swept in across the Indian Ocean. It devastated Mozambique then, still as strong as ever, it turned its black heart angrily on Swaziland and broke upon the Mahlangatsha hills. The Swazi hill people had never seen rain like this. Eight hundred millimetres of water flushed down upon those slopes. It burst their kraals apart and swept away their cattle. Hundred-year-old trees were rooted out of the ground and dashed into the valleys. And in the valleys the rivers rose up in turbulent brown flood: the Ngwempisi, the Mkondo and the little Usuthu took the vandal water and rushed it towards their recipient river – the Suthu River.

It became a monster, that Suthu River – a maddened thing of surf and breakers that burst its banks and tore up bridges. Big bridges with house-thick concrete spans that carried double roadways, were tossed and tumbled kilometres from their posts. And on it surged, gaining strength as every donga and sloot came down in cathartic tribute.

There, tropical cyclone Dorinda did not stop. It reared southwest, then south, then thrashed the Lebombo mountains.

They had wanted rain, those Zulus. They had prayed and sacrificed. They had killed the Pondo wizard, and danced in honour of Nomkubulwana. But what was *this*? This fury – this terror. Was there no love left in the heavens for their tribe?

*   *   *

Peter Gebeza was a Zulu who would never have admitted to such foolish tribal beliefs as Nomkubulwana – the granter of rain. This sort of nonsense had gained his people nothing. He believed what he had been taught at the excellent training centre at Teterow in

East Germany. That was that tropical cyclones result from low atmospheric pressure areas that are attended by strong wind and rain; they are given feminine names in alphabetical order. Another thing that he had learned at Teterow was that enemies of the ANC were harsh, ruthless, and brutally ingenious in the application of their oppression. As a black South African he had had no difficulty with that lesson; nor with the lesson that followed – the precept of retribution.

Thus he stood stoically in the lashing rain of cyclone Dorinda with not a single ache of doubt about the justness of the actions he had planned. His position was upon a little rocky hillock about 50 metres from the home of September Mabutane, and he would surely be along presently as his wife, the lovely Vuloyi, was about to give birth. Peter Gebeza remembered as he stood there the golden voice of Nukwe:

'Ba ni shani – *sa!*

Ba ka hi hla – *pha!*

Ba nwa ma kho – *fi!*

Ba nga hi nyi – *ki!*'

Nukwe who had been so innocent and bright. Eeh! September Mabutane, you put out a lovely flame.

*   *   *

On the morning of the second day of cyclone Dorinda, all work at the Suthu River dam site came to a stop. Neither man nor machine was equal to the conditions. A labourer had been crushed to death and another three injured when a front end loader had slithered out of control down a work-face bank. Another man had been caught up in a mudslide while trying to tow out a compressor unit from the south bank spillway bed. They did not find him, they did not even try. Numbers one and two river flow outlets were discharging in the path of that mudslide – two thunderous hundred-metre-long jets – making man and machine into toy things in their path. They were gone in a swirling instant.

Underground, in the machine hall cavern they could not continue because the ventilation shafts and access tunnels flooded. Electrical systems arced into explosive destruction. The maintenance crews could not cope. Ingram had little option but to shut down the entire operation. And Dorinda thrashed on without respite – without mercy.

The clinic was probably the busiest place at that time. Every bed in the main ward was occupied, and patients who should have been admitted were being treated, then discharged. And more were coming all the time. Splashing and sliding, the vehicles were feeling their way towards the clinic, bearing the injured – the wounded, the contused, and the broken of limb.

There was only one patient in the two-bed female ward, and that person had no right, by gender, to that bed. Clothed in plain green hospital pyjamas he was gazing through the single window. His head was rocking very slightly forwards and backwards, never ceasing, as though hypnotized by the violence of the outside world. He did not turn when the door opened behind him. He did not respond to the man who loosened the nylon restraint straps that bound him to his bed.

'It's a hell of a storm.'

Gray Whitaker gently lifted the unresisting wrist of his patient. It seemed to be a natural thing for a doctor to do, and that was how it was intended. But this doctor did not need a pulse reading. He needed the temperament of trust that touch sometimes engendered.

'I'm going to try again.'

Trying again meant the addition of a further 150 milligrams of Chlorpromazine to the sedative-saturated blood chemistry of the patient. Whitaker had already administered 800 mg of the drug in the past eight hours – another shot might do it.

'There now.'

The hypodermic slid in, the plunger was depressed, then Whitaker sat back on the adjacent bed. From there he too could look through the window. It was impossible to see further than a few grey metres beyond the rain-washed panes. Nevertheless he studied that space for a few minutes – as blank-eyed as his patient. He stared until the sight of it depressed him more than his occupation of the minute. When he turned back, the man had stopped his rocking. A brutal gust of wind shook the building, rattling the asbestos, straining at the guts of the structure. Somewhere a door banged loudly.

'How are you feeling?'

it was difficult to keep his voice as well modulated as he would have liked. The noise of the storm was overpowering.

'How are you feeling?' It sounded better when said close up to the man's ear. 'I'm your friend, Doctor Law. I'm Doctor Whitaker and I'm trying to help you. Can you hear me?'

The unexpected happened – the man's head nodded as though comprehending that question. His lips began to move in the effort to form words. Whitaker put his ear to the man's mouth. There *were* words to be heard – the mutter and slur of the awakening slumberer. 'Help me . . . Doctor . . . itaker.'

'Yes!' Dear God! He had waited so long for this. 'I'm listening. I'm your friend.'

'I'm finished . . . Doctor . . . I'm so low. I don't think I can go on any more. . . . If you are a friend then help me to get away from all this suffering.'

Whitaker thought the voice of his patient was strengthening. He said: 'I'm here to help you, and letting you die is not going to help you, or me . . . or your sister.'

'Kirsten?'

'Yes, Kirsten.'

His voice had definitely improved, both in resonance and articulation. His eyes, too, were more alert. Inquisitively they fastened on Whitaker.

'You're in the clinic at the Suthu River dam site. You were talking about your sister Kirsten.'

'Yes. Can I have some water? I'm so thirsty.'

He passed a tumbler full of water to his patient.

'When did you last see Kirsten?'

'Let me see. Are you her friend?'

'Yes.'

'Ah. It's hard to remember. It's hazy like a dream. Perhaps I saw her. Perhaps I didn't. I don't know. Everything is so muddled. It must be months since I spoke to her, it seems like months. Or was it . . . yesterday?'

As he sought the fugitive memories he raised his hand to meditatively touch his cheek. But the hand at his face was burned to a claw, and as it touched he recoiled from it. In puzzlement and revulsion he held it up. He pleaded:

'What is this? What am I?'

'You're a scientist.'

'*Christ!* Look at me.'

'You're a man who can . . .'

'No!' he shouted Whitaker down. 'I'm a monster. I'm a horror. Look at me. For God's sake *really* look at me.' He sobbed. He threw his hand across his eyes. 'Oh God. I don't want to see it any more. What's happened to me? Oh God, what do you *want* from me?'

'I'm looking at you,' Whitaker said. 'I'm really looking at you. I see a man whose life can never be the same again. I see a man who has the knowledge to alter the future of medicine. What I want from you Doctor Law is the formula of the remedy that you call sontekile. You wrote in your diary that it was a bigger thing than you, and you were right. It is bigger than you. It's bigger; it's more important than any of us – our emotions or our destinies.'

'And that is what you want?' The words came flat and spiritless.

'Yes.'

'And what would you give me in return for sontekile?'

'What can I give you that you want?'

'Death, peaceful death.'

The rain was pelting the window panes; drumming thunderously on the asbestos. The whole prefab was shaking as the squalling wind ripped by. Surely he had not heard the man correctly. He shifted closer to his patient.

'Death, that's what I want from you. Are you prepared to give it to me?'

'I don't believe you.'

'You said our destinies don't matter.'

'I didn't mean it like that.'

'I'm sick, aren't I? I mean my mind is really sick.'

'Yes, but you *can* get well again, believe me.'

'And what about the prognosis for my body?' He held the hand-claw to Whitaker's face. 'Are you going to make this body of mine well again? You don't have to answer me, Doctor Whitaker. Just listen to me. I could no more stand the barbed wire and window bars of a mental hospital than I could the endless surgery that would be needed to make me less of a gargoyle thing than I am at present. I don't want to be exposed to the pitying eyes of my sister as you and your surgeons take a bit from me here, and add a bit there. And to what purpose? So that people will shudder less when they see me; so they won't be induced to vomit at the sight of the face of Montague Law? I know that at the moment I'm probably so high on Phenothiazines that my liver's rotting. What happens when you've got to taper off the dosages or kill me with your therapy? I know of the hell that's waiting for me in the name of civilised behaviour. I don't want it.'

'Do you want to go back to Uhlanga then?'

'Uhlanga? Your drugs have almost robbed me of the memory of the world of isangoma. I know I've been in places that I never want to return to – and yet there was beauty too, and kindness, and compassion. But no. I don't want to go back there. In the life of every man there comes a *best* time for that man to die. I've reached it, Whitaker. I don't want to take another step.'

'Can you remember the formula for sontekile?'

'Oh yes. There was a time when I was not a brain-muddled monstrosity, don't forget.'

'Tell it to me then.'

Their faces were inches apart. Law's eyes met his in question. Whitaker nodded – a gesture of affirmation for the words he simply could not say. From his top pocket he took a pen and a note pad.

'I'm ready,' he said. 'I'm ready because there has to be an end to the misery of this poor bastard. Dear God, he's suffered quite enough.'

*   *   *

Mark Ingram took on the terrible cyclone Dorinda with a vigour and analytical confidence that seemed to reduce its excesses to manageable proportions. He was an inspiration to those of lesser courage.

Davis was of lesser courage. They were standing in the main control room – Ingram, Davis and a paunchy electrical engineer called Simpson. The room was neon lit and painted in restful green. On the walls an array of gauges, meters, dials and other high-tech equipment told all there was to be told about the status of the Suthu River hydro-electric scheme. It was exactly that that had Davis so worried. Simply put, there was too much water coming into the Suthu River dam, too quickly. Davis said as much:

'The inflow is topping 16,000 cubic metres per second and gaining. We're filling at a rate of about three per cent every two hours. That's too quick by far. We wanted this dam to be half full by this time next year. At this rate we'll be half full at midday today. I don't like it. The abutments aren't getting a chance to settle in properly, especially on the south bank. There's a major breccia fault traversing that area. And that is where the thrust of the wall is at its highest. The geo pressures are building up far too quickly for that kind of material to remain stable.'

'Yes,' Ingram stopped him – irritable. 'We all know about the breccia dykes. The point is, Ron, that we're doing everything we can do right now. The river flow outlets allow an outflow of 71 cubic metres per second per channel. Even if all four of them were operational it would only permit an outflow of 284 cubic metres per second. We've got both silt outlets open to the maximum. That's another 375 cubic metres per second outflow. Until the water reaches the spillway shoots there isn't another damn thing we can do. Once it has reached that height we have got the capacity to handle it.'

'The dam will be overflowing by then,' Simpson observed.

'That's right,' Ingram said. 'What we have to do now, Ron, is evacuate the compound, the recruiting office and the clinic. If I remember correctly, they lie only a metre or two above the high water level. A bit of wave action and they'll be in serious trouble.'

'Jesus, I hadn't thought of that,' Davis reached for an adjacent telephone.

'No need for that,' Ingram said to him. 'I don't want any panic messages. The evacuation must be planned and well co-ordinated. Leave the arrangements to me, Ron. I want *you* to stay here in the control room. I'm going to organise things at the compound now,' Ingram glanced at his watch. 'Well, I'd better get things moving.'

'It's a bastard out there,' Davis said. 'Take care.'

Ingram nodded. 'Sure.' He tried to think of some reassuring line on which to peg his exit, but nothing came. The trouble was that Davis was right. An arch dam was not some deadweight concrete thing plonked down in the path of a river. It was a flexible, living piece of engineering. Its strength lay in its ability to move; to take the stress of the water it held and shrug it into the valley sides. This dam had weak spots in the valley sides. It needed to be gradually filled – to squeeze its way into the geophysics of the Lebombos. It was not being given this chance.

Once alone, Mark Ingram allowed this mask of unshakeable optimism to drop away. He was desperately worried about the consequences of tropical cyclone Dorinda, and not only because of what it was capable of doing to his dam – Kirsten Law was out there somewhere. She was tough, that woman of his. But my God, was she tough enough to take on this?

In the foyer of the control complex Ingram zipped himself into an orange storm-parka. For a moment he stood there, looking into the gloom – the flooding sky. Then he pulled the parka hood over his head. He took a deep breath, shoved himself past the doors, and ran. His Land Rover was standing within six quick paces of the control complex entrance. In that distance Dorinda staggered him; drenched him. It took two hands to wrench the car door closed behind him. The cheated storm rocked the vehicle to its springs. Its power was frightening.

He forced himself to relax. He was biting into his lower lip – he stopped that. He eased his grip on the steering wheel, and began to do what he had to do. It was impossible to hear whether the engine had started, so he tested the clutch – there was power.

The drive to the clinic would have taken him minutes on any other day. On any other day he would have smoked a leisurely cigarette and arrived before he had finished it. That morning it took him nearly an hour to cross over the wall and drive those few kilometres. And as slowly, and as doggedly as he drove, he came close to tragedy.

The road had become a phantom thing, hinting at bends where there were none – at straights where there were bends. The wiper blades granted fleeting instants of clarity. His foot hovered in a tiresome dance between brake and accelerator. He nearly ran down a fellow traveller on that road.

A huddled grey shape – he saw it for a moment – then it was gone. Then it was right in front of the Land Rover. He shoved his foot down hard upon the brake. The vehicle slewed; the steering wheel spun and tore loose from his grip. Incredibly, there was no impact.

It was an old Zulu man. He was standing bent beneath his sodden blanket, one hand extended, holding a totally wrecked umbrella above his head as though salvation depended on it.

Mark Ingram, on principle, never offered lifts to pedestrians. This pedestrian, however, did not know the rules. He seemed to think that this vehicle had stopped so hectically for no other purpose than the arrangement of transport. Whilst Ingram was still moribund with shock, the man was wrestling with the passenger door – now seated on the passenger seat. He was shaking with cold. He shed the dripping blanket apologetically, then folded the skeletal remains of his umbrella – very dignified.

He said his name was Ngodini. That much Ingram understood of the spate of animated Zulu that followed.

'I'm going to the compound,' Ingram shouted.

Old Ngodini nodded gravely – replied, '*Yebo*. I will show you the way.'

And he did show Ingram the way; this strangest of navigators muttering his Zulu; his hands forever active, gesturing – pointing. And Ingram, who had never taken an instruction from a black man in his life, obeyed. Perhaps it was the storm that was so potent a leveller.

They reached the compound, then drove on together to the clinic. That seemed to be the old man's destination too. As Ingram was about to exit from the vehicle Ngodini stopped him – he placed a restraining hand across his wrist and spoke to him.

Ingram shook his head. 'It's no good. I don't understand you.' He felt embarrassed by his ignorance. He wanted to be away from this old Zulu now. The man was an insult to him now. 'Thank you for helping me . . . all right?'

There was water streaming downhill past the clinic. It swirled around his ankles and splashed up coldly as he ran towards the shelter of the ambulance port. The cyclone almost threw him and Ngodini through the clinic doors.

Graham Whitaker was not in his office nor was he in the main ward. There were patients in the main ward; every bed was filled. He was not in the dispensary – a buxom nursing sister was in the dispensary. Ingram recalled her name.

'Sister Lubemba,' he greeted her in passing.

Graham Whitaker was in the two-bed ward that was reserved

for woman patients. He was seated on a bed, bowed forward, as though in earnest conversation with the occupant. He was writing in a notebook. As Ingram entered the ward Whitaker looked up angrily. The patient looked up in slow-eyed bewilderment.

It was Montague Law, or one side of him was Montague Law. The other side was deformity beyond belief.

'No.' Ingram denied his own eyes. 'No, no, no.' His features followed his emotions – first disbelief, then disgust.

'Get out!' Whitaker seemed furious. 'For God's sake Ingram get *out* of here!'

The patient just kept staring, puzzled, now mouthing words that were lost like an underplayed flute in the crescendo of that storm. Now pointing. Suddenly screaming. 'Nasiya isitha! *Nasiya! Nasiya!*'

And Whitaker knew that the black eagle uKhosi had taken flight again.

But Ingram had fled and the door was now closed. And the cry died away to a whimper – to a childlike request:

'Can I sleep now? They've all gone away. Can I sleep now? I'm so tired. I'm so, so tired.'

'Yes,' said Whitaker. 'You can sleep now.' He squeezed down on the plunger of his syringe. 'They've all gone now. You're safe with me.'

And just to be absolutely certain of that he tightened the nylon restraint straps once again. Then he left the ward.

Whitaker was expecting to find Mark Ingram waiting for him in his office; he was expecting a confrontation. He found instead smiling Sister Lubemba and surprisingly, the old sangoma Ngodini. Ingram had entrusted Sister Lubemba with a note; handwritten, on clinic stationery.

'He said it was urgent. He said he could not wait for you. He had too much to do.'

Whitaker bridled his curiosity regarding Ngodini. He greeted the sangoma courteously, then read the message. It was the closest thing to an apology that Ingram probably had ever written.

'Graham. It was wrong of me to accuse you of not having had regard for Kirsten's welfare. You, after all are not her nursemaid. I think you could have let Dent and myself know what she had done, but you didn't, you'll have to live with that decision.

'*I was astonished to come across Monty Law like that – so disfigured. I was shocked. That was why I reacted as I did.*

'*We have much to talk about you and I. I think you know what I mean. I would like to have spoken to you today but now there is no time. Things have been pretty hectic since Dorinda struck, and that brings me to the point of this note.*

'*The clinic is going to have to be evacuated. I'm afraid that the waters of the dam are rising so rapidly that you might possibly be in danger there. I am arranging for some vehicles and personnel to move you to higher ground. You have more time than you need, so please – no panic. I know I can rely on you to see that the operation is conducted in an orderly way.*' It was signed: '*Mark Ingram*'.

Whitaker read the note twice, then folded it and pocketed it. Sister Lubemba concluded the missive: 'He said that you can reach him on your radio if you have any queries or problems.'

'Queries?' Whitaker thought about the message he had just read. 'Problems? Yes, Sister Lubemba. I should imagine that we'll have our share. Mister Ingram has instructed us to prepare for an evacuation of the clinic. In the middle of a tropical cyclone, yes we'll have our problems.'

Unmoved, Sister Lubemba said, 'We'll manage.' Then she said something in Zulu to Ngodini. The old man nodded sagely. She was obviously drawing Whitaker's attention to the sangoma's presence.

'I forgot my manners,' Whitaker said. 'Really, forgive me. To what do I owe the honour of this visit? It must be something very urgent.'

'We think so,' Sister Lubemba said. 'Ngodini has heard that Vuloyi, September Mabutane's wife, is already in labour. He says it will be a difficult time for Vuloyi. The *Bula* have fallen very badly for her. The midwives who should be in attendance are afraid of the storm and the river. There is no one to help her. The *Bula* indicate that you, Doctor Whitaker, should be at her side.'

'Sister, am I to believe . . .? Never mind.' Graham Whitaker had learned much in his short stay in Ingwavuma. Never would he forget old Ngodini's pronouncement after the sound of the explosion that day at Lake Mandlankunzi – 'A death sound,' he had said. And so it had proved to be. Two deaths in fact – two ANC guerillas – own goals.

'So his *Bula* predict a difficult delivery. Then we shall have to help, Sister, that's all.'

'I thought you would say that Doctor Whitaker. I can fetch her in the ambulance and bring her here.'

'It's no good bringing her here. Anyway, I wouldn't let you drive in these conditions. No, I'll do it. Does Ngodini know how to find Mabutane's kraal?'

'Yes, yes of course.'

'Then he can show me the way. Tell him that, Sister. Then start preparing all the patients, except the patient in the woman's ward. It would be better if *he* stays with me, Sister. Load him on a stretcher and get him into the ambulance. While you're doing that, I'll pack the instruments I'll require.' Whitaker thought for a minute. There were probably a score of things he had overlooked, instructions he had not given. But there stood Sister Lubemba – need anything more be said?

'I've packed a set of obstetric instruments,' Sister Lubemba said. 'They're already in the ambulance.'

'Good,' Whitaker said. 'Well then, give me a few minutes to pack some personal things, then meet me at the ambulance, with my patient.'

Once alone, Graham Whitaker moved swiftly. From a locked drawer he took the battered diary of Montague Law. He packed that into his doctor's case. In the same drawer, still in its red manufacturer's box, lay the Walther pistol that Dent had bequeathed him; he hesitated, then packed that too. He checked the drug compartments, then, satisfied, he snapped the case shut. That was not all that he intended to save from the flood waters of the Suthu.

Hidden behind the examination screen in his office was a basket; a large *iquthu* basket, not heavy, but cumbersome. He placed it on his desk the better to grasp it. Then with the basket hugged to his chest and the now very heavy doctor's case grasped before him, he left the office.

* * *

September Mabutane stood at the *umsamo* – the sacred place of his *indlu*. With a quiet, respectful voice, his tone subordinate to the storm, he thanked the *amathongo* spirits for his deliverance.

'My father Ndawonye. I am home. I am happy.
You were with me. Your hand guided my hand –
Your feet sought out the safe trail.
Now I see that my wife Vuloyi who worships you,
Vuloyi who you have always looked on with favour,
This woman of whom it is said – a boy awaits in her womb,
She is suffering. Yes, she is crying out with the Zala.
The pains of begetting it seems are great – too great.
The time of begetting has gone on for too long.
Now you know that I will make a big sacrifice
when this child – this boy is born.
Already I have killed a fine goat so that you will not hunger.
Can't you see how she suffers in her labour?
Can't you hear her cry out to you?
What is the good of it if you turn your back on her?
This woman who tries to bring us such honour.
My father Ndawonye I know that already you have carried me
a great distance.
Even the white woman who is with us knows it.
Even Lulele and the girl children know it.
Let the whole of Ingwavuma know that where you are, there the
garden is sweet.
Yes, you who held the buffalo by the horn for me, see here now:
Is the chain to be broken? Are we to be all women in this house?
Eh?'

Mabutane stood there for a while listening to the roar of the angry sky. Then he stood back from the *umsamo*. He had said all he could think of to say.

The *indlu* was gloomy and heavy with lingering, damp smoke. Near the centre pole an embered fire was busy beneath some steaming hunters pots, hissing from the rain drips and the spill. A kerosene lamp, pegged against the centre pole, pruned back the darkness where it could.

'Let it go well with her,' Mabutane said. These words were not addressed to the *amathongo* spirits however. They were intended for those within the *indlu*.

He received no reply.

Where the light was best, Vuloyi lay. Beneath her an *isicephu* mat was spread. Lulele supported her shoulders and Kirsten kneeled between her drawn-up thighs.

'She did everything a pregnant wife should do,' Mabutane went on. 'She wore the *unKhondo* bracelet. She covered herself with the *inGcayi* cloak. She did all that.'

'Of course she did,' Kirsten said. 'This has got nothing to do with what she did or did not do. The baby is positioned wrongly. Instead of his head lying in the birth canal, his feet are there. I can feel them. I've done all I can, externally, to revert the baby's position. It's too late now. He's going to come legs first. It sometimes happens like that. Don't worry; on the farm I delivered a hundred babies.'

She had delivered many babies. That was the truth. The inference that she knew how to handle a footling breech – that was a fabrication. She knew that a vaginal delivery in such circumstances was possible, but dangerous. She knew there was no alternative but to try. Vuloyi needed confidence. She tried to give her that.

'Is the *muthi* ready?' she asked September Mabutane.

It was a simple ceremony and as old as Zululand. Where a woman was long in giving birth, it was the job of the husband to bring the ladle containing the *nqunula muthi*; to hold it to the lips of his wife until the birth spasm took her. This Mabutane did.

Kirsten did not know whether there was any medical value in the practice, nor did she care. If Vuloyi believed it would help her, then that was enough. And Vuloyi did believe that. She relaxed; her eyes adored her beloved husband's face as he held the ladle to her. Then a uterine contraction racked her and she gasped with pain. Kirsten timed the contraction – 60 seconds. The next contraction was just under three minutes in coming. Kirsten inserted her hand. The cervix had dilated, the baby's feet seemed firmer in the canal. She smiled her encouragement to Vuloyi, and Vuloyi smiled back her trust.

'Soon,' Kirsten promised. 'Very soon.'

And as though at that prediction the uterine waters gushed. Vuloyi hugged her swollen abdomen; she arched upwards and screamed. And Kirsten prickled with the sweat of fear.

'Not yet,' she instructed. 'Don't push. Not yet.'

Another contraction – another spasm. Another scream. The

cervix was as wide as it would stretch.

'Now push Vuloyi. Now push, my sister. With every contraction push.'

Vuloyi's vagina was opening, widening in its maternal struggle. One tiny foot, oh thank you God, and then another; a pair of slowly writhing legs. It seemed in agony this warm wet thing.

'Push . . . Oh! Push . . . Oh! Vuloyi push.'

'A boy!' She heard September Mabutane's shout. 'Look – a boy!'

This joy was premature. The moment of crisis was at hand. The baby's head and umbilical cord were now together in the birth canal. The head would squeeze the cord – compress it – render it useless. In this contest for life the very lifeline was in peril. Before its first cry this babe was facing asphyxiation. Hurry Vuloyi – hurry.

It seemed there were others in the *indlu* – a male voice that did not belong to September Mabutane. Kirsten was aware that the door had opened – a gust of wind – a hand on her shoulder compelling her to move; to give up her position. She did it because the voice and the hand belonged to Graham Whitaker. His presence brought calmness to the *indlu*.

He kneeled where Kirsten had kneeled. His hands were quick, supportive and delivering. 'That's fine,' he smiled. 'Just fine . . . yes,' his fingers doing things deep inside the womb. 'Yes,' he reassured, 'yes.' The language of Whitaker's body spoke of these hidden actions – a head being freed – rotated now to fit the ovate passage it had to follow. He visibly rotated the baby's body. 'Easy . . . easy, here we come.'

The cord was pulsing with life. The baby was born.

'*Baba Ndawonye!*' September Mabutane cried. 'I salute you, one and all! It breathes the spirit of life! see . . . it cries! See Inkosikazi, see Ngodini. Look you uWhitaker, you doctor of all doctors. Where is the enemy now? They're not here. They're not there. They can see that the strength of this house has been doubled. My father! *This* is honour!'

Whitaker, with careful cradled hands, presented the baby to its mother. The weariness departed from Vuloyi's pretty face. Lulele and she admired the babe's perfection – its maleness. It was a time for laughter.

'And look what I brought you too, uWhitaker.' September Mabutane took the hand of Graham Whitaker and led him to Kirsten. 'Your eyes were a night pool of worry when last I saw you. Now they shine again. Here she is, this woman that you love, and dressed like a Zulu bride. *Hau*! She is a fine thing this woman of yours. *Hau*! There are princes who would challenge you for this one.'

'I believe you,' said Graham Whitaker. He kissed her very lightly to the applause of September Mabutane. But there was a leanness to his giving – a reticence. He stood beside her stiffly. Then he told her: 'I've got your brother, Kirsten. He's in the ambulance outside.'

'Thank you.' The words seemed inappropriate. What was there that she could say?

He guided her towards the *indlu* door. September Mabutane opened it for them.

'Look,' the Zulu shouted, 'even the rain clouds have parted so that the sun might see the boy child.'

It was true. In the excitement the diminishing of sound had gone unnoticed. It was drizzling lightly, but the rain and the wind had stopped. The Land Rover with the big red crosses on its sides was parked close by, its engine still running, its wipers squeaking across its sprinkled windscreen. The ground was puddled, and riven with gushing brown water. Mabutane waited at the door as Whitaker took Kirsten to the ambulance.

'He's sedated heavily,' Gray Whitaker warned. 'He may not even recognise you. I'm sorry Kirsten. I'm afraid his condition may shock you.'

She felt sympathy, not shock. He was lying on a stretcher; staring at the dome light of the ambulance. Wrists, ankles and pelvis, he was pinioned with nylon straps. He looked so helpless.

'He looks at peace,' Kirsten said at last. 'How . . . why is he here? Where did you find him?'

'Dent had him.' Whitaker related all he could of the circumstances that had brought her brother to his present situation. He spoke about the attack at Abercorn Drift; his argument with Dent. He told her about the cyclone and the call to evacuate the low areas. 'I've got the Inkatha too,' he said. 'I couldn't leave it at the clinic. Look.'

Upon the empty stretcher lay a heap of blankets – not just blankets. The *iquthu* basket accounted for some of the bulk.

Kirsten felt like crying when she saw Fana's basket. She wanted to explain to Gray Whitaker. 'That's where it all began you see, with old Mancoba and his obsession to destroy what's in that basket. It seems so long ago now. I've almost forgotten what the old *madala* looked like. If it hadn't been for Mancoba this basket would still be hidden in a cave in the Suthu River gorge, and the rising waters of the dam would have done his work for him. It's ironic, isn't it? He was a victim of the thing he wanted so badly to destroy. I can't help feeling that Monty was destroyed by the Inkatha too. He is destroyed, isn't he Graham? Look at him. That is my brother that half-human, half-monstrous thing lying there. And the Inkatha, that's the cause of it all. Believe me, I wish I had the courage to destroy this thing myself. I'd do it here and now, I tell you.'

And then she did cry. She pressed her head on Whitaker's shoulder and sobbed. He drew her to him and that felt good. But the tears did nothing for the sadness in her – that was gouged too deeply.

'September Mabutane must take the Inkatha now,' she said. 'Some good must come of this thing now. He must decide what must become of it. I believe that's right.'

'I think so too,' Graham Whitaker said soberly. He lifted the basket and carried it towards the *indlu*. There Kirsten presented the *iquthu* to the Zulu.

'The sacred Inkatha of Shaka Zulu. It's in your charge now, September Mabutane. May you have the wisdom to decide its rightful destiny.'

Solemnly he took the *iquthu* basket and placed it on the *umsamo*. He stood for a while with his back towards them, his head bowed meditatively. Then he straightened.

'It belongs to Abanzanzi,' he said. 'I will take it to Uhlanga and she will use it to unite the nation. That was King Cetchwayo's wish. This is how it must end. And now I would like to be alone.'

'We're leaving,' Kirsten said. 'uWhitaker thinks that it will rain again very soon. The eye of the cyclone is over us, that's why everything is so still at the moment. He says you're safe here because the dam is holding back the flood waters. Your kraal is not in danger from the river.'

September Mabutane nodded. He said to Ngodini, 'Will you stay with me, sangoma? My boy child needs to be strengthened now.'

Ngodini smiled his toothless smile. '*Yebo*, uMabutane. You are right.'

'Visit me often,' September Mabutane told Kirsten. 'I've grown to love you as though you were my daughter. My house is your house, Inkosikazi.'

'And my house is your house,' Kirsten replied. 'Stay well, my father.'

He took her hands and held them tightly for a moment. 'Go well, my daughter.'

She turned away quickly, as one does who has private tears to shed. Her vision shimmered as she walked towards the Land Rover. Graham Whitaker opened the cab door for her.

'Come, my Zulu bride.' He tried to draw a smile, but she could not smile.

'*Sala kahle*,' Whitaker attempted the Zulu greeting.

'*Hamba kahle*,' September Mabutane said. He died with the words of that greeting on his lips.

A rifle cracked and he stumbled against the ambulance. Another shot and his blood was everywhere. Two shots – that was what it took to kill that wonderful man – to pitch him slackly forward into a muddy puddle. A third shot holed the Land Rover and whined away in ricochet. Kirsten was slow to react. Sheer disbelief estranged her from her reflexes. She could not conceive the truth of this. September Mabutane would stand up in a moment and smile and walk back to the *indlu* where the baby was crying. *This* was wrong – impossibly wrong.

The trance of incredulity was hard to dispel. It was with her when she reached the body of September Mabutane, lingered as she helped Graham Whitaker drag the body into shelter.

'September,' she called. 'September . . . *September*,' as if by sheer insistence she would draw him back. There was no such miracle. Whitaker worked hard but not even his skilled hands could move this man to life. Then Lulele began screaming. Another shot struck the ambulance, and another – and these were no ordinary bullets. These glanced away in streaks of lightning blue. These were incendiaries.

'He's gone,' Whitaker shouted. '*For God's sake what's happening?*'

They had been ambushed. That was what was happening. There was a sniper on the little stone koppie that overlooked the kraal. A murderer with an automatic rifle and a magazine full of incendiaries . . . He was sniping at the ambulance – *and Monty was in the ambulance.*

'My God!' said Graham Whitaker. '*Look!*'

The Land Rover was burning. Lazy grey smoke was trickling from the engine compartment. Even as they looked a tongue of flame played upwards. The heat was instant. With a hungry '*Whoof!*' it fired the ambulance. *And Monty was in the ambulance.*

He was thrashing against the restraint straps – helpless and in terror – crying with pain. The inside of the ambulance was savage with searing pain. Kirsten grasped the stretcher, heaved at it. Oh God! How she pulled on those metal bars but it would not come. Then Whitaker was there, and he knew what to do. The stretcher rolled. Gasping for air, they flung themselves from the open rear doors. There was no fresh air just rasping, gagging, smoke. Everywhere there was smoke.

The ambulance siren had tripped on and was wailing loud and long. The agony of Montague Law was equal to it. He was writhing. He was screaming. Whitaker scorched and coughing was fumbling amongst his medical things . . . too slow. Too slow to meet the torment of this man. In anguish she bent to her brother. She tried to comfort him but the task was hopeless. Like some tortured dumb creature he was wrenching to be free. What *could* she say to heal him? She could not bear it. She undid the straps that held his ankles, then started to unstrap his wrists. Whitaker had filled his syringe. He looked up. He shouted desperately:

'Kirsten! *Don't!*'

But Montague Law was free. He stood for a moment, his limbs still jerking in reflex, disbelieving that his arms and legs could move at will – his neck, his head, his eyes. He saw Graham Whitaker advancing on him through the smoke. He seized the ambulance stretcher. Wielding it as though it was a natural weapon he hit out at the oncoming man. Kirsten tried to stop him.

She dragged at her brother's arms. She did not even hinder him. His strength was machine-like. She sprawled. The frame struck Whitaker's face. He threw his hands up and collapsed.

The ambulance exploded – the siren purled slowly into silence. The crack of gunfire became audible again. Lulele's sobbing . . . the baby's crying . . . Kirsten's voice, imploring: 'No! Oh no!'

But it was not her plea that halted her brother's attack. It was Ngodini's shout that stopped him.

'*Yima!* Mvulaba!'

And Mvulaba obeyed. One pace short of homicide he laid down his terrible weapon. Meekly he turned towards the sangoma.

'Come to me,' Ngodini commanded. 'Come here to where I stand. Yes, look at me, Mvulaba. *Look at the baby and remember*. The pain made you forget. Eeh! That is understandable. But look now. Look back into your mind as I have into mine. Do you see the great things that I see, Mvulaba?'

As Ngodini spoke, Kirsten attended to Graham Whitaker. His case lay open; his medical things lay scattered in the mud. She looked for a bandage and found a gun.

The wind came again, roaring at the fire, whipping away the screening smoke. The koppie was suddenly visible once more. A man was standing clear – a black man with a Kalashnikov rifle. He began to advance upon the kraal.

Kirsten took aim, slow, deliberate aim. '*Here is our destination; yours and mine.*' She could hear the voice of Ngodini. She could hear the return of the storm.

> '*Here is the healer of our nation.*
> *Here is the pathway we had lost.*
> *Here is the earth we have forgotten how to love.*
> *We were hungry – now we have food.*
> *We were naked – now we are clothed.*
> *Born of Vuloyi, yet not of Vuloyi –*
> *In the womb of the princess of heaven –*
> *his seed was the prayer of the nation.*
> *He stands in the space between night and day.*
> *On his forehead is the mark of the sun.*
> *We are his – he is ours.*
> *Our hope.*

Our destiny.
Indaba my people
Here is Okhethiwe
This is the chosen one.'